Science and Archaeology

The MIT Press
Cambridge,
Massachusetts, and
London, England

Science and Archaeology   Robert H. Brill, Editor

This book was designed by Muriel Cooper. It
was set in Fototronic Galaxy by York Graphic
Services, Inc., printed on Oxford Sheerwhite
Opaque by Halliday Lithograph Corp., and bound
by Halliday Lithograph Corp. in the United
States of America.

ISBN
0 262 02061 0

Library of Congress
catalog card number:
70-113731

Dedication

This book is dedicated to the late Martin Levey. Doctor Levey, a noted historian of science, was the organizer of two previous symposia on archaeological chemistry sponsored by the American Chemical Society. It was also he who initially suggested that the 1968 symposium, the one presented in this book, be held. Doctor Levey was an outstanding philologist, an historian, a mathematician, and a chemist. It was the combination of these diverse qualifications, unique perhaps in him, which accounts for his accomplishments in the history of science and medicine. Although his work met the most exacting standards of scholarship, there always lay behind it an unpretentious attitude and an insight into the ways of human beings— both those of the past and those of the present.

R.H.B.

Science and Archaeology

Introduction

Robert H. Brill
The Corning Museum of Glass

This book is a compilation of the papers presented at the Fourth Symposium on Archaeological Chemistry sponsored by the Division of the History of Chemistry of the American Chemical Society. The Symposium was held in Atlantic City, New Jersey, on September 9–11, 1968.[1] The program consisted of 22 invited papers covering a wide range of research tools and of archaeological materials.

The term "archaeological chemistry" was taken in a very broad sense in organizing the Symposium, for research in this field now makes use of the techniques and methodologies of many areas of science other than chemistry. In fact, the everyday work of many investigators in this field is far enough removed from being purely chemical that perhaps we would do well to make more regular use of the term "archaeometry" to describe their activities.

It may occur to the reader that there is no one obvious theme connecting all these papers. This is a result of a deliberate decision made while the program was being assembled. Because most research scientists find it difficult to generate much enthusiasm when required to address themselves to some arbitrarily assigned problem, it was decided to allow each participant to choose his or her own topic freely. In doing so, we relied upon the premise that if a problem is sufficiently important to attract the attention and efforts of leading investigators in a field, then it is of sufficient importance to be of interest to all the others. Thus, if there is a theme to the Symposium, it is that of current research. It has turned out that this collection of papers indicates clearly the directions in which the mainstreams of research in archaeological chemistry are presently leading us.

In addition to the scientific content of the papers themselves, perhaps the most stimulating aspect of the Symposium during its actual presentation was the wide variety of approaches and motivations represented by the participants. Several papers made it evident that the great surge of science during the past two decades has not been without an effect in archaeological chemistry, for some of the most up-to-date and complex instrumentation provided by modern science has already been put to work in the study of archaeological materials. Some of these techniques had barely come into existence when the previous Symposium was held in 1962, and we now have at our disposal means for analyzing large numbers of samples, not only more accurately than before but much more rapidly and with greater convenience. On the other hand, in some of the papers a strong emphasis was placed on the detailed handling and autopsy (as our British counterparts would put it)[2] of the objects themselves. There is an important need for both of these types of research in archaeological chemistry, and they obviously complement one another very well.

The names of some of the Symposium participants will be familiar to many readers, even those outside the field. A few have worked in archaeological chemistry for 30 years or more, but the Symposium also welcomed several new workers into the field—workers whose names will undoubtedly become equally well known in the years to come.

In general, editing of these papers has been held to a minimum primarily, of course, because little editing was required but also because this helped the book as a whole to reflect further the fact that research in this area of science bears more distinctively than in most the individuality of the investigator. It is likely, in fact, that along with the pleasure of handling the ancient objects it is this individuality of expression which has attracted many archaeological chemists to their field.

Despite the diversity of subjects included, there are a few different schemes by which these papers could be logically ordered for publication. For example, they could be grouped by the materials studied or the analytical techniques employed, but we have chosen instead to group the pa-

[1] Before this Symposium was organized, several persons were confident that three symposia on the subject had previously been presented by the Division of the History of Chemistry, and thus we arrived at the conclusion that this was to be the fourth. Subsequently, however, memories of only the First and Third Symposia remained clear in the minds of division members. And so we leave it (with a blush) to the historians and archivists of chemistry to decide upon the reality of the elusive Second Symposium and to discover the whereabouts of its contents. The First Symposium on Archaeological Chemistry was held in Philadelphia, Pennsylvania, in April 1950. The papers were published in the *Journal of Chemical Education*, Vol. 28, No. 2, February 1951, pp. 63–96. The Third Symposium on Archaeological Chemistry was held in Atlantic City, New Jersey, in September 1962. The papers were published in *Archaeological Chemistry*, edited by Martin Levey, University of Pennsylvania Press, 1967.

[2] Unlike the Third Symposium, which was truly international in character, all of the participants but one in this Symposium are from American institutions. We were most fortunate that Dr. E. T. Hall, of the Research Laboratory for Archaeology and the History of Art at Oxford University, was in the country at the time of the Symposium and was therefore able to participate. It is to him, too, that we owe the coining of the term "archaeometry" alluded to earlier.

pers according to research objectives. The first part includes six papers that are object-oriented; that is, they describe investigations dealing with individual objects or small groups of objects. These studies were undertaken in order to learn more about how the objects or materials were made or, in one instance, what happened to them while on exhibition. The second part contains what we have described (perhaps inadequately) as analytical surveys. These are investigations of larger groups of fragments or objects undertaken with the intention of uncovering patterns of chemical composition which can be used for the classification of the analyzed specimens according to date or provenience. Among these is a group of papers that in effect amount to a subsymposium on neutron-activation analysis. Needless to say, these groupings are somewhat arbitrary, for there are some papers that could be placed in either section. The third part deals with four techniques used for the dating of archaeological objects.

In a day when meetings and symposia tend to be proliferating too widely, one hesitates to remark that there is a need for further symposia in any field. But such truly seems to be the case with archaeological chemistry. During our discussions at the Symposium, three problems in particular arose, which could form the bases for future symposia. First, more thought should be given to choosing the best means for expressing analytical results. Several analysts now find themselves in the enviable but nonetheless difficult position of having to compare literally hundreds or sometimes even thousands of chemical analyses. The choice of criteria for deciding what is significant and what is necessary is crucial indeed, for the means one chooses for coping with such bodies of data will affect their interpretation and ultimate value.

Another important question carries one to the basic objectives and motivations underlying research in this field. There is a growing feeling, among some of those involved, that archaeological chemistry represents something more than just a service to the archaeologist or curator. Even if we never were to confirm a single attribution, or connect or distinguish between any groups of objects at all, the acquisition of chemical and technological information concerning early objects is, in itself, of value. But such a view is susceptible to the criticism of being too lofty or too vague in its objectives. Therefore, we must ask ourselves, realistically, "In exactly what ways, and to what extent, can our findings be extrapolated beyond simple descriptive enumerations so as really to tell us something new and different about early man?"

In any event, whether one subscribes to this goal and its practicability or not, it still remains a fact that once the laboratory work is completed it is all too easy to abandon the data and leave them in the stage of tabulations and statistical correlations. But if such research is to be something more than just an intellectual exercise, the archaeometrist must not leave the interpretation solely to the historian or archaeologist; instead, he himself must play a major role in interpreting his findings—and this is where we need much further effort. Some further thoughts related to this subject are presented in Prof. Smith's Post-Symposium Notes.

The third problem may be reduced to what sounds simply like a hackneyed plea—a plea for close cooperation between the archaeometrist and the archaeologist. But this plea, so often raised in the past, has begun to take on a new meaning. There was a time when the two lived in distinctly different worlds and to many archaeologists the value of the chemist's efforts did not amount to much more than the occasional identification of a curious mineral or other find. Within the last two decades, however, we have gained one another's confidence and come to a much happier and more fruitful state. The field archaeologist and curator now appreciate more fully the value of scientific research on excavated materials, and the laboratory scientist has finally come to realize that the archaeologist and curator are every bit as capable as he of objective reasoning and critical evaluation of evidence. The danger now faced is that with a capability for analyzing much greater numbers of samples and making ever more complicated types of measurements, the laboratory scientist may unwittingly tend to withdraw into a preoccupation with numerical data and lose some contact with his newly won friends in the humanities. There *is* a need for joint meetings between people from these different disciplines.

It had been our hope to have a number of archaeologists attend this Symposium and to participate in whatever capacity they felt appropriate, but the unfortunate timing of the meeting—pleasant though it is in Atlantic City in September—precluded the possibility of our assembling many archaeologists, for they were, in many cases, just returning from the field. In this sense our Symposium was not as successful as it could have been. I personally am more concerned, however, with perhaps having fallen short of another goal, that of improving modes of communications within this field. But like many goals this one is more easily discussed than achieved. Despite all the contributors' efforts to the contrary, we may have failed here in the published versions of our papers to be always as clear and free of technical jargon as we should, in order to make our findings intelligible to those who recovered, who care for, and who seek to learn more from the objects we have analyzed. To any who feel that this is the case, I, as editor, offer my apologies.

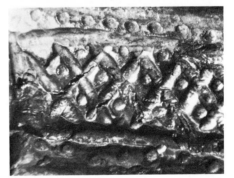

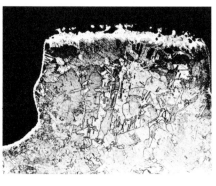

Plate I.
Top: Cemented sheet metal with gold-colored surfaces. Bottom: Uncemented sheet metal with enriched silver surfaces. Both sheets made of 60/30/10 Cu-Ag-Au alloy. (Chapter 1)

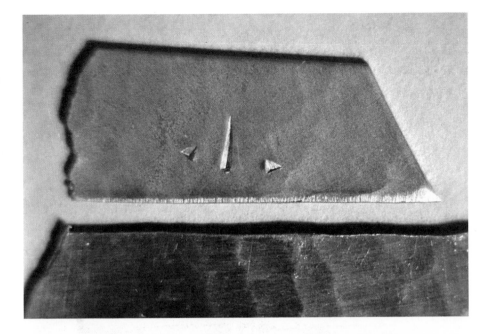

Plate II.
Household religious effigy with Maya blue paint, Mayapan, Yucatan. (Chapter 3)

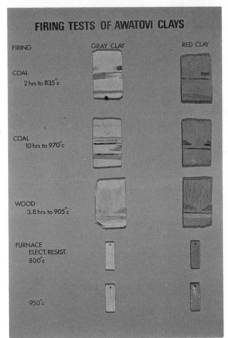

Plate III.
Small cup with bird painted in Zaachila Maya blue, Zaachila, Oaxaca, Mexico. (Photo: INAH) (Chapter 3)

Plate IV.
Firing tests of Awatovi clays. (Chapter 3)

FIRING TESTS OF AWATOVI CLAYS

FIRING	GRAY CLAY	RED CLAY
COAL 2 hrs to 835°c		
COAL 10 hrs to 970°c		
WOOD 3.8 hrs to 905°c		
FURNACE ELECT. RESIST. 800°c		
950°c		

Plate V.
Awatovi pottery types. Rows 1 to 5 correspond to types 1 to 5 as described in text. (Chapter 3)

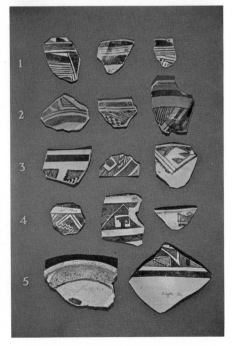

Plate VI.
Color range of Hellenistic and Parthian figurines excavated at Seleucia-on-the-Tigris. (Fired briquettes prepared from Seleucia clay are in the foreground.) (Chapter 4)

Plate VII.
Thin sections in transmitted light (200X): (a) Bead from Lisht North Pyramid site; (b) Another bead from same site as a; (c) Macehead from Nuzi; (d) Sistrum handle; (e) Table top from Timna; and (f) Manufacturing technique VI. (Chapter 5)

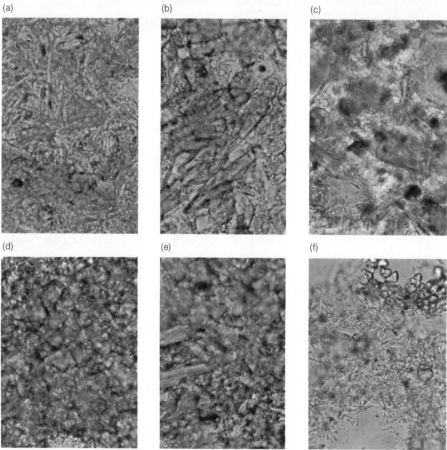

(a) (b) (c)

(d) (e) (f)

Chapter 1

Ancient Methods of Gilding Silver: Examples from the Old and the New Worlds

Heather N. Lechtman
Massachusetts Institute of Technology

Introduction

To illustrate a representative selection of ancient techniques for the gilding of silver, I have chosen material from two distinct geographical regions, the Near East—more specifically Turkey and Iran—on the one hand, and South America—very precisely, the northern coast of Peru—on the other. The objects from the Near East all cluster about the third through the sixth centuries A.D., from the Sasanian empire in Iran and from one of the most splendid periods of the early Byzantine empire with its capital at Constantinople. It is difficult to date the particular Peruvian objects discussed in this paper with the same accuracy as the Old World artifacts. They span a much broader period of time, ranging from the classic Vicus period (ca. 400 B.C.–A.D. 100) through that of the Chimu culture, which was prominent in Peru roughly from A.D. 1000 until the time of the Inca conquest in 1470. But the rigors of precise dating of artifactual material need not be of concern here, for the purpose of this investigation is to demonstrate the ways in which craftsmen, at various points and places in history, have used virtually the same materials but have arrived at totally different yet completely effective solutions to a specific problem, the gilding of silver.

True Gilding and Depletion Gilding

In any discussion of gilding metal, the distinction is usually made between true gilding and processes that may be subsumed under the term depletion gilding, often referred to as gold coloring.[1] True gilding techniques involve the external application of gold to the surface of some other metal. Upon its application the two metals may, in certain instances, undergo interalloying and complete metallic bonding. Processes of depletion gilding, on the other hand, always begin with the gold already alloyed with some other metal. In such cases, the object is to remove enough of the alloying element so that the surfaces become enriched in gold and

eventually appear golden. Depletion gilding techniques are thus based upon chemical reactions that occur only at the surfaces of alloys.[2] They include processes that rely on solid-state diffusion reactions at a moderately high temperature, that is, all *mise-en-couleur* and cementation techniques such as removal of copper from tumbaga, of silver from gold-silver alloys, and of both copper and silver from silver-copper-gold alloys. Electrochemical processes, for example superficial parting, are also included in the term.

The distinction between gilding and coloring is not meaningful from the aesthetic point of view. Both types of process lead to results that, at least under the usual conditions of viewing and handling an object, are similar. But the distinction does have significance from the standpoint of technology, for the metallurgical principles and operations involved are quite different and stem from two approaches to the use of materials that are, in a sense, philosophically distinct. The objects I shall discuss from the Near East are all examples of true gilding, while those from northern Peru may prove to illustrate a unique variety of gold-coloring technique.

Methods of Applying an External Layer of Gold

Aside from the modern processes of electrolytic plating, electrochemical plating, sputtering, and other methods of depositing a thin gold film from solution or from the vapor phase, there have been relatively few techniques for the external application of gold. These have utilized gold in the solid state, in the molten state, and in the form of an amalgam whose properties lie somewhere between those of the other two. Solid gold has been applied most often in the form of thin sheets of foil or leaf, although finely powdered gold has also been used.[3] To differentiate between gold foil and gold leaf, I shall arbitrarily define foil as sheet metal that is greater than about one micron in thickness ($1\mu = 10^{-3}$ mm), while leaf constitutes thicknesses smaller than this value. This definition is not altogether peremptory, since there is a marked difference in the way in which sheet gold handles when it becomes much thicker than about a micron. The metal is as malleable when thick as it is thin, but it cannot follow

[1] Paul Bergsøe's plea for and definition of this clarification of terms is classic. In discussing the process of *mise-en-couleur* he remarks: "However, when this process is described as 'gilding,' a protest must be lodged in the name of metallurgy. By gilding we understand a process by means of which an overlay of gold is applied to the object *externally*. If the gilding proceeds from the gold *in the object itself*, it can at most be called coloration. This, however, is only a question of terminology and has no actual bearing upon the subject, but I call attention to it, as it seems to me a pity that anthropologists and metallurgists make use of a different terminology when speaking of metal." (Reference 2, pp. 35–36.) Rather than use Bergsøe's term "coloration," which has also been used to describe coloring methods that do not utilize metallic gold (see next note), I prefer *depletion gilding* and define it as the enrichment of a surface in gold by removal of other alloying elements already present.

[2] No discussion will be made here of the many recipes for creating golden surfaces on metal without the use of any metallic gold. These abound in the early literature. Some are alchemical in nature, and others involve simple coloring substitutes, but none is a metallurgical process in the strict sense.

[3] I am referring not to the use of gold powder as a pigment in an organic binder which is then painted onto a metallic surface but rather to the rubbing of very finely divided gold onto a clean metallic surface to which it bonds mechanically.

sharp changes of contour easily, tends to buckle perceptibly and to retain the wrinkling upon burnishing, and to become very springy when burnished cold. The mechanical application of thick foil to metal surfaces of widely varying topography is therefore quite difficult, whereas it is easily accomplished with the thinner leaf. Discussion of the first two objects from the Near East shows this difference quite clearly.

Regardless of whether foil or leaf was used, some auxiliary means of attaching the gold to the substrate metal had to be found. The most direct method was that of simple mechanical bonding. Either the surfaces of the substrate were deliberately roughened to accept the applied and subsequently burnished-on gold or the topography of those surfaces, which included all their decorative features, was varied enough to constitute an adequately toothed stratum onto which the gold could be burnished and held mechanically. Once the gold was in place, the entire object might have been heated to cause sufficient solid-state diffusion of the two metals across their common interface so that a zone of interalloyed metal, albeit very thin, might then form an additional and very strong bond to hold the two together. Thin sheet gold has also been applied to metal surfaces with organic binders of various types, a not uncommon practice in ancient Egypt,[4] and, finally, mercury has frequently been used as the agent to facilitate the bonding of leaf to substrate metal.[5]

The application of gold in the molten form to a metallic surface is much rarer chiefly because it is a much more difficult technique, it is more wasteful of gold, and it does not lend itself easily to parcel gilding, that is, to the gilding of only certain areas of a metallic surface for the decorative contrasts produced between gilded and nongilded metal. The technique, akin to tinning of iron or steel, is often referred to as fusion or wash gilding and almost always involves an alloy of gold with copper, which melts at a considerably lower temperature than pure gold itself.[6] The molten metal tends to run over the heated surface of the substrate, and the bond in such cases is usually a fusion

bond caused by the melting together of the metals at their interface. An interesting account of such a technique is given by Paul Bergsøe and is based upon his studies of the gilding practices of the pre-Columbian peoples of Esmeraldas in Ecuador. He concluded that the Indians gilded very small cast copper objects by flushing on the gold-copper alloy of lowest melting point. (Reference 2) It would be well to reexamine this material, both metallographically and with the electron microbeam probe, to reassess Bergsøe's interpretation.

Finally, the peculiar properties of the amalgam of gold have made it an ideal material for gilding metals, one that has been used extensively since at least the first century A.D. and probably even earlier. Gold and mercury, when gently heated, together form an alloy that, on cooling, is of a pasty consistency. As long as the metal to be gilded will also amalgamate with mercury, this pasty alloy can conveniently be spread over those areas of a surface to be gilded. If desired, other areas may be left untreated. When the object is heated to a temperature above the boiling point of free mercury (356°C), the mercury in the amalgam volatilizes leaving the gold behind. The gold is thus held in place as the result of solid-state diffusion between it and the substrate metal, often with the formation of intermediate compounds. Several of the Near Eastern objects illustrated here were gilded by the amalgam process, and the details of the technique are given with the descriptive and analytic material.

The Indians of pre-Columbian Central and South America were master goldsmiths. It is not extraordinary, therefore, to find that, when it came to gilding metals, they employed a wide variety of techniques ranging from the use of gold foils through the fusion gilding procedure described earlier to methods based on coloring procedures. It is in this last category that the peoples of Central America and of northern South America made a unique and important contribution to the development of early metallurgy in the New World. This was the invention, perhaps by the peoples of Colombia, of the gold-copper alloy commonly referred to as tumbaga and the extensive utilization of this alloy by the Indians of Panama, Costa Rica, and eventually Mexico. A wide variety of objects was cast from tumbaga, and the castings were subsequently treated in one of two ways in order to remove the surface copper, leaving the gold behind. When completed, the objects were completely covered with a thin layer of gold and indeed looked golden. The coloring methods involved (1) the formation of copper oxide on the surface of the casting by heating the object in air, followed by chemical solution and removal of the copper oxide, or (2) the slow removal of metallic copper

Depletion Gilding: A Contribution of Pre-Columbian Metallurgy

[4]Lucas describes the plating of copper by attaching gold leaf to this metal with a gum or glue adhesive. He claims that the large marguerites sewn to the linen pall from the tomb of Tutankhamūn were gilded in this manner (Reference 9, p. 232).

[5]One of the earliest references to the gilding of copper with gold leaf applied with the aid of mercury is found in Pliny's *Natural History* (Reference 11).

[6]The maximum depression of the melting point occurs at an alloy composition of approximately 80 percent Au, 20 percent Cu, by weight. This alloy melts at about 900°C, 163 degrees below the melting point of pure gold (1063°C).

from the surface of the casting by allowing the object to remain immersed in a corrosive bath for extended periods of time. The dark, spongy layer of gold formed was later consolidated by burnishing.[7] There is no doubt that similar alloys (coinage alloys, for example) were made in the Old World and that surfaces of most gold alloys were given an improved color in a similar manner, but the technique was never developed and perfected anywhere in the world to the extent that it was in the Americas.

Although the pre-Columbian objects I shall discuss are from Peru, where tumbaga was rarely used, and are examples of gilding alloys that are primarily silver-based, I shall endeavor to show that the gilding methods used by at least some of the North Peruvian peoples were actually coloring methods and that they are analogous to those employed in the more traditional treatment of the copper-based tumbaga alloys.

Objects from the Near East

The Near Eastern material illustrates many, though not all, of the techniques for applying an external layer of gold to a silver surface. The object reproduced in Figure 1.1 is a silver rhyton, in the form of a horse, in the Cleveland Museum of Art (Reference 19). It is from Sasanian Iran, dating to the third century A.D., and is made of several pieces of thin sheet silver carefully fitted together. All the decorated areas, including the trappings, the mane and tail, and the two round phalerae on either side of the chest, were produced by the repoussé technique followed by final chasing with a variety of tracing tools. Many of these traced areas were originally gilded, but most of the gilding has been lost and is now immediately visible only on the muzzle, the straps that secure the saddlecloth, and the hair of the mane. On the other hand, examination under the microscope reveals that the entire saddlecloth was probably originally gilded, although only small fragments of gold remain clinging to some of the rosettes. Similarly, bits of gold can be found on the frames of the phalerae and in other areas within these medallions.

As Dorothy Shepherd has pointed out, the extensive loss of gilding is undoubtedly due to inadequacies in the method of applying the gold. A heavy gold foil, between 8 and 14μ in thickness, was burnished onto the decorated areas of the metal depending mainly on the contours of the traced details to supply the necessary "tooth" to hold it in place. The straight, cut edges of the foil are quite evident in certain areas where they overlap from the heavily traced portions of the metal onto the undecorated, smooth surfaces of the silver. Careful inspection of

Figure 1.1 reveals such an overlap of foil running from the closely hatched, vertical muzzle strap behind the animal's eye onto the ungilded metal just below its ear. The gold is visible here as a highly reflecting, geometrically defined area on a matte silver ground. Figure 1.2, a detail of a similar area of the muzzle, shows a portion of the traced leather strap, which is gilded, and of the ungilt silver below it. The arrow indicates the edge of the thick foil that still covers most of the decoration where that edge has overlapped onto the undecorated smooth silver surface.

Figures 1.3 and 1.4, details of the straps of the harness, reveal quite clearly the extent to which the foil has stretched, cracked, and is peeling away from the underlying silver, demonstrating the inadequacy of even these quite irregular surfaces to hold foil of this thickness in place. Both photographs also illustrate the way in which the gold has buckled badly in the depressions of the traced lines. It never adhered well to the silver even in these declivities. From these observations, it is quite easy to understand why the gold has been lost so extensively within the borders of the saddlecloth where only the traced rosettes offer some interruption to the otherwise broad, smooth surfaces of silver. Moreover, inadequate cleanliness of either metal, inadequate heating, and inadequate mechanical pressure in applying the gold would have resulted in poor bonding regardless of the presence or absence of gross surface "tooth."

Because it was impossible to obtain a sample of some of the silver that still retains its gilding without impairing the integrity of the object, no studies were made which might have shown whether or not the object was heated after application of the gold in order to effect a diffusion bond.[8] The fact that some fragments of gold cling tenaciously even to very smooth areas of silver implies that the silver may have been heated while the gold was being applied and that, in a few places, the heating was sufficient to form such a diffusion bond. This would almost certainly have been necessary to maintain the ductility of the thick foil while it was

[7] Bergsøe used both methods successfully to reproduce the gold coloring of experimentally cast tumbaga alloys (Reference 2, pp. 35–37). See also Reference 14.

[8] Several tiny pieces of the peeling foil were removed and examined, however. Qualitative spectrographic analysis of the gold indicated the presence of between 0.1 and 1.0 percent mercury, by weight. It is likely that the concentration of mercury is near the lower limit of this range, for the electron microbeam probe analyzer found no point within the foil at which counts above background were measured for mercury. The silver concentration within the gold did not show a Au-Ag diffusion zone, but the gold appeared to be contaminated with silver, probably in the form of corrosion products, on both its surfaces. Until it is possible to examine a cross section of the gilded silver, it will be difficult to ascertain whether or not mercury was used in applying the foil. Its level of concentration in the gold raises some doubts as to its presence there as a simple contaminant. (See Appendix.)

1.1
Silver rhyton in the form of a horse 34 cm long x 22 cm high. Iran, Sasanian period, ca. third century A.D. The Cleveland Museum of Art, Purchase, John L. Severance Fund [CMA 64.41].

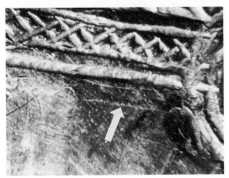

1.2
Horse rhyton. Arrow indicates edge of thick gold foil applied over decorated muzzle strap. Photo by Katharine C. Ruhl.

1.3
Horse rhyton. Wrinkled gold foil is peeling away from traced silver surface. Photo by Katharine C. Ruhl.

1.4
Horse rhyton. The "toothed" surface has failed to bond the foil to the silver. Photo by Katharine C. Ruhl.

being worked and pushed into the traced recesses of the silver. (See the Appendix at the end of this chapter.)

A much more effective use of gold leaf for the parcel gilding of repoussé sheet silver is illustrated by the sixth-century gilt silver book cover shown in Figure 1.5. This book cover, one of a pair now at Dumbarton Oaks, was found in Turkey and may be from a workshop in Constantinople in approximately A.D. 570. (Reference 5) Almost all of the raised design elements are gilded, namely the meander border, the shell niche, the capitals and other portions of the columns, the central cross, and its flanking palm branches. The flat silver field has been left ungilded, producing a brilliant interplay between the silver and the gold motifs.

Simple macroscopic examination of this object affords several clues to the method employed to gild it.[9] As with the horse rhyton, there are a few areas where the cut edge of a piece of leaf has overlapped from a raised, gilded motif onto the flat silver field. Figure 1.6, a detail of one of the palm branches, shows the V-shaped intersection of two gilded, raised areas of metal and the spanning of that intersection by a sheet of leaf that has fallen over onto the silver field. The horizontal edge of the leaf is quite evident in the photograph. Second, peeling away of the leaf from the silver occurs in many areas on this object, especially in the recesses, as can be seen at the extreme lower left corner of Figure 1.6.[10] On the whole, however, the leaf follows the contours of the silver very closely and is well bonded to it. Finally, one of the properties of thin leaf with which the craftsman must always contend is its tendency to tear. If it tears upon application to a metal surface, more leaf must be applied above the tear to hide the underlying metal and to produce an uninterrupted, smooth gold surface upon final burnishing. Occasionally a tear in a sheet of leaf can be found, however, and is incontrovertible evidence that the gold was applied in the form of thin leaf. Figure 1.7 is a detail of a torn piece of leaf noted on the mate to the book cover in question. The light silver metal shows through from below. The fact that this horizontal, irregular band is a tear and not a scratch in the leaf is obvious from the matching contours of its two edges.

The microscopic evidence for the existence on this object of several layers of

leaf, each approximately one micron in thickness, is quite clear. Figure 1.8, a cross section of a gilded fragment of silver, illustrates one part of the surface where at least four separate pieces of leaf are superimposed. The silver is heavily corroded here, which accounts for the peeling away of the leaf. Figure 1.9, another section, reveals other characteristics of the thin leaf, notably its ability to be pushed into broad, shallow depressions on the silver surface, following closely the surface topography (note the way in which three layers of leaf hang down into a surface irregularity, at the left of the photograph, the lowest layer clinging closely to the surfaces of this pit) and the tendency of the leaf to wrinkle upon application. The uppermost layer of gold at the extreme right of the micrograph travels along the surface, folds under itself, travels a little further, folds again, and continues along to the right. This too is a diagnostic feature for the presence of thin sheet metal. Still another photomicrograph, Figure 1.10, illustrates a characteristic of this gilding that was explained only after laboratory experiments were performed to try to reproduce the technique. Once again, the material beneath the gilding is completely mineralized, and the gold now rests on a thick bed of silver corrosion product. Although the micrographs in Figures 1.8 to 1.10 were all taken at the same magnification (1110X), the gold layer in Figure 1.10 appears considerably thicker than in either of the other two illustrations. Furthermore, there appears to be only one continuous layer of gold present, and this thick layer has managed to enter a deep and narrow surface cavity, to line that cavity, and to reemerge onto the surface without breaking. Is this reasonable behavior for a gold sheet of only one micron thickness?

To answer this question, a cross section of a fragment of gilded silver from the book cover was analyzed with an electron microbeam probe.[11] The probe traces for gold, silver, and mercury at the gilded surface and well into the substrate silver are shown in the plot of Figure 1.11. The probe operated at 30 kV, specimen current of approximately $0.007\mu A$, and with a take-off angle of $52.5°$. The gold spectra were obtained with a quartz crystal spectrometer, the silver with ADP (ammonium dihydrogen phosphate), and mercury with LiF. The beam size averaged about $2-3\mu$ in diameter.

It is quite evident from this analysis that

[9] A description of the techniques employed to gild this object was first given at the May 1968 annual meeting of the American Group of the International Institute for Conservation of Historic and Artistic Works, Washington, D.C.

[10] The peeling and eventual loss of gold on this object was most often caused by the formation of silver corrosion products beneath the gilding which tended to push it away from the substrate silver. It was rarely caused by poor initial bonding of the leaf to the metal beneath.

[11] All the electron microbeam probe analyses of the Near Eastern material were performed on an Applied Research Laboratories instrument operated by the X-ray and Electron Optics Group in the Department of Metallurgy and Materials Science at M.I.T.

The probe data for the Peruvian objects were taken on a Materials Analysis Co. instrument at the Ledgemont Laboratory of Kennecott Copper Corp.

the gold leaf was applied to the silver with the aid of mercury. Most probably those areas of the silver to be gilded were amalgamated, the leaf was superimposed, and the entire object was then heated to drive off the excess mercury. The probe traces show that there is a considerable zone of diffusion, approximately 16μ broad, between the gold and the silver and that it is within this zone that the mercury is concentrated. The position of highest mercury concentration occurs several microns inside of the gold peak and falls off slowly through the diffusion zone, finally reaching zero concentration within the silver.[12] The broadness of the interalloyed band of gold and silver indicates that either the metals were heated several times, consistent with multiple applications of leaf, or the object was given a final, prolonged heat treatment to drive off the mercury and perhaps to lighten the color of the gold.[13]

With this much information, reproduction of the leaf gilding was attempted. A piece of thin silver sheet was repeatedly bent until fissures of appreciable depth began to form on one surface. This surface was then amalgamated with pure mercury, and a piece of gold leaf 1.3μ thick was laid on the silver. When the leaf appeared white with mercury, the sample was placed in a small muffle furnace at 540°C for one minute. This sequence was repeated three times, a total of three layers of approximately one-micron-thick leaf having been applied to the silver.[14] A cross section of the unburnished metal is shown in Figure 1.12 at a magnification of 200. Several observations may be made about the structures at or near the surface: (1) It is nowhere apparent that three individual layers of leaf had been applied to the silver; (2) the total thickness of the gilding is considerably greater than 3.9μ; (3) the gold has been drawn down into the deep, narrow surface fissures and has lined these cavities in a continuous fashion just as it did on the book cover itself (illustrated in Figure 1.10). There are two ways in which gold might enter and line these cavities. One is by simple capil-

larity, for if gold leaf is applied to surfaces coated with a limited amount of liquid mercury, surface tension will draw the gold into close contact with the silver, though it is unlikely that the leaf would penetrate very narrow or deep cavities by this means. The second possibility involves the solution of gold in mercury and its diffusion through the liquid and deposition upon the silver surface as a layer of gold-silver-mercury alloy having lower solubility than gold. This layer would thicken as the mercury in the alloy is evaporated, which might also produce a skin upon the surface of the silver. In both cases the gold, though in the form of thin sheets, has been entirely reformed as an alloy and modified by the continuous diffusion into the silver base and subsequently by evaporation of the mercury.

Interdiffusion of gold and silver in the solid state accounts at least in part for the thickened appearance of the gold leaf and for the disappearance of visible junctions between the successive layers of leaf in successfully gilded areas. Two gold surfaces, both joined by mercury, would maintain their metallic continuity even after the mercury had been removed to produce an apparently single layer of coating.[15] Interdiffusion requires good contact between the gold and the silver, and its extent depends upon the temperature and time of heating. Thus, the single thick layer of gold in Figure 1.10 was formed in an area where the layers of leaf were in close contact with one another when heated and in equally good contact with the underlying silver. On the other hand, these conditions were not met in areas such as that shown in Figure 1.8, where, despite the fact that the metal was subjected to the same heating conditions, little or no interdiffusion has taken place, and the layers of leaf remain separate. The apparent thickening of the gold leaf as a result of interdiffusion is shown schematically in Figure 1.13.

[12] Several 2θ scans taken with the probe of the spectra of all elements within the silver failed to reveal the presence of mercury in the metal itself.

[13] Theophilus, in describing the amalgam gilding of a silver chalice, directs that, once the metal has been thoroughly gilded, it must be heated to dryness, that is, until all of the excess mercury has evaporated. Once dry, the metal should be heated'' . . . again until it begins to turn pale.'' The pale color of the gold is caused by the rapid diffusion of silver into the gold layer forming a Au-Ag alloy which is paler than pure gold. Of course, the formation of this diffusion zone also increases the strength of the bond between the gold and the silver (Reference 6, p. 114).

[14] The silver was later given a long anneal of 16.5 hours at 340°C, which undoubtedly accounts for the thickness of the gold and the extent of Au-Ag diffusion at these metal interfaces. (See next footnote.)

[15] The apparent thickening of one metal in a diffusion couple upon heating is known as the Kirkendall effect. (See Reference 20.) It is illustrated for a Au-Ag diffusion couple by the diagram in our Figure 1.13. A series of fixed, inert markers has been placed at the interface between a thin gold film and a much thicker silver sheet. When the two metals are heated, some of the gold diffuses into the silver and some of the silver into the gold. Because the rate of diffusion of silver into gold is greater than the reverse reaction, as indicated by the relative lengths of the arrows in the diagram, after a given period of time there will have been a net transfer of matter in the direction of the gold. This shift of the center of gravity of the system or apparent shift in the position of the inert markers can be interpreted instead as a thickening of the gold layer above the position of the markers. This is why the gilding in Figures 1.10 and 1.12 appears as thick as it does. When measuring the thickness of gold leaf in a cross section, it is important to choose an area where Kirkendall thickening of the leaf has not occurred.

1.5
Silver parcel-gilt book cover. 37 x 30 cm. Byzantine Turkey, ca. A.D. 570. Dumbarton Oaks, Washington, D.C. [D.O. 63.36.9].

1.8 (to right)
Book cover. Cross section through four layers of gold leaf lying above corroded silver surface. Magnification 1050X, etched by 5% KCN + 5% $(NH_4)_2S_2O_8$.

1.9
Book cover. Cross section. Leaf-gilded silver surface shows layers of leaf within surface pit (left) and wrinkled leaf (right). Magnification 1050X, etched by 5% KCN + 5% $(NH_4)_2S_2O_8$.

1.10
Book cover. Cross section of leaf-gilded surface. Thickened gold layer has entered and coated the surfaces of a narrow fissure. Magnification 1050X, etched by 5% KCN + 5% $(NH_4)_2S_2O_8$.

1.6
Book cover. Arrow indicates edge of gold leaf overlapping onto smooth silver ground.

1.7
Book cover. Arrow points to silver showing through tear in gold leaf.

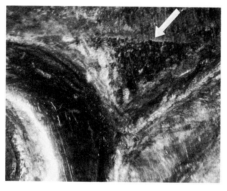

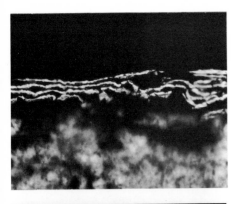

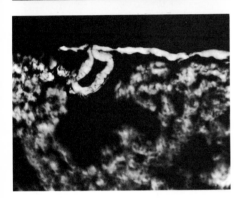

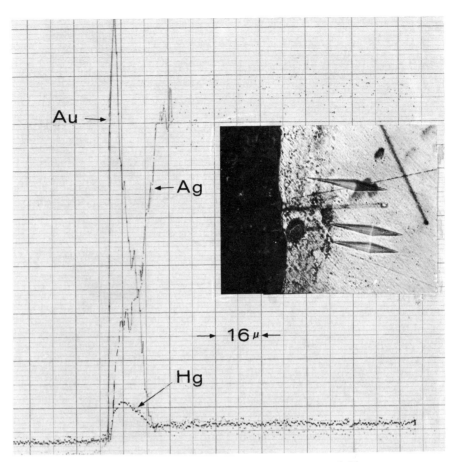

1.11
Book cover. Electron microbeam probe traces of Au, Ag, and Hg across a section of leaf-gilded silver. Photomicrograph (315X) indicates beam path across the gilt surface.

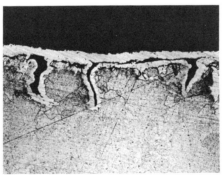

1.12
Photomicrograph of silver sheet gilded in the laboratory with gold leaf and mercury. Section shows penetration of gold into surface fissures and Kirkendall thickening of gilded layer. Magnification: 150X etched by 0.2% H_2CrO_4 + 0.2% H_2SO_4.

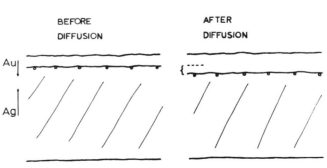

KIRKENDALL EFFECT

1.13
Schematic diagram of the Kirkendall effect in an Au-Ag diffusion couple. The distance through which the inert markers have apparently moved or by which the gold layer has apparently thickened is indicated by the bracket and is known as the Kirkendall shift.

All the phenomena observed in the photomicrographs of the gilded silver of the book cover can, therefore, be explained on the basis of the interactions of gold, silver, and mercury during periods of heating when solid-state diffusion processes and mass transfer in liquid occur.

The next three silver objects were all parcel-gilded by the amalgam method and have been chosen because they illustrate properties of that technique. The silver plate depicting a royal hunting scene, shown in Figure 1.14, is from Sasanian Iran and presumably was made during the reign of King Hormizd II, A.D. 302–309. It is in the Cleveland Museum of Art (Reference 18). Many of the areas of highest relief on this plate, such as the head and torso of the king and portions of both lions and of the horse's body, are actually individual pieces of silver fabricated separately and later set into place on the body of the plate. All the gilding was carried out after these pieces were inserted. The bodies of both lions, the horse's body, and most of the apparel of the king are gilded. The irregularity of the edges of the untarnished gilded motifs, especially in comparison with the precise outlines of the gilding on the book cover, is striking. The gold appears to have spilled over onto the silver background along most of these edges, notably along the proper left side of the king's chest, along his bent right arm, and along the tail of the felled lion. Particular note should be made, however, of places where the amalgam has spilled onto the silver background to such an extent that it traverses the surface of the silver, connecting one gilded area with another. Three prominent spills visible in Figure 1.14 occur between the tip of the king's scabbard and the mane of the slain lion, between the proper right side of the king's torso and the horse's mane, and between the open mouth and the right paw of the attacking lion. A detail of the latter spill is given in Figure 1.15.

Such areas are characteristic of amalgam gilding.[16] Typically, the silver area to be gilded is first amalgamated with mercury, although this is not a necessary step. The mercury diffuses rapidly along the surface of the silver and cannot readily be confined within any prescribed region unless some stopping-out material is used to protect the portions that are to remain free of gold. The pasty gold-mercury amalgam is then spread over the designated area. Some of this amalgam will naturally spill over onto any surfaces where mercury has already alloyed with the silver. It will be difficult to confine even when the pre-

paratory mercury coating is absent. When the object is subsequently heated to drive off the mercury, the gold remains in place. If the gilt edges are particularly rough because of irregular spillage, the excess gold is removed by gently scraping the surface until relatively pure silver is once again obtained. Quite often, however, the gold will have diffused deeply enough into the silver, alloying with it, so that the areas of spilled amalgam always appear slightly pale and shiny owing to the presence of this alloy. Even if not visibly yellow, such areas corrode less severely than pure silver, and with time they stand out by virtue of the contrast between their preserved surfaces and that of the tarnished or otherwise corroded silver. This phenomenon is rarely encountered with leaf, which tends to remain where it is placed even if the mercury may have spread around it.

The gilt silver rhyton of Figure 1.16 with its four representations of the goddess Anahita is also from the early fourth century of Sasanian Iran. It too is among the collections of the Cleveland Museum of Art (Reference 18). Unlike either of the other two amalgam-gilt objects, here it is the background that is golden and the relief design elements that remain silver. In order to accentuate the outlines of these raised areas of metal, a pronounced, deeply traced line defines their contours. When the thick amalgam was spread over the silver background, it tended to accumulate within these deep depressions. Later, after the mercury was volatilized away, the gold was carefully burnished. But burnishing tools are rarely small enough to enter the depressions caused by engraving or tracing tools; thus, the contour lines have remained full of unburnished gold with the characteristic spongy, open, ''bubbly'' look of accumulated, dried amalgam. Figure 1.17 is a detail of the proper right hand of the goddess shown in the preceding illustration. The deep, traced contour groove outlining the edge of the little finger and the beginning of the palm is filled with this spongy gold. It is in striking contrast to the smooth, polished gold of the background alongside it. The bubbly effect occurs primarily in the regions where the amalgam is able to accumulate in relatively thick layers. In such regions the bubble structure forms in the solidifying metal by virtue of the escaping mercury vapor. The sponginess may be typical of even thinner layers of amalgam, however, resulting simply from crystallization of the gold during solidification. This is rarely seen except in surface depressions because it can be burnished smooth elsewhere.

The porous, spongy quality of an amalgamated gold surface is not surprising when one looks at cross sections of silver that have been amalgamated with mercury alone, then dried but left unburnished. Figure 1.18 is just such a section of a

[16] Microbeam probe data of a cross section of gilded silver from this plate indicate the presence of mercury in association with the gold and silver at the surface of the section. The analyses were performed at Case–Western Reserve University under the direction of Prof. Donald F. Gibbons and Mrs. Katharine C. Ruhl. Personal communication, June 1968.

1.14
Silver plate with royal
hunting scene. Iran,
Sasanian, ca. A.D. 302–
309, approximately
20.5 cm diameter. The
Cleveland Museum of
Art, Purchase, John L.
Severance Fund. [CMA
62.150].

1.15
Silver plate. Detail of the
amalgam spill between
the jaws and paw of
the attacking lion.
Photo by Katharine C.
Ruhl.

1.16
Silver rhyton with fig-
ures of the goddess
Anahita, 18 cm high x 11
cm maximum diameter.
Iran, Sasanian period,
early fourth century A.D.
The Cleveland Museum
of Art, Gift of Katharine
Holden Thayer [CMA
62.294].

1.17
Silver Anahita rhyton.
Detail of the spongy,
porous gold accumu-
lated within the traced
groove outlining the
hand. Photo by Katharine
C. Ruhl.

1.18
A section of worked
silver sheet amalga-
mated with mercury in
the laboratory. Magnification 150X, etched by
0.2% H_2CrO_4 + 0.2%
H_2SO_4.

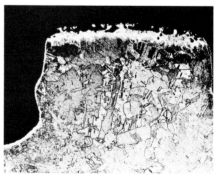

1.19
More highly magnified
detail of section shown
in Figure 1.18. Note
entry of mercury into
grain boundaries. Mag-
nification 370X.

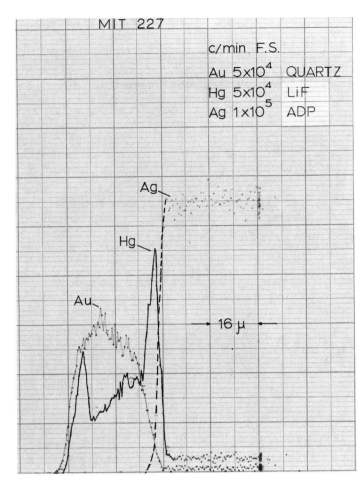

MIT 227

c/min F.S.

Au 5x10^4 QUARTZ

Hg 5x10^4 LiF

Ag 1x10^5 ADP

Ag

Hg

Au

16 μ

1.20
A section of worked
silver sheet gilded in
the laboratory with
Au-Hg amalgam. Magnifi-
cation 75X, etched by
0.2% H_2CrO_4 + 0.2%
H_2SO_4.

1.21
Silver Anahita rhyton,
cross section showing
the thick, surface layer
of gilding. Magnification
375X etched by
$K_2Cr_2O_7$ + NaCl +
H_2SO_4 diluted 1:9.

1.22
Silver Anahita rhyton.
Electron microbeam
probe traces of Ag, Au,
and Hg across the
gilded surface shown in
Figure 1.21.

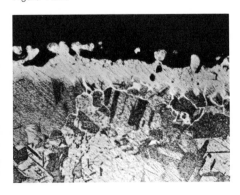
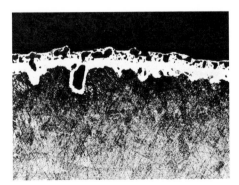
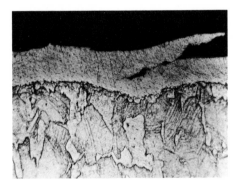

piece of sheet silver that was cold worked until both tiny surface fissures and deeper fatigue cracks were produced. The surface was then amalgamated with mercury and the sample heated in a muffle furnace at 540°C for one minute. The amalgamation and heating were repeated three times. The specimen was then annealed at 340°C for 16.5 hours. The photomicrograph shows, in the first place, how uniformly the mercury has amalgamated with the silver in the deepest surface pits and, second, how open and granular the upper surface of the silver remains. Figure 1.19, a more highly magnified detail of this same specimen, illustrates the extent to which the mercury has cracked the worked metal along grain boundaries and shows even more clearly the spongy nature of the silver.

A similar piece of metal, also worked to produce cracking, was amalgamated with mercury and placed in a furnace at 570°C for half a minute. Afterward it was coated with a layer of Au-Hg amalgam and heated again for one minute at the same temperature. Two further applications of amalgam followed by two identical heat treatments ensued. Figure 1.20 is a photomicrograph of a cross section of this gilded, but unburnished, silver. The porosity of the gold layer is quite apparent here as is the obvious penetration of the mercury and, therefore, of the gold into the surface irregularities.

A cross section was made of a tiny gilded fragment removed from a broken edge of the figured rhyton. A photomicrograph of the gilded surface is given in Figure 1.21. The gold layer superimposed above the worked silver substrate is extremely smooth, indicating extensive final burnishing.[17] It is also extremely broad, measuring approximately 26μ in thickness. Although it is possible that a single layer of amalgam could have resulted in such a thick deposit of gold, it is more likely that a series of applications was made and the final layer burnished and possibly scraped to make it uniform and compact.

Electron microbeam probe traces through this same section are shown graphically in Figure 1.22. It is quite clear that very little diffusion has occurred between the silver and the gold and that the mercury is associated primarily with the gold. A characteristic feature of the mercury traces in all the amalgam-gilded samples studied thus far has been the very high concentration of this element at the interface zone between the gold and the silver. An intermediate compound of mercury-gold-silver must form in this region where the gold concentration is quite low but where the concentration of silver has begun to rise. The peak mercury concen-

tration in this case is approximately 24 percent, while the average concentration of mercury within the gold is approximately 7 percent. The distribution of the three elements in this cross section is nicely given in the set of probe scanning display photographs of Figure 1.23. The high concentration of mercury at the Au-Ag interface is particularly clear in the mercury scan. As a comparison, probe traces were also taken of the experimental sample shown in Figure 1.20; these appear in Figure 1.24. In this case, too, very little diffusion has occurred between the gold and the silver, whereas the mercury has diffused quite deeply into the silver as well as being retained within the gold. The characteristic interface mercury peak, here definitely more closely associated with the silver than in the case of the rhyton sample, is quite apparent. The concentration of mercury at the peak position is approximately 75 percent, while its highest concentration within the gold is about 37 percent.

The third object gilded by the amalgam method is the small (approximately 7 × 4 cm) silver torso shown in Figure 1.25 which is almost identical with that of the king depicted on the hunting scene plate in Figure 1.14 and can safely be said to be from Iran sometime within the fourth to sixth centuries A.D. This torso is one of the separately fabricated pieces of relief decoration described earlier, which was made for insertion onto a silver plate previously prepared to receive it. It is presently in a private collection in Cleveland.

The surface decorative tooling, both traced and engraved, was completed before the gilding was applied. The gilt areas include the sleeve cuff, the shoulder and chest straps, the ''bib'' between the shoulder straps, and the waistband. A small metal sample was removed from the lower proper left corner of the waistband and included the three small, punched tool marks visible there in Figure 1.25. The photomicrograph in Figure 1.26 is a cross section through part of one of these punched depressions. The smooth, burnished layer of gilding on the flat surface of the waistband is located in the upper right portion of the photograph. The average thickness of this layer is approximately 10μ. The unburnished gold within the depression, however, has accumulated in large, spongy clumps, and only that portion immediately adjacent to the underlying, heavily worked silver is closely bonded to it. A set of electron microbeam probe traces taken through the burnished portion of the gilding (Figure 1.27) is comparable with those of Figures 1.22 and 1.24 and is particularly close in profile to the traces through the Anahita rhyton. Here the mercury concentration at the peak position is approximately 15 percent, whereas the average mercury concentration within the gold itself is about 6

[17] The crack in the gilding occurred when the rhyton was damaged. It is not a characteristic feature of an amalgam-gilt surface.

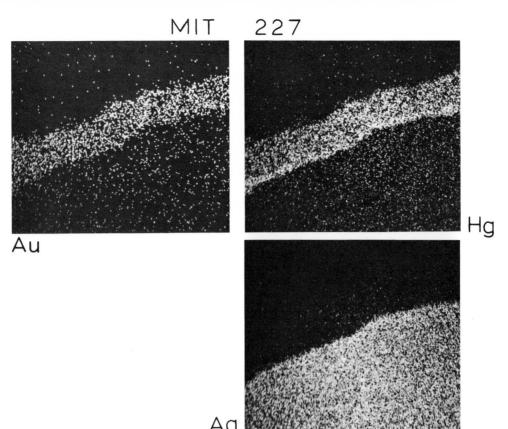

Au

Hg

Ag

1.23
Silver Anahita rhyton.
Electron probe scanning
display photographs
showing the distribu-
tions of Au, Hg, and
Ag in the section of
Figure 1.21.

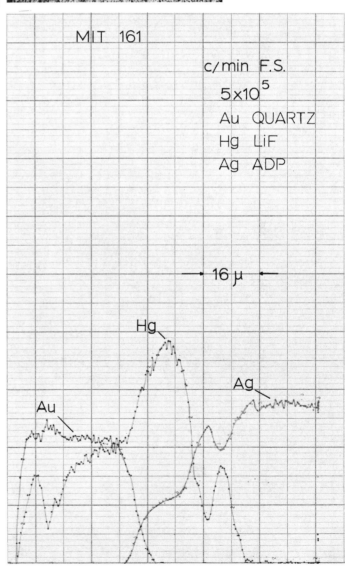

MIT 161

c/min F.S.
5×10^5
Au QUARTZ
Hg LiF
Ag ADP

16 μ

Hg

Ag

Au

1.24
Electron microbeam
probe traces of Ag, Au,
and Hg across the ex-
perimental sample
shown in Figure 1.20.

1.25
Silver torso insert from
a plate. Iran, Sasanian
period, fourth to sixth
century A.D. Private col-
lection, Cleveland.
Photo by Katharine C.
Ruhl.

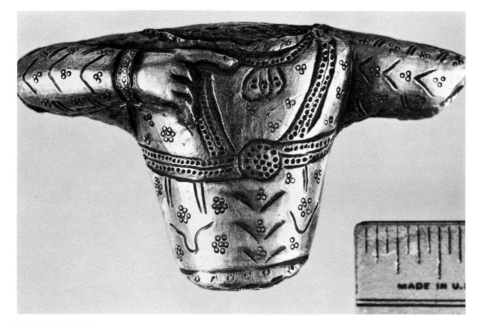

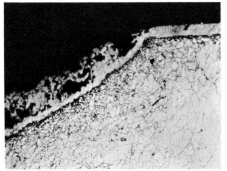

1.26
Torso insert, section
through a decorative
punched hole. Accumula-
tion of spongy gold is
seen within depression.
Magnification 300X,
etched by $K_2Cr_2O_7$ +
NaCl + H_2SO_4, diluted
1:9.

1.27
Torso insert. Electron
microbeam probe traces
of Ag, Au, and Hg
across the burnished
portion of the gilt sur-
face in Figure 1.26.

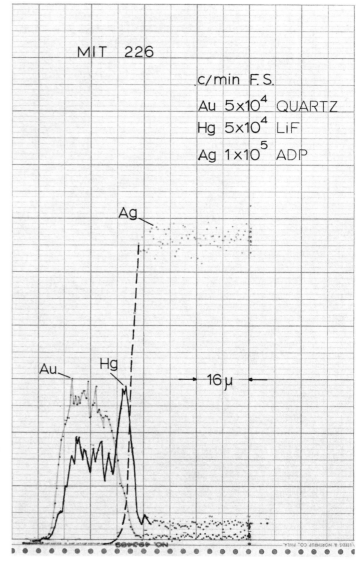

MIT 226

c/min F.S.

Au $5×10^4$ QUARTZ
Hg $5×10^4$ LiF
Ag $1×10^5$ ADP

Ag

Au   Hg

← 16μ →

1.28
Disk thought to come
from Vicus in northern
Peru. Lent for study by
Mr. and Mrs. Dudley T.
Easby, Jr.

1.29
"Vicus disk," detail of a
traced motif on the ob-
verse surface.

percent. The fact that the probe traces from the amalgam-gilded objects and from the experimental sample exhibit such little diffusion between the silver and the gold evidently suggests that the heating that took place after each application of amalgam was both brief and at a relatively low temperature. In the case of the experimental sample, heating the object for a total of three minutes at 570°C was insufficient to allow much Au-Ag diffusion to take place, whereas diffusion and retention of mercury under these conditions proved more than adequate to produce excellent alloying and bonding.

Summary

The gilding techniques exhibited by these five objects from the Near East have certain features in common that may serve, in part, to characterize them.

1. All the objects are parcel gilt, that is, they were gilded only in certain areas in order to take advantage of the highly decorative effect of the juxtaposition of silver and gold.

2. The gold was applied after the surface chasing—by tracing or engraving—was completed. In the case of the horse rhyton, it was the decorative tooling itself that was to hold the gold in place. Gold tended to accumulate in these tooled areas in both the leaf-gilded book cover and the amalgam-gilded objects.

3. The gold layer, regardless of its method of application, is of considerable thickness. Even the leaf-gilded object had several layers of leaf applied to it, creating a gilded coating of about 4μ. Generally the gilding is between 10 and 30μ thick.

4. In four of the five examples, the gold was applied with the aid of mercury. The possible employment of mercury in the gilding of the fifth example has been discussed. See also the Appendix.

Objects from Peru

Analysis of the gilded material from the Near East proved fairly straightforward. Often clues to the gilding techniques employed became evident on a thorough macroscopic examination of the objects, and these were later substantiated by metallographic evidence. The two objects from Peru that have been chosen for discussion were selected precisely because surface examination offered few insights, and they remained puzzling even after metallographic studies were undertaken. Note has been made in the introductory section of the fact that a host of gilding techniques was undoubtedly used in Peru and in South America generally, but a particular type of gilded object which defies simple analysis appears to be characteristic of the development of metallurgy along the north coast of Peru. It is these artifacts that will be treated in this sec-

tion. These particular investigations are in an early stage, and my comments will, therefore, be more in the nature of suggestions as to the gilding techniques employed and indications of the direction that the investigations should take rather than solutions to the posed problem.

The gilded disk that appears in Figure 1.28 is said to be from Vicus, a burial site in the upper Piura Valley very close to the Ecuadorian border. The metal artifacts from this site are extremely difficult to date and to relate to the associated ceramic sequences. Generally speaking, the artifacts tend to group themselves into an early or classic Vicus style, (ca. 400 B.C.–A.D. 100) and a later style, the negative Vicus style (ca. A.D. 100–700), which takes its name from the negative-decorated pottery that characterizes it.[18] Therefore, the disk may fall anywhere within this broad time period. It was kindly lent for study by Mr. and Mrs. Dudley T. Easby, Jr.[19]

The disk is fabricated of thin sheet metal, ostensibly silver, hammered to its present shape with a high central boss and a series of traced motifs that decorate both the front and the back of the object. The gilding covers all its surfaces, and only where the gold has been lost through wear or corrosion of the underlying metal can the silver be seen beneath it. The lighter, pock-marked areas evident in Figure 1.28 are patches of silver that have lost their gilded covering. The gold is extremely smooth and appears to be very thin as well. It is as uniformly deposited within the rather narrow and shallow grooves left by the tracing tool as it is on the smooth, flat surfaces. A detail of one of the decorative motifs is shown in Figure 1.29. The smooth, uninterrupted quality of the gold is apparent except in those areas, such as the eye of the figure, where corrosion has pitted the metal. The surfaces give no indication of the way in which the gilding was accomplished. The only feature of note is that there is no accumulation of gold within the declivities. A uniform, continuous layer appears to cover the entire object. In fact, one has the impression that the gilding was completed before the final decorative tooling was carried out.

[18] The styles and chronological periods followed here are those outlined recently by Alan R. Sawyer, Reference 17.

[19] The disk illustrated in Figure 1.28 may not be from Vicus, however. Two disks, virtually identical with it, have more recently been lent for study by Junius B. Bird. He describes these as having come from a tomb with a relatively dry environment, whereas objects from Vicus are subject to moist soil conditions. He believes, therefore, that these disks are from a site south of Vicus and that their style places them in the Chimu period. (Personal communication, December 1968).

Table 1.1

Analysis of the "Vicus" and Chimu Disks

	Wet Chemical*			Spectrographic (Qualitative)								
	Percent, by weight											
	Ag	Cu	Au	Bi	Fe	Hg	Mg	Mn	Ni	Pb	Si
"Vicus" Disk (MIT 217)	29.2	60.8	10.1	0.01–0.1	N.D.†	N.D.	0.0001–0.001	N.D.	0.001–0.01	0.1–1.0	N.D.
Chimu Disk (MIT 218)	43.4	33.5	6.4	0.01–0.1	0.0001–0.001	N.D.	0.0001–0.001	0.0001–0.01	N.D.	0.1–1.0	0.001–0.01

* The maximum relative experimental error in the determination of Au and Cu is ±0.5%; for Ag it is ±2%. The gold was determined gravimetrically as a residue; the silver was determined as silver chloride by gravimetric analysis; the copper was determined colorimetrically by iodometric titration. See Earle R. Caley, *Analysis of Ancient Metals*, Oxford, 1964, pp. 51–53 and 67–74; Charles M. Dozinel, *Modern Methods of Analysis of Copper and Its Alloys*, Amsterdam, 1963, pp. 87–92.

† Not detected.

The photomicrographs illustrated in Figures 1.30 to 1.32 show, in cross section, the microstructure of a small fragment of metal removed from the edge of the "Vicus" disk. It is immediately apparent from the two-phase structure that the metal from which this object is made is not pure silver. The analysis in Table 1.1 indicates that it is essentially an alloy of silver and copper. Several other features are notable in these photomicrographs. The heavily worked metal has been severely deformed, and the silver-rich (light etching) and copper-rich (dark etching) phases have become narrow, interlayered bands elongated in the direction of working of metal. Figure 1.30, which shows the entire cross section from front to back, also exhibits most clearly the rather thick silver-enriched zones on both surfaces of the metal. A detail of one of the surfaces, given in Figure 1.31, shows this thick, almost copper-free surface zone more clearly. It is almost impossible at this magnification (380X) to discern any gold whatever. It is only in the more highly magnified (750X) detail in Figure 1.32 that the thin gold coating can be seen (see arrow). It is approximately one micron in thickness.

When certain Ag-Cu alloys are made into sheet metal, it is almost inevitable that the final sheet will appear as if it is of pure silver because of the depletion of copper from the surfaces by oxidation during annealing.[20] A reconstruction of the sequence of metallurgical events taking place is given in Figures 1.33–1.35. An alloy resembling that of the metal in the disk, namely a 60/40 Cu-Ag alloy, was cast and allowed to air-cool in a crucible. It is shown in the as-cast condition in the photomicrograph of Figure 1.33. The structure reveals large cored dendrites (dark etching) of the copper-rich, beta solid solution of silver in copper surrounded by the eutectic (light etching) structure of the alpha (silver-rich) and beta phases. The eutectic structure varies from areas where it is quite fine to others where it is reasonably coarse. The cast

alloy was put through a series of 15 courses of hammering, flame annealing, and pickling in order to reduce it from a slab 0.44 cm in thickness to a thin sheet 0.07 cm in thickness, a reduction of 84 percent. A cross section of the resulting sheet is shown in Figure 1.34. The structure is not unlike that of the disk, though it is considerably coarser. In the photomicrograph of Figure 1.35, one can still see vestiges of the original thick dendrites now much reduced and elongated by deformation. The beta phase of the eutectic has tended to ball up as a result of annealing but would, on further hammering, become thin stringers similar to those present in the disk metal. The origin of the banded structure of the disk metal can be explained, therefore, in terms both of the original two-phase microstructure of the cast alloy and of the deformation of those phases through cold or hot working. Figure 1.35 also gives a more detailed picture of the enriched silver surface of the experimental sample. In fabricating the experimental sheet, it was necessary to anneal it repeatedly to soften it. During the course of each annealing operation, the copper within the alloy diffused rapidly onto the surface where it was oxidized. This dark scale of copper oxide was dissolved by pickling the metal in dilute sulfuric acid or in ammonia, and hammering was recommended.[21] After only about three such sequences, enough copper had been removed from the surface so that it appeared silver.[22] The thinner the metal became, the more often annealing and pickling were necessary and the thicker the enriched silver layer grew. It is quite

[20] See Reference 12 for a description of the phenomena involved in this process.

[21] There are many naturally occurring acids such as oxalic or acetic acid which could be used to remove the copper oxide scale. Similarly, urine might have been used by the pre-Columbian Indians for this purpose, ammonia being one of its decomposition products.

[22] The Peruvian Indians utilized this effect in the manufacture of many objects that were meant to look like silver. Copper-silver alloys were often used on the south coast of Peru from the late Ica period onward, and it was a common alloy of the Chimu culture as well. See Reference 13 and also the two Chimu wall plaques from the north coast of Peru, made of silver-copper alloy, illustrated in Reference 3, Figure 45.

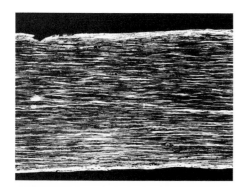

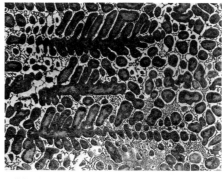

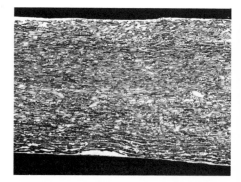

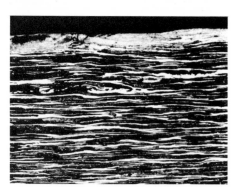

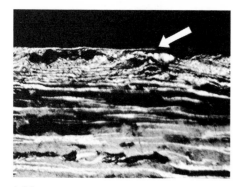

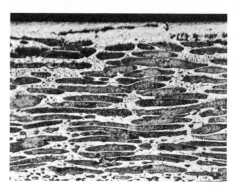

1.33
A section of 60/40
Cu-Ag alloy in cast condition. Magnification
120X, etched by FeCl$_3$.

1.34
A section through sheet
metal hammered from
the casting shown in
Figure 1.33. Magnification 60X, etched by
K$_2$Cr$_2$O$_7$ + H$_2$SO$_4$ +
HCl.

1.35
Detail of Figure 1.34
showing enriched silver
surface layer. Magnification 275X.

1.30
"Vicus" disk, photomicrograph of an entire
section through the
metal. Magnification
120X, etched by
K$_2$Cr$_2$O$_7$ + H$_2$SO$_4$ +
HCl.

1.31
"Vicus" disk. Detail of
Figure 1.30 showing the
enriched surface layer
of silver. Note the tiny,
white precipitates of
silver within the copperrich areas. Magnification 380X.

1.32
"Vicus" disk. Section
through the surface;
arrow indicates thin
gold layer above silver.
Magnification 750X. As
polished.

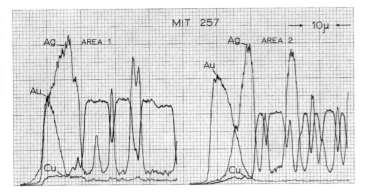

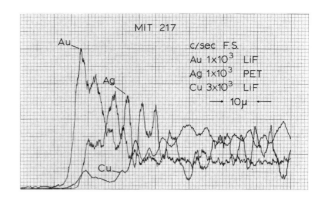

1.36
Electron microbeam
probe traces of Au, Ag,
and Cu across two
areas of a leaf-gilded
silver sheet. Area 1,
single leaf layer: Ag-
PET-1K; Cu-PET-10K;
Au-LiF-1K. Area 2,
double leaf layer: Ag-
PET-1K; Cu-Lif-10K; Au-
LiF-3K.

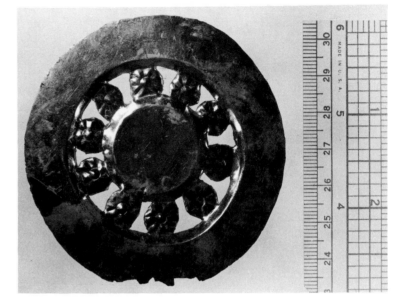

1.37
"Vicus" disk. Electron
microbeam probe traces
of Au, Ag, and Cu
across the gilded sur-
face of a cross section
of the metal.

1.38
Chimu disk. Vicinity of
Trujillo, ca. A.D.
1000–1470. American
Museum of Natural His-
tory [AMNH
41.2/5876].

21

evident that a good deal of the silver metal observable on the disk in areas where the gilding has been lost is simply the silver of these enriched surface zones.

The question still remains as to the manner in which the gilding was formed on the silver surface of the disk. It is entirely possible that the gold was applied in the form of thin leaf of approximately one micron thickness or that it was rubbed onto the surfaces as a finely divided powder. In either case the gold would have had to be applied at or very near the completion of the object. Otherwise the continued heating necessary to anneal the metal would cause such extensive diffusion between the gold and the silver that the gold would become pale and lose its covering power. In order to illustrate this effect, some gold leaf of approximately one micron thickness was burnished onto the silver-enriched surface of a piece of the experimentally prepared Cu-Ag sheet metal. In some areas only a single layer of leaf was applied; in others two layers were attached. The metal was then put through four additional courses of hammering, annealing, and pickling. The leaf work hardened rapidly upon both burnishing and hammering, and it became quite clear that even had it been applied after the object was completed, some annealing operations would have been carried out to soften the metal and to facilitate bonding between the silver and the gold.

A cross section of the gilded sample was analyzed with an electron microbeam probe, and the probe traces for silver, copper, and gold are shown in Figure 1.36. The probe had a 35° take-off angle, was operated at 20 kV and at a specimen current of 0.01 μA. The gold spectra were taken with a LiF crystal, the silver with PET (pentaerythritol), and copper with either LiF or PET. The beam size was about 1–2 μ.

Area 1 is a surface onto which a single layer of gold was applied. Two layers of gold were burnished onto Area 2. Diffusion between the silver and gold is extensive in both areas. In the case of Area 1, however, the gold and silver have completely alloyed, and there is no place where the gold does not contain large amounts of silver. In fact, this is an area where the gold became so pale that one could no longer see that any gold was present. On the other hand, the double layer of gold in Area 2 was thick enough so that about two microns of gold remain that contain virtually no silver. This area appeared very golden at the end of the hammering-annealing sequences.

A similar set of microbeam probe traces was made through the cross section of the disk metal. These appear in Figure 1.37. The profile of these traces is not dissimilar to that of Area 2 of the experimental sample. There is a fairly broad re-

gion at the surface containing virtually no silver as well as a deeper zone in which the gold and the silver are alloyed. The most important information carried by these traces, however, is the fact that there is an appreciable amount of gold within the body of the metal itself (compare the Au trace in the body metal of the experimental Ag-Cu alloy with the trace in the body metal of the disk). The analysis indicates that there is approximately 10 percent of gold, by weight, in the disk metal, and it is evident from the probe traces that this gold is *not* confined to the surface gilding layers but that it is a constituent of the alloy. The disk is a ternary alloy of silver, copper, and gold. The relatively high concentration of the gold indicates that it is probably a purposeful additive. It is certainly present in excess of what one would expect of silver with a high gold impurity level.

The disk illustrated in Figure 1.38 is the second object from Peru. It shares many characteristics with the disk assumed to come from Vicus. It is made of even thinner sheet metal, with pierced, openwork design and with gilding on all surfaces. This object, which is presently in the collection of the American Museum of Natural History, is probably of Chimu origin (ca. A.D. 1000–1470) and is said to come from the coastal region near the modern city of Trujillo. The surfaces of the disk are extremely smooth, although many areas are covered with copper corrosion products that give it the patchy appearance evident in Figure 1.38. The gilded layer appears incredibly thin and also has a pale, greenish hue characteristic of gold alloyed with silver. The traced motifs on the "rosettes" are shallow, and in a number of places the tracing shows strong evidence of having been accomplished after the gold was already in place. Nowhere is there any accumulation of gold within these depressions. As with the "Vicus" disk, there are no observable indications on the surfaces of this object as to the gilding method employed.

The composition of the metal is given in Table 1.1. As is evident from the microstructure of a cross section of the metal (Figure 1.39), the copper has corroded extensively and exists mainly in the form of cuprous oxide within the body of the object. This undoubtedly explains why the sum total of the major metallic constituents of the metal is only about 83 percent by weight. Normalizing this to 100 percent, the uncorroded metal contained approximately 51 percent Ag, 39 percent Cu, 7.5 percent Au. The microstructure of the unetched section is virtually identical with that of the "Vicus disk." Here, however, it is the corroded copper-rich phase that provides the contrast to the lighter silver-rich areas. The broad, enriched silver surfaces are also quite evident. Examination of the section with the optical microscope at a magnification of 1000X did not reveal any distinct layer of gold above the silver.

The electron microbeam probe traces taken across this section are shown in Figure 1.40. The gold trace reveals the extremely thin surface gilding, indicates quite clearly that this layer is entirely associated with the silver-enriched surface zone, and explains why it does not appear as a discrete layer in the cross section. The gold and silver are interalloyed, which accounts for the pale greenish color of the disk itself. The probe profile of this disk is similar to that of Area 1 in Figure 1.36, and the same arguments that might account for the "Vicus" gilding in terms of an extremely thin, externally applied gold layer—in this case completely diffused into the silver—could be equally valid for the Chimu object. Once again, however, it should be noted that the gold is present throughout the body of the metal, the gold trace indicating quite clearly that this metal is a ternary Ag-Cu-Au alloy.

There is at least one other method by which both these disks might have been gilded, however, a method that would explain the macroscopic characteristics of the gold surfaces and that would satisfy the data provided by the probe traces. Such a method involves depletion gilding, that is, surface enrichment of the gold already present in the alloy by selective removal of the silver. We may conservatively assume that the pre-Columbian Indians did not have available to them a reagent, such as nitric acid, which has been used in Europe since the twelfth or thirteenth century for parting silver and gold. The removal of silver from the alloy by simple acid dissolution is highly unlikely.[23] On the other hand, it is perfectly plausible that the Indians may have used some operation akin to cementation to remove some of the surface silver. Cementation has traditionally been used for the purpose of purifying gold containing impurities such as copper and silver. It is undoubtedly a process of great antiquity, but literary evidence for its use in Europe and the Near East before the early Middle Ages is scant. Descriptions which seem to relate to it are to be found in both Strabo and Pliny, but the details are hard to follow. By the twelfth century, in the treatise of Theophilus, we have a detailed account of the method, and its use thereafter is documented in many sources. See References 1, 6, 7, 10, 21, 22, and 23.

In all cementation recipes, the gold is packed in a reactive powder (the cement),

which, when heated, combines chemically with the impurities on the surface of the gold and eventually, by diffusion, with the impurities throughout the entire body of the metal. The cement, which invariably contains salt, reacts to form chlorides of silver and other impurity metals, leaving the gold unattacked. Both the reagent and the reaction products are absorbed in the largely inert matrix of brick dust or some similar material. Additional ingredients may be ammonium chloride, potassium nitrate, copper sulfate, iron sulfate, vinegar, or urine. The most direct method is simply to place the salt-clay mixture in an earthenware crucible, add a layer of gold in some form with a high surface area such as granules or thin sheet, then another layer of cement, and alternate layers until the crucible is filled. It is then luted and placed in a furnace at a temperature well below the melting point of the alloy, generally for from 12 to 24 hours. The copper and silver in the gold are attacked by the chlorine generated and react to form copper and silver chlorides. Depending upon the furnace temperature, these salts either will melt and be taken up by the clay matrix or by the walls of the crucible itself or will remain solid and can be dissolved later from the surface of the gold. The process may be repeated as many times as necessary and is a drastic and thorough procedure for the removal of all the impurities.

To my knowledge, there is no evidence that cementation has ever been used for purposes of gilding by surface enrichment of gold in an alloy of low gold content. A somewhat similar technique has been used, on the other hand, to improve the surfaces of alloys that are rich in gold but contain some silver as well. Gowland describes such a coloring procedure that has been used in Japan since the sixteenth century. At that time it was employed to color the surfaces of gold coins, minted by the government, containing approximately 25 percent of silver. The mixture used in the reaction contained iron and copper sulfates, potassium nitrate, calcined sodium chloride, and resin rather than powdered brick dust. These were mixed with water to make a paste that was painted onto the pale-colored coins. The coins were "heated to redness" on a grate over an open charcoal fire, later immersed in a strong solution of salt to remove the reaction products that had formed on the surfaces, and dried. The surfaces were pure gold at the end of this treatment.[24]

Furthermore, we also know that by the time of the Spanish conquest of Mexico in the sixteenth century the Aztec goldsmiths were well aware of the effect of

[23] One should keep in mind, however, the possibility that certain acid solutions such as aqueous ferric sulfate or ferric sulfate and salt might have been used. Their effectiveness in both removing the silver and in creating a coherent gold layer on alloys of low gold content will have to be tested in the laboratory.

[24] See Reference 4. I am grateful to Professor Cyril Stanley Smith for having called my attention to this practice.

clay and salt as an agent for enrichment of the surface color of an object cast in gold or in tumbaga. Fray Bernardino de Sahagún, a Spanish priest living among the Aztecs of preconquest Mexico, compiled a manuscript between the years 1558 and 1569 entitled "Historia general de las cosas de la Nueva España." In it are recorded detailed accounts of the mode of life of the Indians, as related by the Indians themselves, including a section devoted to metalworking. In a passage describing the finishing operations used to smooth and clean the surfaces of a cast gold object, the Indian craftsman recounts burnishing it, treating it with alum, and heating it over a fire. Subsequently, ". . . when it came forth, once more, for the second time, it was at once washed, rubbed, with what was called 'gold medicine.' It was just like yellow earth mixed with a little salt; with this the gold was perfected; with this it became very yellow."[25] Although we have no way of knowing how early such coloring techniques were used in South and Central America, the notion that some form of cementation was practiced and had become a traditional operation by the sixteenth century is not an unreasonable one.

Obviously if the Peruvian alloys were gilded by cementation, the cementing mixture must have been mild and the action relatively slow so that it could be controlled easily. Only the outermost surface silver in these objects had to be removed in order for a uniform gold layer to form. That layer, as we have seen, need be no thicker than about one micron for the metal to appear golden. A delicate balance had to be achieved between the rate at which the chloride reacted with the metal and the rate at which the silver diffused to the surface. If the action was too drastic, too large a proportion of silver and copper would be removed, the gold formed would be powdery and noncohesive, and the surface would appear severely pitted and irregular.

Laboratory experiments indicate that the process is indeed feasible and not difficult to perform. An alloy containing 60 percent Cu, 30 percent Ag, 10 percent Au was cast and subsequently hammered into a thin sheet in the manner previously described. The formation of enriched silver surfaces occurred after only a few annealing and pickling sequences. The microstructure of a cross section of the resulting sheet is shown in Figure 1.41. It should be compared with that of the disk presumed to come from Vicus, Figure 1.31, as well as with that of the experimental Ag-Cu alloy in Figure 1.35. The

deformed, copper-rich dendrites in both gold-containing alloys are filled with fine white specks that represent tiny precipitates of silver formed within the beta solid solution during some stage of the annealing operations and suggest that the solubility of gold in the copper-rich phase varies considerably with temperature. By contrast, the binary alloy contains none of this precipitate.

Pieces of the sheet metal were placed in fireclay crucibles, surrounded by a cementing mixture. The cement comprised two parts of ground (approximately 50 mesh) common brick dust and one part of similarly ground rock salt. It was very slightly dampened with either water or urine immediately before use in the crucibles. The crucibles were luted and placed in a furnace at 350°C. After ten minutes, those pieces of metal exposed to the salt-clay-urine cement had formed a continuous, compact, and smooth layer of surface gold, while it took twice that length of time to develop a similarly cohesive layer on the pieces surrounded with cement dampened with water. When the metal was allowed to remain in the furnace for longer than these brief periods, the gold layer became associated with the corrosion products of the copper and silver, which in turn adhered firmly to the siliceous matrix of the cement. The reactions had gone too far, and the gold layer pulled away from the underlying metal, remaining in association with the metallic salts and the matrix. Undoubtedly the cementing mixtures were too strong, and the action was too rapid. Further experiments will have to be designed to determine the optimum conditions under which cementation can be carried out. Nevertheless, reasonably successful results were obtained with the cement and heating conditions described, and the color photograph in Plate I shows a gold-covered, cemented piece of metal alongside an uncemented piece with enriched silver surfaces. The gold layer is obviously very thin, and there are a few areas where the silver shows through. The color of the gold is not dissimilar to that of the Chimu disk, but it is nowhere near as rich and deeply golden as the surface of the disk from "Vicus," which has a much thicker layer of gold. Before cementation, several decorative marks were made on the metal with a tracing tool. The gold layer has formed quite evenly over the surfaces of these depressions. Obviously these same tool marks could have been made after the gold layer had been formed. As long as the metal was simply displaced and not cut by the tool (the usual distinction between tracing and engraving), the gold surface would be retained within the depressions formed.

Electron microbeam probe traces were taken across sections of several pieces of gold-colored metal. One such trace is

25 This manuscript is known as the *Florentine Codex* and was written originally by Sahagún in his transcription of Náhuatl, the language of the Aztec. It has recently been translated into English by Dibble and Anderson (Reference 16).

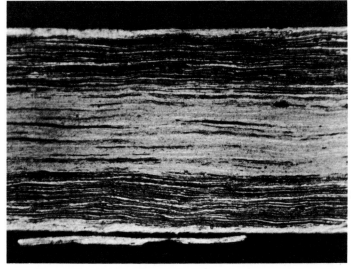

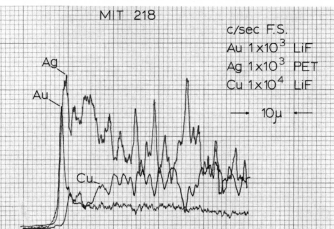

MIT 218

c/sec F.S.
Au 1×10^3 LiF
Ag 1×10^3 PET
Cu 1×10^4 LiF

→ 10μ ←

Ag

Au

Cu

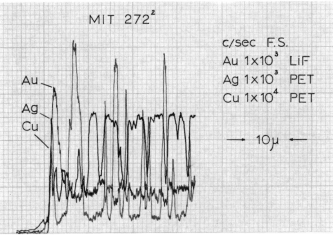

MIT 272²

c/sec F.S.
Au 1×10^3 LiF
Ag 1×10^3 PET
Cu 1×10^4 PET

→ 10μ ←

Au

Ag

Cu

1.39
Chimu disk. Photomicrograph of an entire cross section through the metal. Magnification 495X, As polished.

1.40
Chimu disk. Electron microbeam probe traces of Au, Ag, and Cu through the gilded surface of the section shown in Figure 1.39.

1.41
A section through sheet metal hammered from a 60/30/10 Cu-Ag-Au alloy. Compare with microstructure of "Vicus" disk in Figure 1.31. Magnification 570X, etched by $K_2Cr_2O_7$ + NaCl + H_2SO_4 diluted 1:9.

1.42
Electron microbeam probe traces of Au, Ag, and Cu across the surface of a section of cemented sheet metal (60/30/10 Cu-Ag-Au alloy).

25

shown in Figure 1.42. Its profile is similar to the traces of both the "Vicus" and the Chimu disks. There is a high, narrow gold peak at the surface containing virtually no silver or copper. (The very narrow silver and copper peaks at the extreme surface of the gold are undoubtedly due to the presence of bits of silver and copper corrosion products adherent to the metal.) Although the gold is only $1-2\mu$ thick, once optimum conditions are established for the formation of this layer, it should be possible to produce much thicker surface coatings.

Summary

The characteristics of the gilding on these Peruvian objects will be treated in the same order as were those of the earlier Near Eastern material in order to facilitate direct comparison between the two.

1. The gilding covers all surfaces of the objects in a smooth, uniform, and continuous layer as if the craftsman clearly intended to have the objects look golden.

2. It is difficult to ascertain whether the gilding was completed before or after the decorative tooling. The gold in the tooled depressions is as thin and as smooth as it is elsewhere on these objects, which suggests that depletion gilding rather than leaf gilding was the method employed.

3. The gilding is very thin, only about 2μ thick in the case of the Chimu disk and 4μ on the "Vicus" artifact.

4. Mercury was not used to facilitate the gilding of these objects. In fact, no analyses of gilded metals from pre-Columbian America have ever demonstrated the presence of mercury.

Conclusion

The intent of these investigations has been not only to document as closely as possible the ways in which an individual craftsman confronted the materials and tools of his craft in the manufacture of particular objects but to try to demonstrate the variety of technical solutions that can arise in response to a given objective. There has not been time to discuss the traditions of metalworking in the two geographic areas treated here, but certainly the heritage of technical style is very important in the sense that it conditions the way in which an individual meets the range of alternatives open to him. The materials he has available will also, obviously, color the breadth of technical diversity of which he is capable. But we ought not to see a given technical solution as governed solely by the state of the technology itself. It is evident that the Peruvians and the Iranians were after two very different effects when they gilded metal and that the techniques they devised were as much a part of the economics, the aesthetics, the religion, the utilitarian objectives of their respective milieus as they

were part of their technical capability or point of view. For example, one cannot explain the differences merely on the basis of the presence of mercury in one setting and its absence in another.

The two most outstanding features of the gilt silver objects from the Near East are, it seems to me, on the one hand the purely aesthetic presence of the gold in juxtaposition to the silver, and on the other the purely technical expedient of applying the gold with the aid of mercury. The use of mercury for gilding metal, once it was introduced into this region, was rapidly adopted, widespread, and longstanding. It was a particularly simple and economic way of using gold and of obtaining its glitter in just those areas on a metal surface where it was desired. Certainly in the case of Byzantine art gold was used in mosaics, in icons, on metal objects not only as a representation of an imperial or a sacred color but for the effect it had in generating different atmospheres of light—light creating the space surrounding figures in a mosaic, light emanating from an icon, or light glittering from the surface of a golden cross on the cover of a holy book. Being able to control with relative ease the placement of gold on the surface of a silver object was important, because it was precisely the interplay between the gold and the silver that was to produce the desired life of that surface.

On the other hand, one ought to raise the question of whether or not methods other than mercury gilding were used by silversmiths in the Near East at this time, and if so when and why they were used. All the objects I have illustrated, both Byzantine and Sasanian, were either ecclesiastical or, if not imperial, at least elegant possessions of persons or institutions of some significance. Most of them were probably made in imperial workshops. Were other, less prestigious objects or objects made in provincial workshops fabricated in the same way? It would be instructive, for example, to examine gilt silver jewelry, although little remains, or other small, occasional objects that may have had greater circulation and may have been more generally available. Imperial jewelry and jewelry of the wealthy in Byzantium was made of gold. But silver and gilt silver were used for the more popular varieties and gilded bronze for the really inexpensive kinds. Apparently the affluent often wore gilt bronze jewelry in the streets rather than their valuable possessions that might have been attractive to thieves! (Reference 15) Was gilding with mercury the technique used on such minor objects, or were other available methods employed? Although it was available to the more privileged artisan, was it a common material supplied to the average workshop?

The kinds of economic considerations that must have governed the use and distribution of gold in the Near East were not those of Peru. Native gold was found there in great quantity and was plentiful also in the neighboring states of Ecuador, Colombia, and Bolivia. From the variety of surviving artifactual material made of gold it seems apparent that the metal was widely available. Although there are a good many bimetallic objects that take advantage of the decorative juxtaposition of gold and silver as well as some silver objects that are parcel-gilt, for the most part the uninterrupted expanse of a gold surface was the quality most desired. This predilection reached its peak at the time of the Chimu kingdom and later during the Inca empire when the walls of palaces and of the sun temples were covered with plaques or sheets of gold. It is not surprising, therefore, to find that when an object was gilded—by whatever process—its entire surface was covered with gold. The use of gold foil for this purpose is one of the most efficient methods in the sense that it utilizes the least amount of gold and wastes little. On the other hand, we have seen that the Chimu disk contains about 7 percent of gold and that from ''Vicus'' approximately 10 percent. Regardless of whether these disks were gilded by leaf or by cementation, the presence of these amounts of gold in the alloys indicates some lack of concern with efficient use of this metal. By A.D. 1000 when the era of the big city began, the quantity of gold being mined and distributed must have been enormous, and economizing on the metal could not have been a vital consideration. One of the more intriguing aspects of the proposed cementation process is precisely that it is suitable to gilding large expanses of metal easily and quickly.[26] Even a vessel already shaped so that access to its hollow interior is difficult can readily be gilded in this manner. Once we are able to date the metal artifacts from Vicus more securely, we may find that the gilding of large areas of metal, especially metal in the form of thin sheet, is considerably earlier than we now consider it.

Another observation that warrants consideration is the fact that, thus far, the examples of gilded sheet-metal objects of silver-copper-gold alloys have all come from the north of Peru. If these artifacts were indeed gilded by the cementation coloring method proposed. I believe we are justified in regarding the philosophy behind this technique as very similar to that behind the manufacture of tumbaga, discussed in the introductory section. We know that tumbaga was rarely used in Peru. It has been argued that on the northern coast of Peru copper was plentiful and gold scarce, that objects of pure copper and later of bronze were covered with gold leaf when they were gilded, and that, therefore, there was probably little or no trade between Colombia and Peru. (Reference 14) While this may be true in the sense of the movement of metals, it seems not at all unreasonable to suppose that there was a strong metallurgical tradition in the north of South America, common to Peru and Colombia and, to a lesser extent, Ecuador, which resulted in the application of a characteristic set of metallurgical principles and attitudes to the particular problems at hand. The concept of removing silver from the surface of a hammered sheet of Ag-Cu-Au alloy is not really very different from the concept of removing copper from the surface of a cast Cu-Au alloy. The methods are different both because of the alloys involved and the fact that some are worked while others are cast. Tumbaga was used primarily for castings, whereas the ternary alloy appears to have been more suitable for sheet metal. But the rationale behind the methods is really quite similar. If, after further experimental work and examination of more objects of this kind, it becomes apparent that depletion gilding was the process employed, we may wish to address ourselves more seriously to a consideration of the extent to which the northwest corner of South America was a region of shared metallurgical principles and procedures. The movement of metalworkers rather than of metals may have been the substance of any such common tradition.

[26] If cementation was used for gilding, it supposedly was also used for the purification of gold in bulk. Bergsøe argued for the likelihood of the Indians' acquaintance with cementation in Reference 2. He points out that in Samuel K. Lothrop's description of the metal artifacts from Coclé, Panama, there is mention of 16 items made of Au-Cu alloys that are free from silver. (See Reference 8.) Bergsøe argues that it is entirely possible these alloys were made with gold from which the silver had been extracted by cementation. His own successful experimental attempts to cement powdered gold with clay and salt are described.

Acknowledgments

This paper is dedicated to William C. Root, whose death in June 1969 has meant the loss, to those of us engaged in the study of pre-Columbian metallurgy, of one of the field's most active and enthusiastic scholars. It was he who gave me the first bits of gilt metal from South America with which to begin my research into early gilding techniques, and in his suggestions and criticisms he gave me as well the benefit of his many years of experience in studying the technologies of these cultures. He was a pioneer in a field still largely unexplored. The kindest tribute to him will be to pursue that exploration with the rigor and the excitement that were the substance and the motivation of his work.

I should like to thank, first, those individuals whose scholarly interest and delight in the objects I have studied made it possible for me to pursue my own enthusiasm for the technology of this material. They are: Junius B. Bird, Elizabeth H. Bland, Mr. and Mrs. Dudley T. Easby, Jr., Dorothy G. Shepherd, and John S. Thacher. I am especially grateful to Dorothy Shepherd for her kind cooperation and generosity during the course of this study.

The assistance I have had in the analytical examination of the objects was no less valuable. None of the electron microbeam probe data in connection with the Peruvian material could have been assembled without the assistance, advice, and patient skill of Stephen L. Bender and John K. Hill of the Ledgemont Laboratory, Kennecott Copper Corporation. At M.I.T., I would especially like to thank Donald L. Guernsey, Stephen M. Nagy, and Walter W. Correia, who were responsible for the wet chemical and spectrographic analyses of the Peruvian objects; Joseph A. Adario, who ran all of the microbeam probe traces of the Near Eastern artifacts; and Richard A. Berry for his assistance in casting the alloys used to reproduce the pre-Columbian techniques. I am particularly grateful to Katharine C. Ruhl of the Cleveland Museum of Art for having taken all the color slides of the Sasanian objects that I showed at the conference as well as the details of the Iranian objects which illustrate this paper.

Finally, my warm thanks to Cyril Stanley Smith for sharing with me his wealth of knowledge of metallurgy, materials, and man—but especially for his encouragement during all those hours when ancient technology seemed to defy modern resolve.

Table A.1

Composition of Metal Samples Removed from Surface of Horse Rhyton*

Sample Type	No. and Site of Sample		Composition† (weight percent)			
			Au	Ag	Cu	Hg
1	8	Loose fragment of gold foil	90.5	6.8	1.0	1.7
1	1	Gilding: chest harness, proper right side	57.4	40.0	0.5	2.1
1	4	Gilding: nose harness	65.9	32.0	0.5	1.6
2	6	Gilt area, gilding lost: medallion strap on proper right chest	8.4	89.2	1.6	0.8
2	2	Probable gilt area, gilding lost: top right strand of mane	1.2	97.6	0.9	0.3
2	7	Possible gilt area, gilding lost: roping on saddle, proper right front edge	0.6	97.9	1.2	0.3
3	3	Ungilt silver: body, near hoof of proper right leg	0.8	98.2	1.0	<0.02
3	5	Ungilt silver: proper right hock	0.7	98.5	0.8	<0.02

* A tiny fragment of gold foil (Sample #8), similar to that analyzed by emission spectrography, was the only "bulk" sample studied. All the other samples were taken by Sayre, who used an essentially nondestructive technique he has developed for removing minute quantities of metal from a surface by stroking the surface lightly with a small quartz plate or cylinder. (See E. V. Sayre, "The Nuclear Age and the Fine Arts," *Proceedings of the 1967 Youth Congress on the Atom,* Chicago, 1967.)

† Approximate composition calculated upon the assumption that the elements determined are the only components in significant concentrations.

Appendix

Since this paper was written, further studies of the gilding on the Cleveland Museum horse rhyton have been most generously undertaken, at the request of the author, by Edward V. Sayre and Pieter Meyers at the Chemistry Department of Brookhaven National Laboratory. Three types of sample were removed from the rhyton: (1) metal from gilded areas; (2) metal from areas that appear to have been gilded but have lost their gold foil; (3) metal from areas presumed never to have been gilded. The composition of these samples was determined by neutron activation analysis, and the results are given in Table A.1.

The analyses show that mercury was used in applying the gold foil to the silver surfaces. Furthermore, the concentration of mercury in the silver presumed to have been gilded is at least ten times as great as the trace amount in the ungilded silver, demonstrating that the sampled areas must have been either covered with gold at one time or preamalgamated with mercury. The loose fragment of foil contains very little silver in comparison with the silver concentration in the gilding still in situ. This may indicate that the flake never adhered to the surface and little or no Au-Ag diffusion occurred when the metal was heated to drive off the mercury. By contrast, the high concentration of silver in Samples 1 and 4 and the tenacity of this gold to the surface of the rhyton may indicate extensive interdiffusion resulting in effective bonding. The inability of the thick gold foil to make close contact with the irregular contours of the rhyton surface still remains the primary reason for poor bonding in spite of the presence of mercury.

References

1.
Barba, Alvaro Alonzo

El Arte de los Metales, R. E. Douglass and E. P. Mathewson, Trans. and Eds., New York, 1923, pp. 272–273.

2.
Bergsøe, Paul

"The Gilding Process and the Metallurgy of Copper and Lead among the Pre-Columbian Indians," *Ingeniørviden-skabelige Skrifter Nr. A 46,* 1938.

3.
Emmerich, André

Sweat of the Sun and Tears of the Moon, Seattle, 1965, p. 30.

4.
Gowland, W.

"Metals and Metal-Working in Old Japan," *Trans. Japan Society,* **13,** 1915, pp. 30–32.

5.

Handbook of the Byzantine Collection—Dumbarton Oaks, Washington, D.C., 1967; Entry and Figure No. 70.

6.
Hawthorne, John G., and Smith, Cyril Stanley

On Divers Arts, The Treatise of Theophilus, Chicago, 1963.

7.
Hoover, Herbert C., and Hoover, Lou Henry

De Re Metallica of Georgius Agricola, New York, 1950, pp. 453–457.

8.
Lothrop, Samuel K.,

Coclé—An Archaeological Study of Central Panama, Memoirs of the Peabody Museum, 7, Cambridge, 1937, p. 74.

9.
Lucas, A.

Ancient Egyptian Materials and Industries, J. R. Harris, Ed., 4th ed., London, 1962.

10.
Percy, John

Metallurgy: Silver and Gold, Part 1, London, 1880, pp. 397–402.

11.
Pliny

Natural History, H. Rackham, Ed., Loeb Classical Library, Vol. 9, Cambridge, 1961, Section XXXIII. 99.

12.
Rivet, P., and Arsandaux, H.

La métallurgie en Amérique précolombienne, Travaux et Mémoires de l'Institut d'Ethnologie No. 39, Paris, 1946, pp. 94–100.

13.
Root, William C.

"The Metallurgy of the Southern Coast of Peru," *American Antiquity,* **15,** 1949, pp. 10–37.

14.
Root, William C.

"Gold-Copper Alloys in Ancient America," *J. Chem. Ed.,* **28,** 1951, pp. 76–78.

15.
Ross, Marvin C.

"Byzantine Goldsmith-work," *Byzantine Art, A European Art,* Catalogue 1964 Exhibition, Athens, p. 360.

16.
Sahagún, Bernardino de

General History of the Things of New Spain, Charles E. Dibble and Arthur J. O. Anderson, Trans. and Eds., Monographs of the School of American Research and The Museum of New Mexico, No. 14, Part 10, Book 9, Sante Fe, 1959, p. 75.

17.
Sawyer, Alan R.

Mastercraftsmen of Ancient Peru, Exhibition Catalogue, Solomon R. Guggenheim Foundation, New York, 1968, pp. 24–35.

18.
Shepherd, Dorothy G.

"Sasanian Art in Cleveland," *Bull. Cleveland Museum of Art,* **51,** 1964, pp. 66–95.

19.
Shepherd, Dorothy G.

"Two Silver Rhyta," *Bull. Cleveland Museum of Art,* **53,** 1966, pp. 289–311.

20.
Shewmon, P. G.

Diffusion in Solids, New York, 1963, pp. 115–117.

21.
Sisco, A. G., and Smith, C. S.

Trans. and Eds., *Probierbüchlein,* New York, 1949, pp. 144–147.

22.
Sisco, A. G., and Smith, C. S.

Lazarus Ercker's Treatise on Ores and Assaying, Chicago, 1951, pp. 182–189.

23.
Smith, Cyril Stanley, and Gnudi, Martha T.

The Pirotechnia of Vannoccio Biringuccio, New York, 1959, pp. 202–205.

Chapter 2

The Techniques of the Luristan Smith[1]

Cyril Stanley Smith
Massachusetts Institute of Technology

From the nomad graves of Luristan in western Iran come many iron or, rather, steel objects that are of considerably greater interest from a technical standpoint than the aesthetically superb and hence more famous bronzes with which they are associated. The bronzes were made by techniques that had been in use for more than a millennium, whereas the iron objects—bracelets, maces, and especially swords—have some unique technical features, for their rugged elaborateness derives directly from the process of manufacture and reveals both high skill and unexpected ignorance.

The Luristan iron and steel objects were made for a people who had not learned to appreciate the shapes that arise naturally under the hammer, and many of the designs emulate more complicated shapes easily possible in a casting. The smith, therefore, who had not yet learned how to hammer-weld, devised a technique for assembling preshaped pieces by mechanical joining.

Although a number of technical studies of the swords have been published in the past (the most important of which are listed in the references at the end of this chapter), they have mainly involved museum objects that could not be damaged in the examination. The objects used in the present study were purchased specifically for the purpose. Moreover, they were heavily corroded, and it was therefore possible to cut out substantial samples for chemical analysis and metallographic studies without aesthetic loss.

Figures 2.1 to 2.5 show the general appearance of eight of the objects used for the present study, some of them both before and after electrolytic cleaning to remove the heavy layers of rust.[2] The provenance of the objects, listed in Table 2.1, is not certainly known. They were purchased as Luristan material from dealers in Tehran in 1961, 1962, and 1967, but only the most interesting sword (No. 105) and the maces uniquely conform stylisti-

cally to Luristan.[3] Except for No. 102; which is much later, the other pieces were approximately contemporary with the Luristan irons (ninth to seventh centuries B.C.) and are metallurgically similar although they probably originated in other parts of Iran.

Chemical analyses were made at the Applied Research Laboratory of the United States Steel Corporation, through the courtesy of Dr. Max Lightner. The results are reported in Table 2.1. The mace head No. 106 contained nickel, and the dagger No. 102 (of late origin) contained phosphorus, but otherwise the steels are all free from significant amounts of any kind of alloying element except carbon and nitrogen.[4] Sulfur is low in all the samples, as would be expected with charcoal-smelted ores.

The carbon content of the steel is highly variable from place to place within one object, and the average analyses given are locally without meaning. The Luristan smith clearly operated his smelting fire under conditions that were frequently highly carburizing; he made true steel. There are zones with as much as 1 percent carbon (estimated from the amount of iron carbide seen in the microstructure) but carbon-free areas are to be found adjacent to them in the same piece, and everything in between, with no special relationship between location and carbon content. Probably the smith was unaware of these local differences; certainly he did not (as later smiths have done) select and use the harder metal in areas where strength was needed or a softer metal for decorative parts.

The silicon is, presumably, mainly in non-metallic form in the inclusions, which, as in all ancient iron, are numerous. Figures 2.7 to 2.11 show the appearance under the microscope of four different types of inclusions that have frequently been encountered. The mixed wüstite (FeO), fayalite ($2 FeO \cdot SiO_2$), and glassy silicate inclusions are perhaps simply residual from the ore, the silica having been fluxed by unreduced oxide. The wüstite content is highly variable from place to place and

The Steel

---

[1] Paper presented at the Fifth International Conference on Iranian Studies, Tehran, April 1968, and the A.C.S. Symposium on Archaeological Chemistry, Atlantic City, September 1968.

[2] Cleaning was done by electrolyzing in 5 percent aqueous sodium hydroxide solution, the specimen being cathodic and the current density about 40 mA per square cm. The action was continued for about 4 days by which time all loose oxide had been reduced or had fallen away without effect on the solid metal. The objects were then removed, washed, scoured with a steel wire brush, warmed, and coated with wax. Such cleaning destroys whatever evidence might lie in the corrosion products and is generally to be discouraged except for objects intended for exhibition or those believed to contain internal chlorides.

[3] The author is grateful to Dr. Peter Carlmeyer, Munich, for help in identification.

[4] The presence of nitrogen was not always shown in the chemical analysis for it was distributed with extreme irregularity. Microscopic examination, however, left no doubt that there were considerable quantities in some areas for it was revealed, especially in low carbon zones, as tiny crystallographically oriented plates (needles in section) characteristic of the nitride Fe_4N, and the more profuse precipitation of Fe_8N. Figure 2.6 shows the richest field that was encountered in any specimen. The structure is comparable to published photomicrographs of iron containing about 0.05 percent nitrogen.

Table 2.1

Identification and Composition of Objects Studied*

M.I.T. Designations	Type of Object and Presumed Provenance	Location of Sample for Analysis	Chemical Composition (percent by weight)							
			C	Mn	P	Si	Cu	Ni	Co	N
101	Dagger (Fig. 2.1D, 2.2D). Medean western Iran, seventh century B.C.	Section of blade 4 to 10 cm from hilt	0.57		0.025					0.007
103	Dagger (Fig. 2.1B, 2.2B). Talish or Giyan area, ninth or eighth century B.C.	Section of blade 6 to 10 cm from hilt	0.089	<0.01	0.028	<0.04	0.02	0.05		0.004
104	Dagger (Fig. 2.1A, 2.2A). Talish or Giyan area, ninth or eighth century B.C.	Square portion of handle 2 to 8 cm below "bobbin"	0.23		<0.01					0.003
105	Short sword (Fig. 2.3). Luristan ca. eighth century B.C.	Section of blade 2 to 10 cm below ricasso	0.63	0.02	<0.01	0.02	<0.01	0.01	0.01	0.002
		Section through lion head attached to ricasso	0.39	0.04	<0.01	0.08, 0.17	<0.01	0.01	0.03	0.003
106	Mace (Fig. 2.4B, 2.5B). Luristan ca. eighth century B.C.	Section through square handle 22 to 29 cm from top end of head	0.063	0.02	0.031	0.03, 0.14	0.02	0.48, 0.58	0.25	0.005
107	Mace head (Fig. 2.4A). Luristan, ca. eighth century B.C.	Equatorial section normal to hole	0.23		<0.01					0.006
113	Mace head (Fig. 2.5A). Luristan, ca. eighth century B.C.	Equatorial section normal to hole	0.10	<0.03	0.023					0.006
102	Dagger (Fig. 2.1C, 2.2C). Uncertain, ca. ninth century A.D., perhaps European.	Section of blade 4 to 10 cm from hilt	0.098	<0.01	0.24	<0.01	0.05	0.05	0.03	0.004

* *Note:* Additional elements analyzed for, but not detected in any sample, were sulfur in all cases less than 0.01 percent; tin less than 0.002 percent; columbium, molybdenum, titanium and vanadium all less than 0.005 percent. The silicon is present mainly in the form of silicate inclusions.

Analyses made in the Applied Research Laboratory, U.S. Steel Corporation, courtesy M. W. Lightner. The analyses for carbon, phosphorous, and nitrogen were made chemically on millings cut transversally from the entire cross section. The other determinations were done by emission spectroscopy on areas ground parallel to the widest surface of the piece, avoiding the areas richest in slag inclusions. A blank means element not determined. The accuracy of the determination (apart from sampling errors) is ±2 on the last digit stated.

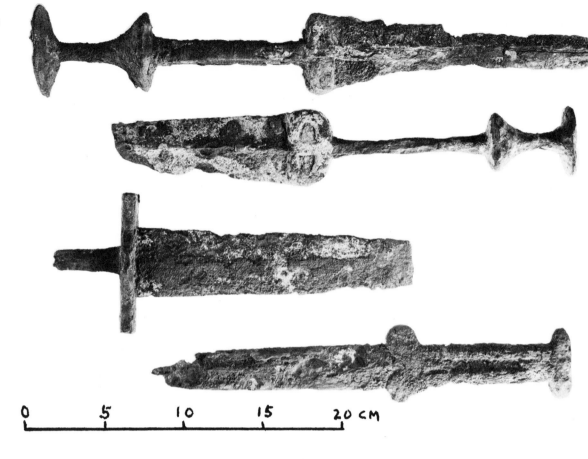

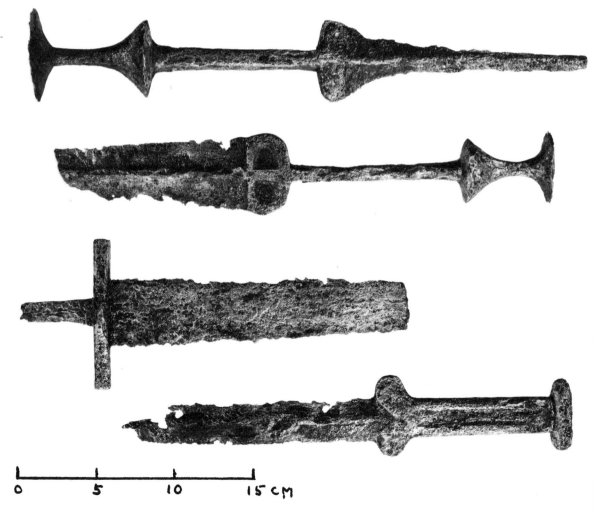

2.3
No. 105. Short sword
of classic Luristan type.
Ca. eighth century B.C.
After electrolytic cleaning.

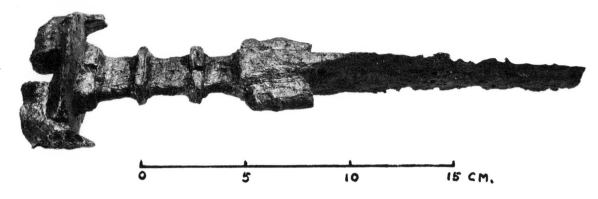

2.4
(A) Mace head, No.
107, and (B) Mace,
No. 106. Luristan, Ca.
eighth century B.C. Elec-
trolytically cleaned.

2.5
(A) Mace head, No.
113, (B) Mace head,
No. 106 (Cf. Figure 4),
(C) Mace head of uncer-
tain provenance, proba-
bly Luristan, eighth cen-
tury. (A and C, un-
cleaned; B after electro-
lytic cleaning.)

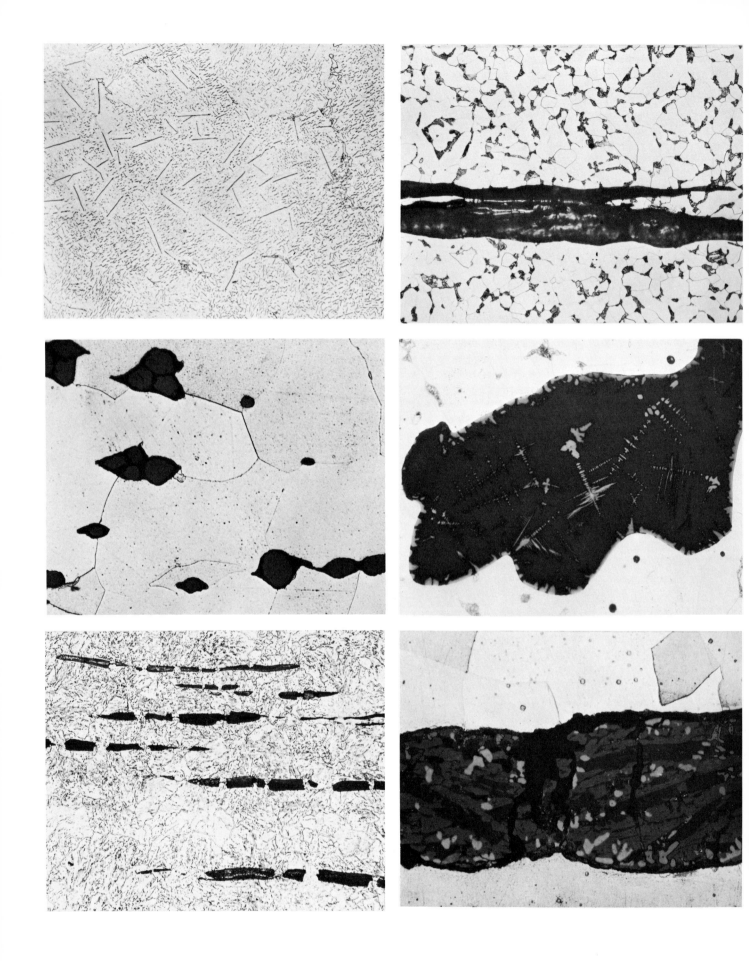

2.6
Microstructure near inner surface of lion attachment, No. 105, showing low-carbon area with heavy precipitation of iron nitrides. Etched, 580X. (Note: This and all subsequent photomicrographs are of specimens metallographically polished and etched with a 2 percent solution of nitric acid in alcohol)

2.7
Slag inclusions in dagger, No. 103. Spherical particles of wüstite (FeO) partly surrounded by silicate in matrix of carbon-free ferrite grains. Etched, 580X.

2.8
Slag inclusions in a high-carbon area in No. 105. The silicate slag had been first elongated when plastic (perhaps liquid) and subsequently broken by deformation at a lower temperature. Etched, 230X.

Column 2

2.9
Stringer of transparent glassy slag in center of pommel, No. 104. Longitudinal section. Etched, 230X.

2.10
Large slag inclusion in No. 104, showing well formed dendrites of wüstite in glassy silicate matrix. Etched, 580X.

2.11
Complex crystalline slag inclusion in No. 102. (Note, this dagger is later and the steel less pure than the Luristan material.) Etched, 580X.

is roughly in inverse amount to the carbon content, as would be expected since wüstite cannot exist under highly reducing conditions. Compare Figure 2.7, showing mainly wüstite (perhaps residual particles of partly reduced unmelted oxide from the ore) surrounded with a little glassy slag in a carbon-free area, with Figure 2.8 which shows a wüstite-free silicate slag in a zone having high carbon content. Most of the inclusions had been deformed in a plastic (probably liquid) state, but quite frequently well-elongated stringers of slag had been later broken up mechanically when solid, with the fragments unchanged in shape by either spheroidization or deformation and separated by metal forced between them (Figures 2.8 and 2.9). The metal, therefore, must have been first worked at a high temperature and subsequently extensively deformed when much colder. The two stages probably correspond to the initial reduction and consolidation of the iron sponge and to the final shaping operations, respectively.

Many of the slag inclusions have the glassy transparent character that denotes high silica content. Figure 2.9 shows such slag in No. 104. In Figure 2.8, the smallest stringers are glassy while the larger ones have partially crystallized— more likely as a result of nucleation than of differences in composition. Many ancient irons contain minute spherical particles (about 1 to 10μ diameter) of a clear glassy material, seemingly different from the larger inclusions. Their origin is obscure—they may represent small isolated silica inclusions in the ore that were fluxed and later reduced while entirely surrounded by metal, or they may be residual ash from charcoal fragments that became incorporated in the metal and were subsequently deprived of carbon by diffusion.

It is more common for the slag to have one or more phases in a dendritic or crystalline shape that could only form from the liquid state. (See Figures 2.10 and 2.11 and also Figures 47 to 51 in Smith, Reference 12.) Figure 2.11 is of the dagger No. 102, of a much later date than the others, and shows in the slag three distinctly different crystalline phases which have not yet been identified positively.

Slag inclusions carry with them much evidence regarding the details of metallurgical processing and their analysis is to be the next stage of this research. But whatever the composition and structure of the slag, its distribution, like that of the carbon, provides an index of local metal flow and gives clues to the deformational history of the metal which, in turn, reveals much about the smith's practice in making the objects (see Figures 2.12 to 2.17, 2.32, and *passim*). Though one cannot rule out the possibility that several different pieces of sponge iron were combined together to give a big enough bloom to forge these objects, or even the possibility that scrap from previous operations was faggoted into the new metal at this stage, there has been no later welding. Except for mechanical attachments each of the objects, with its blade, handle, pommel, and decoration, is a single piece, metallurgically intact. Although the long seams of high and low carbon metal do rather suggest the welding together of pieces of different but more or less uniform composition, the stringers of slag are not related to the boundaries between areas of different carbon contents. The general heterogeneity is entirely of the type that could have originated in the original spongy bloom of iron as it left the reduction hearth or furnace, modified with the subsequent shaping of the entire piece and some diffusion of carbon. In the Luristan sword examined by Maxwell-Hyslop and Bird in collaboration with Hodges (References 7 and 1), the hilt had been composed by hammering a stack of irregular flat strips into a compact mass; this had obviously been done hot but at a forging heat not at the much higher temperature needed for welding.

The carbon content in the swords is not related to the position in the weapon, that is, the cutting edges vary just as much in carbon content as do the decorative parts. There is no evidence whatever of superficial or local carburization of the finished piece, and, surprisingly, very little evidence of surface decarburization during forging.

The objects examined were so heavily corroded that no fine surface detail was visible. The decorative heads on the Luristan short swords illustrated by Lefferts (Reference 5) and Ternbach (Reference 13) seem to have been finished by both chiseling and chasing and perhaps by some use of abrasive, but in general the objects owe their shape entirely to the simple percussive tools of the smith. The general symmetry and surface characteristics of the Luristan steel objects make it almost certain that some kind of round or flat swages were used rather than free hammer work, and perhaps large shaped sets. Sections through the length of the blades (Figures 2.12 to 2.15) show the metal flow, and the cross sections of the blades (Figure 2.16) show—excepting again No. 102—an irregularity of structure that comes from simple forging without any major laminations or welds.

The ends of several of the pieces had been transversely cut to shape by the use of a saw or, more likely, by grinding, not with the blacksmith's cold chisel. This is easily seen particularly in Figure 2.17, the head of the short sword No. 105. Both the main handle itself, which is integral with the blade, and the decorative heads have slag lines terminating abruptly at the

General Shaping Techniques

2.12
Axial section through
handle in No. 104. The
flow of the metal during
forging is revealed by
the distribution of the
slag streaks and zones
of higher carbon (dark
etching) metal. Etched,
90% of actual size.

2.13
Section through shoul-
der of blade, No. 104.
Etched, 3.9X.

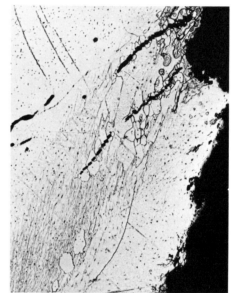

2.14
Microstructure showing
surface deformation and
partial recrystallization
beneath ridge in No.
104 (Cf. Figure 2.13).
Etched, 190X.

2.15
Transverse section
through ricasso of short
sword, No. 105, showing
manner of attachement
of the decorative lions.
Etched, 1.4X.

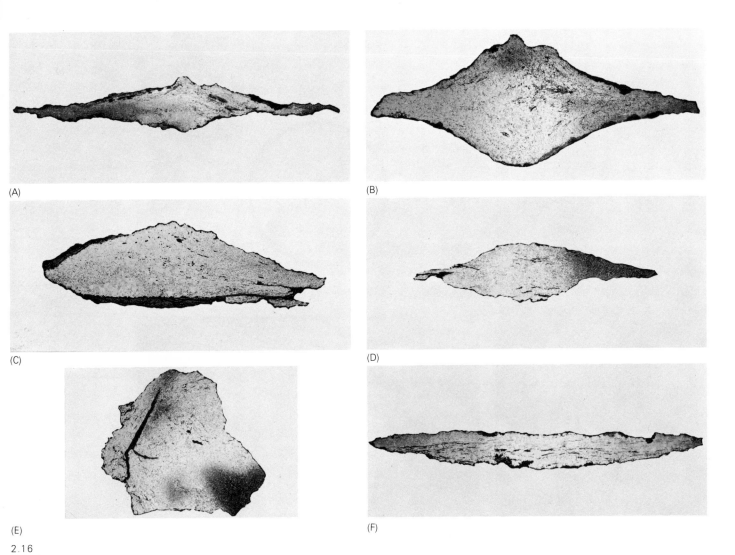

(A)

(B)

(C)

(D)

(E)

(F)

2.16
Etched transverse sections of dagger blades showing distribution of carbon and slag content
(A)
No. 101, 4X;
(B)
No. 103, 4X;
(C)
No. 104, 8X;
(D)
No. 105, 4X;
(E)
No. 106 (Mace handle), 4X;
(F)
No. 102, 3.25X.

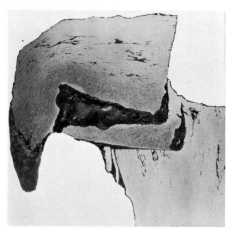

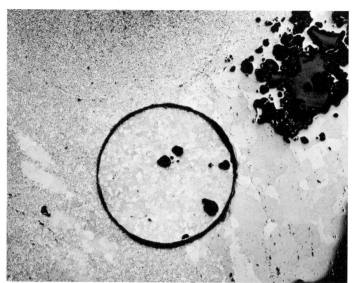

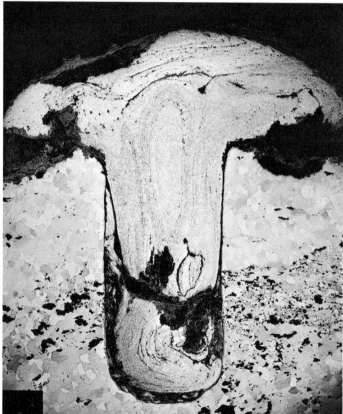

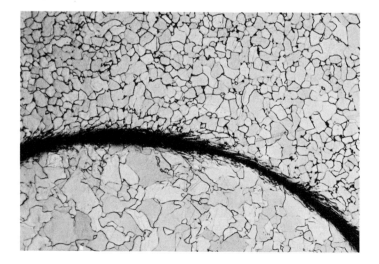

2.17
Section through end of·
hilt, pommel and attached
heads, No. 105. (See
Figure 2.34 for section
normal to this). Etched,
1.4X.

2.18
End of handle, No.
101. Shows tang fitting
into accurately cut hole.
Lightly polished and
etched, 1.4X.

2.19
Longitudinal section
through handle of
mace, No. 106, showing
transverse drilled hole.
Etched, 3.5X.

2.20
End of mace head No.
107, ground flat and
polished. Shows section
through decorative pin
fitted in drilled hole.
Note large variation in
grain size. Etched,
11X.

2.21
Axial section through
decorative pin in mace
head, No. 113. Etched,
9X.

2.22
Edge of pin shown in
Figure 2.20 at higher
magnification. Etched,
55X.

end with almost no deformation as they approach the surface (Figure 2.17). Even more remarkable is the ability of the smith to make well-shaped holes. A rectangular hole with slightly rounded ends was cut in the pommel of No. 101 (Figure 2.18) and No. 105 (seen in cross section in Figures 2.17 and 2.32). A round hole tapering from about 4 to 4.5 mm diameter had been drilled neatly through the handle of the mace, No. 106 (Figure 2.19), with little distortion of the adjacent metal. Such a hole could have been made by using a soft metal tool loaded with abrasive and rotated by means of a bow drill.

Particularly interesting are the holes in the mace heads, Nos. 107 and 113, that were made to accommodate little decorative pins (Figures 2.20 to 2.22). Both of these are 3.2 mm in diameter and were drilled into a depth of about 7.0 mm. The surface metal is locally displaced and the structure distorted (Figure 2.22) but not in the same direction of rotation everywhere, which suggests an oscillating drive for the drill. The distortion, which is reflected in locally increased hardness (Figure 2.48), may also have arisen when the pin was driven. The shape of the bottom of the hole in No. 113 (Figure 2.23) shows that the drill had a narrow rounded protrusion on its head or that the hole was drilled in two stages. The head of the pin had clearly been formed by upsetting the protruding end of a length of wire of a diameter to fit into the hole. Both the structure and the hardness of the body of the pins show a gradient from the center to the outside, and it is probable that the final shaping of the pin had been done cold. The pin body is accurately circular in section, but it is unlikely that it could have been made by drawing, for neither enough power nor suitable die materials would have been available. The iron used for the pins was very malleable, for it had withstood with only slight cracking the further extension to about 9 mm diameter during the flattening of the head. These pins marked the only significantly cold-worked metal found in any of the objects.

The microstructure of the body of the pin in No. 107 (Figure 2.20) shows a larger grain size and less obvious deformation than that in No. 113. Only the surface of this pin showed any distortion, actually to about the same extent as the matching surface of the inside of the hole (Figure 2.48). The pin in No. 113 (Figure 2.23) was slightly tapered, and the end was irregular and broken. There are some irregular metal fragments wedged into the hole, which had been intensely cold-worked but have recrystallized to an extremely small grain size (Figure 2.24). These may have been formed by abrasion when the pin was driven in, but possibly they are chips from engraving or filing operations that had

been put into the hole to wedge the pin. The other mace head, No. 107 (Figure 2.21), contained no such material but had intact, well-fitting pins.

The pommel on No. 101 was attached by peening over of a projecting tang in an accurately fitted hole. Both tang and hole are flat rectangular shapes, the short sides heavily rounded (Figure 2.18). Because the semicircular ends partially overlap the parallel slot in between, the holes were clearly *not* shaped by drilling two holes and cutting out the metal in between, but both half-round and flat files seem to have been used.

The mace heads are of three types. No. 106 (Figures 2.4B, 2.5B) was forged integrally with its iron haft; No. 266 (Figure 2.5C) was forged with an internal conical hole evidently to fit on the end of a pointed rod; and the third type, of which there are two examples, Nos. 107 and 113 (Figures 2.4A and 2.5A), had a cylindrical haft-hole passing transversely through its center. All had deep flutes except No. 107, which had been heavily damaged by corrosion. These flutes seem rather definitely to have been formed by a fuller or other special tool, for they are beautifully shaped and well finished.

The slag distribution in the sections of Nos. 113 (Figure 2.24) and 107 revealed a complicated pattern of metal flow, suggesting a sequence of forging operations somewhat as follows: A lump of sponge iron was forged into a cylindrical rod about 4 cm diameter and 7 cm long. A hole was then made with a cold drifting iron, and the piece swaged cylindrical again. The ends were then enlarged by upsetting (with the center of the shank in a hole or split ring) to give a dumbbell shape. Finally, the flutes were shaped by the use of a special curved V-shaped swage struck at an angle roughly 45° to the original axis, perhaps also finishing in a concave die. The surfaces do not show individual hammer marks. The lower faces (normally invisible) of some of the flutes revealed unwelded cavities, and the sections of both 113 and 107 disclosed some internal unconsolidated metal.

The pins inserted in laboriously drilled holes in the mace head (discussed in the previous section) served a purely decorative function and disguised the fact that all the grooves and flutes did not meet exactly at the common center; a forged projection at this place would have interfered with the finishing of the fluted surfaces.

In the mace head No. 266 (Figure 2.5C), of uncertain provenance, there is a smooth conical axial hole extending the full length, 9.2 cm, tapering uniformly from 2.2 cm diameter at the bottom to 0.80 cm at the top, leaving the metal thickness, except for the flutes, tapering from about 2.5 mm to about 8.0 mm.

The Mace Heads

41

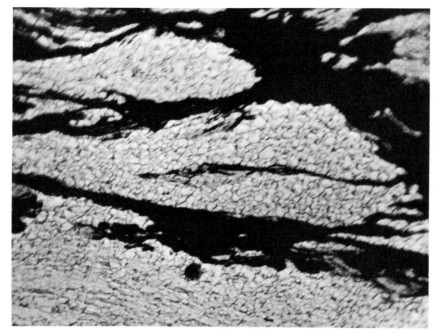

2.23
Metal chip between pin and body of mace head, No. 113 (Cf. Figure 2.21), shows re-crystallized metal of ex-tremely small grain size. Etched, 1350X.

2.24
Midsection through mace head No. 113, in place of fluting slightly above the pin shown in Figure 2.21.

0   1   2 CM

2.25
Attachment of guard to hilt of dagger, No. 102. 75% of natural size.

2.26
Sketch showing con-struction of handle of dagger No. 101. Traced from a radiograph.

The collar of small projections is matched by a slight depression on the inside, but the forging of the longitudinal flutes left no internal marks.

The Daggers

The decoration of most of the daggers is of a type that would come naturally to a smith using a hammer and a few sturdy tools such as fullers and swages. A common form of dagger (not here investigated) consisted of a simple, nearly flat, forged blade of steel with a tang onto which was cast a decorative hilt in bronze. Birmingham et al. (Reference 8) have described Luristan sword blades of wrought bronze with cast-on hilts, also bronze. Our late dagger, No. 102 (Figure 2.2C), has an effective guard in the form of a cross piece of rectangular section with an elongated slit fitting over the tang. Despite its appearance (Figure 2.25) this guard was not welded, but is a single piece of solid metal in which a hole was apparently drifted and subsequently flattened on the tang.

In the dagger No. 101 (Figure 2.2D) the entire blade and handle with its decoration was forged from a single piece of steel, except for the small cross piece at the end which is perforated to fit a small tenon (Figure 2.18). In view of the intricacy of the surfaces forged at the other end of the handle (Figure 2.26), this joint seems almost unnecessary, but it was perhaps used to allow the tool used in forging the longitudinal grooves in the handle to have full run, for much the same reason as the pins in the mace heads. The bobbin-shaped handles of daggers 103 and 104 (Figures 2.2A and 2.2B) seem to have required special dies or swage blocks for their shaping. No. 104 was sectioned and shows (Figures 2.13 and 2.14) that the detail at the shoulder of the blade was achieved mainly by deformation (forging), not cutting, though the metal at the extreme surface is distorted in places, and there was probably some abrasive finishing.

The Short Sword: Mechanical Joints

The most interesting object was the complicated short sword No. 105 (Figure 2.3), of the type unique to Luristan. In the less corroded examples that have been published, the lumps flanking the ricasso are seen to represent crouching lions, and those bent over the edge of the pommel are compound human and animal heads. As Naumann (Reference 9) and others have shown, these swords are composed of many pieces separately forged and mechanically joined together by a kind of crimping operation. The process is curiously unblacksmithlike in nature, but it called for considerable skill in shaping the parts with sufficient accuracy. Our sword was sacrificed completely in order to obtain cross sections for study from all significant places, thereby gaining more information about its construction than was

possible with the museum-owned objects studied by earlier investigators.

Figure 2.27 is a radiograph of the entire hilt, showing the spaces between many of the parts. There was no visible hint of these joints on the sword as received, but most of them became visible to some degree after electrolytic cleaning had removed the rust. Figure 2.28, which is based on the radiographs but incorporates the information provided by later sectioning, shows the manner of construction. Six pieces (which served more of a decorative than a functional purpose) were attached directly to the integrally forged blade and handle,[5] and two pieces to the pommel. All the joints are purely mechanical, the matching male and female parts being carefully shaped and held in place by a final local plastic deformation of the metal. Because of the fine tool work needed on the decorative heads, it is easy to see why the smith might choose to make these separately and attach them in much the same manner as an inlaid carved gemstone, but the use of a similar technique on the pommel itself and the plain bands encircling the hilt indicates a curious unwillingness to forge details that could more easily have been shaped integrally with the hilt.

The simplest joints to describe are the two bands surrounding the hilt transversely. These are pieces of rectangular iron bar about 6.5 mm square, cut to length and bent—bent hot, for the metal at the bends is not significantly cold-worked. These bands fit closely into accurately shaped grooves that had been precut all around the handle and provided with raised flanges at the side that had been finally hammered back to grip the ring tightly. This can be seen in the cross section, Figure 2.29, and in the general view of a groove after its ring has been removed, Figure 2.30.[6] Figure 2.31 shows the microstructure of the joint at higher magnification. It should be noted that there is no flow of metal except in the immediate vicinity of the flanges near the surface. The flanges seem to have been raised with a chisel-like tool driven almost parallel to the surface of the handle, stopping before the raised-up chip broke away, yet there are no visible chisel marks even in the uncorroded area. The bottom of the groove is slightly convex and is remarkably uniform in shape all the way round the hilt (Figure 2.30).

[5]In the majority of the swords described by other writers, the blades are separate pieces, inserted into a slot in the hilt. The single-piece integrally forged construction of the present weapon is both simpler and mechanically better.

[6]The flange is similar to that on the sword illustrated by Maxwell-Hyslop (References 7 and 1). The heavier squarer flanges on the Philadelphia and New York hilts involve more substantial displacement of metal.

43

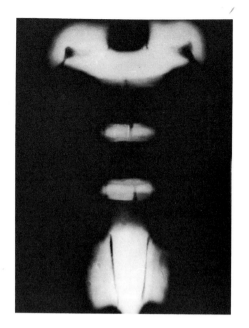

2.27
Radiograph of handle of short sword No. 105.

2.28
Sketch showing construction of short sword No. 105. Traced from a radiograph, with details supplied by examination of the sections cut for metallographic examination.

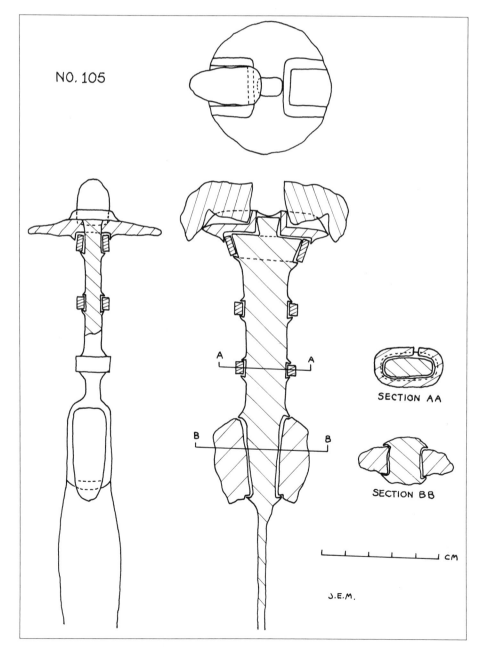

NO. 105

SECTION AA

SECTION BB

CM

J.E.M.

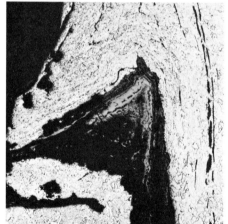

2.29
Transverse section of hilt, No. 105, showing attachment of encircling band. Etched, 6X.

2.30
Appearance of hilt after removal of decorative band, showing groove cut to receive it. Etched, 2X.

2.31
Same specimen as Figure 2.29 at higher magnification. Shows detail of metal flow in cleat. Etched, 48X.

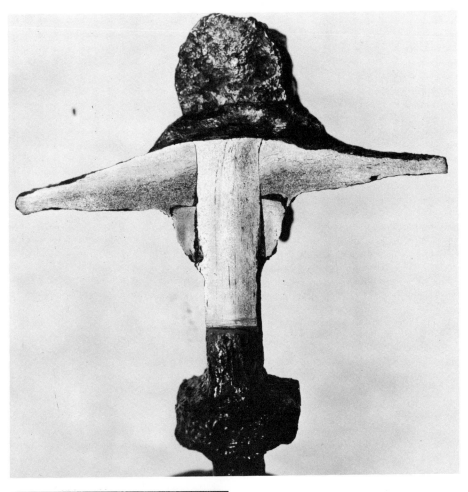

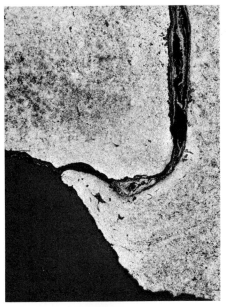

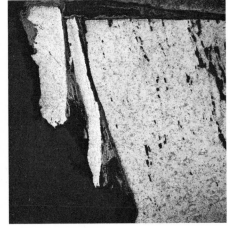

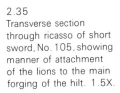

2.32
Section through pommel
and hilt in No. 105,
parallel to smallest di-
mension of hilt, at right
angles to section
shown in Figure 2.17.
Etched, natural size.

2.33
Junction of hilt and
pommel in No. 105.
Same section as Figure
2.17, at higher magnifi-
cation. Etched, 7X.

2.34
Section through head
attachment and pommel,
No. 105. (Section cut
parallel to that in Figure
2.32, but near circum-
ference of pommel.)
Shows deep socket
forged to receive the
head. Etched, 1.5X.

2.35
Transverse section
through ricasso of short
sword, No. 105, showing
manner of attachment
of the lions to the main
forging of the hilt. 1.5X.

2.36
Detail of section shown
in Figure 2.35, showing
clinching of flange into
groove of attachment. 9X.

2.37
The socket on the hilt
(partly sectioned) with
the lion boss removed,
and (above) the boss,
inverted, showing the
groove in the matching
surface.

At high magnification, it can be seen that the flat bottom of the groove had been heavily cold-worked, but only superficially so—to a depth of about 0.2 mm. Though the flange is highly distorted (Figure 2.31) and seems to have been accumulated by lateral displacement of metal, the depth from which it had come was shallow, for the slag stringers beneath the cut are almost undistorted.

The manner of attachment of the disk-shaped pommel to the hilt will be clear from the transverse section through it, Figures 2.17 and 2.34 and the sketch, Figure 2.28. A tang the full thickness of the hilt (7.9 mm) but only a third as wide projects through a rectangular hole piercing the pommel and is slightly peened over at the top end. For added security or for decoration it rests not only on the shoulder of the hilt but also on a ring, very similar to those in the middle of the hilt, which abuts a flange cut on the hilt and nests within a similar flange raised on the underside of the pommel. Both flanges had been produced in the same way as those discussed in the last paragraph, and they had the same heavily distorted surface microstructure. Figure 2.33, of a section (Cf. Figure 2.17) through the junction between hilt and pommel normal to Figure 2.32, shows the shoulder of the hilt—which the slag streaks prove to have been cut, not forged—and the ring fitting against a flange, now corroded away. Because of the strong taper of the hilt in this plane, a thin wedge had been driven inside the ring to secure it.

The pommel is much more elaborate than appears in the section Figure 2.32, for at the right angle to this on top, it has raised flanges or sockets to carry the decorative heads. The inserts do not fit snugly, but the flanges allow for this by their height—they extend to a distance of 9 mm above the bottom of the groove. Unlike the smaller flanges on the hilt, these flanges were shaped by gross forging, for slag inclusions (Figure 2.34) show metal to flow up into them for a distance and there is no superficially cold-worked layer. Some die or punch was almost certainly used. It could not have been an easy operation.

The crouched lions mounted on the ricasso were set into complete rectangular cells that were made by forging over a shaped punch in the same way as the three-sided cavities for the heads on the pommel. Figure 2.35 shows a cross section entirely through the ricasso, and Figure 2.36 a detail of the joint. Figure 2.15 is a longitudinal section, normal to Figure 2.35, and reveals a poorer fit. Breaking open the joint after the sections had been made revealed the true shape of the two matching surfaces (Figure 2.37). Note the rounded corners of the insert and the rather deep groove punched

around it to provide good anchorage for the matching flange.

Altogether these swords are astonishing. I cannot accept the statement of Maxwell-Hyslop (Reference 9) that the smiths were not competent; I regard them as having been extremely adept in complicated shaping, but since they were unable to weld they developed elaborate methods of mechanical joining. The maces indicate that the gross convex form of the decoration on the short sword could have been forged, and there even exist some swords (for example Maxwell-Hyslop, Reference 7, Plate L, No. 5, and Ternbach, Reference 13, Plate XIII, No. 3) in which some decorative detail was forged as an integral part of the pommel. The decoration resembles in part a jeweler's inlay, in which a separately carved piece made by a different worker was inserted. This would indeed be preferable to the performing of elaborate finishing work on a forged sword.

The microstructure and hardness of iron carbon alloys are both very sensitive indices to the heat treatment that the metal has received. Although the objects examined present a number of different structures, none of them corresponds to intentional hardening by quenching or other rapid cooling. At most, cooling was accelerated by waving around in the air. The hardness numbers given in Table 2.2 confirm this.[7]

As mentioned before, the carbon content varies almost randomly through the steel. Typical microstructures of low carbon areas are shown in Figures 2.38 to 2.40 and ones of higher carbon content in Figures 2.41 to 2.43. The former (omitting the slag discussed in an earlier section) consist of more-or-less well formed grains of ferrite (alpha iron). The straight-line Neumann bands (mechanical twins), which are shown in the large grains in Figure 2.39, could be found in the low carbon areas of most samples. They are

Heat Treatment

---

[7] For comparison with the hardness values given in Table 2.2, it might be noted that pure iron-carbon alloys with 0.1 to 0.8 percent carbon have hardnesses in the annealed condition between about 80 to 200 VHN, while if rapidly quenched in water they range about 350 to 950 VHN. Poor quenching or partial reheating (tempering) would give intermediate values. Like bronze, iron can also be hardened by cold-working. See also the next subsection.

A tiny fragment ostensibly from a Luristan axe that came from a well-known museum had a well-laminated texture and the microstructure (reproduced in Figure 43 of Reference 11) corresponding to quenched steel. It was hard (400 VHN, in places). Since all the other samples examined were unhardened and not laminated, it is safer to question the origin of this sample than to suppose that Luristan smiths did sometimes quench their steel. It would, in fact, be a rather frustrating operation to quench-harden steel as variable in carbon content as typical Luristan material.

2.38
Transverse section of blade, No. 102. Shows irregular grain size and faint ghosts of previously existing alpha-gamma structure caused by phosphorous segregation. Etched, 74X.

2.39
Ferritic structure in hilt of No. 103 (Cf. Figure 2.12). The straight lines in the larger grains are mechanical twins (Neumann bands). Etched, 74X.

2.40
"Mild steel" structure in transverse section of blade of No. 105. Etched, 190X.

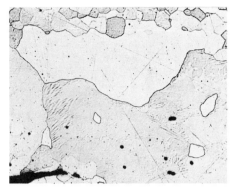

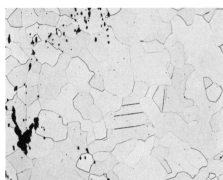

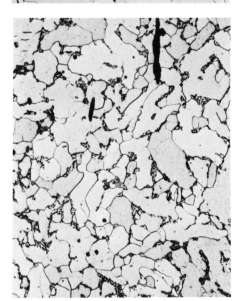

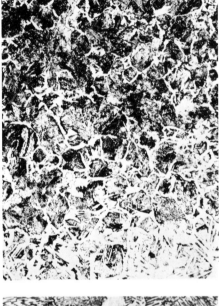

2.41
Transition between high and medium carbon area in handle, immediately below pommel of No. 104 (Cf. Figure 2.16C). Etched, 96X.

2.42
Gradient in structure of high carbon area in No. 106. Etched, 96X.

2.43
Typical well-formed pearlite in handle of dagger No. 104. Etched, 960X.

47

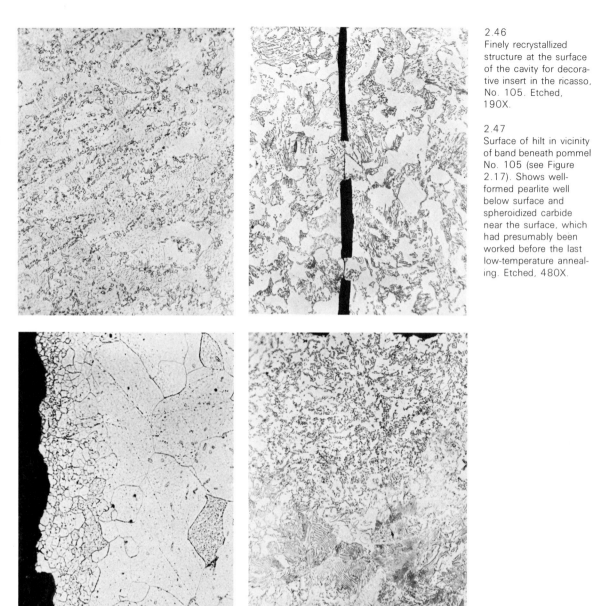

2.44
Slightly spheroidized pearlite in hilt of No. 105. Shows also fragmented slag (Cf. Figure 2.8). Etched, 480X.

2.45
Spheroidized carbide and precipitated nitrides in hilt of No. 105. Etched, 480X.

2.46
Finely recrystallized structure at the surface of the cavity for decorative insert in the ricasso, No. 105. Etched, 190X.

2.47
Surface of hilt in vicinity of band beneath pommel No. 105 (see Figure 2.17). Shows well-formed pearlite well below surface and spheroidized carbide near the surface, which had presumably been worked before the last low-temperature annealing. Etched, 480X.

2.48
Local variation of microhardness in Mace head, No. 113. Lower traverse A is in the thickest part, parallel to the axial hole, about 1 cm from it (Cf. Figure 2.25). Upper curve B is across the body of the pin, Figure 2.21.

2.49
Microhardness in various regions of the short sword, No. 105. Curves A, B, and C represent a continuous traverse across the three parts of the ricasso, Figure 2.14. A and C are the lion inserts; B is the central portion of ‛ the hilt. D represents the diagonal traverse across the head attachment to the pommel, Figure 2.36, E the vertical traverse across the center of ricasso, Figure 2.37 center, F the vertical traverse through section of pommel, directly above right edge of ring insert, Figure 2.34, and Curve G is the transverse section through handle, 1.5 cm below top, Figure 2.34.

Table 2.2
Hardness
Measurements

Object No.	Location	No. of Readings Taken	Microhardness (VHN)*		
			Minimum	Maximum	Average
101	Transverse section of blade, Figure 2.16A	24	111	260	161
102	Transverse section of blade, Figure 2.16F	13	158	187	163
103	Transverse section of blade, Figure 2.16B	28	100	185	140
104	Transverse section of blade, Figure 2.16C	13	103	158	129
105	Cross section of blade near top, Figure 2.16D	14	102	189	141
	Section of blade 15 mm below ricasso, Figure 2.14	10	89	124	108
	Section of hilt, 1.5 cm below top, Figure 2.34	10	85	148	110
	Section of pommel, traversed parallel to hilt of both ring insert, Figure 2.34	10	147	212	189
	Pommel sectioned near periphery, Cf. Figure 2.36	25	91	172	131
	Transverse section through base of decorative head attached to pommel, Cf. Figure 2.36	16	97	210	160
	Transverse section through center of ricasso, Figures 2.37 and 2.52E	16	78	226	145
	Lower part of hilt, beneath attached lions, Figures 2.14 and 2.52B	10	81	123	105
	Section of right lion, Figures 2.14 and 2.52A	10	83	113	103
	Section of left lion, Figures 2.14 and 2.52C	10	88	108	94
	Traverse through left lion attachment, Figure 2.37	12	81	113	98
	Section through lower band surrounding hilt	26	101	136	118
106	Transverse section of handle, 2 cm from end, Figure 2.16E	20	99	169	117
107	Transverse section through thickest part, normal to hole	16	79	127	97
	Axial section through decorative pin, A	10	135	173	153
	Axial section through decorative pin, B	8	144	173	158
113	Transverse section through thickest part, parallel to axis of the hole, Figures 2.25 and 2.51	22	75	147	87
	Cold-worked head of inserted decorative pin, Figure 2.23	19	212	271	235
	Shank of inserted pin	19	153	271	207

* The microhardness numbers, in kilograms per square millimeter, were measured with the Vicker's indenter using a 200 g load. Indentations were spaced at intervals of 0.25 to 2.0 mm, usually in two traverses at right angles to each other representing the entire section at the place noted.

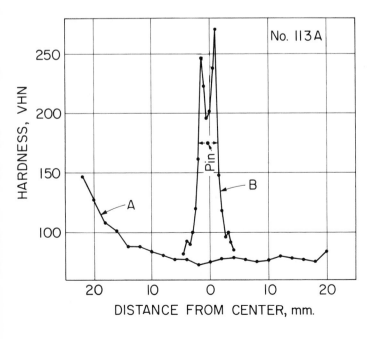

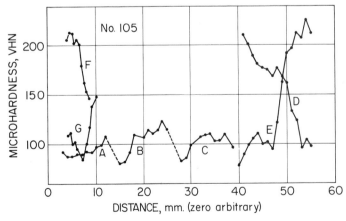

presumably due to shock in manufacture or in use, for they are easily produced by a hammer blow. They are found to some extent in most ancient irons of low carbon content and large grain size.

The grain size varies considerably. Some of the grains large enough to be seen by the naked eye as in Figures 2.15 and 2.21 are almost certainly a result of exaggerated grain growth occurring during the annealing of a purely ferritic sample at a temperature below the critical point (910°C in pure iron), but most of the ferrite grains had the slight irregularity associated with their production by transformation of austenite. The structures in Figures 2.41 to 2.43 are typical of air-cooled samples of steels of medium carbon content. Light-etching areas of ferrite have formed around the grain boundaries of austenite, and there is further growth of ferrite into the body of the grains in a more geometric form. The dark areas represent eutectoid pearlite (fine alternating lamellae of iron carbide and ferrite resulting from transformation just below the critical point at 723°C).

Several photomicrographs of Luristan steel that have been published—for example, Brick (cited by Maryon, Reference 4) Naumann (Reference 2) and Smith (Reference 11)—have shown the carbide to be spheroidized to a greater or less degree. This could have resulted only from heating below the transformation temperature, though the degree to which spheroidization occurs is very sensitive to deformation and the structure therefore differs considerably in different parts of the objects. Much of the carbide in short sword No. 105 was in well-shaped pearlitic form (Figure 2.43), but in other areas it was somewhat spheroidized (Figure 2.44). It seems probable that the spheroidized structures resulted simply from forging at a slightly lower temperature than usual, for the smith could hardly have been aware of the abrupt critical point.

Spheroidized carbide mixed with nitride was encountered in one part of No. 105 (Figure 2.45) but it is usually difficult to recognize the nitride when much carbon is present. In the dagger No. 102 there were many areas in which the ferrite in the microstructure revealed ghost markings (Figure 2.38) obviously related to segregation occurring in a preexisting alpha-gamma microstructure that has disappeared during cooling. This is the only one of the objects studied to contain a significant amount of phosphorous, which diffuses slowly and is distributed in quite different amounts in the alpha and gamma phases.

Although most of the pieces examined had, both internally and on the greater part of their surfaces, structures associated with simple air-cooling from tempera-tures well above the critical point (725° to 910°C depending on carbon content) without any further treatment, there is evidence of later heating to a lower temperature.

It was mentioned earlier that the steel in the grooves cut to receive the bands on the hilt and pommel of No. 105 had been superficially cold-worked in a manner that suggested working with a chisel. Actually the ferrite in the most heavily cold-worked areas has recrystallized to an extremely small grain size (Figure 2.46) and in similar areas that are pearlitic the carbide has become spheroidized (Figure 2.47). This indicates that the mechanically finished dagger had been heated for a short time to a temperature perhaps as high as 650°C. A similar effect was encountered on the surface of the shaped shoulder of No. 104 (Figure 2.14). The recrystallization of the heavily distorted chips alongside the pin (itself unaffected) in the mace head No. 113 (Figure 2.23) suggests a similar if less intense thermal history. The objects had been forged mainly at the usual supercritical temperatures, and the fine recrystallization occurred only in regions that had been subjected to severe and highly localized surface deformation. Was the final fitting together of the parts perhaps done just below a red heat? The fact that the effect occurs on several of the objects makes it unlikely that it resulted from heating in a cremation or an accidental fire; perhaps it marks the use of bluing or some other low-temperature chemical treatment carried out to produce an attractive corrosion-resisting surface on the finished objects. There are no records describing the surface appearance of iron objects in the period under discussion, but it seems somewhat unlikely that they would have been bright.

Hardness

Table 2.2 summarizes microhardness measurements on the objects. The average hardness numbers are misleading, for there is considerable variation from place to place. Figure 2.48 presents a number of measurements across various sections of the short sword No. 105. The hardness in local regions is roughly what would be expected for metal of carbon content revealed by the local microstructure after air-cooling from temperatures somewhere in the range 750 to 900°C.

Locally enhanced hardness caused by cold-working is clearly shown in Figure 2.49, which summarizes measurements on the mace head No. 113; Curve A is a traverse across the head in an area that is mainly recrystallized low-carbon iron, and Curve B traverses the stem of the cold-worked pin. The latter shows the high, local hardness in both the body of the pin and the sides of the hole drilled to receive it. Although this metal is of low-carbon content, it is harder than any other metal encountered in the investigation. The

Luristan smith (in common with most other iron workers at any time) did not exploit the superior mechanical properties of cold-worked steel in sword blades or other objects.

A cold-worked bronze containing 10 percent tin could easily surpass the hardness of any of the present steels, and even a cast bronze (with a hardness of about 110 VHN) would be superior to most of them. The advantage of iron over cold-worked bronze must have been mainly an economic one. The ores of iron are far more widespread than are those of copper and especially those of tin, though when making complicated shapes this advantage would have been partly offset by the greater labor needed in forging iron than when casting bronze.

Summary and Conclusions

Iranian smiths in the period 800 ($\pm$200) B.C. were highly skilled, although they were unacquainted with some of the basic methods of ironworking. Their forging, which involved the use of special swages, is magnificent, but there is no evidence of welding, and the smith assembled shapes as complicated as those of bronze castings by using elaborately fitted mechanical joints, locked by peening or crimping. Holes were drilled and surfaces were accurately cut by a technique, supposedly using abrasives, that only superficially distorted the adjacent metal.

Chemical analysis showed the steel to be unusually free from impurities, though one sample contained nickel, and iron oxides and silicates were generally present as slag inclusions. The carbon content, as estimated from the microstructure, varied between 0 and 1.0 percent in different parts of the objects, reflecting uncontrolled local variations of carburization in the reduced iron sponge as it came from the smelting hearth. No significant carburization or decarburization had occurred either during forging or after. The microstructure showed the pieces to have been air-cooled after forging, not quenched for hardening. The hardness, averaging about 130 VHN, varied locally between 80 and 270 VHN, the highest values being only in a few regions that had been locally cold-worked. There was some evidence of a final low-temperature heat treatment, perhaps to confer corrosion resistance by surface oxidation.

Until many more studies of a comparable kind have been made on material from other cultures, it is premature to draw general conclusions. Nevertheless, the Luristan smith's curious combination of skill in forging and ignorance of either welding or quench hardening seems rather clearly to denote a transitional period in the knowledge of iron. Furthermore, the iron objects whether swords, daggers, maces, or bracelets are all of a decorative design that is more appropriate to the mold

of the foundryman and the chaser's chisel than to the hammer of the smith. It seems that the economic advantage that lies in the greater abundance of the ores of iron compared with those of copper and tin was offset to a considerable extent by the greater labor involved in the forging operation and by the apparent inability to use scrap. Homer's legend of the blinding of Polyphemus proves that the quench-hardening of steel was known at the time (at least in Greece), but the Luristan smith either did not know it or preferred not to use it because of the extreme difficulty of consistently producing steel of a suitable quality and of properly controlling the quenching operation. In the unquenched state, steel is little better than bronze: indeed, it is inferior to cold-worked bronze, and it would probably not have been used had not economics accelerated its introduction. Some bronze swords at the time were cold-worked; had the iron been so treated, its mechanical properties would have been considerably enhanced. The absence of such processing except in trivial parts suggests that sufficiently powerful hammers and sufficiently resistant anvils for cold-working large objects had yet to be developed. (When these did become available later, comparable properties were more easily obtained by heat treatment.)

Acknowledgments

The photomicrographs in this paper are mainly the work of Mrs. Betty Nielsen of the University of Chicago, Mrs. Katharine Ruhl and Mrs. Judith Moore of M.I.T. Their careful work is gratefully acknowledged. The United States Steel Corporation through the courtesy of Dr. M. W. Lightner performed the chemical analyses. Support for this study was provided by the Sloan Fund for Basic Research, M.I.T., and by the U.S. National Endowment for the Humanities.

Addendum

By far the most important paper on Luristan steel yet to appear was published after the present paper was written (early in 1958). This is Albert France-Lanord, "Le fer en Iran au premier millénaire avant Jésus-Christ," *Revue d'Histoire des mines et de la métallurgie*, 1, 1969, pp. 75–127. France-Lanord includes photographs of two typical short-swords in unusually fine condition showing fine traced decoration and many photographs of metallographic sections of similar swords. All were assembled without welding, but the number of parts and the details of their attachment differ. In one of the short swords, rivets were used to secure the decorative heads on both pomel and ricasso, and also to fix the blade to the handle. France-Lanord notes the lack of welding and points out that the forging, shaping, and riveting techniques were essentially those of the bronze worker. He concludes that there was a complete separation between those men who smelted iron as an article of commerce and those

51

who shaped objects from it, using old methods on a newly introduced material.

France-Lanord also describes daggers with cast-on bronze hilts, axes, spears, horse bits, and several sword and knife blades. Most of the objects are irregularly carburized, although France-Lanord observed that harder metal was generally selected for blades and softer iron for decorative parts. One blade (No. 10, of unspecified origin) seems to have been carburized locally on its cutting edge, though a fortuitous fluctuation of carbon content is not excluded. Another (No. 14, of the seventh to sixth century B.C.) has a laminated composite structure somewhat reminiscent of later Damascus swords. France-Lanord believes that the structure could not have resulted from the simple forging of an unmelted sponge and suggests possible origin either in a Wootz-like material (high-carbon steel, melted, and slowly cooled to give a coarse crystalline segregation) or in stacks of iron plates impregnated with molten cast iron as in Needham's co-fusion process used in the Far East some centuries later. However, it seems to the writer that the making of "natural" steel by operating the refiner's hearth under highly reducing conditions must at least occasionally involve the transitory production of some liquid cast iron, and structures like that of France-Lanord's No. 14 could easily result from the irregular distribution of liquid metal within a poorly consolidated sponge. Even large gradients of carbon content in hyper-eutectoid steel would not be eliminated by diffusion as long as working was done at a temperature low enough to retain some carbide everywhere. I have seen Iranian iron in which heavy carburization locally follows deep seams and cracks in a distribution that could not possibly occur by gas transfer but would easily result from eutectic material being carried by capillarity into these regions. Though the chemistry is identical with co-fusion it does not require the prefabrication of plates of iron and their immersion into separately-made cast iron, but is simply a result of differing degrees of carburization at different locations within a single, somewhat porous, lump of metal.

References

1. Bird, V., and Hodges, H. W. M. "A Metallurgical Examination of Two Early Swords from Luristan," *Studies in Conservation,* **13,** 1968, pp. 215–233.

2. Birmingham, J., Kennon, N. F., and Malin, A. S. "A 'Luristan' Dagger: An Examination of Ancient Metallurgical Techniques," *Iraq,* **26,** 1964, pp. 44–49.

3. Damien, R. "Sur des épées en fer provenant du Luristan," *Revue Archéologique,* **2,** 1962, pp. 17–27.

4. Godard, A. "Bronzes du Luristan," *Athar-e Iran,* **3,** 1938, pp. 233–263.

5. Lefferts, K. C. "Technical Notes on Another Luristan Iron Sword," *Amer. J. Arch.,* **68,** 1964, pp. 59–62.

6. Maryon, Herbert "Early Near Eastern Swords," *Amer. J. Arch.,* **65,** 1961, pp. 173–184.

7. Maxwell-Hyslop, K. R., and Hodges, H. W. M. "Three Iron Swords from Luristan," *Iraq,* **28,** 1966, pp. 164–176.

8. Naumann, F. K. "Untersuchung eines eisernen luristanischen Kurzschwertes," *Archiv fur das Eisenhuttenwesen,* **28,** 1957, pp. 575–581.

9. Naumann, F. K. "Die Untersuchung alter eiserner Fundstücke und die dazu verwendeten Verfahren," *Archaeological Chemistry,* M. Levy, Ed., Philadelphia, 1967, pp. 181–203.

10. Pleiner, R. "Untersuchung eines Kurzschwertes des luristanischen typus aus der Sammlung des Deutschen Klingenmuseums [Solingen]," to be published in *Arch. Anzeiger (Jahrb. Deutschen Arch. Inst.).*

11. Salin, E., Le Clerc, J., Steichen-., and Hoang, C. "Etudes physique, chimique et metallographiques d'une Epée du Luristan," *Revue d'Histoire de Sidérurgie,* **3,** 1962–1963, pp. 209–217. (This is a slightly altered version of the technical portion of Reference 3, with fewer illustrations.)

12. Smith, C. S. "The Interpretation of Microstructures of Metallic Artifacts," in *Application of Science in Examination of Works of Art,* W. J. Young, Ed., Boston, Museum of Fine Arts, 1967, pp. 20–52.

13. Ternbach, J. "Technical Aspects of the Herzfeld Bent Iron Dagger of Luristan," in *Dark Ages and Nomads. Studies in Iranian and Anatolian Archaeology,* M. J. Mellink, Ed., Nederlands Historisch-Archaeologisch Instituut, 1964, pp. 46–51.

A Post-Symposium Note: Science in the Service of History.

This conference on archaeological chemistry has been unusually interesting and stimulating; yet, as it nears its end, I feel a slight unease and wish to make a plea for a change in attitude on the part of scientists who devote time to the service of the humanities.

Most of the papers in this conference have been written by physical scientists with the express purpose of assisting their colleagues in the social sciences—of answering questions previously raised by archaeologists, anthropologists, art historians, and historians generally. We have heard of the most modern analytical techniques being used to provide patterns of characteristic trace elements that serve as indices equaling or surpassing the stylistic criteria that have been used by historians and cultural anthropologists to trace migrations and cultural influences. It is indeed exciting to see science provide "fingerprints" that establish beyond doubt Neolithic contacts between the Baltic and the Aegean, and seventeenth-century trade between a Devon village and an early settlement in the New World.

All this constitutes a contribution of which scientists can be extremely proud. But is it enough? To my mind, typing studies, however ingenious and admirable their analytical basis may be, can serve only to help answer old questions, not to enlarge the scope of history. Analytical chemistry was at the forefront of science until recently, but now it is seen that even gross composition is not enough—it is simply the first step toward getting a structure that has desirable properties.

The aim of the humanist generally is to explore the nature of man. The art historian tries to follow the development of inconography and design, to find the interaction of the entire cultural milieu with aesthetic expression, and the general historian tries to analyze man's whole experience, though he has not heretofore paid much attention to man as scientist and even less to his technological life. This neglect has resulted, at least in large part, from the fact that the records available for such study are rarely the written records cherished by historians but are usually objects. Nevertheless, such artifacts do carry within themselves a rich store of information that can be read only by recently developed laboratory methods for revealing the structural characteristics of matter and for studying the dependence of structural details upon composition and especially upon the mechanical and thermal treatment to which the material has been subjected.

The reading of this record is what scientists alone can do, and in so doing they extend the range of possible historical questions: such studies provide primary information on what men did in the past,

quite different in kind from the purely incidental or geographical information conveyed by trace-element analysis and the temporal data provided by C^{14} and fission-track studies. Should we not go far beyond the development of scientific methods to serve present archaeology, however valuable this may be, and work to develop a better understanding of the history of our own side of human activity—a history of how man made and used things, revealing his knowledge of the diversity and nature of materials and enabling the reconstruction of a most intimate part of his experience? Surely this is one of the very bases of culture and not a bit less essential to understanding man than the development of his political, economic, and even intellectual organizations.

The "fingerprinting" of artifacts by trace-element analysis and their dating by measuring the effects of nuclear transmutation enables the movements of peoples, or more often peddlers, to be reconstructed. But artifacts are far more than indices. Is it not an equally important part of human history, not just to know that at one time and place there existed a people enjoying the external form of a glazed ceramic pot, using iron daggers to kill each other, or bedecking their women with gold and amber, but also to study the knowledge possessed by the man who made these things and to trace the rise and decay of technical skills in different cultures? By careful scientific study of the details of structure of an object, it is possible to form a very good idea as to the sequence of thermal, mechanical, and chemical operations that brought it to being. It is possible almost to relive the experience, sensually if not intellectually, of the artist or artisan.

Obviously this is only a small part of history. It is more important to understand the entire cultural milieu, including its effect on the craftsman, than it is to see what the craftsman contributes to the environment of others. The studies advocated leave untouched even many aspects of technology itself. Being by nature small-scale, they can contribute only indirectly to an understanding of the social and economic factors involved in organized schemes for transportation, architecture, or military operations. Any one study, by itself, can answer only limited questions. But scientists know well that crystals and biological organisms are hard to understand without atoms and cells. My plea is just that we should try to bring into the scene something that has hitherto been grossly neglected.

The lack of concern with technology has produced a common view of history that is utterly unrealistic and one that provides a singularly poor basis for understanding the predicament of the present world. Scientists should themselves be more interested than any other group in correcting the perspective, for they are the direct inheritors of the old tradition. It is particularly appropriate for them to do so at the present time because they alone are familiar with the recently developed analytical procedures that are necessary.

Let scientists, therefore, ask and answer their own historical questions as well as help to answer those presently posed by the archaeologist and general historian. In so doing not only will they come to understand their own profession better but they will also extend the range of what is called history. Historians have always exploited the contents of libraries, and they are beginning to make more professional use of museums: With initial help from scientists they will come to use the laboratory also, and the more they do so, the more they will be able to understand the origin of ideas and the forces for cultural change.

C. S. S.

Chapter 3

**Ceramic Analysis:
The Interrelations of Methods;
the Relations of Analysts and
Archaeologists**

Anna O. Shepard
United States Geological Survey

**The Interrelation
of Methods**

Pottery is a great challenge to the analyst because of its complexity. The basic material of pottery, clay, is in itself highly variable. Moreover the properties of clay encouraged, and sometimes forced, potters to modify its composition. Then, in the process of firing, bodies of wares and pigments underwent extensive changes. Consequently, the student of pottery needs to draw on every pertinent, available analytical method.

In the ceramic technology project, sponsored for many years by Carnegie Institution of Washington, mineralogical analysis with the petrographic microscope was extensively used. This was an easy approach in the study of New World pottery and proved especially useful for postulating the sources of pottery when the general geology of an area was well known. In these studies the importance of chemical analysis was never ignored, but the interdependence of chemical and mineralogic methods was not effectively illustrated.

I have chosen the investigation of the ancient pigment Maya blue to illustrate the interdependence. Maya blue was used extensively by the Indians of Mexico and Central America. It is best known from Yucatán, where it was used for temple murals and postfiring paint of household religious effigies (Plate II). The temple murals at Bonampak, Chiapas, Mexico, are a well-known example of Maya mural painting and illustrate the extensive use of Maya blue. They are reproduced in color in Reference 11.

The period of use of Maya blue was from the florescent stage to postconquest times. The dating of the florescent stage is problematic. It may be estimated as in the eighth century A.D. Postconquest murals were preserved in a Christian chapel at Dzibilchaltun, Yucatán.

**The Properties of
Maya Blue**

The color of the pigment is green blue; it has been called cerulean. It varies in value with the amount of calcite the clay mineral base contains as an impurity.

Maya blue has the remarkable property of color stability in boiling nitric acid, first noted by Merwin (Reference 10). The study of Maya blue has been pursued by a number of investigators beginning with Merwin (Reference 10) and is continuing in the present. The pigment was studied extensively by Gettens, who, with Stout, first named it Mayan blue (Reference 6). Its basic component, the clay mineral palygorskite (attapulgite), was identified by FitzHugh (then Elisabeth West) (Reference 5).

The composition of the colorant was a subject of long debate among specialists: Was the pigment a natural mineral or some clay organic complex, as suggested by physical properties and thermal reactions? (Reference 13) Natural samples of palygorskite having the color of Maya blue suggested a natural mineral, but all these samples lost their color when dry, and it was not restored by rewetting. Finally three archaeological samples threw evidence strongly in favor of a synthetic product. The first was from an early excavation near the Cathedral of Mexico; the specimen was found by Gettens at the American Museum of Natural History. The second, also found by Gettens at the same museum, was labeled "Aztec." Later the third sample was recovered in the excavation of Gallegos at the site of Zaachila, Oaxaca, Mexico (Reference 4). In addition to vessels painted with the pigment, this discovery included plaques of it, evidently offerings. The most spectacular painted artifact from the tomb represents a "hummingbird" perched on the rim of a small cup (Plate III).

The sample from the Cathedral of Mexico was a mixture of palygorskite and sepiolite, a clay mineral structurally similar to palygorskite but differing in Al:Mg ratio (Reference 13). The "Aztec" sample was identified by FitzHugh as sepiolite (unacknowledged in Reference 5). The Zaachila sample was a palygorskite but differed sufficiently in relative intensity and number of X-ray reflections for Bradley, who first defined the structure of palygorskite (Reference 1), to suggest that it is a distinct variety of the mineral (personal communication) (Figure 3.1). The X-ray diffraction pattern of the Sapillo Creek, New Mexico, palygorskite is identical to that of the Zaachila pigment. The Zaachila Maya blue is deeper in color than most Yucatecan Maya blues, a difference that may be related to crystal structure. A paper defining differences in palygorskite structures, "Palygorskite: New X-ray Data" by Chris, Hathaway, Hostetler, and Shepard, has recently been published.

Since we had failed to find a natural palygorskite with the properties of Maya blue, it was highly improbable that these three examples of Maya blue with distinct clay bases were natural minerals. Nevertheless, attempts to synthesize Maya blue with palygorskite and indigo (known in Pre-Columbian America) that had been made by several chemists were unsuccessful; the pigment was off-color, and the color was immediately destroyed by hot mineral acids. It remained for a specialist in clay-organic complexes, who was familiar with the properties of palygorskite, to synthesize a palygorskite-indigo com-

Natural Mineral or
Synthetic Product

plex with the essential properties of Maya blue (Reference 16). Although van Olphen did not claim that his synthesis proved that indigo is the colorant or that the Maya followed a method of preparation similar to his, his discovery does afford a valuable working hypothesis for the study of Maya blue.

Clays of Yucatán

In order to explain the status of our knowledge of Maya blue in 1966, I will backtrack. A large proportion of Maya blue samples is from Yucatán. Acquaintance with the ceramic resources of Yucatán is therefore important. As an introduction, clay samples from eight pottery-making villages were analyzed by X-ray diffraction. These samples had been collected by R. H. Thompson (Reference 15). The villages extend across the peninsula from Valladolid in the northeast to Lerma in the southwest. Palygorskite was potters' clay in the village of Mama. It was also used as tempering material there and in the villages of Ticul and Becal. Location of the pottery-making villages on a geologic map indicates that those using palygorskite as clay or for temper (Mama, Ticul, and Becal) are in or adjacent to the Eocene formation (Figure 3.2) (Reference 2). The other clays include montmorillonite, kaolinite, and mixed layer clay. The clay deposits are exposed in sinkholes, the well-known cenotes of Yucatán, occurring three to four meters below the surface, which is limestone. The clays are mainly colloidal in texture and altered; consequently they give poor X-ray diffraction patterns.

Chemical Analysis

The inadequate X-ray patterns led us to test the classifying value of alumina-silica ratios as determined by quantitative spectrochemical analysis. Analyses of the clays and a few potters' clay temper mixtures were made by Norman Suhr, Pennsylvania State University (Figure 3.3).

The Lerma clay is the nearest to a kaolinite that has a weight percent silica:alumina ratio of 1:2. The higher ratio indicates the presence of some montmorillonite. An electron micrograph shows fine hexagonal plates of kaolinite (Figure 3.4). Ticul clay was recognized by X-ray diffraction as a mixed layer clay. The silica:alumina ratio indicates that the components are kaolinite and beidellite.

X-Ray diffraction identifies Becal clay as kaolinite-montmorillonite mixed layer. Mérida and Valladolid had been identified as montmorillonites by X-ray diffraction, but Mama clay was established as a palygorskite. (The ratio of magnesium to aluminum in palygorskites is variable; therefore the silica:alumina ratio does not apply in the classification of these clays.)

It is clear that both mineralogical and chemical analyses are essential and that silica:alumina ratio alone is not a reliable means of clay classification.

The only potters' clay-temper mixtures analyzed for silica:alumina ratios were from Ticul and Valladolid. The small deviation is attributable to chemical composition of the temper; calcite would not affect the ratio.

The spectrographic analyses also revealed an unanticipated result. The palygorskite clay from Mama contained nearly twice the percentage of potassium of Attapulgus palygorskite (0.95 compared with 0.47) suggesting admixture with some illitic clay not detected in the X-ray analysis. Other reported analyses indicate a range in percent potassium (Attapulgus 0.39–0.69, Quincy, Florida 0.76). There is no mention of a test for minor illite in any of these reports. Thus far only preliminary tests have been made to identify minor illite in palygorskite by a proposed thermal X-ray method (Reference 8).

Significance of Maya Blue

Especially interesting questions relating to Maya blue are the original places of production and the extent of trade in the pigment. These questions can be investigated by X-ray diffraction using the powder camera method for small, unoriented samples. The two distinct structures of palygorskite, the sepiolite, and sepiolite-palygorskite mixtures will be clues to sources.

A chemical approach may also be possible if each clay mineral has a distinct pattern of associated trace elements. The question of relation of trace elements to conditions of genesis is raised, but the chemical approach is yet to be tested.

The success of the projects on places of production and extent of trade will depend on discoveries of new samples by archaeologists, careful sampling, and accurate documentation. The justification of the project rests on gain in knowledge of the contacts and relations of the originators of Maya blue.

Historically the fields of geology and chemistry have supplemented each other inseparably. Geological samples are the source of much of the raw material of chemistry; the reactions by which rocks and minerals originate and are altered follow the laws formulated by chemists, a relationship effectively illustrated by Keller (Reference 9). A knotty problem such as Maya blue is thus an effective means of convincing both analysts and archaeologists of the necessity of using every pertinent analytical method.

Relations of Analytical Specialists and Archaeologists

Among the many archaeologists who have invited specialists to join them in the field, the Middle East projects under Dr. Braidwood, University of Chicago, are noteworthy for the number of different specialists he enlisted in order to study environmental factors conditioning development. These projects were, however, devoted largely to preceramic cultures. Covering more advanced periods, archaeologists have enlisted the cooperation of specialists in pottery, metals, and glass.

To illustrate the advantages of field association, I will draw on an American project of some thirty years ago, Peabody Museum's excavations at Awatovi, Arizona. For this project, experiments were made in the field during the period of excavations.

Awatovi is in the Hopi country, southwest of Mesa Verde. The site covers 23 acres on the rim of a mesa overlooking the Jeddito Valley (Figure 3.5). It was occupied during the time of Pueblo III, IV, and part of Pueblo V (estimated dates: Pueblo III, about 1150 to 1300; Pueblo IV, about 1300 to 1630 (coming of the Spaniards); Pueblo V, about 1630 to 1700 (historic period)). The Awatovi Expedition field research was conducted in 1935–1939. The desire of the project's director, Dr. J. O. Brew, for technological ceramic assistance arose from interest in the relation between color of pottery and the fuel used in firing. There was a sequence of orange and yellow wares at Awatovi, although the earliest pottery of the site was gray like the prevalent types in the northern Pueblo area. There were outcroppings of coal in the Awatovi region (Reference 7) and an area on the site where pottery had been fired. Hence the archaeologists wondered if use of coal as fuel facilitated oxidation of pottery.

Concepts of the effects of firing had been influenced by the hypothesis of Harold Colton, who drew an analogy between the zones of a bunsen flame and firing atmosphere (Reference 3). He postulated that the gray wares of the northern Pueblo area were fired in a reducing atmosphere and the southern area red or brown wares were fired in an oxidizing atmosphere, a hypothesis that ignored the original oxidation state of the clay and the variability of atmosphere during the progress of open, nonkiln firing.

My immediate purpose in going to Awatovi was to test the effects on native clays of firing with coal and with wood. As studies progressed, broader objectives emerged. These are reviewed following the description of the firing tests.

My field equipment was simple: a chromel-alumel thermocouple with a portable pyrometer, and a Leitz binocular microscope.

During the project I had much invaluable cooperation. Dr. Brew was keenly interested in the tests and alerted the archaeologists to pertinent objects they might find in excavation, such as iron-manganese nodules that could have been used for

pigment. Dr. John Hack, then a graduate student at Harvard under Kirk Bryan, supplied the coal fuel and gave general information about the occurrence of coal in the region (Reference 7). My father, a chemist, who had followed my ceramic technological work for some years, took part in all stages of the experiments.

After collecting and making preliminary firing tests of clays that occurred near the site, I chose six out of eleven for the firing tests. Most of the clays were gray, fine textured, and dense. The two red clays were sandy and contained some gypsum. For the firing test, plaques were prepared with a mixture of clay and ground potsherd comparable to the ratio of clay to temper that had previously been found in petrographic analysis of Awatovi pottery. Mineral and organic pigments were applied on the plaques for tests of their firing properties, and the effect of alkali on the clay was also tested.

The Clays

The effects of coal and wood (juniper to avoid high pitch) were compared. Methods of contemporary Pueblo potters served as a model for placing fuel. The Pueblos place their fuel (dung chips) around the pottery in a dome shaped "kiln." In the Awatovi test pottery was protected from direct contact with fuel by large potsherds. The coal, which was in slablike pieces, was easily placed. The wood was set either in teepee fashion or interlaced horizontally on a hexagonal outline after the style of building a Navajo hogan.

The Firing Tests

The coal burned without replenishment and the fuel kiln was sufficiently open to permit good draft. The wood burned rapidly, required replacement, and ashes collected around the pottery. The tests were supplemented in the laboratory with duplicate samples in an electric resistance furnace. The tests illustrated for the archaeologist the importance of the original oxidation state of the clay together with texture of the body, and the variable composition of the firing atmosphere. The results of the tests are illustrated with an average gray and average red clay (Plate IV). On firing with coal the red clay that was fully oxidized in its natural state retained that condition. The gray clay was not fully oxidized on short firing with coal. The typical colors of full oxidation are shown with longer coal firing. With wood firing the gray clay was unoxidized, and the red clay was reduced. All samples were fully oxidized on firing in the laboratory, and the color variations with temperature increase in the potter's range were not marked.

As the Awatovi project developed, our interests grew beyond the question of the relation between coal fuel and firing color. We wanted to know the history of pottery development at Awatovi, the effects of

57

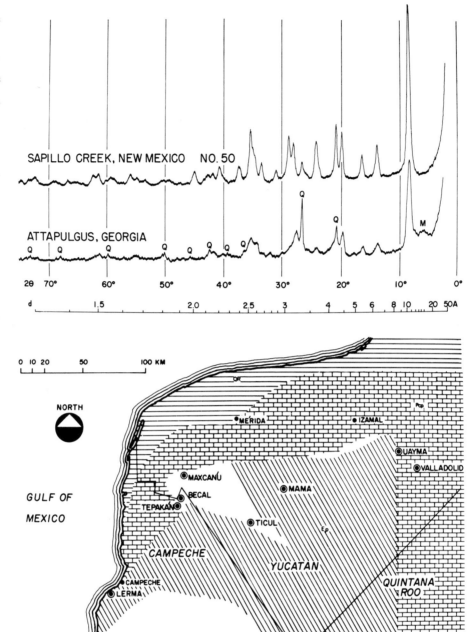

3.1
X-Ray diffraction patterns of palygorskite from Sapillo, New Mexico and Attapulgus, Georgia. The patterns of Sapillo and Zaachila attapulgites are identical. Impurities in Attapulgus attapulgite are montmorillonite (M) and quartz (Q).

3.2
Pottery-making villages of Yucatán, in their geologic setting. Pottery-making villages as of 1951, circled dots. Capitols of states, solid dots (Izamal included because of theoretical interest). Political divisions between states, solid lines. Tentative time estimates of formations: Quaternary, QR; Upper Miocene? or Pliocene? Pep; Middle Eocene, Ep; Paleocene to Mid Eocene, blank area.

POTTERY MAKING CENTERS

3.3
Silica-alumina ratios, potters' clays and clay-temper mixtures.

3.4
Electron micrograph of Lerma kaolinitic clay. (1.25 x 10⁶X)

CLAYS CLASSIFIED BY SiO_2/Al_2O_3 natural, tempered (+)

SiO_2/Al_2O_3

LERMA

+TICUL

BECAL

MÉRIDA

+ VALLADOLID

MAMA

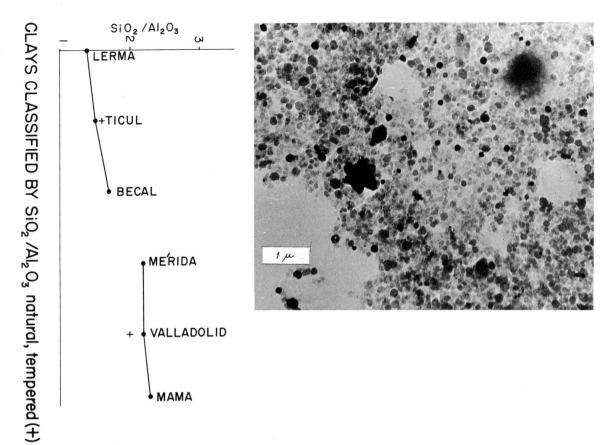

1 μ

3.5
Location of the site of Awatovi, Arizona. Central Part of South-west Showing Location of Awatovi

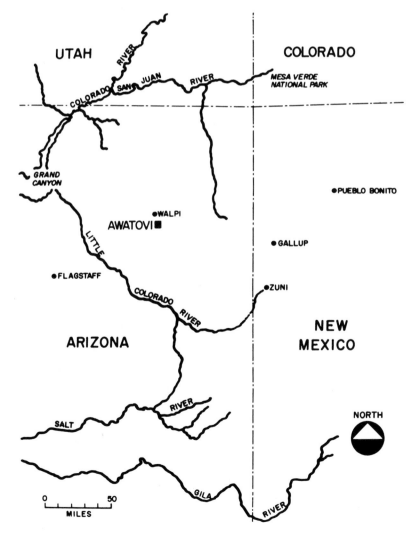

UTAH

COLORADO

COLORADO RIVER

SAN JUAN RIVER

MESA VERDE NATIONAL PARK

GRAND CANYON

●PUEBLO BONITO

●WALPI

AWATOVI■

LITTLE

●GALLUP

●FLAGSTAFF

COLORADO RIVER

●ZUNI

ARIZONA

NEW MEXICO

RIVER

NORTH

SALT RIVER

GILA RIVER

0   50
MILES

natural resources, and the influences of neighboring people with different ceramic traditions.

Major steps in ceramic advancement were indicated when knowledge of the clays and their firing properties was related to the sequence of pottery types archaeologists had defined, indicating them by place name and descriptive phrases. Sherds will illustrate the characteristics of the types (Plate V):

1. Awatovi black-on-white: buff-firing clay tempered with sand or sherd, carbon paint, unoxidized.

2. Jeddito black-on-orange: red-firing clay tempered with sand or sherd, iron-manganese paint, oxidized.

3. Awatovi black-on-yellow: buff-firing clay tempered with sand or sherd, iron-manganese paint, oxidized.

4. Jeddito black-on-yellow: buff-firing clay untempered, iron-manganese and iron oxide paints, oxidized.

5. Sikyatki polychrome: buff-firing clay untempered, iron-manganese and iron oxide paints, oxidized.

There were two major changes in ceramic practice: development of a firing method that fully oxidized the clay and discovery of a clay that did not require tempering material.

A firing method that resulted in full oxidation of the clay was established with Awatovi black-on-yellow. The preceding type, Jeddito black-on-orange, did not prove development of oxidizing firing, because Awatovi red clays are oxidized in their natural state. The firm establishment of an oxidizing firing method with Awatovi black-on-yellow is demonstrated by its persistence in the two succeeding types, Jeddito black-on-yellow and Sikyatki polychrome.

Small chips of the illustrative sherds were refired to test color effects of firing atmosphere. The oxidized chips of Awatovi black-on-white show the cream color of the paste and also the resistance of the carbon paint to oxidation. Chips of the red-clay type, Jeddito black-on-orange, were reduced to check color change; they turn a deeper gray than the clay of Awatovi black-on-white (see Plate V).

Use of an untempered clay that led to a flowering of decorative techniques was generally adopted by the time of Jeddito black-on-yellow. Estimates of the dates of these changes are only very general: oxidizing firing with Awatovi black-on-yellow, early 1300s; untempered paste, late 1300s or early 1400s.

Some speculation can be suggested. The color of Jeddito black-on-orange must have appealed to Awatovians, but red clays were rare in the immediate vicinity of the settlement; therefore potters developed a firing method that would give their common gray clays a warm color. Our firing experiments had shown that use of coal as fuel was a practical procedure.

The exuberance of painting techniques, including spatter and black outline of red motifs, which coincided with the adoption of untempered clay and production of elaborate design must reflect the creative resources of Awatovians at this time. A smooth vessel surface would facilitate painting and would develop pride in the ware. But this cannot be a full explanation. The part that may have been played by religious concepts is suggested by the study of Kiva paintings (Reference 14). But in the final analysis, we return to the creativity of the people themselves.

Our general reconnaissance for raw materials largely answered the question of natural resources: The gray clays corresponded in thermal behavior to the clays of types 3 to 5; the red clays duplicated the thermal properties of type 2. Iron-manganese nodules, which would yield the inorganic pigments used after type 1, were common in the sediments.

The influence of people with distinct pottery making traditions was of particular interest because of Awatovi's important ceramic developments: Were the ideas behind them Awatovi's own or did trade wares sow the seed? (For tentative identification of trade ware, I relied on petrographic identification of nonplastic inclusions.) Red trade wares were uncommon at Awatovi. They could have been made from red clays oxidized in their natural state. There is no record in my notes of an untempered trade ware. Indications that Awatovians initiated the two major changes in technique are therefore reasonably clear.

There is some evidence of Awatovi's influence in other parts of the southwest, especially at a site on the Rio Puerco where abundant Sikyatki type polychrome pottery suggests settlement of Awatovi people.

An unanswered question: Awatovi black-on-white was made with a clay that differed from the gray clays of the Awatovi region. We knew from previous extensive experiments with pigments and clays that a carbon paint requires a clay with an expanding lattice, such as a montmorillonite (Reference 12, p. 33). The carbon from an organic extract burns off readily from a kaolinitic type clay. In our tests this paint type burned off from all the Awatovi gray clays collected. In a search for clues to the source of Awatovi black-on-white, I studied heavy minerals in the clay, a technique that holds possibilities but requires more effective means of separation of mineral and clay than were available at the time of the project.

Conclusions

The Awatovi experience suggested that establishment of satisfactory communication may well be the principal value of association of specialists and archaeologists in the field. Questions and discussions follow immediately as problems arise, and the informality of camp life frees participants from restraint. The more specific advantages are easily recognized: The analyst needs familiarity with natural resources and environmental conditions; he needs to know the historical background of the potters and the conditions of excavations; the archaeologist needs to watch the results of experiments, to share the surprises of unexpected results, and to sense the necessity of finding different approaches when the obvious method fails. Through these experiences, the archaeologist gains an appreciation of the philosophy of the specialist's research, and a sound ground for mutual understanding is developed.

Field Experience

Although the early work at Awatovi established the advantages to ceramic specialists and archaeologists of close association in the field, it was focused on New World conditions that may or may not be universal. Old World ceramic history presents striking differences from the New World record. Ceramic discoveries were made much earlier in the Old World, and they marked important steps in progress. Familiar examples are the potter's wheel, a permanent kiln, glazes, and glass. In order to learn whether experience in the American field would apply in this more complex ceramic world, I spent six months in the Near and Middle East in 1966. Studies were directed toward the effects of environment and natural resources, evidence of the genesis of inventions, the response of potters to cultural pressure and change, and finally to the attitudes and interests of archaeologists active in that area. Highlights of these experiences will indicate the results of the comparison.

Initial studies of Bronze Age pottery from Arad, Israel, revealed many parallels in adaptation of materials to vessel function and to finishing processes. Location of sources of clay was essential in the study and was carried out through the excellent cooperation of the Geological Survey of Israel. Classes of clay and of added nonplastics differed from familiar ones reflecting differences in natural resources, but there was consistent similarity to the New World in potters' recognition of the relation of material properties to vessel function.

Studies made with the cooperation of a skilled Israeli potter and of Arab potters illustrated the advantages of experience in the craft, both in understanding processes and in establishment of mutual respect of native potter and observer. A technical feature of interest was the Arab's use of sea water in mixing clay. Although the practice is unknown in the New World, the questions it raises about effects on qualities and properties of the ware and the role of firing conditions are not outside the ceramic technologist's experience.

In a review of ceramic advances, it was apparent that some had incipient beginnings in the New World. An example made familiar through the studies of George Foster in southern Mexico is the unpivoted wheel, which is also known in a distinct form in Yucatán. These incipient potter's wheels may make a contribution in the study of slow and fast wheel techniques and especially in establishment of the criteria of each technique.

In the study of glazes, America's contribution is in a long stratigraphic record of lead glazes for painted design in the Southwest. These record a detailed sequence of compositions that controlled viscosity and color of the glaze.

The incipient vitrification of a clay slip or paste known in the Roman ware Terra Sigillata has long been a subject of debate. This ware has a counterpart in the Plumbate ware of Latin America. The experiments and failures of the Latin American potters afford opportunity to study clay composition in low-fired vessels and the effects of variations in firing atmosphere. These records are lost when only successfully made examples are available for analysis.

We have no proof of the existence of permanent kilns in pre-Columbian America. Contemporary native kilns are simple. On the other hand, kiln development in the Old World is a reminder of the common aspects of ceramics and metallurgy and is a warning against the pitfalls of overspecialization.

Summary

The ceramic analyst trained in the American field who turns to the Old World archaeology will find much that is familiar in materials utilization and inventive processes, he will be challenged by some new analytical problems, and he will find inspiration and guidance in the archaeologist's historical insights.

In the realm of collaboration, I was impressed by Old World archaeologists' sound, thorough historical background. This is a stimulus to the specialist and an enrichment of his work. I experienced this advantage in working with archaeologists in Israel, with American archaeologists excavating in Jordan, and with British archaeologists in Iran.

The ceramic specialist in the potter's world will recognize problems that would not have occurred to him in the laboratory. He will consider the kind of pottery needed, what substitutes there were for pottery, how satisfactory available resources were for pottery making, how pottery fitted into the life of the people, whether its function was only utilitarian or whether it extended beyond into the realm of religion and aesthetics. The new ideas that will arise in the search for answers will also be new to the archaeologist because they are outside the immediate demands of digging.

The specialist, in following the archaeologist's work, will appreciate his problems and recognize his ingenuity in meeting them; also, he will gain understanding of the history of the site, which will illumine his grasp of its ceramic record.

There is excellent balance between the training and responsibilities of the archaeologist and those of the specialist on which mutual understanding will grow through field association.

Acknowledgments

Dr. H. E. D. Pollock, Carnegie Institution of Washington, has given foundation and breadth to my study of Maya blue through his scholarly review of Mexican historical records and through his continual alertness to every form of evidence.

My experience in archaeological camps has been enriched by each of the archaeologists I have mentioned.

Chemists and mineralogists of the Geophysical Laboratory, Carnegie Institution of Washington, and of the U.S. Geological Survey, Denver, have contributed generously to analyses and ideas. Finally Dr. R. H. Brill as editor has given much help and encouragement.

References

1.
Bradley, W. F.

"The Structural Scheme of Attapulgite,"
Amer. Mineralogist, Vol. **25,** 1940, pp.
405–410.

2.
Butterlin, J., and
Bonet, F.

"Mapas Geologicos de la parte Mexicana
de la Peninsula de Yucatán," *Ingenieria
Hidraulica en Mexico*, Mexico, Vol. **17,**
No. 1, 1963, pp. 63–82.

3.
Colton, H. S.

"The Reducing Atmosphere and Oxidizing
Atmosphere in Prehistoric Southwestern
Ceramics," *Amer. Antiquity*, Vol. **4,** 1939,
pp. 224–231.

4.
Gallegos, R.

"Zaachila: The First Seasons Work," *Archaeology*, Vol. **16,** 1963.

5.
Gettens, R. J.

"Maya Blue: An Unsolved Problem in Ancient Pigments," *Amer. Antiquity*, Vol.
27, Salt Lake City, 1962, pp. 557–564.

6.
Gettens, R. J., and
Stout, G. L.

Painting Materials: A Short Encyclopedia,
Van Nostrand, New York, 1942.

7.
Hack, J. T.

"Prehistoric Coal Mining in the Jeddito
Valley, Arizona," *Paper of the Peabody
Museum*, Vol. **35,** No. 2, 1942.

8.
Heller, L.

"An x-ray method for the determination of
small quantities of palygorskite in clay
mineral mixtures," *Acta Universitatis, Geological supplementum* **1,** 1961, pp.
173–180.

9.
Keller, W. D.

Chemistry in Introductory Geology, 1963.

10.
Morris, E. H.,
Charlot, J., and
Morris, A. A.

"The Temple of the Warriors," *Carnegie
Institution of Washington*, Washington,
Pub. 606, Contrib. 60., 1931.

11.
Ruppert, K., Thomp-
son, J. E. S., and
Proskouriakoff, T.

Bonampak, Chiapas, Mexico, Carnegie
Inst. Wash., Pub. No. 602., 1955.

12.
Shepard, A. O.

"Ceramics for the archaeologist," *Carnegie Institution of Washington*, 1965,
Pub. 609.

13.
Shepard, A. O., and
Gottlieb, H. B.

"Notes from a ceramic laboratory," *Carnegie Institution of Washington*, 1962,
Washington, Note 1.

14.
Smith, W.

"Mural Decorations at Awatovi and
Kawaika-a, Report of the Awatovi Expedition No. 5," *Papers of the Peabody Museum of American Archaeology and Ethnology*, Vol. **37,** Harvard University, Cambridge, 1952.

15.
Thompson, R. H.

"Modern Yucatecan Maya Pottery," *Soc.
for Amer. Arch.*, Memoir 15, Salt Lake
City.

16.
van Olphen, H.

"Maya Blue: A Clay-Organic Pigment?,"
Science, 1966, Washington, Vol. **154,**
pp. 545–546.

Chapter 4

A Study of Temperatures Used in Firing Ancient Mesopotamian Pottery

Frederick R. Matson
The Pennsylvania State University

Introduction

Fragments of pottery and sometimes of figurines are found in abundance at most archaeological sites in the Near East occupied after about 6000 B.C. The variation in the color of such potsherds and figurines can indicate the range in temperatures to which they were fired, provided that one undertakes the color sortings with a background knowledge of the color changes that can take place when the local clays of the region are fired. (See Plate VI.) An adequate sample is needed, so such sortings should preferably be done at the excavation camp after the sherds have been washed and before any of the materials have been discarded. If this cannot be done, the nature of the samples studied must be well-considered when interpreting the results.

Data are presented in this paper showing the changes in some physical properties of a Tigris River clay as it was fired to successively higher temperatures. The color changes of this high lime clay serve as indicators for estimating the degree of firing of ceramic products in ancient Mesopotamia. Color sortings of sherds and figurines can then provide information on technological aspects of the culture producing the ware. Most of the laboratory work was completed some years ago, and the conclusions then reached but not published are modified here in the light of additional field work and visits with potters working today in Near Eastern villages. In a concluding section I should like to sketch broadly my present impression of the variation in firing temperatures used in pottery manufacture by the successive cultures in wide areas of the Near East where the clays are rich in lime. These interpretations will surely be modified or refined as additional ceramic materials become available at well-excavated, stratified sites.

Much of the data presented here has been available on microfilm for many years (Reference 6). I should now like to use it to provide information that may be of help to those concerned with the uses of pottery in the study of man's technological development.

In 1936–1937, I was privileged to be a member of the field party excavating at Seleucia-on-the-Tigris during the sixth and final season of the University of Michigan's work at that site. I am most grateful for the training and academic stimulation that I received from Professor Clark Hopkins, Director, and Dr. Robert H. McDowell, Field Director. Seleucia is now a complex of mounds twenty miles south of present-day Baghdad on the west bank of the Tigris River. It had been the capital city of the Seleucid Empire and a major city dur-

ing Parthian times but sharply declined in importance when the Sassanians established their capital immediately across the river at Ctesiphon. The four major occupation levels at Seleucia represented a span of five centuries, from 295 B.C. to A.D. 216. My major assignment at the site was to excavate a temple area with the aid of 140 Arab workmen. I also had the opportunity to become acquainted with all of the pottery excavated in several parts of the city during the last season and to collect clay samples at many sites in Iraq. During the next two years, as a part of the work for my doctoral dissertation, I made extensive laboratory tests and studies of the clay samples and sherds and had available for examination all of the ceramic material from Seleucia allocated to the University of Michigan.

The clay used in these studies came from an undisturbed stratum immediately below the lower level of the temple which I was excavating. Thus it was clay that was at, or quite near, the surface at the time that the site was occupied. It all passed through a 120-mesh sieve and was a good plastic clay with which to work. An X-ray diffraction study showed that the principal clay mineral was illite. The differential thermal analysis was inconclusive. The chief mineral inclusions in the clay were calcite, quartz, flint, gypsum, magnetite, biotite, and sericite. Accessory minerals were chlorite, sillimanite, red iron-stained lumps, serpentine, diallage, and actinolite.

The chemical composition of the Seleucia clay was determined by Miss Mildred Parrish in the Research Laboratories of the Armstrong Cork Company, and is shown in Table 4.1. The low alumina and high calcium oxide content are explained by the presence of calcite and gypsum in the clay. A separate analysis of acid-treated clay, in which the amount of calcium present was determined by titration with

Firing Changes in the Physical Properties of the Seleucia Clay

	Seleucia (%)	Samarra (%)
SiO_2	40.28	39.90
Al_2O_3, TiO_2	9.52	20.07 (with a little oxide of iron)
Fe_2O_3	6.36	
CaO	16.43	16.75
MgO	4.20	Trace
BaO	0	
Na_2O	0.58	
K_2O	1.41	
SO_3	0.78	
Loss on Ign.	19.36	23.49
Total	98.92	100.21

Table 4.1
The Chemical Composition of Two Tigris River Clays

65

$KMnO_4$, showed that it contained about 30 percent $CaCO_3$. A similar lime-rich Tigris River clay underlying the conglomerate at Samarra, about 70 miles northwest of Baghdad, was reported by Willcocks (Reference 18, p. 93, analysis by A. Lucas). It, too, is shown in Table 4.1.

Soluble salts present in clays can have an important role in the development of colors when pottery or brick are fired. In the ancient city area of Seleucia, there is a salt encrustation on the surface of the ground at the beginning of the dry season that breaks as one walks over it. The village and desert Arabs use washed salts from some areas as flavoring for their food. In one spot near Seleucia, the surface salts were so rich in nitrates that they were said to have been used in making crude gun powder. The improvement of Iraqi agricultural yields is greatly hindered by the difficulties encountered in effectively reducing the salt content of the soil. A qualitative analysis of soluble salts extracted from the Seleucia clay showed the presence of small amounts of chlorides and phosphates and a significant amount of sulfate, doubtless from the gypsum present in the clay. The salt content of the clay is because of the saline waters of the Tigris which include the effluent from sulfur and naphtha springs. One must keep in mind the effect of the variable salt content of the Mesopotamian clays when discussing color developments during firing.

Clays rich in lime that also contain sufficient iron to be an important factor in color development are frequently used in the brick industry. Both Ries (Reference 11) and Salmang (Reference 12) have summarized some of the studies of the roles of lime and iron in the progressive color changes in such clays when they are fired. Shepard (Reference 13, pp. 213-224) has provided an excellent discussion of the firing of pottery, particularly of wares such as those of the American Southwest where kilns were not used. High lime clays containing iron were not important raw materials for the Indian potters she studied.

The final stages in the color development during the firing of the lime and iron bearing clays so widely available in the Near East will be briefly outlined:

1. *Black to gray*. The organic materials present in many clays will cause the bodies to darken during the initial stages of firing. Gradually the surface and finally the core lighten, the rate depending on the amount and form of the organic material present, its bond relation to the surfaces of the clay particles, the porosity of the body, and the time-temperature-atmosphere conditions of firing. Many surface clays, particularly in arid regions, are very low in organic materials, so surface

and body darkening caused by the presence of carbon may not appear. Then the lack of a black surface or core in sherds may not indicate higher temperatures or longer firings. The Seleucia clay, however, which was taken from a deposit two meters below the present land surface, showed progressive loss of the carbon black. The appearance of the Seleucia test pieces has been discussed and illustrated (Reference 7, pp. 34-35; Reference 8, pp. 492-493, Pl.XXIV). The deposition of grease or soot on and near the surfaces of cooking ware or on vessels trapped in the char and ash of burning buildings must also be considered.

An additional aspect of the dark coloration aided by the presence of carbon and carbon monoxide can be the reduction of the iron present to Fe_3O_4 which is black in color. Further reduction to FeO provides iron in the state of an active flux which will react chemically with the clay. Dark-colored silicates thus formed will not reoxidize at higher temperatures if the kiln atmosphere remains generally reducing in nature, and permanent dark cores can develop which are not indicative of low firing temperatures for the ware.

2. *Pale brown to pink*. When the clay is fired to increasingly higher temperatures up to about 1000°C under oxidizing conditions, the iron present has a chance to become fully oxidized and exert its strong coloring effect. When conditions are less oxidizing, gray-browns may develop. The length of time at which a temperature is maintained influences the color development, and the rate of cooling has a strong influence on color development. If the cooling is too rapid in parts of poorly sealed or cracked kilns, the optimum color will not appear. The form and grain size of the particles in which iron is present in the clay body as well as the total amount of iron will have a strong influence on the fired color.

3. *White skin on pink body*. The soluble salts in the clay will tend to concentrate on the surface of the ware as it dries, having migrated there in the water which evaporates from the unblocked surfaces. Salts, particularly chlorides, will react with the iron present to form $FeCl_3$ which volatilizes readily at about 800°C. This leaves an iron-free surface that has the appearance of a white slip (and has too often been mistakenly called a slip by archaeologists). I have discussed this phenomenon together with other color changes elsewhere (References 5 and 6).

4. *White body*. The lime in the clay becomes an active coloring agent once the $CaCO_3$ has decomposed. Paler shades and finally white colors start to develop above about 850°C as the CaO begins to react effectively with the clay, particularly under reducing conditions. Gypsum, too, decom-

poses under reducing conditions in this temperature range (Reference 16). This complex series of reactions is familiar to ceramic engineers who have to deal with the color problems relating to the scumming of brick. Brownell (Reference 2) has provided a good summary statement of the nature of scumming. Clays rich in lime, particularly those also containing soluble salts, develop pale pinks and then whites in the general temperature range of 850° to 1000°C, the exact temperature depending on many factors such as chemical composition of the clay and the time-temperature-atmosphere. Frequently one will find sherds with pink cores and white surface zones.

5. *Pale yellow*. Above about 1000°C as vitrification approaches, the calcium-ferro-silicates that have been developing in the clay appear pale yellow in color and at times even olive. The temperature at which this occurs will be strongly affected by the fluxing action of iron in a reducing kiln atmosphere and by the salt content of the clay. Pieces of pottery may become warped as the body softens, and some vessels may stick together if they have been in contact in a very hot zone of the kiln.

In this brief survey of color changes, temperatures have been intentionally mentioned in an imprecise manner so as to emphasize the fact that many variables are involved. Temperature zones rather than precise degree markers are most useful for archaeological studies. The color terms are those used with the Munsell Soil Color Charts (Reference 10).

The test briquettes made from the Seleucia clay were fired in an electric furnace heated by means of SiC resistance rods. The furnace atmosphere could be established through the introduction of air, natural gas, or air-gas mixtures by means of gas and air manifold controls. Three types of firings with differing kiln atmospheres, here termed R, O, and R-O, were used. The R represents the reducing atmosphere firing in which the kiln was brought up to the desired temperature and held there for 30 minutes in a strongly reducing atmosphere. The briquettes were then removed from the kiln and quickly placed in a box of sand so that they might cool with little air being present. An analysis of the reducing atmosphere by means of an Orsat apparatus showed that it was CO, 16.0 percent; CO_2, 4.0 percent; and O_2, 0.8 percent. Sixteen percent CO is about the maximum that can be maintained in a kiln without producing too much smoke and having carbon deposition. The O signified the oxidizing atmosphere which was also held for 30 minutes at the maximum temperature of the run. The briquettes were cooled to about 350°C in the kiln and were then placed in a dessicator for the final cooling. In the R-O firing, after the at-

mosphere had been reducing for 30 minutes at the maximum temperature, it was changed to oxidizing and the temperature was held for another 30 minutes. This procedure introduced as a variable a longer time of firing, but it demonstrated the color changes that could be produced in a kiln such as those used in many Mediterranean and Near Eastern villages today in which strongly reducing atmospheres are produced when fresh fuel is added. At the higher temperatures when the interior of the kiln becomes incandescent the atmosphere is oxidizing for the time intervals between the introduction of additional straw, brush, or wood, etc., as fuel.

When the color changes of the Seleucia clay briquettes with increasing firing temperatures under three different kiln atmospheres were first determined, the Ridgway color system was used. This is now obsolete, and the Ridgway manual is unobtainable. Therefore, in the present restudy for publication, the colors were redetermined using the Munsell Soil Color Charts (Reference 10). Since the Munsell system has frequently been described and discussed, it will be noted here only that one can think of colors grouped in the shape of a sphere with an irregular surface. The *Hues*—red, yellow-red, yellow, etc.—vary around the circumference of the sphere in the order of the spectrum and may be thought of as segments of an orange. The vertical axis of the sphere shows gradations in gray, with black at the base and white at the top, the *Value* or lightness of the color is then indicated numerically from 1 (black) to 10 (white). The strength of the color, its position between neutral gray and its maximum brightness at the same numerical value (in a horizontal plane from the axis to the surface) is termed the *Chroma*. The Chroma increases in numerical value from 1 (gray) to 8 on the Soil Color Charts which are published in a loose-leaf handbook. The directions for the use of the charts and the notes on the determination of soil color provide all the information needed for the effective use of the Munsell system. Shepard's discussion (Reference 13, pp. 107–113) contains useful suggestions for archaeologists who are describing the colors of sherds. (I find that partly closing one's eyes helps when making the final color match.) Broader aspects of color descriptions and measurements are discussed in the two symposia organized by the American Ceramic Society in 1941 and 1947 with Weyl and Balinkin as the chairmen (see References 1 and 17).

A series of color names appears opposite the Munsell Soil Color Charts. These non-exotic simple names were selected after much consultation and compilation as basic color terms. Many of the names are applied to a cluster of two to four colors on the charts, so are not precise, but are simply classificatory. Color descriptions of pottery should make use of these terms despite one's personal predilections, for extremely precise color descriptions are inappropriate, even irrelevant. Colors often vary in shade on different parts of the surface of one vessel, and certainly among vessels from one firing. Therefore, if one wishes to describe pottery colors in a useful way it is best to avoid false precision.

The color descriptions for the Seleucia briquettes appear in Table 4.2. To simplify the summary of the color analysis, the Munsell color notations are used in the left-hand portion of the table, and the color names for the same series are listed separately on the right side.

In the R-series fired in a reducing atmosphere and cooled in a box of sand, a gray core first appears at 500°C and continues to be present throughout the series with little variation in color. Beginning at 850°C, a lighter surface skin appears that is related to the action of the soluble salts, as has already been discussed, and possibly to a slight oxidation of the surfaces as the briquettes cool quickly in the sand. Water quenching might have been a better way to cool these briquettes. Above 950°, the surface color is paler, and at 1100°, it acquires a pale olive gray Hue to the eye although it is still termed white in the Munsell system. These shades of color frequently occur on Near Eastern pottery. The light gray cores of sherds in contrast to the surfaces are best seen on freshly fractured or saw cut edges, and they are intensified when the cross sections are moistened with water. Since flames can play directly on some of the ware in simple up-draft kilns such as those used in the Near East, it is quite possible to have some strongly reduced ware that was stacked near the hearth in the kiln, while more oxidized pieces are produced in most of the kiln-load from the same firing. By 1170°, the clay has melted into a gray slag and is useless.

In the O-series the color changes from very pale brown to pink with increasing temperatures, and becomes noticeably lighter in Value at 900°. At 1100°, a pale yellow surface and body have developed.

In the R-O series the gray cores have been entirely eliminated by the 30 minute final period of firing in an oxidizing atmosphere, but there is still a difference in color Value between the core and surface. It has been found when refiring sherds that it is seldom possible to eliminate completely the effect of the reducing period on the core color because some fluxing has usually occurred. The colors developed in the R-O firings are the same as those of the O-series through 800°. Above this temperature the R-O briquettes are less pink, and the color differences between the two series are clearly seen above

950°. At 1100°, the color is lower in Value, approaching a pale olive.

The test briquettes whose color changes have just been discussed were tempered with distilled water in accordance with good laboratory practice when they were prepared. The colors developed were, therefore, influenced only by salts already present in the clay. However, the Tigris River water has a bitter taste, and the Arabs working in the excavations at Seleucia preferred to get their drinking water from irrigation canals whose water came from the Euphrates River, some 18 miles to the southwest. Thus additional salts may have been included in the potter's plastic clay through the tempering water or because surface clays including the salt crust were used for the production of pottery and figurines.

As a first check on the effect of salted tempering water on fired color development, sodium chloride and plaster of Paris were boiled in water and the filtrate was used to temper the clay. The fired briquettes of this salted series showed the same color developments through 850° as the basic series under the three atmospheric conditions. At higher temperatures they were more strongly bleached with shades in the range of the Munsell "white," being well developed by 950°. These colors are commonly seen on Mesopotamian vessels and sherds.

In the past four years we have been systematically adding salts under controlled conditions to a series of Near Eastern clays. The results of these studies will be discussed in another paper, but they confirm and enrich the data of these first studies. They strikingly show that salts in lime-rich ferruginous clays accelerate the development of white bodies at firing temperatures above about 900°C. The white surface skin on brown to pink clay ware, often mistakenly termed a slip, appears in the 800°–900°C temperature zone. This white surface indeed looks like a slip when first seen, but if one examines freshly fractured edges of sherds with a hand lens, no differentiation in the fracture pattern will be seen at the color interface. If doubt persists, thin sections of sherds should be prepared. When they are examined under a petrographic microscope at high magnification the presence or absence of a surface coating can quickly be determined. There are indeed slips applied to some ware, but the term should not be indiscriminately used for white-surfaced pottery.

Ten figurine fragments were refired to 1000°C for 30 minutes under oxidizing conditions to determine the changes in their color. The series consisted of three that were pink to reddish yellow in surface color (using the Munsell terminology) with pinkish gray cores; three with a white sur-

Table 4.2
Firing Changes in
Color of the Seleucia
Clay

Temp. (°C)		Furnace Atmosphere*			Furnace Atmosphere		
		R	O	R-O	R	O	R-O
		(Munsell Color Notation)			(Munsell Soil Color Names)		
Unfired		10YR 7/2	10YR 7/2	10YR 7/2	Light Gray	Light Gray	Light Gray
300°	Surface	—	10YR 7/3	—	—	Very Pale Brown	—
	Core	—	10YR 7/3	—	—	Very Pale Brown	—
400°	Surface	10YR 7/3	10YR 7/3	—	Very Pale Brown	Very Pale Brown	—
	Core	10YR 7/2	10YR 7/3	—	Light Gray	Very Pale Brown	—
500°	Surface	—	7.5YR 7/4	—	—	Pink	—
	Core	—	7.5YR 7/4	—	—	Pink	—
600°	Surface	10YR 5/1	7.5YR 7/4	7.5YR 7/4	Gray	Pink	Pink
	Core	2.5Y 7/0	7.5YR 7/4	7.5YR 7/4	Light Gray	Pink	Pink
700°	Surface	10YR 7/2	—	7.5YR 8/4	Light Gray	—	Pink
	Core	2.5Y 7/0	—	7.5YR 7/4	Light Gray	—	Pink
800°	Surface	2.5Y 5/0	7.5YR 7/5	7.5YR 7/5	Gray	Pink	Pink
	Core	2.5Y 7/0	7.5YR 7/4	7.5YR 7/4	Light Gray	Pink	Pink
850°	Surface	2.5Y 8/2	5YR 7/5	7.5YR 8/4	White	Pink	Pink
	Core	10YR 8/1	5YR 7/6	7.5YR 7/4	White	Reddish Yellow	Pink
900°	Surface	2.5Y 8/2	5YR 8/4	7.5YR 8/4	White	Pink	Pink
	Core	2.5Y 7/0	5YR 8/4	7.5YR 8/4	Light Gray	Pink	Pink
950°	Surface	5Y 8/1	5YR 8/4	7.5YR 8/4	White	Pink	Pink
	Core	5Y 8/1	5YR 8/4	7.5YR 7/5	White	Pink	Pink
1000°	Surface	2.5Y 8/2	5YR 8/4	10YR 8/4	White	Pink	Very Pale Brown
	Core	2.5Y 7/0	5YR 8/4	10YR 8/5	Light Gray	Pink	Very Pale Brown
1050°	Surface	5Y 8/1	—	2.5Y 8/4	White	—	Pale Yellow
	Core	2.5Y 8/0	—	2.5Y 8/4	White	—	Pale Yellow
1100°	Surface	5Y 8/2	2.5Y 8/4	5Y 7/4	White	Pale Yellow	Pale Yellow
	Core	5Y 7/1	2.5Y 8/4	5Y 7/4	Light Gray	Pale Yellow	Pale Yellow
1170°	Surface	10YR 5/1	—	—	Gray	—	—
	Core	2.5Y 5/0	—	—	Gray	—	—

* Note: Furnace Atmosphere: R, Reducing throughout the firing; maintained for 30 minutes at the highest temperature. O, Oxidizing throughout the firing; maintained for 30 minutes at the highest temperature. R-O, Same as R, but followed by 30 minutes in an oxidizing atmosphere at the highest temperature.

4.1
A fired brick pavement
of neo-Babylonian times
at Ur. The low-fired
brick have disintegrated.

face over a pink to very pale brown core; two that were white throughout; and two with a grayish-green tinge, although they are classed as white in Munsell's terms. They all fired to 2.5YR 8/4 or 7/4, both termed pale yellow. There were, however, reddish yellow to red stains on some ancient fractured and original surfaces. It would appear that materials absorbed by the fired ware while it remained buried at Seleucia for almost 2000 years had an influence on the refired colors. This is a phenomenon well-known to brick manufacturers. They term it "flashing" when a surface coloring effect is developed because of the chemothermal reactions of volatile fluxing and coloring ingredients that are on the brick surfaces. The formation of $FeSO_4$ could account for this discoloration.

The tests so far reported in this paper have established a basis for estimating firing temperatures of ware made from a Tigris River clay, and by extension to similar clays. Color sortings of Seleucia pottery, lamps, and figurines will be discussed shortly, but mention should first be made of the results of the measurements of some of the other physical properties of the briquettes insofar as they might be of use in determining firing temperatures.

The hardness of pottery is reported in some archaeological papers. Presumably the hardness will increase with the higher firing temperatures, particularly as the vitrification stage is approached. The measurement is made by attempting to scratch the test surface with a series of ten minerals ranging from talc to diamond. This is, of course, Mohs' mineral-hardness scale so commonly used by mineralogists. The scratch hardness is really a measure of abrasion resistance, so the grain size distribution of the ingredients in the clay body, the effective packing of the particles, the bonding strength of the clay, and the force with which the test scratching is done can all affect the results. Shepard (Reference 13, pp. 113–117) has useful comments on hardness testing. Mohs' scale with the refinements suggested by March (Reference 4, p. 20) was used to test the fired Seleucia briquettes, and the scratches were all examined with a hand lens so as to increase the accuracy of this subjective measurement.

The results, summarized in Table 4.3, suggest that in the usual firing range of Mesopotamian pottery, 600°–1000°C, differences in scratch hardness are not of diagnostic value in estimating firing temperatures. Small changes occur at temperatures known from the color shifts to be critical. They can first be recognized in the surface hardness, then at the next higher temperature in the core. Thus knowledge of the variations in hardness can help characterize pottery. For example, Seleucia ware exposed to a reducing atmosphere

Table 4.3

Scratch Hardness of the Seleucia Clay

Temp. (°C)		Furnace Atmosphere		
		R	O	R-O
Unfired		2.5	2.5	2.5
500°			2.5	
600°	Surface	2.5–3	2.5+	2.5–3
	Core			2.5
700°	S	3		3
800°	S.C	3	2.5+	3
850°	S.C	3	3	3
900°	S.C	3	3	3
950°	S	3.5	3	3.5+
	C	3	3	3
1000°	S	3.5	3.5	3.5+
	C	3.5	3	3.5
1050°	S	3.5–4	3.5	3.5–4
	C	3.5	3.5	3.5
1100°	S	5	5	5.5
	C	5	3.5–4	5.5
1170°	Slag	5.5		

during some stage of its firing may be slightly harder than that fired under oxidizing conditions, possibly because of the fluxing action of FeO. This difference in hardness was noticeable when the test briquettes were sectioned with a diamond-embedded saw blade. Low-temperature ware will be less abrasion-resistant, and can break or disintegrate readily. The fired brick pavement of Neo-Babylonian times at Ur that is seen in Figure 4.1 illustrates this point. The brown brick in the foreground have crumbled, while the higher-fired white brick with greater bond strength are intact. Undoubtedly the crystallization of salts in porous pottery and brick during the dry season accelerates the disintegration of those pieces with low-fired bodies.

Hardness measurements of potsherds can be of use to help resolve specific problems, and they certainly should be made on the test pieces when studying the firing behavior of local clay. However, they are of little diagnostic value when studying the range in firing temperatures.

It is encouraging to report that Wright has recently published extensive tabulations of hardness and color measurements of the sherds found in the excavation of an Early Dynastic Mesopotamian town near Ur (Reference 19, Appendix I). He says (p. 123), "This appendix should encourage more detailed comparisons between Early Dynastic ceramic assemblages than has been usual. It should also provide data for the rapidly developing field of mathematical topology."

The percent loss of weight upon firing is another physical measurement that might be of use in determining the firing temperatures of ancient pottery. When clays such as that from Seleucia are fired, they lose weight below about 600°C because of the volatilization of the chemically com-

Table 4.4
Percent Loss of Weight of the Seleucia Clay

Temp. (°C)	Furnace Atmosphere		
	R	O	R-O
600°	3.1%	3.2%	3.2%
700°	7.4	—	8.4
800°	12.5	10.4	12.4
850°	17.1	16.2	17.3
900°	17.9	17.5	17.5
950°	18.2	17.5	17.5
1000°	18.1	17.5	17.9
1050°	18.2	17.6	17.9
1100°	18.3	17.6	18.0

bined water present in the clay, plus a small amount of water from the gypsum, chlorite, and biotite that occurred in the clay deposit. Between about 600° and 900°C, the thermal decomposition of calcite from the limestone and possibly of gypsum will cause significant weight loss. (West and Sutton, Reference 16, have shown that gypsum in the presence of carbon and under reducing conditions can decompose in this temperature range.) The calcined limestone present in fired pottery will rehydrate and gradually revert to the carbonate form if the ware has not been fired high enough, usually about 900°C, so that the CaO can react with the clay and form part of a complex silicate structure. Therefore, loss of weight studies of potsherds and figurines, refiring them at successively higher temperatures, may not always give reliable results if there was much limestone present in the potter's clay. A test series of figurines, however, gave surprisingly good results.

The loss of weight of the Seleucia clay briquettes measured in this series of firing experiments is reported in Table 4.4. The percent loss is expressed in terms of the unfired dry weight so that there will be a common base for comparison. Below 600°C, there was a small loss in weight, but the great loss occurred between 600° and 850° in the zone of calcite decomposition. Above 900°, there was no further significant loss. It is noticeable that the R and R-O series lost weight more rapidly than those briquettes fired under oxidizing conditions and that the reactions were almost completed at 850°. In the O-series it was not until 900° that the weight became constant, and the total weight loss by 1100° was less than that for the briquettes which had been subjected to reducing atmospheres. These

notes indicate trends but should be confirmed by further testing of several samples at each temperature. This experiment does indicate, as did the color changes, that clays rich in both lime and iron are sensitively influenced in their chemothermal reactions by the kiln atmosphere.

The ten figurines selected for special study have already been characterized in terms of their colors. They were first refired to 400°C in an oxidizing atmosphere for 30 minutes to establish base weights, for they might contain some partially hydrated material after burial for almost 2000 years. They lost 1–2 percent in weight. In the second refiring they were held at 1000°C in an oxidizing atmosphere for 30 minutes. The results are shown in Table 4.5a where it can be seen that the weight losses agree well with the color indications of low, medium and high fired wares.

The data in Table 4.4 were used to calculate the approximate weight losses of the Seleucia test briquettes were they to be refired to 1000°C. The difference in weight between the 1000° firing and that at 600°, 700°, 800°, and 850° was expressed as the percent based on each of these lower temperatures. (Calculations were not made for the firings above 850° because the weight losses were so small.) The results are shown in Table 4.5b aligned with the appropriate figurine groups of Table 4.5a.

The percent loss of weight of the refired figurines agrees in rank order of color indications with the calculated data for the briquettes but not closely enough by 100° to use this approach for actual temperature estimates. The amount of lime originally present in the figurines compared with that in the test briquettes as well as the degree to which it had reverted to the carbonate form would be affected by the ever-present factors of the time-temperature-kiln atmosphere when the figurines were originally fired. The correlation is surprisingly good when one considers the effect of these variables upon the results. Percent loss of weight upon refiring could serve as a useful check procedure in the study of specific problems.

The true specific gravity of the Seleucia clay and of a series of figurine fragments

Table 4.5
(a) Percent Loss of Weight of Seleucia Figurines Refired to 1000°C; (b) Percent Loss of Weight of Seleucia Test Briquettes Refired to 1000°C. (calculated).

(a)

Figurine Color Group	% Wt. Loss
Pink surface, pinkish gray cores	12.1, 11.3, 9.1
White surface skin, pink cores	8.7, 6.2, 5.0
White	2.4, 1.0
White with olive-gray tinge	0.1, 0.04

(b)

Orig. Firing Temp. (°C)	% Wt. Loss at 1000°C
Unfired	17.5
600°	14.9
700°	10.1
800°	6.0
850°	0.5

Table 4.6
True Specific Gravity of the Seleucia Clay

Firing Temp. (°C)	Furnace Atmosphere		
	R	O	R-O
Unfired	2.75	2.75	2.75
800°	2.85	2.79	2.84
900°	2.90	2.93	2.89
1050°	2.93	2.94	2.94
1100°	2.97	2.95	2.97
1170° (slag)	3.00		

was accurately measured using calibrated pyncnometers for the tests. Selected results, those at the temperatures where significant changes occurred, are shown in Table 4.6 with the values rounded off to two significant figures. As in the other tests, the briquettes fired under oxidizing conditions showed less chemical reaction resulting in increase in true specific gravity by 800° than did those under reducing atmospheres, and their final approach toward vitrification may have been a little less complete by 1100°.

Fragments of six figurines from the selected color series were powdered and their true specific gravities were determined. The moderately fired pieces were found to have values of 2.75, 2.80, and 2.88; the highest fired, to judge from their color, had results of 2.96, 3.03, and 3.03. The comparison between these figures and those in Table 4.6 is in good agreement, even though the composition of the figurines and the briquettes may have differed somewhat. Therefore, it would be possible to measure the true specific gravity of carefully selected samples for the estimation of the ancient firing temperatures, but the amount of work involved in these time-consuming measurements would rarely be justified. The fired colors of the ware can usually provide the information with sufficient accuracy.

The firing shrinkage of most clays used by potters is not great nor progressively uniform. It will be influenced by the amount and grain size of any sand present in the body that occurs naturally or has been added as tempering material by the potter. Some clays are washed to remove sand from them. The volume firing shrinkages of the fine textured Seleucia clay briquettes were measured, and the data were then recalculated to express the values as percent linear firing shrinkage. Warping would thus not influence the shrinkage measurements. The detailed results will not be presented as they are not useful for the estimation of firing temperatures. In general the clay had a linear expansion of 0.2–0.4 percent at 600° and 700°C, followed by less than 3 percent shrinkage through 1050°, and 4–7 percent shrinkage between 1050° and 1100° as incipient vitrification began. It is possible to measure the additional

shrinkage of sherds and figurines that have been refired in the laboratory, but the results do not justify the effort. For highly siliceous bodies such as those of special types of glazed Islamic pottery studied by Kiefer and referred to later, shrinkage measurements can give an indication of the original firing temperatures.

A decrease in porosity might be an indication of increased firing temperature as the clay body begins to shrink but before the overfired vesicular structure develops. (The porosity of a ceramic body is expressed as the percent water absorbed under standard test conditions per unit of volume of the test piece.) The results of the porosity measurements of the briquettes, ranging from 28 percent to 40 percent, did not show any clear trends save at the highest temperatures. The small size of the pieces tested and the small number of examples would in part explain this. There was a marked decrease in porosity between 1050° and 1100° caused by incipient vitrification. There was also a slight tendency for the R-O series (with 60 minutes at the highest firing temperature) to be lower in porosity than those of the R and the O series which had but 30 minutes at the highest firing temperature. A series of 43 figurine fragments selected to represent the major color differences indicative of degree of firing were tested for their porosity, but the results, ranging from 24 percent to 44 percent, gave no useful correlation with fired clay color. It would therefore seem that the firing temperature, save for very high temperature overfiring, had no important influence on the porosity of the ceramic products.

The study of thin sections of the fired briquettes, some figurines, and many sherds from Seleucia under the petrographic microscope confirms the temperature indications provided by the color of the fired products. Changes in the birefringence of the clay, the alteration of the calcite, and the appearance of ferruginous inclusions are temperature indicators. Such detailed studies, however, are made for other purposes and cannot be considered a primary means of estimating firing temperatures, although they can provide confirmation. Shepard (Reference 13, pp. 27–31) has useful comments on the effects of heat on nonplastics.

This survey of the results of some of the physical measurements made on Seleucia clay briquettes and figurines indicates that changes in color because of firing temperature and atmosphere can serve as the most useful and simple guide for the estimation of the original firing temperatures. The percent loss of weight on refiring may at times be useful; hardness and true specific gravity determinations have limited application.

The Firing Temperatures of Seleucia's Ceramic Products

The large quantity of figurines, clay lamps, and almost complete pieces of pottery from the six seasons of excavations at Seleucia that was available at the University of Michigan made it possible to study firing temperatures in terms of clay colors on stratigraphically controlled large samples. Selected materials from this extensive study will be presented to illustrate some of the results. Five arbitrary color categories were established based on Munsell's soil color names. It might be well to comment on the terms selected. *Brown* indicates at least the surface color of the objects, and often their core color as well, although this may shade into grays. This arbitrary color range includes Munsell's pinks as well. *White on brown* is used for the objects that have a white surface skin with a brown body beneath it. *White* includes the pale colors, some of which observers not oriented toward the Munsell terminology might call pale pink to yellow. Villagers in Greece and the Near East today term a wide range of shades as white and do not differentiate between them when discussing pottery. *Olive* includes the higher fired white wares that are verging on yellow-green shades of color. It includes the colors grouped on Munsell's Hue 5Y plate. The term yellow might have been used, but it is too close to white for useful distinctions to be made in large sortings. The category used for the pieces that cannot be classified into the other groups is *X*. They may vary greatly in surface color, have been discolored by burial in hearth debris or in burned buildings, or have been made of clays which developed a different series of colors when fired. Consistent results are best obtained when one person or two people working together make the classification. In the Seleucia studies all of the color groupings were determined by one person under reasonably uniform lighting conditions. The results of several color sortings of the Seleucia ceramic materials are presented in Table 4.7.

The large number of almost whole pieces of pottery available (969) made it unnecessary to use sherds in this study. Since several sherds could have come from one vessel, it was thought best not to group them with the pottery. Most of the pottery (70 percent) fired white, and very little showed evidence of overfiring. The low percentages of white on brown and of brown point to a good ceramic tradition of kiln firing in which the ware had an opportunity to mature at 900° to 1000°C before the firing ended. The kiln temperature probably dropped quite rapidly after the firing ceased, judging from the pale neutral color of the ware. The pottery from the sixth season constituted about one-third of the sample. Since the excavations in the last season included some new areas, this group was compared with the materials from the other seasons and the color distributions were found to be almost identical. This would suggest that there was a long-established tradition of pottery manufacture at Seleucia that was consistent in the several parts of the large city in terms of degree of firing of the wares.

Small lamps are found in large quantities in excavations of the Hellenistic and Parthian periods and show little variation in shape or design. The 97 lamps brought back to the University of Michigan after the last season were sorted as to color distribution. The distribution was about the same as that for the pottery, with fewer low fired pieces and several more that were quite high fired. This parallel distribution would indicate that the small lamps were fired in the same kilns with the pottery. Today the Greek and Near Eastern potters fill the interstices in the kiln load with small vessels. It is likely that lamps were placed in the voids between vessels when the Seleucia kilns were loaded.

Table 4.7
Color Distribution of the Pottery, Lamps, and Figurines Found at Seleucia.

	No. of Test Pieces	Brown	White on Brown	White	Olive	X
(a)						
Pottery	969	14.24%	9.60%	70.38%	1.55%	4.23%
Lamps	97	11.34	7.22	70.10	8.25	3.09
Figurines, Total Series	2927	32.83	30.92	27.37	4.20	4.68
(b)						
Figurines, Block G-6 (by Levels)						
I (120 A.D.–216 A.D.)	200	42.5%	25.5%	23.0%	3.5%	5.5%
II (70 A.D.–120 A.D.)	336	36.3	34.5	20.8	4.5	3.9
III (143 B.C.–70 A.D.)	686	34.4	36.9	22.6	3.3	2.8
IV (295 B.C.–143 B.C.)	79	22.8	46.8	22.8	6.3	1.3
(c)						
Figurines, Block G-6						
Late III (Postrevolt)	291	39.9%	32.6%	19.9%	4.8%	2.7%
Early III (Prerevolt)	367	29.2	40.6	25.9	1.9	2.5

Almost 3000 figurines were available for color sorting. Their distribution is quite unlike that for the pottery and lamps, and indicates a different tradition of firing. The colors are distributed about equally among low-, medium-, and high-fired groups. This would suggest that a different type of kiln was used, probably with less uniform heat distribution. It is likely that the duration of the firings was also less. We will return to this discussion later after having looked at some subgroups of the figurines and examined Dr. Van Buren's figurine color distribution.

One of the areas excavated at Seleucia for several seasons was G-6, a large residential block with small shops facing the streets around its periphery. Three major levels of occupation in this city block had been excavated through a depth of over 30 feet of deposits below the surface during the earlier field seasons. In the last campaign a start was made on the excavation of Level IV. The color distribution of the 1301 figurines that were sorted from Block G-6 in terms of their levels is shown in Table 4.7b. The earliest materials (but by far the smallest sample) were the best fired. The latest materials were the lowest fired although the increase in the brown figurines was only six percent. Grouping together the brown plus the white on brown, one finds that the percentage is about the same as in the earlier levels. Other factors such as the size and shape of the figurines and variations in the amount of soluble salts in the clay should also be considered when assessing the meaning of the slight increase in lower-fired figurines. Level I covers a final century of unrest for the city of Seleucia, a time when it was sacked by three Roman generals—Trajan, Verus, and Septimius Severus—so a decline in production standards or in the availability of fuel might not be surprising.

A further test was made by sortings of the G-6 figurines. After Seleucia was conquered by the Parthians, it remained an autonomous Hellenistic city in culture and architecture, paying tribute to the new overlords but living for the most part in its old ways. During a seven-year period, A.D. 36–43, the city experienced great unrest with severe power struggles going on with varying success between the native party and the aristocratic party. The latter eventually won but had been so weakened that, according to McDowell, it had to request royal domination. McDowell (Reference 9, pp. 225–226) has described and interpreted this struggle in terms of the series of coins that were minted during this period of unrest. As a result of these disturbed years, the loss by Seleucia of autonomy in government, and the development of a strong native party that was frequently in power, there was a marked change in the cultural life of the city,

judging from the archaeological evidence. Hellenistic types of architecture, figurines, pottery, etc. that had still been common in early Level III, were replaced by types characteristic of the oriental culture of the Parthians. These new types continued through Levels II and I.

It was possible to select 658 figurines from Level III that could be approximately divided into the prerevolt and the postrevolt periods. The color sortings in Table 4.7c clearly show a change for the worse in the manner of firing the figurines after the time of the revolt. They were fired at lower temperatures, and there was less experienced control of the kilns; for there was a marked increase in the number of overfired pieces. It is easy to speculate on the reasons for this decline in the degree of firing of the figurines. Without elaborating on them, a few ideas can be suggested: Fuel may have become scarcer or more expensive to obtain, there may have been a decline in standards of craftmanship because of untrained assistants or added responsibilities in the homes (if women made the figurines) with the shift in cultural orientation toward the East, and probably there was a depression. It is interesting to note that the color distribution of postrevolt Level III is almost identical with that of Level II.

A postscript can be added to these color distribution studies of some of the ceramic products from Seleucia. In the spring of 1955, I was able to return to the site at the suggestion of and with the help of the late Dr. Naji al Asil, then Director General of Antiquites for Iraq. The Tigris River had changed its course near Seleucia as a result of severe floods in 1938, and parts of the city, including the temple I had excavated, were irretrievably under water. As I walked about the extensive site, I was surprised to note the large number of brown sherds that lay on the ground. My recollection, based in part on the pottery sortings in which 70 percent of the vessels were white, was that brown materials were scarce. I examined the surface sherds and realized that the materials lying on the ground to a large part represented soft low-fired vessels that had broken easily in antiquity. Few of these would be among the restorable pots that would have been saved by the excavators. Many would have crumbled due to the crystallization of salts in the porous bodies, a destructive process of low-fired ware that is illustrated in Figure 4.1. Spalling or disintegration in less than a year after the vessels were fired would occur for those pieces containing coarse grains of limestone that had been calcined during firing if the CaO had not reacted with the clay to form a calcium silicate but was free to hydrate.

It is a good idea to observe the sherd detritus on the surface of a site and on

Table 4.8

Color Distribution of the Van Buren Figurines

Site	No. of Figurines	Brown	White on Brown	White	White plus White on Brown	Olive	Miscellaneous
Total Van Buren Series	750	30.8%	11.5%	40.7%	52.2%	11.9%	4.1
Seleucia	2927	32.8	30.9	27.4	58.3	4.2	4.7
Assur	41	31.7	14.6	36.6	51.2	7.3	9.8
Babylon	39	33.3	10.2	30.8	41.0	12.8	12.9
Kish	77	28.6	13.0	50.7	63.7		7.7
Nippur	103	27.2	13.6	42.7	56.3	8.7	7.8
Tello	34	32.3	8.8	26.4	35.2	29.4	3.1
Warka	34	17.7	2.9	50.0	52.9	20.6	8.8
Ur	109	14.7	20.2	40.4	60.6	21.1	3.6
Susa	28	17.8	3.6	50.0	53.6	14.3	14.3

the dumps from the excavations to judge whether the sample one collects for color distribution studies truly reflects the range of products coming from the kilns. Figure 4.2 shows such a sherd-strewn surface in southern Iraq at Tell Uqair. Much high-fired Ubaid pottery had been obtained at this excavation, but it was amazing to see the large number of chips of low-fired ware intermingled with the white sherds.

While this paper was in press, Wright has published an extensive series of Munsell color identifications for both paste and surface color of Early Dynastic sherds excavated near Ur (Reference 19, Appendix I). It would be interesting to group them for comparison into the five categories used in this report.

Van Buren Figurine Colors

One of the few early publications in which the color of the clay objects is consistently given is that of the helpful and energetic late Elizabeth Douglas Van Buren (Reference 15). In her study *The Clay Figurines of Babylonia and Assyria* many terms were used to describe the colors. I have attempted to group them into five categories using Munsell soil color names, so that her data can be compared with color distributions for the Seleucia figurines. Some of the Van Buren color designations had to be arbitrarily squeezed into this simple classification. The results appear in Table 4.8. The white on brown category is very low compared to that of the Seleucia figurines, and the white group is high. This is doubtless because the surface color often was used to characterize a piece without reference to its core color, which may not have been visible were some of the figurines complete. To compensate for this, an additional column has been added to the table in which these two categories are grouped together. With this addition the color distribution of Van Buren's series agrees well with that from Seleucia. The olive category seems high, but some pieces so termed might have been classified as

white by another observer. One value of the Seleucia series is that the color sortings were all carried out by one person. The high percentage of olive figurines could also indicate that these high-fired and therefore durable pieces had good survival value.

Of the 750 figurines described by Van Buren, 62 percent of them came from but eight sites, and their color distributions are included in Table 4.8. Although the individual samples reported from these sites, 28 to 109 figurines, cannot be considered representative of all of the materials excavated, and they may have been made in widely different time periods, it is interesting to compare them for they show surprising consistencies. Assur, Babylon, Kish, and Nippur are sites in upper and central Mesopotamia, the region roughly between present-day Mosul and Diwaniya. Their color distributions are similar to those of the Seleucia figurines. Tello is to the southeast. If the color designations are accepted, there is a remarkably high number of olive pieces. One wonders about increased salt content of the clay or a difference in techniques of firing. It would be interesting to examine an extensive series of ceramic materials from Tello. Warka and Ur are southern sites, and in the sample reported, which certainly is but a tiny part of the materials from these great excavations, the pieces tend to be white to olive in color. Again, this may be due to increased salt content in the soil. Susa is in a different geological region, but its color distribution is like that of Warka, judging from the very small sample from both sites.

This analysis of the Van Buren color designations suggests what could be done with better samples. It would be interesting to examine large collections of figurine fragments from stratigraphically well-controlled excavations to see if differences in the degree of firing could be related to method of manufacture, workshops, types

4.2
Sherd-strewn surface in southern Iraq at Tell Uqair. The softer low-fired ware is broken into the smaller pieces.

4.3
Pottery fired on open hearth with dung cakes as fuel in Iraqi Kurdistan.

4.4
Kiln used in 1968 in village of Charikar in Afghanistan.

4.5
Hearth of kiln in Figure 4.4.

4.6
Early Dynastic III vessels from Ur.

of figurines, etc. The eight classes into which Van Buren divided the 750 figurines used in her study—male, female, gods, goddesses, divine couples, religion and magic, animals, and daily life—bore no relationship to the degree of firing.

The good agreement between the color distributions for the Van Buren and the Seleucia sortings certainly indicates a consistent tradition in the firing of the figurines, one different from that used in pottery manufacture. Speculation as to the type of kiln used when there is at present no archaeological evidence is rather fruitless, but one wonders if it was not small and more like a bread oven than a potter's kiln. A craft tradition different from that of the potters must be recognized for the manufacture of the figurines. Possibly it continued as a household art carried on by the women long after the potters had established separate working establishments.

Kilns and Firing Temperatures

Early pottery of the Near East in the time range 6000–4000 B.C. was fired on open hearths with dung cakes, straw, or brush as fuel. The tradition still continues today in remote villages. I have observed such firings in Kurdistan in northeastern Iraq at the village of Diyana which is near the Rowanduz gorge. A bed of ash served as a hearth, and dung cakes were used both as the fuel and as the kiln. They were stacked to form a vault above the nested vessels, as can be seen in Figure 4.3. This picture was made at the end of the firing as the ashed cakes crumbled and the vessels were ready for removal from the kiln to be decorated with painted lines and dots applied with tar. After the ware had cooled, it had a dull pale brown color similar to that of briquettes made from the same clay that had been fired in the laboratory for 30 minutes at temperatures of 600° and 700°. The ware is sufficiently durable to be used today as water jars and cooking pots. It had not been fired high enough to decompose much of the fine grained limestone in the clay, so disintegration of the vessels due to the rehydration of the lime was no problem. Shepard (Reference 13, pp. 83–84) inserted a thermocouple in the similar hearth loads of pottery as Pueblo women fired their wares. She found that the firing temperatures ranged from 625°–940°C. In Guthe's detailed study of the manufacturing processes of the potters at the Pueblo of San Ildefonso in New Mexico, the pioneer work in ethnographic ceramic studies, he described the simple ovens used to fire the pottery. He found that each firing took about half an hour, the end point being determined by the appearance of the progressively lighter surface color of the pottery. (Reference 20, p. 72.)

It is not yet possible to pinpoint the development of permanent kilns in the ancient Near East, but it was probably in the last half of the fifth millennium B.C. Scott has summarized the archaeological evidence for early kilns (Reference 21, pp. 391–397). Ubaid pottery was consistently high fired to white and often to olive colors (although low-fired ware also existed as the sherds in Figure 4.2 illustrate). Kilns were square or cylindrical tubular structures with a firing chamber at the base into which the fuel was intermittently placed. The perforated roof of this chamber formed the hearth of the kiln on which the ware was stacked. The flames and heat from the burning fuel rose through the hearth holes to fire the ware. The crown of the kiln, judging from present-day practices in villages, was often a temporary structure formed of fragments of fired pots that were placed over the top of the load of green ware. A kiln of this type in use in 1968 near the village of Charikar in Afghanistan is shown in Figure 4.4. One can see the pattern of sunlight that penetrated down through the hearth holes of the empty kiln into the firing chamber. A stack of sherds is waiting to be used to top the next load of unfired ware as a temporary crown for the kiln. The appearance of the hearth can be seen in Figure 4.5 as one looks down from the open top. One casserole from the previous firing still remains in place inverted between flue holes.

In kilns such as that just described there can be great variation in the final firing temperature from the hearth to the temporary crown to the center of the load to the kiln walls. Drafts on windy days can wreak havoc with firings and cause much of the ware to be overfired. A series of Early Dynastic III vessels from Ur can be used to illustrate this point. They appear in Figure 4.6. A large series of such pots, identical in form, were stored in the Mustansarriyah in Baghdad, the supplementary storage area formerly used by the Iraq Museum. I was permitted to select the five pieces shown and place them in the courtyard to photograph them. They range in color from brown with a spot of surface white, seen on the left, through white on brown, white, very pale olive, and overfired olive. The smaller size of the last piece is probably not accidental; firing shrinkage has occurred.

Kiln design seems to have changed little in the Near East except for the building of permanent crowns on the kilns. But kiln control developed with experience. In general the firing range of 800°–1050° was standard in the simple structures, the end of the firing being determined by the appearance of the ware when viewed through a peep hole. Color changes under approximately black body conditions can be recognized by experienced potters. Thus they can terminate their firings in a consistent temperature pattern.

The development of glazes led to further problems of kiln control. I have suggested elsewhere (Reference 6, p. 91) that 800°–900°C was sufficient temperature to melt the glazes. I have the general impression but no statistical support for the observation that brown to white on brown bodies are characteristic of many of the glazed pieces of Islamic times, for the potter had to avoid the highest temperatures if he were to produce good glazed ware. Kiefer has published an excellent technological study of some glazed Anatolian ware whose body is a siliceous paste rather than clay, a body ineptly termed "faience" by archaeologists (Reference 3). From his analyses of the thermal expansion and contraction of his test pieces as they were fired to increasingly higher temperatures until they began to fuse, he was able to estimate the probable original firing temperatures of the wares. He found that many of them were in the range of 850°–900°C but that the total range was about 750°–1050°C.

In this report suggestions have been made as to some of the many factors that influence the firing temperatures of the pottery of the Near East and of their influences on the colors of the wares. No formal color chart has been developed based on the extensive laboratory experiments, as the intent is to emphasize the need for further studies of local clays and statistically significant samples of sherds, pottery, figurines, bricks, and lamps. As they appear, it will be possible to refine the general statements as to firing temperatures for specific plain, painted, and glazed wares, successive time periods, and regional differences.

References

1.
Balinkin, I. A.
(chairman)

"Symposium on Color," *Amer. Ceramic Soc. Bull.*, **27** (2), 1948 pp. 43–63. (Discussion of these papers appears *ibid*, **27**(5), 1948 pp. 185–187.

2.
Brownell, W. E.

"Scum and Its Development on Structural Clay Products," Research Report No. 4 of the Structural Clay Products Research Foundation, Chicago, 1955.

3.
Kiefer, C

"Les Céramiques Siliceuses d'Anatolie et du Moyen Orient," *Bull. de la Société Francaise de Céramique* **1,** no. 30, 1956, pp. 3–24; no. 31, pp. 17–34.

4.
March, Benjamin

Standards of Pottery Description, Occasional Contributions from the Museum of Anthropology of the University of Michigan, No. 3, University of Michigan Press, Ann Arbor, 1934.

5.
Matson, Frederick R.

"Technological Notes on the Pottery," in Nicholas Toll, *The Green Glazed Pottery. The Excavations of Dura Europos.* Final Report 4, Part 1, Fasicle 1, Yale University Press, New Haven, 1943, pp. 81–95.

6.
Matson, Frederick R.

"A Technological Study of the Unglazed Pottery and Figurines from Seleucia on the Tigris." Ph.D. Dissertation, University of Michigan, 1939. University Microfilm no. 660, Ann Arbor. 1945.

7.
Matson, Frederick R.

"Ceramic Archaeology," *Amer. Ceramic Soc. Bull.*, **34,** 2, pp. 33–44, 1955.

8.
Matson, Frederick R.

"Some Aspects of Ceramic Technology," in *Science in Archaeology,* Don Brothwell and Eric Higgs, Eds., Thames and Hudson, London, 1963, pp. 489–498; 2nd ed. 1969, pp. 592–602.

9.
McDowell, Robert H.

"The Excavations at Seleucia on the Tigris." *Papers of the Michigan Academy of Science, Arts and Letters* XVIII, 1932 pp. 101–119, published 1933.

10.

Munsell Soil Color Charts, Munsell Color Company, Inc., Baltimore, 1954.

11.
Ries, Heinrich

Clays, Their Occurrence, Properties and Uses, John Wiley & Sons, Inc., New York, 3rd. ed., 1927.

12.
Salmang, Hermann

Ceramics-Physical and Chemical Fundamentals, translated by Marcus Francis Butterworths, London, 1961.

13.
Shepard, Anna O.

Ceramics for the Archaeologist, Publication 609, Fifth Printing, Carnegie Institution of Washington, Washington, D.C., 1965.

14.
Stone, J. F. S.

"The Use and Distribution of Faience in the Ancient Near East and Prehistoric Europe," (with notes on the spectrochemical analysis of Faience by L. C. Thomas), *Proc. Prehistoric Soc.*, New Series XXII, (5) 1956, pp. 37–84.

Clay Figurines of Babylonia and Assyria, Yale Oriental Series, Researches, XVI. Yale University Press, New Haven, 1930.

15.
Van Buren,
E. Douglas

"Thermography of Gypsum," *J. Amer. Ceramic Soc.*, **37**, 5, 1954, pp. 221–224.

16.
West, Richard R.,
and
Sutton, Willard J.

"Symposium on Color Standards and Measurements I–V," *Bull. Amer. Ceramic Soc.*, **20**, (11) 1941, pp. 375–402.

17.
Weyl, Woldemar A.

The Irrigation of Mesopotamia, E. & F. N. Spon, Ltd., London, 1911.

18.
Willcocks, W.

The Administration of Rural Production in an Early Mesopotamian Town. Anthropological Paper No. 38, Museum of Anthropology, University of Michigan, Ann Arbor, 1969.

19.
Wright, Henry T.

Pueblo Pottery Making. A Study at the Village of San Ildefonso. Papers of the Southwestern Expedition, Number 2, Department of Archaeology, Phillips Academy, Andover, Mass. Published by Yale University Press, New Haven, 1925.

20.
Guthe, Carl E.

"Pottery." In *A History of Technology*, vol. I, Charles Singer, E. J. Holmyard, and A. R. Hall, eds., Oxford, 1954, pp. 376–412.

21.
Scott, Sir Lindsay

Chapter 5

Egyptian Blue as a Pigment and Ceramic Material

W. T. Chase
Freer Gallery of Art

Introduction

My interest in Egyptian blue stems from the arrival at the Metropolitan Museum of two excavated objects discovered at Hasanlu in the 1964 season (Figures 5.1 and 5.2). (See Reference 15.) One of these is a goblet, 4 13/16 inches high, made of a hard body material with blue, red, and black tinges. It arrived in fragments. The other is an object of unknown function which I will call a sistrum handle. At one time the Department of Ancient Near Eastern Art of the Metropolitan referred to this as a handle for a sistrum, and it seems to me preferable to use this shorter term to avoid repeating the longer, "object of unknown function."[1] Both of these objects when received were badly blackened by carbon from a fire, and in order to oxidize and remove the carbon it was decided to refire them to 400°C. During refiring the sistrum handle broke, and it became obvious that we should learn more about the behavior of Egyptian blue as a modeling or ceramic material. Incidentally, we later decided that the breakage occurred because of thermal shock from an overly rapid increase in temperature caused by a malfunctioning temperature control and not because of any property of Egyptian blue. These new breaks also gave us ample opportunity for sampling, of which we took full advantage as you will see later.

Definition

So far we have not answered the primary question: What is Egyptian blue? Egyptian blue is a calcium-copper tetrasilicate with the formula $CaCuSi_4O_{10}$ (or $CuO \cdot CaO \cdot 4SiO_2$). (See Reference 16.) So Egyptian blue is a definite chemical compound with a definite composition and crystallographic properties, just as malachite or salt are definite compounds.

The use of the term "Egyptian blue" has had some unfortunate consequences, as it leads to confusion with Egyptian faience which is usually bluish or greenish and which was made from some of the same raw materials: sand, natron, and a copper salt. Faience and its fabrication is a study in itself, and we must leave this for other investigators. (References 23 and 10). What makes Egyptian faience blue, however, is not Egyptian blue but a blue glaze formed by the migration of the soluble salts to the outside of the porous body where they were vitrified (turned into a glaze) in the firing, or by investing the pieces to be glazed in a mixture of various materials. Objects of Egyptian blue can also be confused with blue glass, but unlike glass Egyptian blue is very opaque, even at thin or broken edges.

Since Egyptian blue was the most important blue pigment in antiquity, it has been studied for a long time. Chaptal started about 1804 (Reference 6), and Sir Humphrey Davy investigated it in 1815 (Reference 11). In the 1880s, mineralogists in France became interested in it, and in 1889, Foqué established the composition as the calcium-copper tetrasilicate $CaCuSi_4O_{10}$. (See Reference 11.) He also synthesized the mineral and reported that the specific gravity is 3.04, that the substance belongs to the quadratic (now called tetragonal) system, that it appears in the form of scales flattened parallel to the base of the prism, sometimes of rectangular outline (Figure 5.3), that the optical properties are uniaxial negative, and that "these scales, seen under the microscope on their edge, with interposition of a nicol [or polarizer], offer a very remarkable pleochroism. With the rays vibrating parallel to the axis they are of a pale rose color; with vibrations in a direction perpendicular to the axis they are of an intense blue." A thin section from an Egyptian blue bead from the Lisht North Pyramid site illustrates this very well (Reference 9). The Egyptian blue in the bead crystallized in large plates, and the thin section happened to cut some of these plates parallel to the {110} face shown in Figure 5.3. Seen edge-on, the maximum pleochroism is visible; in a microscope slide made from an Egyptian blue pigment the plates most often lie with the {001} face parallel to the slide so that pleochroism is not easily visible. Pleochroism is still one of the best diagnostic features to determine the presence of Egyptian blue. The refractive indexes of Egyptian blue (ϵ 1.605 and ω 1.635) (see Reference 11) are higher than balsam, like those of azurite (Reference 7), and like azurite it is quite birefringent. The blue-lavender pleochroism of the prismatic plates of Egyptian blue seen on edge, however, immediately gives it away. A microchemical test with dilute HCl will, of course, immediately dissolve azurite with effervescence but will not affect Egyptian blue at all.

One of the best and most convenient ways to identify pigment materials is by means of X-ray powder diffraction. This technique is especially useful because only very small samples are required. X-Ray powder diffraction measurements can be used both for identification and for elucidation of the structure of a material. Some prints of X-ray powder diffraction films are shown in Figure 5.4. The films are all taken of Egyptian blue samples from different sources, except for the last which does not match, showing that it is a different material. A. Pabst of the University of California, Berkeley, has done the most comprehensive work on Egyptian

Identification

[1] The Department of Ancient Near Eastern Art now calls this a "spade-shaped object," but for brevity I shall retain the term "sistrum handle" here.

5.1
Goblet, ninth century
B.C., made of Egyptian
blue, height 4-13/16
inches. Found at Hasanlu
in 1964 in burned
building II. (Metro-
politan Museum of Art,
Rogers Fund, 65. 163.
36.)

5.2
Spade-shaped object,
possibly a sistrum han-
dle, ninth century B.C.,
made of Egyptian blue,
height 6-1/8 inches.
Found at Hasanlu in
1964 in burned build-
ing II. (Metropolitan
Museum of Art, Rogers
Fund, 65.163.37.)

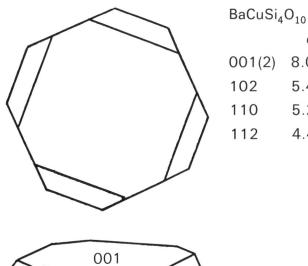

$BaCuSi_4O_{10}$

	d
001(2)	8.06Å
102	5.44
110	5.25
112	4.41

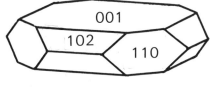

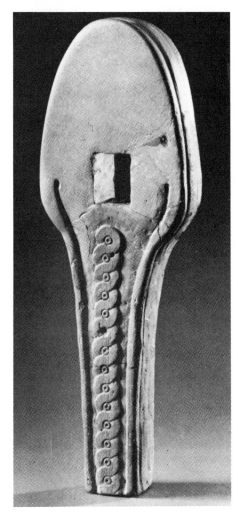

5.3
The crystal habit of Egyptian blue is identical to
that of $BaCuSi_4O_{10}$ as
represented by this idealized drawing. (Pabst
"Structures of some tet-
ragonal sheet silicates,"
Acta Crystallographica,
12, 1959, p. 738, fig.
2.)

5.4
X-Ray powder diffraction
films of Egyptian blue.
From top to bottom:
Synthetic Egyptian blue;
Egyptian blue from
Tel-el-amarna (1370
B.C.); Egyptian blue from
Nuzi (1500 B.C.);
Egyptian blue from
Ptolemaic statue (FGA
0.899); Diopside from
base of Egyptian statu-
ette of the Roman
period (FGA 0.862).

blue with X-ray diffraction. (See References 16 and 13.) By mixing $CaCO_3$, CuO, and amorphous silica in a pellet with 10 percent of borax for a flux, heating this to 850°C for about a day and slowly cooling it, then leaching the pellet with HCl and gently crushing it, perfect platy tetragonal crystals of Egyptian blue about 0.1 x 0.03 mm in size were formed. This material was found to be isostructural with gillespite ($BaFeSi_4O_{10}$); and Egyptian blue, gillespite, and the Sr and Ba analogues of Egyptian blue ($SrCuSi_4O_{10}$ and $BaCuSi_4O_{10}$) all crystallize in the space group $P4/ncc$-D_{4h}^8. These are all tetragonal sheet silicates. Pabst took special care to eliminate effects dependent on preferred orientation in measuring the intensities of the diffracted lines. He remarks that, "patterns made from ordinary powder mounts with preferred orientation of particles show markedly different intensity relations." (Reference 16.) Mazzi and Pabst also established that Egyptian blue and the natural mineral cuprorivaite are indeed the same material, as postulated by Minguzzi (Reference 13).

Let us see how Pabst's measurements of the d spacings (spacings between planes of atoms) correspond to those taken from objects and to other samples. Table 5.1 shows the d spacings and intensities of reflections from various samples of Egyptian blue. The samples were taken from as many different places as possible. The first four columns represent the Egyptian blue synthesized by Pabst (Reference 16), with Miller index, intensity, and d spacings, both observed and calculated from the structure. The next two columns were determined by William J. Young of the Boston Museum of Fine Arts from Egyptian blue pigment from the ninth dynasty in Egypt. The next two, Schippa and Toracca determined on a Roman blue pigment from the first century A.D. (Reference 18). The next two, I determined on blue that I made according to the formula published in Laurie, McClintock, and Miles (Reference 11). A. M. Rosenquist determined the next on blue found on a shield in the Bø grave above the Arctic Circle in Norway (ca. A.D. 250) (Reference 17). The last are reflections of α quartz from the A.S.T.M. powder diffraction file. One spacing of about 7.6 Å appears strongly in four patterns. A spacing of about 3.78 Å appears in all five patterns strongly. And a spacing of about 3.3 Å also appears in four patterns, but more strongly in Young's, mine, and Rosenquist's than in Pabst's, suggesting that it comes in part from the quartz spacing of 3.343 Å. Pabst carefully picked single crystals of his synthetic blue to use for his measurements. This would eliminate effects caused by quartz. Archaeological samples of Egyptian blue. like most archaeological samples, are, however, often impure and will often contain quartz and other materials. From this cursory examination of these measurements, we can conclude that Pabst's published measurements are correctly those of Egyptian blue and are adequate to identify the material beyond any doubt. These measurements also represent cuprorivaite and can be found on A.S.T.M. card 12–512 in the powder diffraction file. This, then, is how Egyptian blue is identified.

History of Use

As mentioned earlier, Egyptian blue has a long history of use as a pigment. Its earliest recorded use was in the fourth dynasty in Egypt (Reference 12). The use of Egyptian blue lasted throughout the Dynastic period in Egypt and continued on into the Roman period; it spread to Rome, Pompeii, and in ca. A.D. 250 as far as Norway (see above). The Etruscans used it in their wall-paintings, and in Pompeii it is found in abundance (Reference 1). The range of blues available to the Pompeiian painters was very wide, as Augusti illustrates. In the colors found in excavated shops in Pompeii and Herculaneum, he found three main hues; one was supplied in large crystals in spheres, and two were supplied in small crystals as powders. After about the fourth century A.D., the secret of the manufacture of Egyptian blue was lost, to be rediscovered in the nineteenth century.

Ancient Texts

The ancient texts shed some light on the manufacture and use of Egyptian blue. Vitruvius says that the manufacture of Egyptian blue was discovered in Alexandria which was actually not built until 2000 years after the discovery of the pigment:

Methods of making blue were first discovered in Alexandria, and afterwards Vestorius set up the making of it at Puzzuoli. The method of obtaining it from the substances of which it has been found to consist, is strange enough. Sand and the flowers of natron are brayed together so finely that the product is like meal, and copper is grated by means of coarse files over the mixture, like sawdust, to form a conglomerate. Then it is made into balls by rolling it in the hands and thus bound together for drying. The dry balls are put in an earthen jar, and the jars in an oven. As soon as the copper and the sand grow hot and unite under the intensity of the fire, they mutually receive each other's sweat, relinquishing their peculiar qualities, and having lost their properties through the intensity of the fire, they are reduced to a blue colour. (Reference 21)

These balls were discovered at Pompeii. Vitruvius did not know that the sand had to contain $CaCO_3$ to work correctly, but we can forgive him that because of his accurate description of the process. "They mutually receive each other's sweat" poetically expresses what we know today as solid solution.

Theophrastus delineated two types of *kyanos*, one of which was natural and one of which was manufactured in Egypt (Egyptian blue), and he notices that the finer it is ground, the paler the blue (Reference 4). He also uses the word *kyanos* to define a blue precious stone—probably lapis lazuli. The same confusion existed in ancient Egypt, where the word *ḫsbd* means Egyptian blue and the semiprecious stone lapis and its imitations (Reference 8). In fact, the Egyptians did have modifiers to denote qualities of the pigment and to separate genuine lapis or imitation; *ḫsbd* was the most valuable of the semiprecious stones, and there are many references to it in Egyptian texts. A quote from Harris's book is appropriate here:

It has not seemed desirable, or indeed altogether feasible, to separate the various words for faience, glass, frit, etc. from the semiprecious stones. It is not a distinction of which the Egyptians themselves were ever acutely conscious, and it is evident that the name of almost any stone could equally well be applied to its imitation in faience or glass, it being quite impossible in many cases to tell which is meant. (Reference 8)

So we should not be chagrined when we cannot immediately tell what an ancient blue object is made from, as it seems that the equivalent of "valuable blue material" was good enough for the Egyptians.

Fabrication of Egyptian Blue

Now to the primary questions of this paper: How was Egyptian blue made into objects? What changes have the objects undergone since their manufacture? To answer these questions I used two approaches: I attempted to duplicate ancient Egyptian blue objects in the laboratory, and I examined the ancient objects closely to ascertain how they were made. First, let us consider the Egyptian blue made in the laboratory.

I tested a number of compositions (see Table 5.2) and Laurie's formula turned out to be a very good one:

Laurie's Formula (Reference 11)
(Our Formula II)

64.6 g silicic acid (powdered silica)

7.2 g synthetic natron
(3.2 g sodium sesquicarbonate
2.1 g sodium sulfate
1.5 g sodium chloride)

15.4 g copper carbonate (malachite)

12.4 g calcium carbonate

Firing this to 830°C for 45 minutes produced a nice blue which gave an X-ray diffraction pattern (see Figure 5.7) corresponding to the blue from the sistrum handle, with some remnant lines from the quartz, synthetic natron, and calcite, showing that they had not all combined in this short firing time. This figure also shows the correspondence between the synthetic natron used as a flux or fusion mixture in our experiments and the natron found in mummy wrapping bags from the tomb of Tutankhamūn, now in the collection of the Metropolitan Museum. The state of division of the silica has a great deal to do with the rate of the reaction. Using quartz sand in the same proportions, one gets a granular, spongy mixture with particles of blue, which, when ground and refired, develops the characteristic powder-blue color. Schippa and Torraca also observed this fact.

Time and temperature of the reaction have a great deal to do with the formation of the Egyptian blue crystals. (See Table 5.2.) Figure 5.5 shows the X-ray diffractometer traces of the various crystalline phases which arise from firing Formula II at different temperatures. The Egyptian blue phase disappears at around 1000°C and a glassy phase forms, with quartz lines still showing up. All of these temperatures were held for about one hour, and therefore the transformations may not in all cases have proceeded to equilibrium. Egyptian blue crystals can be regenerated by soaking the glassy mixture at a temperature of 850°C for a prolonged period of time.

So far we have been talking about the changes that take place in an oxidizing atmosphere. What happens in a reducing atmosphere? Even at a relatively low temperature (900°C) the Egyptian blue crystals reduce to red copper oxide and other products, as is clearly shown in Figure 5.6. The transformation of Egyptian blue to a copper oxide and quartz can easily be made with the material held in a platinum spoon in a reducing flame. The blue phase can, however, be regenerated by soaking in an oxidizing atmosphere at 850°C. The reaction products of the reduction are colored a deep reddish-brown. The particles look like red clinkers under the microscope. This is apparently what happened in the case of the goblet, and in the case of two pieces of a table top excavated at Timna by the Smithsonian Institution Division of Old World Anthropology and called to my attention by Dr. Gus Van Beek (Reference 20). Both of the fragments show corners, and so we can infer that the table top must have been at least 16 × 21 × 5.3 cm and possibly much larger. This may well be the largest piece of Egyptian blue in existence. A section across the table from the top reveals that the blue has changed to red on the surface, and in fact the blue crystals have disappeared in the area of the outer surface. The alteration could be caused by damage from a fire, and in fact we know that all three of these objects (the goblet, the sistrum handle, and the table top) have been in contact with fire. The goblet and sistrum handle were recovered from burned building II at Hasanlu, and the

Table 5.1

d Spacings of Egyptian Blue (in Angstroms) from Various Sources

hkl	I	d observed	d calc	I	d	I	d	I	d	I	d	I	d
		Egyptian Blue, Synthesized. Pabst (Reference 16, page 735.)			Egyptian Blue Pigment, Eighteenth Dynasty. W. J. Young, B.M.F.A		Egyptian Blue Pigment, Roman, First Century A.D. Schippa and Toracca.		Egyptian Blue Made According to Laurie et al. W. T. Chase.		Egyptian Blue from Shield in Bø Grave. Rosenquist.		Quartz ASTM Card 5-0490.	
								13	8.55				
								100	7.86				
002	4	7.63	7.56	4	7.56	S	7.630			M	7.6		
						VW	6.070						
								8	5.54				
102	1½	5.22	5.25	1	5.28	W	5.300						
110			5.16							VW	5.15		
								10	4.47				
								98	4.43				
112			4.26	5	4.27					S	4.25	35	4.26
				3	4.05					VW	4.05		
004	9	3.78	3.78	7	3.79	VS	3.810	100	3.83	S	3.78		
200	2½	3.66	3.65					18	3.71	VW	3.65		
								16	3.55				
104	8	3.36	3.36	10	3.35			100+	3.39	VS	3.34	100	3.343
202	10	3.29	3.29	2	3.28	S-M	3.310	87	3.31	M	3.28		
211	5	3.19	3.19	3	3.20	M	3.210	33	3.23	M	3.19		
114	4	3.05	3.05	8	3.05	S	3.060	58	3.09				
212	9	3.00	3.00			M	2.990	86	3.04	VS	2.99		
				1	2.87			20	2.85				
213	½	2.736	2.740	1	2.71								
204	4,	2.629	2.626	2	2.64	M-W	2.636	23	2.65	M	2.61		
220	4	2.585	2.581	2	2.59	W	2.600	21	2.60	M	2.57		
006	½	2.518	2.520	3	2.50			31	2.55				
214	½	2.471	2.471	2	2.46			40	2.48	M	2.45	12	2.458
222			2.442										
106	2	2.386	2.382	3	2.39	M-W	2.390	27	2.40	VW	2.37		
302	3	2.321	2.316	1	2.32			25	2.34	VW	2.31		
310			2.308					43	2.30				
311			2.282	6	2.28	M	2.285	55	2.29	S	2.28	12	2.282
116	5	2.270	2.265										
												6	2.237
								13	2.225				
215			2.218										
312			2.208										
224	1	2.136	2.132	2	2.14			40	2.143	M	2.12	9	2.128
313			2.099					13	2.096				
206	½	2.069	2.074					13	2.069				
304			2.051										
								16	2.024				
321	2	2.007	2.007					20	2.011				
216			1.995					15	2.000				
								17	1.998	W	1.99		

Table 5.1
d Spacings of Egyptian Blue (in Angstroms) from Various Sources (Continued)

Egyptian Blue. Synthesized. Pabst (Reference 16. page 735.)				Egyptian Blue Pigment, Eighteenth Dynasty. W. J. Young, B.M.F.A.		Egyptian Blue Pigment, Roman, First Century A.D. Schippa and Toracca.		Egyptian Blue Made According to Laurie et al. W. T. Chase.		Egyptian Blue from Shield in Bø Grave. Rosenquist.		Quartz ASTM Card 5-0490	
hkl	l	d observed	d calc.	l	d	l	d	l	d	l	d	l	d
				3	1.98			18	1.981			6	1.980
314	2	1.970	1.970					17	1.973				
322			1.956										
				3	1.92			62	1.907				
008	1½	1.890	1.890			M-W	1.895						
323			1.879	4	1.88								
315			1.835					60	1.845				
108	6	1.831	1.830	6	1.83	S	1.835	68	1.831				
										S	1.82	17	1.817
												1—	1.801
								20	1.797				
	4	1.784		2	1.79	M-W	1.787	25	1.787	S	1.78		
								13	1.778				
								18	1.771				
	2	1.758						16	1.762	W	1.75		
	4	1.704		2	1.71	M-W	1.710	30	1.713	M	1.70		
								13	1.691				
				3	1.68			12	1.675	M	1.67	7	1.672
								16	1.667			3	1.659
	2	1.636		1	1.63			16	1.639	W	1.63		
				3	1.61			17	1.614				
	4b	1.603				W	1.605	18	1.605			1—	1.608
								17	1.601				
								17	1.585	W	1.59		
	½d	1.573								VW	1.57		
				3	1.54			25	1.548	M	1.53	15	1.547
	1	1.528						17	1.521				
	1	1.483		2	1.49			-end-		VW	1.47		
	½	1.462											
	½	1.456								W	1.45	3	1.453
				1	1.44								
	½	1.435								VW	1.43		
	½	1.426		1	1.42					VW	1.42	1—	1.418
	2	1.398		1	1.40					W	1.39		
	2	1.380		3	1.38							7	1.382
				3	1.37					S	1.37	11	1.375
												9	1.372
	2½	1.336		2	1.34					M	1.33		
	1	1.315											
	Plus fifteen or more lines, mostly weak and diffuse.									Plus thirteen more lines, mostly weak.		Plus twenty-one lines to 0.9825.	

Table 5.2

Summary of Firing
Experiments on
Synthesis of
Egyptian Blue Objects

Note: In each case, the starting material in each firing is given, followed by the color and sometimes the consistency of the product of the firing. Where the atmosphere was controlled, the condition (oxidizing or reducing) precedes the starting materials. Abbreviations: For. = formula, Fir. = firing, subscript o or r = oxidizing or reducing. Thus, in column Formula II, Firing VII the first starting material was Formula II which had been run through firings IA, II, and III (reducing). In all cases the reducing atmosphere was attained by surrounding the material with charcoal in a porcelain crucible. In Formula II, Firing IV reducing, all of this charcoal had oxidized before completion of the firing and the ash might have contributed to accidental fluxing of the mixture. This table is a shorthand compilation of months of work which we are not able to present here in greater detail. Most of the products were examined microscopically and analyzed by X-ray powder diffraction also (see Figures 5.5 and 5.6).

Firing	Firing Conditions	Formula I	Formula II	Formula III	Formula IV	Glass Mix α	Glass Mix β
	Maximum temperature Average change in temperature per minute Time held at maximum temperature	64.6 g sand 7.2 g synthetic natron 15.4 g $Cu_2CO_3(OH)_2$ 12.8 g $CaCO_3$	64.6 g silicic acid 7.2 g synthetic natron 15.4 g $Cu_2CO_3(OH)_2$ 12.8 g $CaCO_3$	60.6 g sand 9.2 g synthetic natron 18.0 g $Cu_2CO_3(OH)_2$ 12.2 g $CaCO_3$	60.6 g silicic acid 9.2 g synthetic natron 18.0 g $Cu_2CO_3(OH)_2$ 12.2 g $CaCO_3$	180 g silicic acid 400 g K_2CO_3 15 g KNO_3 16 g $CaCO_3$	180 g of glass mix α 20 g CuO
IA	830°C Δt 5.5°/min 45 min	Raw For. I Some particles of blue formed.	Raw For. II Grey.	Raw For. III Some particles of blue formed.	Raw For. IV Grey.		
II	850°C Δt 6.2°/min 6 hours	For. I, Fir. IA Black, green, and blue in clinker-like mass.	For. II, Fir. IA Egyptian blue-light blue.	For. III, Fir. IA Black, green, and blue in clinker-like mass.	For. IV, Fir. IA Egyptian blue; light-medium blue, a little darker than For. II.		
III	900°C Δt 4.6°/min 1 hour		Oxidizing For. II, Fir. IA, II; bluer and slightly more sintered but still powdery. ——— Reducing For. II, Fir. IA, II; dark reddish-brown, powdery.		Oxidizing For. IV, Fir. IA, II; very blue, powdery. ——— Reducing For. IV, Fir. IA, II; dark reddish-brown, powdery.		
IV	1000°C Δt 3.3°/min 70 min		Oxidizing For. II, Fir. IA, II; still bluer. ——— Reducing For. II, Fir. IA, II; greenish cake—possibly due to accidental fluxing.		Oxidizing For. IV, Fir. IA, II; bluer, powdery. ——— Reducing For. IV, Fir. IA, II; reddish and powdery.		
V	1100°C Δt 3.0°/min 1 hour		Oxidizing For. II, Fir. IA, II; some green glass, black, and dark blue. ——— Reducing For. II, Fir. IA, II; greenish-black with quartz and CuO(?).		Oxidizing For. IV, Fir. IA, II; greenish-black with traces of blue. ——— Reducing For. IV, Fir. IA, II; very glassy blackish with green tone.		
VI	1150°C Δt 2°/min 1 hour		Oxidizing For. II, Fir. IA, II; grey, powdery. ——— Reducing For. II, Fir. IA, II; black, partly sintered.		Oxidizing For. IV, Fir. IA, II; grey, powdery. ——— Reducing For. IV, Fir. IA, II; reddish-black, partly sintered.		
VII	850°C Δt 3°/min 24 hours	A number of samples were run including:	For. II, Fir. IA, II, III$_r$ For. II, Fir. IA, II, IV$_o$ For. II, Fir. IA, II, IV$_r$.		For. IV, Fir. IA, II, III$_r$ For. IV, Fir. IA, II, IV$_o$ For. IV, Fir. IA, II, IV$_r$.	Plus four samples from firing V; all turned blue.	

Table 5.2

Summary of Firing
Experiments on
Synthesis of
Egyptian Blue Objects
(Continued)

Firing	Firing Conditions	Formula I	Formula II	Formula III	Formula IV	Glass Mix α	Glass Mix β
VIII	850°C not observed 1 hour				For. IV, Fir. II, III, reoxidized to Egyptian blue.		
IX	850°C Δt 3°/min 6 hours	Batch Firing	225.3 g silicic acid 25.0 g synthetic natron 48.2 g Cu(CO₃)₂ 44.1 g CaCO₃		Gave nice, bright blue powder. This was ground for use in manufacturing experiments (Firing X).		
X	850°C Δt 2°/min 2 hours	Manufacturing Experiments	(1) 10 g Fir. IX 4 cc H₂O Product blue and friable but holds shape H = 2 (Moh's scale).	(2) 10 g Fir. IX 4 cc 5% gum arabic Product blue, less friable than 1 H = 3.	(3) 10 g Fir. X 4 cc of 1:30 gelatin solution Product blue, friable H = 2.	(4) 10 g Fir. X 5 g slaked lime Product bluish-grey, friable, soft H = 2.	(5) 10 g Fir. X 10 g plaster of Paris Product bluish-grey, but bluer than 4, very easily cut H = 2−	(6) 10 g Fir. X 10 g soda-lime glass 4 cc 3% gelatin Product greenish-blue, hard, vitreous H = 6.
XI	1000°C Δt 1°/min 1 hour					Raw Glass Mix α Hygroscopic light blue to white glass.	Raw Glass Mix β Hygroscopic dark blue to black glass.
XII	850°C Δt 5°/min 1 hour						Glass Mix β Fir. XI Some devitrification but no Egyptian blue formed.

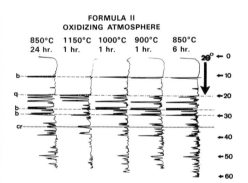

FORMULA II
OXIDIZING ATMOSPHERE

850°C 24 hr. 1150°C 1 hr. 1000°C 1 hr. 900°C 1 hr. 850°C 6 hr.

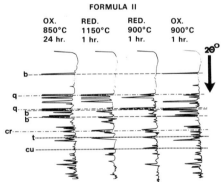

FORMULA II

OX. 850°C 24 hr. RED. 1150°C 1 hr. RED. 900°C 1 hr. OX. 900°C 1 hr.

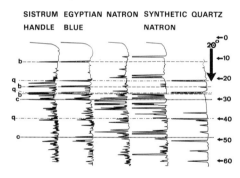

SISTRUM HANDLE EGYPTIAN BLUE NATRON SYNTHETIC NATRON QUARTZ

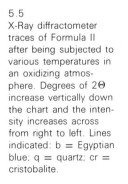

5.5
X-Ray diffractometer traces of Formula II after being subjected to various temperatures in an oxidizing atmosphere. Degrees of 2Θ increase vertically down the chart and the intensity increases across from right to left. Lines indicated: b = Egyptian blue; q = quartz; cr = cristobalite.

5.6
X-Ray diffractometer traces of Formula II after oxidation and reduction. Lines indicated: b = Egyptian blue; q = quartz; cr = cristobalite; cu = cuprite; t = tenorite.

5.7
X-Ray diffractometer traces of various materials. Lines indicated: b = Egyptian blue; q = quartz; c = calcite.

table top was rescued from a spot at Timna where the local peasants had been burning marble for lime. Lucas mentions the alteration of Egyptian blue to black (Reference 12), but in my experience, the black surfaces are usually soot.

Internal Evidence of Manufacturing Techniques

What can we infer about the manufacturing techniques from the objects themselves? The body of the goblet is mostly composed of a glassy substance, quartz, and air holes—a very porous body. This may be evidence for a high temperature in the fire when the burned building was destroyed. No Egyptian blue can be seen in this section, because it was all altered in the fire. Microscopic examination of a smear (that is, a powdered sample mounted in Canada balsam) taken from another portion of the goblet revealed a few particles of Egyptian blue, small and crystalline, apparently not ground-up particles. These facts and the blue color indicate that the goblet was originally made from Egyptian blue, and possibly made with an addition of glass. The body is still quite hard, and firing to 400°C removed the carbon on the surface, leaving a red and blue object. The central fragment at the rim of the goblet was given this treatment. Unfortunately, this object will not regain its blue color in prolonged firing to 850°C, as a test firing of a small fragment showed. The reason could be that the copper, being changed to cuprite, may have been leached out of the goblet, or the flux of sodium carbonate or potash may have been removed by the action of ground water, so that the transformation back to Egyptian blue could not take place. We could have attempted to add some flux or copper compound, but this would have changed the chemical composition of the object and refiring would have been very dangerous; so we decided to leave well enough alone.

This brings us back to the question of how these excavated objects were made. I experimented with six different techniques of manufacture using Egyptian blue with the composition of Formula II: (1) adding water; (2) adding gum arabic solution; (3) adding gelatin solution; (4) adding slaked lime; (5) adding plaster of Paris; (6) adding a modern soda-lime glass and gelatin. I fired all of these up to 850°C and held this temperature for one hour. The only composition that developed the hard, stonelike surface of the excavated objects was that with the glass admixture. This composition molded well, released from the mold well and gave after firing a hard (Moh's hardness = 6), elastic product that seemed superficially similar to the excavated objects. The large bubbles which occur in the excavated objects also are visible in the test pieces made from this composition although they also show up in the other test pieces. Our manufacturing technique with gum arabic has a microscopic appearance similar to those

of the excavated objects, while the manufacturing technique using glass has a fused, glassy appearance. (See Plate VII f.) I probably used way too much glass (ca. 50 percent) and a composition with 10–15 percent should work fine. All of the manufacturing techniques yielded a modelling material that was plastic enough in the wet state to roll beads from easily (Reference 2). The size of gelatin or gum arabic was necessary, however, when one desired to get a modelling material that would release from a mold. I removed the molds before firing in all cases.

Interestingly enough, this idea of a glass admixture finds a tenuous confirmation in the historical evidence brought to my attention by John D. Cooney of the Cleveland Museum of Art (private communication). He pointed out that seal cylinders and beads were made of Egyptian blue in Old Kingdom Egypt, but that the use of Egyptian blue for a wide variety of objects becomes frequent in Dynasty XVIII. Some of these pieces are inscribed for Amenhotep III. He notes that early examples of Egyptian blue

Other Evidence of Fabrication Techniques

are invariably a light, almost a French, blue the texture of which is almost always granular with an appearance of softness strongly resembling chalk. The surface is always matt. Sometime late in Dynasty XVIII or soon afterwards this material is largely, though not entirely, replaced by Egyptian blue with different characteristics. In this later material the color is darker, even a deep blue, the body has lost its granular appearance and structure and appears to be a solid uniform mass of very fine grain resembling stone, while the surface frequently has a low gloss.

This change coincides with the first great period of glassmaking in Egypt in Dynasty XVIII (Reference 5); it is not inconceivable that the burgeoning glass industry contributed the impetus to manufacturing Egyptian blue objects with a glass admixture, or, conversely, that experimentation with methods of making Egyptian blue might have led to the discovery of glass (see Reference 3). The difference between the microstructure of Egyptian blue made before and after this postulated change is shown in Plate VII. Plate VII a and b show thin sections through beads probably from Old Kingdom strata in the Lisht North Pyramid site. Plate VII c shows a section through an Egyptian blue macehead from Nuzi (Reference 19); these three were made before Dynasty XVIII. Plate VII d and e show the sistrum handle and table top at the same magnification as a and b. Plate VII f shows the thin section of manufacturing technique 6 (Table 5.2). The later pieces have a closer-grained and denser body with a little glass in the interstices.

The technique of adding glass to a body finds a parallel in the modern pottery of Iran, described by Wulff (Reference 22). He says that the stone paste potter makes his pottery from 70–80 percent quartz, 10–20 percent fine clay, and 10 percent frit. The frit is a kind of alkaline glass, compounded from flint, quartz, and potash. This body is plastic enough to be thrown on the wheel like clay. If this technique works with quartz, then it should work with Egyptian blue.

The fabrication of Egyptian blue also has affinities with those of faience and glassy faience; the raw materials are the same and the firing temperatures are similar (Reference 23). Wulff says that the glazing temperature of modern faience is near 1000°C, which is considerably higher than the formation temperature of Egyptian blue, 850°C. The techniques have so many similarities that parallel investigation of them along with that of glassy faience might lead to some interesting conclusions.

Egyptian blue as a ceramic, or fired composition material, has clear affinities with faience, glassy faience, and glass, and possibly with gem carving, yet its production remains a separate and little-explored chapter of the sumptuary arts of the Near East. Many questions still remain unanswered. We would like to have conducted more experiments in the manufacturing techniques to see if prolonged soaking at temperatures around 850°C or a little higher could bring about sintering of the individual grains of Egyptian blue and allow a body to be formed without the glass admixture. (Dr. Brill has informed me that he has been able to form hard, compact molded objects of Egyptian blue by extended heating. The material itself was prepared from a formula not very different from our Formula I.) More molding and firing should be done to find out the limitations of that technique. Chemical analysis of objects should be done for a number of reasons; it might confirm the glass admixture and could possibly distinguish provenance. Egyptian blue from Egypt should be low in potassium content because of the supposed employment of natron as the flux. If potash was used to manufacture Egyptian blue in other parts of the Near East, the potassium contents of these materials should be distinguishably higher. And a concerted search of museums and the literature for a broader statistical base of Egyptian blue objects from Egypt, Iran, Arabia, and other areas would be extremely helpful in defining the locations and dates of manufacturing centers of this material. These questions I must leave for future investigators.

Acknowledgments

The major portion of the work discussed here was performed under a Chester Dale Fellowship at the Metropolitan Museum of Art during February to August 1966, while the remainder of the work and preparation of the photographs and text was done at the Freer Gallery of Art in 1968 and 1969. I should like to thank Kate Lefferts of the Metropolitan Museum of Art for initiating these researches, and Seymour Lewin of New York University for enabling me to carry out the X-ray diffraction studies described here. I greatly appreciate the cooperation of the Department of Ancient Near Eastern Art and the Department of Egyptian Art of the Metropolitan Museum in allowing me to sample the objects under their care. R. J. Gettens, Robert Brill, Frederick Matson, John D. Cooney, and others gave me much help and encouragement. The Mineral Sciences Department of the Smithsonian Institution deserves many thanks for the generous help it has given the Freer. Five of the thin sections photographed here were prepared by Grover Moreland of this department; and John White, Edward Henderson, and William Melson also have been very helpful. William J. Young of the Museum of Fine Arts, Boston, kindly supplied X-ray diffraction data; and Gus Van Beek of the Department of Anthropology, Smithsonian Institution, brought to my attention a unique piece of Egyptian blue found in South Arabia, a piece which he consented to let me study in detail. To these and all of the other researchers whose work has contributed to this paper, I give many thanks.

References

1.
Augusti, Selim

I Colori Pompeiani; Studi e Documentazioni I, Ministero della Pubblica Istruzione, Direzione Generale delle Antichità e Belle Arti, Rome, 1967.

2.
Beck, H. C.

"Glass before 1500 B.C.," *Ancient Egypt,* 1934, p. 3. (See also, L. Hodgson in *Papers of the Society of Mural Decorators and Painters in Tempera,* **3,** 1925–1935, p. 36.)

3.
Brill, Robert H.

"Ancient Glass," *Scientific American,* **209,** 1963, p. 123, 126, passim.

4.
Caley, Earle R., and Richards, John F. C.

Theophrastus on Stones, Columbus, Ohio, 1956, paragraph 55 and pp. 183–187.

5.
Cooney, John D.

"Glass sculpture in Ancient Egypt," *J. Glass Studies,* **2,** 1960, p. 12.

6.
Eibner, Alexander

Entwicklung und Werkstoffe der Wandmalerei vom Altertum bis zur Neuzeit, Munich, 1926, p. 203.

7.
Gettens, Rutherford J., and Stout, George

Painting Materials: A Short Encyclopaedia, New York, 1966, p. 148b.

8.
Harris, J. R.

Lexicographical Studies in Ancient Egyptian Minerals, Deutsche Akademie der Wissenschaften zu Berlin Institut für Orientforschung Veröffentlichung Nr. 54, Berlin, 1961, pp. 124ff and 148f, and 13.

9.
Hayes, William C.

The Scepter of Ancient Egypt, New York, 1960, p. 395; *Bulletin of the Metropolitan Museum of Art,* **9,** No. 10, October, 1914, p. 207 and **3,** October, 1908, pp. 184–188.

10.
Kiefer, Charles, and Allibert, A.

"Les céramiques bleues pharaoniques et leur procédé revolutionnaire 'd'émaillage'," *Industrie Céramique,* No. 607, May, 1968, pp. 395–402.

11.
Laurie, A. P., McClintock, W. F. P., and Miles, F. D.

"Egyptian Blue," *Proceedings of the Royal Academy,* **89,** 1914, p. 419.

12.
Lucas, A., and Harris, J. R.

Ancient Egyptian Materials and Industries, London, 1962, p. 341.

13.
Mazzi, Fiorenzo, and Pabst, A.

"Reexamination of cuprorivaite," *The American Mineralogist,* **47,** March–April, 1962, pp. 409–411.

14.
Minguzzi, Carlo

"Cuprorivaite: un nuovo minerale," *Period. Mineral,* **8,** pp. 333–345.

15.
Muscarella, Oscar White

"Hasanlu 1964," *The Metropolitan Museum of Art Bulletin,* **25,** 3, November, 1966, pp. 132–133.

16.
Pabst, A.

"Structures of some tetragonal sheet silicates," *Acta Crystallographica,* **12,** 1959, pp. 733–739.

"Analyser an skerd og skjold fra Bø-funnet," *Viking,* 1959, pp. 33–34.

17.
Rosenquist, A. M.

"Contributo alla conoscenza del 'bleu egiziano'," *Bollettino dell'Istituto Centrale del Restauro,* **31–32,** 1957, p. 105.

18.
Schippa, Giovanni, and Torraca, Giorgio

Nuzi, Cambridge, Mass., 1939; description of this bead by R. J. Gettens, Vol. 1, p. 460.

19.
Starr, Richard F. S.

This object will be published in detail in *Timna Temple.*

20.
Van Beek, G. W., and Van Beek, A. G.

The Ten Books on Architecture, Tr. Morgan, Cambridge, Mass., 1926, 7, 11, 1, p. 218.

21.
Vitruvius

The Traditional Crafts of Persia, Cambridge, Mass., 1966, p. 165ff.

22.
Wulff, Hans E.

"Egyptian Faience—A possible survival in Iran," *Archaeology,* **21,** 2, April, 1968, pp. 98–107.

23.
Wulff, Hans E., Wulff, Hildegard S., and Koch, Leo

Chapter 6

Calclacite and Other Efflorescent Salts on Objects Stored in Wooden Museum Cases

**Elisabeth West FitzHugh
and Rutherford J. Gettens**
Freer Gallery of Art

The titles of most of the papers presented in this symposium volume clearly indicate that archaeological chemistry is mainly concerned with the materials and the making of ancient objects. We think, however, it should also concern itself with the conservation of objects recovered from the ground, the sea, or other environments, which are now housed in museums or private collections. It has long been observed that a few ancient objects of stone, brick, and plaster, especially those brought from dry countries to the more humid temperate zones, eventually become more or less covered with white crystalline deposits called efflorescent salts. As the dictionary defines it, to effloresce is "to burst forth . . . , as if flowering," and "to form or become covered with powdery crust." Most efflorescences that we see are on porous materials which absorb moisture or deliquesce at times of high humidity, and soluble salts are then drawn in liquid form to the surface by capillary forces. In dry weather the water evaporates and the salts are left behind in clusters or tufts of white needlelike crystals or whiskers. Usually, as previously indicated, the salts are inherent in the material of the objects. They are mainly chlorides, nitrates, sulfates, and carbonates of the alkali and alkaline earth metals, and their movement is entirely caused by fluctuations of temperature and humidity at the surface of the object. There is an extensive literature on efflorescence phenomena, because it is of importance to the building and ceramic trades. However, we do not plan to deal here with the general problem of efflorescence on walls and masonry. We wish to draw attention to a special type of efflorescence stimulated more by outside factors than internal ones and observed almost exclusively in museums. This type of efflorescence includes salts formed by reaction of the material of the object, or impurities within it, with corrosive acidic vapors given off by wood, or other materials of the exhibition cases that house the objects. These formations can cause quite mysterious behavior of objects and can harm them seriously.

In 1899, in the *Journal of Conchology*, Mr. Loftus St. George Byne (Reference 3) reported the formation of white crystals on shells in the National Collection in South Kensington, London. At the time they were identified as a mixture of calcium butyrate and calcium acetate; traces of organic matter in the shells were suggested as the source of butyric acid. The acetic acid was thought to have originated in the gum adhesive used to attach the shells, because at that time acetic acid was used as a preservative for gum. A little earlier the effect of sea atmosphere was blamed

for the deterioration of shells in a collection in Tasmania (Reference 7). Dr. Alexander Scott, founder of the British Museum Laboratory, some years later, in 1923 and 1926, described and gave analyses of various salts which were found as efflorescences on stone specimens from all over the world. He found that sodium chloride was the most common salt. He further illustrated an ancient carved limestone foot with such a growth of long filamentous crystals that, "until these were removed it was impossible to tell whether it was a right or left foot." (Reference 15). M. F. Taboury in 1931 described a calcium acetate efflorescence occurring on minerals in museums in the form of fine needles or snowy flakes and suggested that their formation was caused by the presence of acetic acid vapor from the oak wood cases in which the minerals were stored (Reference 16). Oak is again mentioned by Nicholls in 1934 as a source of acetic acid, even when the wood is thoroughly seasoned (Reference 11). He suggested that traces of sea water in the shells previously described by Byne were a source of hygroscopic salts which absorbed the acetic acid vapors and then reacted with the clacium carbonate to form calcium acetate.

In 1945 René Van Tassel (Reference 17) called attention to a white silky acicular efflorescence forming on calcareous rock specimens stored in oak cases in the Musée royal d'Histoire naturelle de Belgique in Brussels. He identified (Reference 13) this salt as calcium acetate chloride pentahydrate ($Ca(CH_3COO)Cl \cdot 5H_2O$) and gave it a mineral name, *calclacite*. The material had formed on a specimen of Carboniferous Age limestone from Yvoir, Belgium (Figure 6.1). The stone specimen was collected in 1930 and was placed untreated in a practically hermetically sealed oak wood box. In 1958, he published (Reference 18) crystallographic data, including *d* spacings of the X-ray powder patterns, on a sample of synthetic calclacite prepared in the Freer Gallery Laboratory (Table 6.1). This same salt was also observed by Van Tassel (Reference 19) on another Carboniferous Age limestone fossil from Soignies, Belgium which had been collected in 1943; the specimen was washed with dilute hydrochloric acid and afterward kept in a closed wood museum case.

Calclacite also occurs on man-made objects in museums. Possibly the most spectacular occurrence was on a Babylonian baked clay truncated cone bearing a cuneiform inscription of Nebuchadnezzar (605–561 B.C.) which was acquired by the Semitic Museum of Harvard University in 1913 and sometime later placed in a

Calclacite

fairly confined space in a flat glass-topped cherry wood exhibition case. Fibrous crystal growth on the surface was observed several years before the cone was removed from the case in 1947 (Figure 6.2). The whiskery crystals growing from the surface, some reaching a length of 15–20 mm, were concentrated on one side of the object giving it the appearance of being covered with white fur. Microscopically the fibers varied greatly in width and were striated lengthwise as though extruded from tiny holes in the surface of the baked clay. Microchemical tests showed that Ca^{++}, Na^+, Cl^- and CH_3COO^-

ions were present. The bulk of the crystal mass was removed mechanically, yielding about 0.2 g, and after careful sorting was wet-analyzed by a commercial analyst (Table 6.2). The principal constituents are approximately in equivalent ratio suggesting that the formula of the salt is $CaClAc \cdot 3H_2O$. This corresponds to somewhat less water than the 5 molecules of water found by Van Tassel. The X-ray diffraction pattern of the clay cone efflorescence, however, is that of calclacite. After sampling, the salt efflorescence was completely washed away by repeated immersion of the object in distilled water (Figure 6.3).

Calclacite was also found in two Greek terra cotta vases (Figure 6.4) in the G. H. Chase Collection in the Fogg Museum in 1950; these crystals had the familiar extruded appearance, tested positive for Ca^{++}, Cl^-, and CH_3COO^- ions microchemically, and had a refractive index of about 1.50. The vases had been stored in wooden cabinets. Both efflorescences were confirmed by X-ray diffraction as calclacite. Four potsherds from Ur in the British Museum, sampled in 1960, which also had been stored in wooden cases, showed calclacite efflorescence. The powder patterns made by the authors, however, contain more lines than were reported by Van Tassel because they were taken on a 11.46 cm camera (Table 6.1).

At the time that the calclacite efflorescence on the Babylonian clay cone was noticed, a similar-appearing efflorescence was seen on inscribed and decorated South Arabian limestone fragments in the same gallery in the Semitic Museum at Harvard. They had been placed in glass and cherry wood wall cases in 1936, and the efflorescence was sampled in 1950. The fibrous crystals proved to be weakly birefracting, with n slightly above 1.50, and to contain Ca^{++}, Cl^-, CH_3COO^-, and some $SO_4^=$ ions.

Efflorescence Similar to Calclacite

Table 6.1
X-Ray Diffraction Data on Calclacite

Synthetic Calclacite Van Tassel, 1958*			Calclacite Efflorescence on Potsherd from Ur†	
d(Å)	I	hkl	d(Å)	I
			11.763	10
8.27	s	110	8.264	100
			7.017	50
6.87	m	020	6.86	50
6.15	w	001,111		
			6.077	10
			5.187	5
4.86	vw	210,121	4.818	20
			4.537	1
			4.217	20
4.16	m	221,220	4.166	30
3.67	w	031	3.647	2
			3.421	2
			3.336	5
			3.268	5
3.24	s	112,212	3.247	40
			3.173	5
3.06	w	002	3.065	15
3.00	w	222	3.009	15
2.94	vw	012,22$\bar{1}$	2.936	10
			2.878	10
			2.824	20
2.65	w	23$\bar{1}$	2.651	20
			2.571	2
			2.503	2
			2.441	20
2.43	s	340	2.431	30
			2.404	10
2.30	m	060	2.302	15
			2.252	10
2.22	w	33$\bar{1}$		
2.14	w	113	2.153	1
			2.122	1
2.04	m	510,003,052,41$\bar{1}$	2.04	30
			1.995	10
			1.968	1
			1.946	1
1.907	vw	360,15$\bar{2}$	1.909	1
1.876	vw	450,530,171,601	1.873	5
1.842	w	270,10$\bar{3}$	1.84	5
			1.73	1
1.704	w	460,600	1.705	3
1.560	vw	470,35$\bar{2}$		
1.486	w	024	1.488	1

* René Van Tassel, "On the crystallography of calclacite," *Acta Crystallographica*, 11, Part 10, Oct. 1968, pp. 745–746. 5.73 cm diam. camera; visually estimated intensities: s-strong; m-medium; w-weak; vw-very weak.
† Sampled at British Museum 1960. Freer film F995. Measured by W. T. Chase.

Table 6.2
Analysis of Calclacite*

	Percent	Percent at. wt.	Molecular Ratio
H_2O	24.66	1.37	ca. 3
Cl	17.25	0.483	1
CaO	27.12	0.483 (for Ca)	1
Na_2O (alkalies as)	3.79	—	—
SO_3	1.20	—	—
NH_3 (by distillation)	3.66	—	—
$HC_2H_3O_2$ (as volatile acids)	26.18	0.436	1
Total	103.86		
Less equivalent O for 17.25 g Cl	3.89		
Corrected total	99.97		
Loss on ignition	52.05		

* In 1948, by H. J. Hallowell of Danbury, Connecticut.

Table 6.3
X-Ray Diffraction Data on Efflorescence X

British Museum Potsherd (B.M.842.44232; Freer film F326)		Roman Pottery Lamp (U.S.N.M. 305.934; Freer film F691)	
d(Å)	I	d(Å)	I
11.95	8	11.95	8
6.92	10	6.96	10
6.19	3	6.11	6
5.44	3	5.44	2
5.22	3	5.22	4
4.55	2	4.55	1
4.27	1	4.27	2
		3.97	4
3.99	5	3.88	1
3.74	3		
3.48	1	3.47	1
3.40	5	3.39	6
3.30—		3.29—	
3.27*	4	3.26	5
3.16	5	3.15	6
3.07	1	3.05	1
2.84	4	2.79	1
2.61	4	2.61	4
		2.56	<1
2.52	1	2.49	1
		2.45	<1
2.41†	4	2.40	4
2.36	1	2.35	1
2.32	1	2.31	1
2.26	1	2.26	1
2.24—		2.22—	
2.22*	3	2.20*	2
2.11	1		
2.05	1	2.04	1
2.00	3	1.98	1
1.97	1	1.95	1
1.91	1	1.91	1
1.87	1	1.87	1
		1.69	<1
1.63†	1	1.66	1

* Wide line.
† Indistinct line.

Later observations showed that this salt occurs as widely as calclacite and is similar to it in that it contains the same three ions and often occurs in the same needlelike form. It is different crystallographically, however. The X-ray diffraction powder pattern is not the same (Table 6.3). Twelve potsherds now in the British Museum from various sources, some Near Eastern, had formations of this salt. One of these efflorescences (from B. M. 1907, 1–12, 842.44232) was examined optically by Dr. Van Tassel who provided the following data: "Fibrous crystals showing polysynthetic twinning, negative elongation, monoclinic or triclinic symmetry, oblique extinction about 20°, refractive indices $\delta = 1.504$ and $\alpha = 1.492$" (Reference 19). The same salt was later found on a number of other pieces, all well scattered: on two classical pottery objects in the U.S. National Museum, Smithsonian Institution, Washington, one a Roman terra cotta lamp (U.S.N.M. 305.934) which was stored in a pine drawer in a mahogany and walnut case for some years until the efflorescence was noted in 1958, the other a Greek miniature lecythos (U.S.N.M. 391.050) given to the museum in 1947 but not examined until 1960 (Figures 6.5 and 6.6); on a fragment of a clay mold for casting Chinese bronzes in the Royal Ontario Museum, Toronto, examined at Toronto in 1955; on three potsherds from Nubia seen at the University Museum, Philadelphia in 1962; and finally on two geological samples noted by Van Tassel (Reference 19), one on a carbonate rock from Orleansville, Algeria, and the other a calcareous sandstone from Belgium, both samples having been stored in wooden museum cases in the Musée royale d'Histoire naturelle de Belgique.

For convenience we are calling this unknown salt "efflorescence X." We have tried to identify it precisely but so far without success because of insufficient samples. The X-ray powder patterns of all samples of this type of efflorescence compare well visually. When a fairly pure specimen of the unknown can be collected in sufficient quantity for analysis, so that we can determine its chemical formula, we hope to name it. It may be a different hydrate or it is remotely possible that it is dimorphous with calclacite.

Lead Formate

We shall now describe a quite different type of efflorescence which, however, appears to have a similar cause. In August 1956, a white snowflakelike growth was noted on three sixteenth century Renaissance lead medals in the National Gallery of Art, Washington, D.C. One of those is shown in Figures 6.7 and 6.8. The X-ray diffraction powder pattern (Table 6.4) was identified as that of lead formate. (Control samples of known lead formate were obtained from two chemical companies, and lead formate was also prepared in the Freer Gallery Laboratory in two ways: by exposing lead to formic acid vapor in a closed space for 48 hours, and by reaction of formic acid with lead carbonate.) The medals had been put on exhibition in April 1956 after being cleaned with a combination of organic solvents; no protective coating was applied. They were displayed in flat cabinet cases where they could be viewed from above and were lighted with fluorescent tubes which were partly concealed by baffles inside the case. The cases were made of birch wood, the cloth lining was cellulosic in origin, the lacquer sealer had a nitrocellulose base, the assembly glue was hide glue, and the laminating glue was a urea-formaldehyde resin. The temperature inside one case ranged from 86°F at the bottom to 103°F

6.1
Needles of calclacite growing on the surface of a rock specimen from Yvoir, Belgium. (2.5X) (Courtesy Musée royal d'Histoire naturelle de Belgique, Brussels)

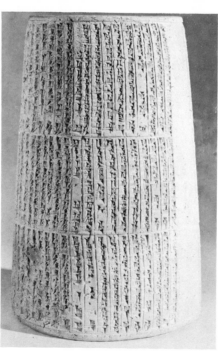

6.2
Whiskers of calclacite growing from the surface of a cuneiform inscribed Babylonian clay cone of the time of Nebuchadnezzar (605–561B.C.). The characters are partially hidden under the salt efflorescence.

6.3
The Babylonian clay cone after the calclacite crystals were washed away with water. (About 1/3 natural size) (Photographs Fogg Art Museum, Harvard University)

6.4
Crystals of calclacite
growing from the sur-
face of a small Greek
vase in the Fogg Art
Museum (1939.250).
(5X) (Photograph: Fogg
Art Museum, Harvard
University)

6.6
In the detail (12X) of
the efflorescent salt on
the miniature Greek
vase (Figure 6.5); the
needlelike crystals have
a silky appearance.
(Photograph: Freer Gal-
lery of Art)

6.5
Crystals of an efflores-
cent salt similar to calclacite ("efflorescence X")
growing from the sur-
face of a miniature
Greek vase in the U.S.
National Museum, Smith-
sonian Institution
(U.S.N.M. 391.050).
(Photograph: Freer Gal-
lery of Art)

6.7
A lead medal of Caspar Winntzrer by Friedrich Hagenauer (dated 1526) in the National Gallery of Art, Washington, D.C. (A1450.710A) became partially covered with a crystal growth of lead formate. (Courtesy National Gallery of Art)

6.8
In this magnified detail (5X) the snowflake appearance of the crystals on the lead medal (Figure 6.7) are plainly visible. (Courtesy National Gallery of Art)

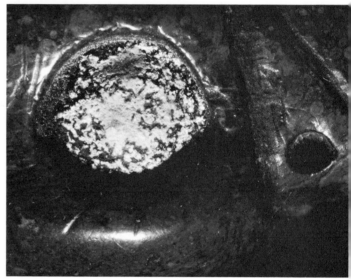

6.9
The inlaid lead eye of an American Indian serpentine pipe in the Brooklyn Museum also became encrusted with crystals of lead formate. (Photograph: Freer Gallery of Art)

6.10
A magnified detail (7.5X) of one of the lead eyes of the stone pipe (Figure 6.9). (Photograph: Freer Gallery of Art)

Table 6.4
X-Ray Diffraction Data on Lead Formate

Lead Formate*		Lead Formate Efflorescence on Lead Medal†	
d(Å)	I	d(Å)	I
5.7	80	5.72	7
5.2	100	5.22	10
4.37	40	4.42	6
		4.27	6
		3.87	6
3.71	40		
3.26	60	3.27	10
		3.12	1
3.03	80	3.04	9
2.83	20	2.85	6
2.72	40	2.72	10
2.60	20	2.60	4
		2.47	4
2.45	20	2.46	4
2.36	20	2.37	3
2.22	10	2.24	4
2.18	10	2.18	5
		2.14	3
2.07	10	2.09	3
		2.04	6
2.02	40	2.00	5
		1.98	2
		1.95	2
		1.92	1
1.87	30	1.89	5
1.80	10		
1.74	20	1.75	3
1.71	20	1.73	3
1.63	20	1.64	3
		1.61	3
1.59	30	1.60	3
1.54	20	1.52	3
		1.50	2
		1.47	1
		1.43	3

* J. D. Hanawalt, H. W. Rinn, and L. K. Frevel, "Chemical Analysis by X-Ray Diffraction," *Ind. Eng. Chem., Anal. Ed.* **10,** 1938, pp. 437–512.

† Lead medal, National Gallery of Art, Washington, D.C. (U.S. Nat. Gall. A1409.669A; Freer Film F254). Further X-ray diffraction data on lead formate are given in "Standard X-Ray Diffraction Powder Patterns," NBS Circular 539, Vol. 8, Issued April 1, 1959, p. 30.

had been first noticed in 1957, but the owner (the object was on loan to the museum) says that it was not always present. No information was available about the material of the exhibition case. The eyes were cleaned mechanically and washed with water but after eight months storage at the Freer Gallery Laboratory under well-ventilated conditions the efflorescence reappeared. This would indicate that the cause of its formation is somehow inherent in the object itself. Possibly it might be related to some modern adhesive used in resetting the eyes.

Other Formate and Acetate Efflorescences

In 1960 a white efflorescence of sodium formate was observed on many areas of an early sixteenth-century Limoges enamel triptych in the Walters Art Gallery (W.A.G. 44.159) in Baltimore. The enamel was flaking away in spots and short fibers and cauliflowerlike clusters of white material showed under low magnification. It is recalled that a calcium formate efflorescence was reported by Komarek on $CaCO_3$-containing fossils in Prague (Reference 10). However, this may have been caused by the treatment of the fossil shells with formaline to remove living organisms from the dirt remaining in the shells.

Other acetate efflorescences besides calclacite and its related compound have been noted. Calcium acetate was found by Van Tassel (Reference 19) on shells and bird's eggs, and the efflorescence sometimes resulted in the complete destruction of the object. He also found sodium acetate on tertiary mollusks from Reims, France, but he does not know if these mollusk shells were subject to chemical treatment.

Wood, Coatings and Adhesives as Sources of Corrosive Acidic Vapors

On stone and pottery objects, it is easy to understand where the inorganic ions of soluble efflorescent salts come from, but it is not so easy to explain the organic ions like acetate and formate.

at the top under the fluorescent tube. The manufacturer's chemist reporting on the material used in the construction of the cases said, "It is possible that formaldehyde was absorbed by the wood fiber and that over a period of time [was] released in minute quantities to the atmosphere within the case." There is another occurrence of lead formate. In 1961 a white efflorescence was noticed on the inlaid lead eye of an American Indian bird-shaped serpentine pipe (Figures 6.9 and 6.10) in the Brooklyn Museum (Brooklyn Museum L49, 3-1). The white material was identified by X-ray diffraction as lead formate. It

It has of course long been known that acetyl groups, which take part in the metabolic cycle of wood hemicellulose formation, can easily hydrolyze to free acetic acid. In fact, acetic acid was at one time produced commercially by the destructive distillation (or pyrolysis) of hardwoods and perhaps still is. When these studies on efflorescence were first begun over twenty years ago there was little published information on acidic vapors given off by wood, but fortunately in recent years much has been written, mostly in England. Research has been stimulated by corrosion problems in the packaging industry. Sawdust of most woods when moistened with distilled water gives glass electrode pH values lying between 4.0 and 6.0 (Reference 12). Experiments by Clarke and Longhurst (Reference 4) show that acetic acid in air can promote corrosion of metals in concentrations as low as 0.5 ppm or less. As in other atmospheric corrosion phenomena, a certain relative humidity must be exceeded to start the attack. This appears to be in the region of 70 percent RH for most metals, but for some, including copper, the critical RH is about 85 percent. These authors also conclude that the kiln-dried wood evolves more corrosive acidic vapors than air-dried wood. M. K. Budd (Reference 2) is authority for the statement that at the elevated temperature of 48°C (118.4°F) as much as 7 percent of the original weight of oak wood can be released as acetic acid vapor over a period of two years.

Perhaps the most important paper yet published on purely technical aspects of the problem is that of Arni and coworkers (Reference 1) on work done at the Arthur D. Little Research Institute in Scotland. By gas chromatography and spectrophotometry they have analyzed the vapors emitted by certain freshly felled hardwoods and softwoods and they found that sawdust samples of various woods incubated at 48°C and 100 percent RH for six months evolve several volatile fatty organic acids. For instance in the case of oak heartwood, the amount of formic acid is 137 ppm (based on the weight of wood as dried), acetic acid 1094, propionic acid 1.7, and isobutyric acid 1.7 ppm. The acid substances evolved from nonincubated oak heartwood at 48°C for 48 hours is much less, namely: formic acid 5.2, acetic acid 36.5, and isobutyric acid 1.7 ppm. Sweet chestnut heartwood gives still higher figures; some of the other woods measure lower. The authors suggest that formic acid may come from formate ester groups in the wood, but it is also possible that it is produced from the splitting of pyruvic acid during the metabolic processes of wood formation. The demonstrated presence of formic acid in these volatiles testifies to the improved analytical methods made available in recent years.

There are other possible sources of organic vapors: These are paint, varnishes, glues in plywood and joins, plastic fittings, and fabric linings. Urea-formaldehyde glues have been suspect but not proven as the cause of lead formate efflorescences on the lead medals in the National Gallery. Donovan and Moynehan in a recent article in *Corrosion Science* (Reference 5) report their studies on the behavior of zinc sheet specimens exposed over a variety of paints and coatings. Results showed that all drying-oil-based paints tested induced a high level of corrosion. Analysis of the corrosion products resulting from attack by vapors from drying-oil-based paints have invariably shown the presence of formate, together with varying proportions of acetate, propionate, and/or butyrate groups. The corrosion product from acrylic and nitrocellulose coatings showed acetate but no formate. These authors present interesting graphs that show the rate of evolution of formic

acid from air-drying paints. The overall results of their tests demonstrate that even under conditions of low humidity drying oil paints continue to evolve volatile degradation products, which constitute a corrosion hazard for a very long time after paint application. Donovan and Moynehan say that the level of formic acid release, even after extended periods of air drying, is of the order of 0.0025 percent of the weight of the paint film per day.

Rance and Cole (Reference 14) made a survey of specific instances of attack on metals by organic vapors from wood, paints, and insulating materials, and adhesives and have suggested ways of minimizing it. They report briefly on further laboratory work being conducted by the Corrosion and Electrodeposition Committee of the (British) Inter-Service Metallurgical Research Council.

As mentioned earlier, all efflorescences on limestone or pottery objects long stored in wood museum cases are not necessarily induced by acidic vapors from wood or other enclosure materials. Whiskers may form from salts already present which are extruded from pores in the material. A common one is sodium nitrate. It has been noted on objects from a wide variety of locations: a clay mold fragment for an early Chinese bronze in the Royal Ontario Museum, Toronto; on three objects in the U.S. National Museum, Smithsonian Institution; an American Indian pot (probably prehistoric Hopi, fourteenth to fifteenth century) collected near Winslow, Arizona, in 1896 (U.S.N.M. 292.714); a fragment of worked stone from Abiquiu, New Mexico (U.S.N.M. 314.194); and a Han pottery sculpture of a headless figurine (Figures 6.11 and 6.12) from a cave tomb, Kiating, Szechuan Province, China (U.S.N.M. 341.398). Sodium nitrate has also been reported on a Buddhist carved stone figure in situ in a cave at the Oya-ji Temple in Japan (Reference 6).

Komarek observed a calcium nitrate efflorescence on tertiary limestone containing fossil shells in the National Museum, Prague (Reference 8). He notes that this is the same efflorescence that occurs on farm stable walls.

Common salt, sodium chloride, can occur as an efflorescence. Four American Indian pots in the U.S. National Museum (two bowls, U.S.N.M. 157.208 and 157.380, a jar, U.S.N.M. 157.302, and a cup, U.S.N.M. 157.303) had been exhibited for over 30 years in a glass and wood case at the time that an efflorescence was noted in 1958. The whiskers on one bowl (208) are sodium chloride, and those on the other three pots are a mixture of sodium chloride and sodium nitrate.

A curious mixed efflorescence is reported also by Komarek (Reference 9) who de-

**Other Efflorescences
not Dependent on
the Presence of
Organic Acid Vapors**

6.11
Whiskery crystals of sodium nitrate on the surface of a Chinese pottery figurine of the Han dynasty in the U.S. National Museum (U.S.N.M. 341.398).

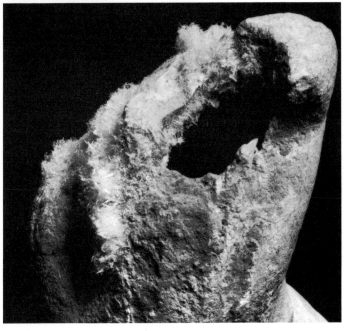

6.12
The needlelike crystals on the Han figurine shown here in 1.8X detail grow as if extruded from pores in the pottery surface.

99

6.13
X-Ray powder patterns
of calclacite, ''efflores-
cence X'' and lead for-
mate.
Calclacite
F373
Synthetic calclacite
E. W. Fitzhugh

F421
Calclacite Corinthian
vase
Fogg Museum of Art

''Efflorescence X''
F655
Efflorescence Potsherd
British Museum 435991

F691
Efflorescence Roman
pottery lamp
U.S.N.M. 305934

Lead Formate
F290
Lead formate Commer-
cial

F254
Efflorescence on lead
medal
U.S. National Gallery
A1409.669A

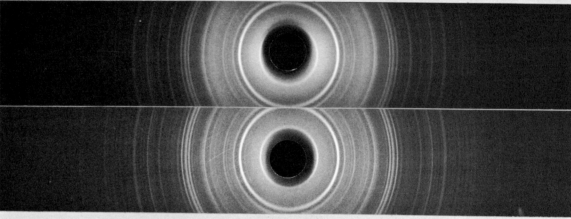
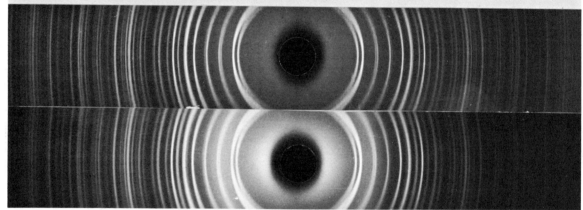

Calclacite and Other
Efflorescent Salts on
Objects Stored in
Wooden Museum Cases
100

scribes a mixture of sodium bicarbonate and calcium chloride which had deeply corroded the surface of a calciferous fossil. He suggests that sodium chloride already in the limestone reacted with the calcium carbonate to produce these two salts. The hygroscopic calcium chloride attracts moisture from the air to supply the water necessary for the progress of the reaction.

Conclusion

It has long been known that common glass and wood exhibition cases within museums do not always provide an ideal environment for objects. Too much light gets through from the outside and often illuminants within a case can be injurious. Silver tarnishes from sulfur gases that diffuse through imperfect joins; bronze and iron corrode from moisture that enters the same way. The studies of this chapter point to another danger less commonly recognized. The only answer is continuous vigilance on the part of the curator. Control of temperature and humidity by modern air conditioning equipment has improved the environment of galleries but still has not provided adequate protection from pollutants in modern urban atmosphere. Because of increased interest in urban air pollution, sensitive instruments have been developed to identify and measure the noxious gases of urban atmosphere. It is time to think of adapting those improved methods of analysis to the study of air in museum galleries and even to the microclimate of exhibition cases.

Acknowledgments

The authors are grateful for generous assistance: first, to Professor Clifford Frondel of the Department of Mineralogy and Petrography, Harvard University, who helped initiate this study; to Dr. René Van Tassel of Brussels, who has supplied information and specimens; to Professor Mojmir Frinta of the State University of New York at Albany, who translated articles in Czechoslovakian journals; and to Miss Mavis Bimson of the British Museum, who gave specimens of efflorescent salts. Several friends have given wise counsel.

References

1.
Arni, P. C., Cochrane, G. C. and Gray, J. D.
The emission of corrosive vapours by wood. I. Survey of the acid-release properties of certain freshly felled hardwoods and softwoods. II. The analysis of the vapours emitted by certain freshly felled hardwoods and softwoods by gas chromatography and spectrophotometry. *J. Applied Chemistry* (London), **15** (1965), pp. 305–13, 463–468.

2.
Budd, M. K.
Corrosion of metals in association with wood. *Appl. Mater. Res.* (Eng.), **4** (2), 124–125 (1965).

3.
Byne, Loftus St. George
The corrosion of shells in cabinets. *Journal of Conchology*, **9** (1899), pp. 172–178, 253–254.

4.
Clark, S. G., and Longhurst, E. E.
The corrosion of metals by acid vapors from wood. *J. Applied Chemistry*, **11** (Nov. 1961), pp. 435–443.

5.
Donovan, P. D., and Moynehan, T. M.
The corrosion of metals by vapours from air-drying paints. *Corrosion Science*, **5** (12) (1965), pp. 803–814.

6.
Emoto, Y.
On "Iwashio" in an acidic tuff at the Oya-ji Temple. *Science for Conservation* (Tokyo), No. 2 (1966), pp. 39–43. In Japanese.

7.
Kenyon, Agnes
Notes on the effects of the atmosphere on the shells of mullusca. *Papers and Proceedings of the Royal Society of Tasmania for 1896*, (July 1897), p. 88.

8.
Komarek, Karel
Chemical problems in museology. *Casopis Narodniho Musea* (Bulletin of the National Museum, Prague), **122** (1953), pp. 140–151.

9.
Komarek, Karel
Chemistry and museum material. *Casopis Narodniho Musea* (Bulletin of the National Museum, Prague), **123** 1954), pp. 32–38.

10.
Komarek, Karel
Chemical research on deterioration of minerals in museums. *Chemie* (Prague), **9** (1957), pp. 917–924.

11.
Nicholls, John Ralph
Deterioration of shells when stored in oak cabinets. *Chemistry and Industry*, **53** (1934), pp. 1077–1078.

12.
Packman, D. F.
The acidity of wood. *Holzforschung*, **14,** No. 6 (Dec. 1960), pp. 178–183.

13.
Palache, Charles Berman, Harry and Frondel, Clifford
Dana's system of mineralogy. New York, John Wiley, 7th ed., Vol. II (1951), p. 1107.

14.
Rance, Vera E., and Cole, H. G.
The corrosion of metals by vapours from organic materials. London, H. M. Stationery Office, 1958, p. 22.

15.
Scott, Alexander
Third Report upon investigations conducted at the British Museum. The cleaning and restoration of museum exhibits. London, H. M. Stationery Office, 1926.

16.
Taboury, M. F.
Des modifications chimiques de certaines substances calcaires conservées dans des meubles en bois. *Bulletin de la Societé Chimique de France,* **49** (1931), pp. 1289–1293.

17.
Van Tassel, René
Une efflorescence d'acétatochlorure de calcium sur des roches calcaires dans des collections. *Bulletin du Musée royal d'Histoire naturelle de Belgique*, **21,** No. 26 (Dec. 1945), Bruxelles, 11 pp.

18.
Van Tassel, René
On the crystallography of calclacite, $Ca(CH_3COO)Cl \cdot 5H_2O$). *Acta Crystallographica,* **11,** Part 10 (Oct. 1958), pp. 745–746.

19.
Van Tassel, René
Private communication.

Chapter 7

Analyses of Some Metal Artifacts from Ancient Afghanistan

Earle R. Caley
Ohio State University

Although Afghanistan is unusually rich in ancient remains, specimens of ancient materials from that country, especially those obtained by systematic excavation, have rarely been available for analysis. The specimens for the present investigation were kindly supplied by Dr. Louis Dupree of the Pennsylvania State University. At various times since 1950, Dr. Dupree has been exploring and excavating caves and other sites in Afghanistan that were occupied in ancient times by successive groups of people. The chemical analyses here reported are probably representative of the composition of the metals and alloys in use at these sites. Most of the artifacts that were analyzed were found at Snake Cave, which was occupied from very early times. Most of the others were found at Shamshir Ghar, another cave site, which was occupied only after the beginning of the Christian Era. The remainder came from various nearby sites. The sites, located on the accompanying map (Figure 7.1), have been described in detail in the archaeological literature (Reference 2.)

The analytical methods that were used have been described in detail elsewhere (Reference 1). Most of the analyses were made by the author and the others by former students working in his laboratory. Three of the artifacts from Shamshir Ghar were analyzed by the late Dr. Wallace H. Deebel, and all the analyses of Chinese objects, used for comparison, were made by Mrs. In Soon Moon Chang.

Copper

Contrary to what might be expected from the early history of metals in other regions, only two of the artifacts, or about 6 percent of the whole group, were originally composed of unalloyed copper. They may be described as follows:

1. This had the form of a roughly oval disk (12 × 9 mm). It weighed 0.73 g and still contained some uncorroded metal. On one side faint traces of some design appeared and on the other a small central boss. It may have originally been a button. (Date: ca. A.D. 300)

2. This was not an intact object but consisted of a number of fragments of various sizes that had the appearance of being the end result of the complete corrosion of folded sheet metal or crushed tubing. The total weight of the material was 5.0 g. (Date: ca. A.D. 300)

The results of the analyses are shown in Table 7.1. Except for the presence of sulfur, there is nothing unusual about these results. It seems quite unlikely that such proportions of sulfur were present in the original metals, especially the high proportion found in Artifact No. 2. The sulfur

Component	No. 1 (%)	No. 2 (%)
Insoluble Siliceous Matter	1.42	1.80
Cu	86.20	60.58
Fe	0.10	0.67
Ni	0.03	0.01
Zn	0.10	0.00
Sn, Pb, Ag, Au	0.00	0.00
S	1.10	4.59
Other Nonmetals	11.05	32.35

Table 7.1
Analyses of Copper Artifacts from Snake Cave

Component	Percent
Silica and Silicates	1.8
Malachite	87.6
Covellite	9.1
Limonite	1.3
Total	99.8

Table 7.2
Mineralogical Composition of Artifact No. 2

Component	No. 1 (%)	No. 2 (%)
Cu	99.73	98.89
Fe	0.12	1.10
Ni	0.03	0.01
Zn	0.12	0.00

Table 7.3
Original Composition of Copper Artifacts

occurred in the form of cupric sulfide in the corrosion products (as was confirmed by chemical tests), and this was very probably produced by the action of ground water, containing sulfide, on the normal corrosion products of the copper, more especially on those containing copper in the cupric state. Artifact No. 1 contained some cuprous oxide as well as basic copper carbonate (as was confirmed by chemical tests), and a much smaller total proportion of corrosion products than Artifact No. 2. This difference in the nature and proportion of corrosion products may largely account for the widely different proportions of sulfur found in the two objects from the same site. The nonmetals other than sulfur, estimated by difference, consisted mostly of the carbon and oxygen in the green basic cupric carbonate, which was the predominant corrosion product in both artifacts. Table 7.2 shows the mineralogical composition of No. 2 calculated from the analytical figures. The satisfactory summation is an indication of the correctness of this calculated composition. The approximate original composition of the metal of both artifacts, also calculated from the analytical figures, is shown in Table 7.3. It seems probable from the presence of zinc in No. 1 and the presence of over 1 percent iron in No. 2 that the original metal of both artifacts was not native copper but copper produced by smelting.

7.1
Archaelogical sites in
Afganistan.

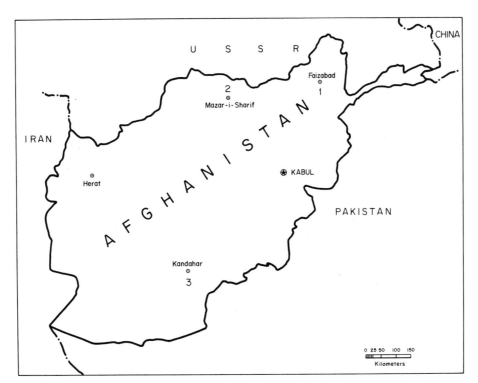

1. Dara-i-Kur }
   Hazer Gusfand } Same Area

2. Horse Cave }
   Snake Cave } Same Area

3. Shamshir Ghar

Low-Tin Bronzes

Three of the artifacts were composed originally of low-tin bronzes, for they contained only about 5 percent tin, with lead absent from one, and present only in low proportion in the other two. The first of those listed and described below came from the Snake Cave, the others from Dara-i-Kur.

No. 1. This was in the form of three completely corroded pieces of sheet metal, which were probably parts of a single object, for faint traces of a similar embossed design were visible on all three. Since these fragments came from the deepest layer of deposit in Snake Cave and apparently belonged to the earliest period of its prehistoric occupation, they are of special archaeological interest. (Date: ca. 5000 B.C.)

No. 2. This was in the form of two completely corroded pieces of a rod or pin. One piece was 18 mm long and the other 13 mm long. Both had a diameter of about 3 mm. It seems likely that they were parts from the same object. (Date not yet available.)

No. 3. This artifact was a tapered rectangular rod broken off at one end and having a conical tip at the other. Its overall length was 125 mm, and the cross section at the broken end measured 8 × 6 mm. It tapered gradually to the tip, which was 10 mm in length. This object appeared to be an ornamental spike, or at least part of one. It was coated with a rough green patina which was underlain with a thin layer of cuprous oxide. Although the metal core was essentially intact, some intergranular corrosion was apparent throughout. The samples of metal taken for analysis were freed as much as possible from corrosion products. (Date not yet available.)

The results of the analyses are shown in Table 7.4, and the approximate original compositions, calculated from the analytical figures, in Table 7.5. It will be seen that lead was not found in No. 1, although a trace may have escaped detection. This absence of lead coupled with a low-tin content is characteristic of the composition of early bronze in various regions. This may also be true for Afghanistan in view of the stratigraphic evidence for a very early date for Artifact No. 1. The similar tin content and its very low lead content may also indicate an early date for Artifact No. 2. The composition of No. 3 was found to differ distinctly in some respects from that of the other two. The tin content is a little lower and the lead content considerably higher. Moreover, the nickel content is higher and silver is present as an impurity. Spectrographic tests showed that this artifact also contained small proportions of antimony and arsenic, but exact quantitative determinations were not made. The percentages

Component	No. 1 (%)	No. 2 (%)	No. 3 (%)
Insoluble			
Siliceous			
Matter	2.61	0.25	0.00
Cu	68.32	70.98	90.44
Sn	5.15	4.91	5.23
Pb	0.00	0.65	2.56
Fe	0.17	0.07	0.17
Ni	0.01	0.01	0.08
Zn	0.00	0.03	0.00
Ag	0.00	0.00	0.08
Au	0.00	0.00	0.00
Various			
Nonmetals	23.74	23.10	1.44

Table 7.4 Analyses of Low-Tin Bronze Artifacts

Component	No. 1 (%)	No. 2 (%)	No. 3 (%)
Cu	92.76	92.60	91.76
Sn	6.99	6.41	5.31
Pb	0.00	0.85	2.60
Fe	0.23	0.09	0.17
Ni	0.02	0.01	0.08
Zn	0.00	0.04	0.00
Ag	0.00	0.00	0.08

Table 7.5 Original Composition of Low-Tin Bronzes

of these elements are included in the 1.44 percent of nonmetals. Artifact No. 3 contained a higher proportion of uncorroded metal than any of the other copper or bronze artifacts from Afghanistan. Perhaps its greater thickness may account for the better state of preservation. Another possible factor is its composition. Bronzes containing a small-to-moderate proportion of lead along with tin are often better preserved than those from the same site that contain little or no lead.

Unlike bronzes from other regions, none of those in this series from Afghanistan contained a moderate proportion of tin, i.e., around 10 percent. In the artifacts in which the percentage of tin was above the low range, the percentages were very high. All these high-tin bronzes were completely corroded. They are listed and described below.

High-Tin Bronzes

No. 1. This artifact was in two flat thin pieces slightly thickened along one edge. Since they joined exactly, it was obvious that they were once part of the same object. From their curvature along the thickened edges and from the way they fitted together, it was also obvious that they came from the outer part of a flat circular object that had a raised rim. One of the pieces weighed 3.2 g and the other 1.7 g. (Date: ca. A.D. 300)

No. 2. This also consisted of two flat pieces that joined exactly. However, these pieces were much smaller and there was no indication of the shape of the original object. (Date: ca. A.D. 300)

Table 7.6
Analyses of High-Tin Bronze Artifacts from Snake Cave

Component	No. 1 (%)	No. 2 (%)	No. 3a (%)	No. 3b (%)	No. 4 (%)
Siliceous Matter	0.21	0.00	0.00	0.00	0.00
Cu	56.32	52.00	51.56	56.84	48.19
Sn	18.94	19.28	19.63	20.02	20.54
Pb	0.01	0.00	0.00	0.02	0.00
Fe	0.01	0.14	0.10	0.11	0.08
Ni	0.01	0.01	0.01	0.01	0.00
Zn, Ag, Au	0.00	0.00	0.00	0.00	0.00
S	0.00	0.00	0.00	0.00	1.39
Various Nonmetals	24.50	28.57	28.80	23.00	29.80

Table 7.7
Original Composition of High-Tin Bronzes

Component	No. 1 (%)	No. 2 (%)	No. 3a (%)	No. 3b (%)	No. 4 (%)
Cu	74.82	72.80	72.42	73.82	70.03
Sn	25.15	26.99	27.43	26.00	29.85
Pb	0.01	0.00	0.00	0.03	0.00
Fe	0.01	0.20	0.14	0.14	0.12
Ni	0.01	0.01	0.01	0.01	0.00

No. 3. This was also in two pieces, but unlike the two previous artifacts the two pieces were curved and did not fit together. The larger piece (3a), which weighed 6.0 g, was thickened along one edge and was apparently part of the rim and side of a cup, or some object of similar shape. The other piece (3b) weighed 1.5 g. Though designated as part of a bracelet, this piece had the same curvature and the same diameter as the thickened rim of the first piece, which indicated that it may have been part of the same cup-shaped object. Samples from both pieces were separately analyzed. (Date: ca. A.D. 300)

No. 4. This artifact was a rod or part of a rod. It was 23 mm long and about 3 mm in diameter. (Date: ca. A.D. 550)

The results of the analyses are shown in Table 7.6, and the approximate original compositions, calculated from the analytical figures in Table 7.7. In these tables the analyses of No. 3 are designated as No. 3a and No. 3b, the first being based on a sample from the larger piece. From Table 7.6 it will be seen that the percentages of tin in the artifacts fall within a narrow range, whereas from Table 7.7 it is evident that the calculated percentages of tin in the original bronzes vary over a wider range. This discrepancy is apparently caused by variations in the proportions of the copper corrosion products in the artifacts, as is indicated by the variations in the percentages of copper and the various nonmetals. Note that the calculated percentages of copper in the original bronzes vary less than those in the artifacts. Although the percentages of copper in No. 3a and No. 3b differ considerably, the calculated percentages of copper, and those for tin and iron, are close enough to support the visual indication that the two pieces of No. 3 came

from the same object. The proportions of lead and nickel are very low in all the artifacts. Artifact No. 4 was found to contain a small proportion of sulfur. This component probably entered the corrosion products in the same way as the sulfur found in the copper artifacts. The approximate mineralogical composition of No. 4, based on a qualitative identification of the corrosion products and in the analytical figures, is shown in Table 7.8.

Table 7.8
Mineralogical Composition of No. 4

Component	Percent
Malachite	52.8
Cuprite	17.2
Covellite	3.8
Cassiterite	26.1
Limonite	0.1
Total	100.0

Copper-tin alloys containing proportions of tin in the range indicated by the analyses have the same general properties and melt at about the same temperature, which is much below the fusion temperatures of simple bronzes that contain moderate-to-low proportions of tin. Bronzes containing such high proportions of tin are almost white in color and are highly reflective when polished. Because of these properties, such bronzes are very suitable for mirrors. The shape of Artifact No. 1 and the calculated composition of the uncorroded alloy indeed suggest that the original object was a mirror. If not a mirror, it was very probably an ornamental or ceremonial object of some sort, for bronze of this composition is too brittle to be used for objects that are subjected to much stress. Because of this property and the hardness of the alloy, this object could not have been made by any method other than casting. The same conclusion as to restriction of use and method of manufacture applies to the original objects

Table 7.9
Percentages of Certain Key Metals in High-Tin Bronzes of China

Object	Sn	Pb	Ni
Chou Dynasty or Earlier			
Blade	16.59	12.74	0.10
Chariot Fitting	17.51	12.04	0.12
Handle	19.25	0.29	0.15
Ceremonial Vessel	19.33	0.24	0.00
Spear	19.84	9.54	0.00
Han Dynasty			
Mirror	25.56	6.46	0.33
Mirror	25.85	4.00	0.05
Mirror	25.98	4.20	0.10
Mirror	26.55	4.71	0.11
Mirror	27.00	4.55	0.09

High-tin bronzes were widely used in ancient China, and it is therefore tempting to infer that China was the source of the high-tin bronzes of Afghanistan. However, there are sharp differences between the composition of the high-tin bronzes from the two regions, as may be seen by comparing the figures in Table 7.7 with those in Table 7.9. All the analyses cited in Table 7.9 were made on samples taken from objects that were not much corroded, so that the percentages of the components listed are close to those in the original bronzes. It will be seen that the range of tin content in the group of miscellaneous early Chinese objects is much below that calculated for the original alloys of Afghanistan. Moreover, there are large differences between the two groups in respect to the percentages of lead and nickel. Additional pertinent information on the composition of ancient Chinese high-tin bronze is provided by the recently published analyses of many samples of metal taken from ceremonial vessels of a wide range of date. (Reference 3.) These analyses show that such vessels were often cast from high-tin bronze, but the highest proportion of tin reported is 21.5 percent, and even this is exceptional, for the tin content of such bronze is generally below 20 percent. However, as is shown by the second group of analyses in Table 7.9, the range of tin content in ancient Chinese mirrors is about the same as that in the high-tin bronzes of Afghanistan. But here also the percentages of lead and nickel are very different. The only other point of similarity is the apparent absence of nickel from two of the miscellaneous objects and the frequent very low nickel content of the high-tin ceremonial bronzes. Since the nickel in ancient bronzes is associated with the copper and since the ratio of nickel to copper varies in the copper obtained from the ores of different deposits, a common source of copper for some of the high-tin bronzes of China and Afghanistan may be

represented by all the other artifacts in this group.

indicated, but it seems certain that the bronzes themselves did not have a common place of origin. In fact, the high-tin bronzes of Afghanistan appear to be unique in their composition, for no other ancient alloys of like composition are known from elsewhere. Perhaps this is an indication that they were made locally.

Leaded Bronze

Only two of the artifacts were found to be composed of leaded bronze, i.e., an alloy in which the proportion of lead exceeds the proportion of tin. Both were from Shamshir Ghar and both were of very late date (ninth or tenth century A.D.). They may be described as follows:

No. 1. This was a bronze coin having a diameter of 17–18 mm and weighing 2.4 g. It was covered with a uniform layer of green corrosion products so dense that no trace of a design was apparent before cleaning. After electrolytic cleaning, parts of a crude design were visible, but the coin could not be attributed with certainty. The surface layers were filed off and the blank was cut in half in order to obtain two samples for analysis. Some intergranular corrosion products were present in the metal of both samples.

No. 2. This artifact was a piece of corroded sheet metal weighing 2.0 g. Its greatest length was 25 mm, its greatest width 15 mm, and its thickness about 1 mm. It appeared to be a segment of a disk, but the complete object could have had some other shape. Faint traces of an ornamental design could be distinguished on the surface, which was covered with a thin layer of soil mixed with corrosion products. Two samples were prepared in the same way as for No. 1. The metal of these samples also contained intergranular corrosion products.

The results of the analyses are shown in Table 7.10. It will be seen that the results obtained for the major components in the two samples of No. 1 are in good agreement, whereas the percentages of copper and lead in the two samples from No. 2 are in poor agreement. This lack of agreement in duplicate samples taken from a bronze containing a very high proportion of lead is by no means unusual, for it is well known that such bronze is often grossly heterogeneous. The presence of silver indicates that the lead used in making the alloys was not desilverized, or was desilverized incompletely. Furthermore, the constancy of the ratios of the percentages of silver to the percentages of lead in the two alloys, shown in Table 7.11, indicate the use of lead of the same quality, and possibly from the same source, in their manufacture. It is very probable that the zinc was also introduced into the alloys as an accidental impurity in the lead. The percentages of zinc are in the same order as the percentages of lead, but the ratios are different for the

Table 7.10
Analyses of Leaded
Bronzes from
Shamshir Gahr

Component	No. 1a (%)	No. 1b (%)	No. 2a (%)	No. 2b (%)
Cu	76.86	77.07	67.22	64.54
Sn	5.75	5.78	3.36	3.29
Pb	14.96	15.14	25.53	28.29
Fe	0.12	0.06	0.49	0.52
Ni	0.15	0.11	0.11	0.11
Co	0.08	0.03	0.13	0.12
Zn	0.20	0.14	0.66	0.74
Ag	0.12	0.16	0.20	0.22
Au	0.00	0.00	0.00	0.00
Nonmetals	1.79	1.51	2.30	2.17

Table 7.11
Ratios of Silver to
Lead in Leaded
Bronzes

Artifact No.	Pb (%)	Ag (%)	Ag/Pb
1a	14.96	0.12	0.008
1b	15.14	0.16	0.011
2a	25.53	0.20	0.008
2b	28.29	0.22	0.008
Average			0.009

Table 7.12
Ratios of Nickel to
Copper in Leaded
Bronzes

Artifact No.	Cu (%)	Ni (%)	Ni/Cu
1a	76.86	0.15	0.0020
1b	77.07	0.11	0.0014
2a	67.22	0.11	0.0016
2b	64.54	0.11	0.0017
Average			0.0017

two alloys. Numerical ratios involving proportions of zinc are not, however, quantitatively reliable because of the volatility of this metal. The amount of zinc left in ancient metals and alloys as an accidental impurity depends to some extent on the heat treatment during manufacture.

The nickel entered the alloys as an accidental impurity in the copper. As shown in Table 7.12, the ratios of the percentages of nickel to the percentages of copper in the two alloys are very similar. This indicates that copper from the same source was used in their manufacture. The presence of cobalt in such high proportions is very unusual. Ordinarily the proportion of this metal in ancient bronzes is much below 0.01 percent. Expecially unusual is the presence of cobalt in a proportion about equal to that of nickel, as in the two samples from No. 2. This element also entered the alloy as an accidental impurity in the copper. Although the ratios of the percentages of cobalt to the percentages of copper in the two alloys are different, the very fact that cobalt was present in unusually high proportions in both alloys would seem to be another indication that the copper used in their manufacture came from the same source.

Pewter

One artifact submitted as an example of ancient silver from Afghanistan was found on analysis to be composed of a tin-lead alloy. It came from Shamshir Ghar and its date was ca. tenth century A.D. This object was in the form of a rough irregular rod that appeared to be a fragment of some sort of ornamental pin or clasp. Its length was 32 mm and it weighed 3.8 g. Mold marks on its side indicated that the original object had been formed by casting in a two-piece mold. This artifact was

coated with a thin, almost uniform layer of greyish white corrosion products that were found to consist mostly of stannic oxide and basic lead carbonate. Two samples were taken for analysis after filing away the layer of corrosion products. However, it was not possible to obtain clean metal for analysis because intergranular corrosion products were present throughout.

The results of the analyses are shown in Table 7.13. These are only partial analyses, for the main purpose at the time they were made was to demonstrate that the artifact was not composed of silver. Undoubtedly the samples contained accidental impurities other than the ones listed. However, in view of the obvious presence of intergranular corrosion products in the samples, the percentages listed as other elements must consist mostly of the carbon and oxygen that were present in these products. The results show clearly that the original alloy was a tin-lead alloy that may be classed as a kind of pewter. It is interesting that the ratio of tin to lead is very close to 2.0, which may indicate that the alloy was not the result of an accidental or careless combination of the two components but the result of the deliberate combination of measured amounts.

Table 7.13
Analysis of Corroded
Pewter from
Shamshir Ghar

Component	Sample 1 (%)	Sample 2 (%)
Sn	63.87	63.64
Pb	32.64	32.89
Fe	0.03	0.02
Zn	0.08	0.07
Other Elements	3.38	3.38

Iron

Over half the artifacts, nineteen in all, were originally iron objects or parts of iron objects. Nine of them were completely rusted, but in most the corrosion products were so compact that the original shape of the objects could be readily discerned, especially after removal, by a combination of chemical and mechanical treatment of the loose outside layers of soil mixed with corrosion products. Seven of the objects in this group came from Snake Cave, one from Horse Cave, and the other from Shamshir Ghar. The absence of residual metal was established by magnetic and chemical tests. No iron carbide or graphitic carbon was detected in any of them, which indicates that the original objects were composed of wrought iron.

The other ten artifacts contained various proportions of metal, mostly in the form of small cores imbedded in a mass of corrosion products. This residual metal was isolated by a combination of chemical and mechanical treatment, and the metal so isolated was tested for malleability, both before heat treatment and after heating to redness and plunging into cold water. The untreated metal was very malleable when hammered, and no difference in malleability was found after heat treatment in the metal of eight objects from Snake Cave, one from Hazer Gusfand (near Dara-i-Kur, Badakhshar), and one from Shamshir Ghar. This showed that these objects were originally composed of wrought iron. Two of the artifacts from Snake Cave contained a high proportion of uncorroded metal. One had the form of a rough irregular rod 52 mm long. Corrosion products were present only as a compact, hard, thin layer on the surface of the metal. This is an indication that the soil conditions were exceptionally favorable for its preservation, or that the iron was exceptionally pure. Possibly both may account for it, but the latter factor seems more likely to have been the cause in view of the condition of other artifacts found near the second object. This was a thin rectangular piece of iron 45 mm long and 20 mm wide that appeared to be part of a blade. This object also was coated with only a thin layer of corrosion products. It was found in the same stratum as one of the completely corroded iron objects and completely corroded high-tin bronze Artifact No. 4. The survival of so much of the iron of an object under conditions that corroded bronze completely indicates that high purity of the iron was the chief factor in its preservation.

One of the iron objects from Shamshir Ghar, dated seventh or eighth century A.D., had a thin metal core that was but slightly malleable. This object was in the form of a rod 53 mm long. After heating the isolated core to redness and plunging it into water, the metal was found not to be malleable at all and very resistant to a file. This indicates that the metal was a steel. One other iron artifact from Shamshir Ghar, dated tenth to thirteenth centuries A.D., contained metal that was not malleable at all. This object was a flat piece of irregular shape coated with a thin compact layer of corrosion products. It weighed 48.6 g and was 3 mm thick along one side and 5 mm along the opposite side. It was evidently a fragment broken from a larger flat piece, possibly the flat bottom of a dish or pan. The fact that its thickness decreased regularly from one side to the other indicates the latter possibility. This object broke when tapped with a hammer, and it could not be drilled or filed with ordinary steel tools. The fractured edges had the bright crystalline structure of white cast iron. No internal corrosion products were visible, but a few small blowholes were present. Five separate samples were taken for the determination of the significant components of cast iron. The results are listed in Table 7.14.

Component	Percent
C	4.25
Si	0.13
P	0.11
S	trace
Mn	trace

Table 7.14
Analysis of Cast Iron From Shamshir Ghar

These results show the metal to be a white cast iron with a carbon content almost exactly that of the most easily fusible alloy of carbon and iron. This alloy melts at 1140°C., a temperature not difficult to reach in a primitive furnace. The percentages of the components other than carbon are lower than in modern cast iron. Iron of such purity could have been produced by reducing a carefully selected iron ore, or a pure mineral such as hematite, with charcoal in a primitive blast furnace at a relatively low temperature by the use of a carefully regulated flow of unheated air. The higher proportion of impurities in modern cast iron are caused by the use of ordinary ore, coke as a fuel, and the higher temperatures arising from the use of a blast of preheated air. From the standpoint of chemical quality the iron of this artifact is superior to modern cast iron, and its composition explains its resistance to corrosion. Modern white cast iron is valued for its resistance to corrosion in the ground, but iron having the composition of the metal of this artifact should be even more resistant. In fact, the excellent state of preservation of the artifact clearly demonstrates how well the iron did resist corrosion.

General Remarks

This analytical study of 31 artifacts from Afghanistan indicates that the metals and alloys used in that region in ancient times differ in certain respects from those in contemporaneous use elsewhere. Most distinctive in composition are the high-tin bronzes, for alloys of like composition were apparently not used in any other region. Differences in the proportions of the various classes of metals and alloys are also evident. Only a little over 6 percent of the artifacts were originally composed of copper, whereas some 60 percent were composed of iron or iron alloys. This unusual distribution may be accounted for in various ways. The most obvious is that this group of artifacts is not representative of the proportions of the several classes of metals and alloys in use in ancient Afghanistan, even though they range widely in date. Whether this unusual distribution is fictitious or real can only be determined by the analysis of many more artifacts from a larger number of sites.

References

Analysis of Ancient Metals, Pergamon Press, Inc., New York, 1964, pp. 81–93.

1.
Caley, E. R.

Shamshir Ghar: Historic Cave Site in Kandahar Province, Afghanistan, Anthropological Papers of the American Museum of Natural History, 46 (2), New York, 1958, pp. 141–179; Dupree, L. "Prehistoric Surveys and Excavations in Afghanistan." 1959–1960 and 1961–1963. *Science* 146 (3644), Washington, 1964, pp. 638–640; Dupree, L. The Prehistoric Period of Afghanistan, *Afghanistan* 20 (3), Kabul 1967, 8–27; Dupree, L. Prehistoric excavations in Afghanistan. *The American Philosophical Society Yearbook: 1967*. Philadelphia, 1968, pp. 504–508.

2.
Dupree, L.

The Freer Chinese Bronzes, **I**, Washington, 1967.

3.
Pope, J. A.
Gettens, R. J.
Cahill, J., and
Barnard, N.

Chapter 8

Compositions of Some Copper-Based Coins of Augustus and Tiberius

Giles F. Carter
Eastern Michigan University

Each ancient coin bears a record, more or less determinable, of the ore from which the metal was obtained, the method by which the metal was won and alloyed, the economics and special governmental policies of the period in which it was made, and its time and place of manufacture. Chemical analyses and metallographic studies of ancient coins are adding to the information obtained from archaeology and numismatics.

Several nondestructive or essentially nondestructive methods for analyzing coins have been developed. Analyses numbering in the tens of thousands are now feasible and should yield valuable information about ancient coins and the men who were involved with their production.

In the past there have been many incomplete and inaccurate wet chemical analyses of ancient coins. However, Caley's analyses of Greek and Roman coins are by far the most numerous analyses of high accuracy (References 1 and 2). Three nondestructive or essentially nondestructive methods are being used to analyze ancient coins: optical spectrometry, X-ray fluorescence, and neutron activation. Spectrometric analysis requires removal of at least a small amount of metal representative of the whole coin. In X-ray fluorescence the metal content is determined in a very thin surface layer, usually less than 0.0005 cm. Therefore accurate X-ray fluorescence analyses require removal of the patina or surface oxide, and usually 0.001 to 0.002 cm of metal from the surface, preferably by abrasion with aluminum oxide powder in a stream of air; this metal removal is necessary to expose at the surface metal which has the same composition as the entire coin (References 3 to 6). Neutron activation analysis is completely nondestructive, but the analyses represent an average composition of the patina and any dirt on the surface of the coin and the metallic substrate. The composition of the patina can be far different from that of the metal in the coin, and the patina composition is partly dependent on the environment with which the coin has come into contact.

No one analytical method is perfect, and it is not the purpose of this paper to argue the superiority of one method over the others. Each method should be used whenever it can effectively and economically contribute to the store of information on ancient coins. In this work all the coins were analyzed by X-ray fluorescence according to previously described methods (References 3 to 6).

Undoubtedly one of the most important generations in all history was the period in which the Roman Empire was established.

This was the same generation that saw the beginning of Christianity. This period is interesting not only historically but also in the field of numismatics. Very few copper-based coins were minted for over fifty years before Augustus' reign. Romans must have been both bored and dissatisfied with the crude, impure copper-based coins that had circulated for so long. The coinage of Augustus was as different from the preceding Roman coinage as was his form of government.

Augustus issued a premium copper-based coinage including two denominations in brass: *Sestertius* and *Dupondius*. The production of brass coins was a breakthrough dating from about the reign of Julius Caesar. Augustus initiated at first one and later a second denomination of pure copper: the *As* and then the *Quadrans*. It should be emphasized that the pure copper asses and quadrantes were nearly as important a breakthrough in coinage as the brass denominations. Pure copper coinage was both metallurgically and psychologically important. The favorable contrast between Augustus' new copper and brass coins and the old impure, crude Republican coinage must have been noticed by the entire Empire.

In Rome the copper-based coinage of both Augustus and Tiberius was sporadic with gaps of one or two to fifteen years between periods of minting. It is important to determine whether the compositions of copper coins change from one period to another. This paper will answer this question.

A second important question of the early Empire is the policy of the emperor towards copper coinage in the colonies. Were minting procedures in colonies similar to or different from those used in Rome at about the same time? Coins were propaganda pieces for the emperor and they comprised different alloys of copper from that found in Rome. The composition of Roman colonial coins is the second main investigation reported in this paper.

In this report all coins have been identified by catalog number as far as possible. A few of the coins were unidentifiable because of poor condition or because of obscurity of type. Catalog numbers of coins are necessary to facilitate future compilations and comparisons of results. Table 8.1 contains the coin identifications, weights, and densities. Coins alloyed with lead usually have higher densities than pure copper. Brass and bronze (Cu-Sn) have lower densities than pure copper.

Figures 8.1 and 8.2 illustrate the copper-based denominations of ''*as*'' and ''*ses-*

Identifications, Weights, and Densities of Coins

8.1a
Obverse of *As* minted
at Rome (R281) (2X).

8.1b
Reverse of *As* minted at
Rome (R281) (2X).

8.2a
Obverse of *Sestertius*
minted at Rome (R-78)
(2X).

8.2b
Reverse of *Sestertius*
minted at Rome (R-78)
(2X).

8.3a
Obverse of Dupondius
minted at Lugdunum
(R-81) (2X).

8.3b
Reverse of Dupondius
minted at Lugdunum
(R-81) (2X).

8.4a
Obverse of *As* minted
at Lugdunum (R-255)
(2X).

8.4b
Reverse of *As* minted at
Lugdunum (R255) (2X).

Table 8.1

Identification and
Physical Properties
of Coins

Coin No.	Catalog No. *	Weight (g)	Density (g/cm³)†	Denomination	Date	Emperor§
Rome					**B.C.**	
R-281	BMC 145	11.4577	8.90	As	23	A
R-257	BMC 143? C470	8.0495	8.85	As	23	A
R-259	BMC 137	9.3654	8.85	As	23	A
R-262	BMC ?	20.6763	8.59	Sest.	23–17	A
R-78	BMC 175	21.1433	8.62	Sest.	21	A
R-261	BMC 193?	8.6225	8.58	Dupon.	17	A
R-298	BMC 220	9.5230	8.85	As	ca. 13	A
R-297	BMC 226	8.5145	8.93	As	ca. 13	A
R-254	BMC 226	8.1643	8.90	As	ca. 13	A
R-253	BMC 214-5	8.5377	8.96	As	ca. 13	A
R-600	BMC 220,209, or 226	10.3891	8.89	As	13 or 7	A
R-80	BMC 261	3.1269	8.89	Quad.	ca. 5	A
R-516	?	6.3651	8.97	As.	?	Agrippa?
					A.D.	
R-245	BMC 151	9.9549	8.87	As	ca. 15	T(A)‖
R-258	BMC 68	8.6864	8.95	As	ca. 15	T
R-299	BMC 99	9.4509	8.90	As	22–3	T(Dr)
R-60	BMC 99	10.1244	8.88	As	22–3	T(Dr)
R-249	BMC 99	8.6015	8.92	As	22–3	T(Dr)
R-250	BMC 91-4	8.9338	8.95	As	22–3	T
R-251	BMC 91-4	8.6886	8.91	As	22–3	T
R-605	BMC 149	7.6745	8.94	As	22–8	T(A)
R-252	BMC 149	7.9433	8.95	As	22–8	T(A)
R-96	BMC 147-9	9.0654	8.94	As	22–8	T(A)
R-476	Im-BMC 149	6.9633	8.84	As	?	T(A)
R-97	BMC 106-7	10.6898	8.91	As	34–5	T
R-256	BMC 121 or 106	9.9327	8.92	As	34–6	T
R-79	BMC 155	10.6977	8.92	As	34–7	T(A)
R-260	BMC 155	8.4787	8.85	As	34–7	T(A)
R-518	BMC 155	10.4140	8.95	As	34–7	T(A)
R-606	BMC 158	9.5934	8.93	As	34–7	T(A)
R-95	BMC 158 (var)	10.3218	8.91	As	34–7	T(A)
R-63	BMC 158	9.7288	8.94	As	34–7	T(A)
Lugdunum					**B.C.**	
R-94	BMC 549	8.8366	8.87	As	10–6	A
R-517	BMC 550	8.6147	8.83	As	10–6	A
R-255	BMC 550	10.4656	8.88	As	10–6	A
R-233	BMC 550	8.4533	8.72	As	10–6	A
R-171	BMC 549?	9.7480	8.71	As	10–6	A
R-179	BMC 550	10.3176	8.89	As	10–6	A
R-602	BMC 559	10.0526	8.88	As	10–6	A
					A.D.	
R-604	BMC 585	6.4803	8.95	As	12–14	A(T)
R-603	BMC 585	7.9419	8.78	As	12–14	A(T)
R-81	BMC 583	11.7954	8.54	Dupon.	12–14	A(T)

Table 8.1
Identification and
Physical Properties
of Coins (Continued)

Coin No.	Catalog No.*	Weight (g)	Density (g/cm³)†	Denomination	Date	Emperor§
Nemausus					**B.C.**	
R-170	S.444 or C.10	6.2266	9.03	AE 25**	after 27	A and Ag
R-424	Sears 454	9.1648	8.92	AE 25	after 27	A and Ag
R-178	S.445 or C.8	13.0822	8.68	AE 25	after 27	A and Ag
R-234	Sears 454 or C.7	13.3762	9.00	AE 25	after 27	A and Ag
R-601	?	19.3515	9.08	AE 28	?	A
Spain					**B.C.**	
R-522	H. 36-10	11.0178	9.22	As	?	A
R-175	H. 14-8	10.6132	9.27	As	6	A
R-172	Sears 437	6.4975	8.31	As	?	A
R-520	Sim. H.33-2	10.7365	9.12	As	?	A
R-173	H. 10-4	6.3941	9.41	Semis	?	A
R-174	?	17.1448	8.72	As?	?	?
					A.D.	
R-521	Mun. Ital.	9.4729	8.85	As	14–37	T
R-280	H. 27-1	14.1791	8.53	AE 28	14–37	T
R-523	H. 37–1	11.6638	8.74	As	14–37	T
Greece and Near East						
R-126	BMC 70? Lac.‖‖	3.1551	8.78	AE 17	27 B.C.– A.D. 14	A
R-526	Grose 3267§§	4.5471	8.93	AE 17	?	A
R-527	BMC 47-9 Thes.‖‖	5.7542	9.22	AE 21	?	A?
R-528	BMC 55 Thes.	2.4304	8.80	AE 17	?	A
R-180	BMC 210 Cyz.‖‖	2.1034	9.06	AE 15	27 B.C.– A.D. 14	A
R-279	BMC 739 Perg.‖‖	10.6934	8.92	As	23 B.C.	A
					A.D.	
R-458	BMC 174 Com.‖‖	10.8878	9.10	AE 30	20–1	T
R-459	BMC 174 Com.	12.0517	8.64	AE 30	20–1	T
Antioch						
R-534	BMC 128 Syria	13.8167	8.94	AE 27	23 B.C.– A.D. 14	A
R-530	BMC 128 Syria	13.2713	8.72	AE 27	23 B.C.– A.D. 37	A
					A.D.	
R-525	BMC 160 Syria	6.8534	8.93	AE 21	14–37	T
R-536	BMC 155 Syria	12.0399	8.95	AE 27	14–37	T
R-316	BMC 154 Syria	16.1160	8.87	AE 26	33	T
R-460	BMC 154 Syria	15.1769	8.89	AE 26	33	T

* BMC = British Museum Catalog: H. Mattingly, *Coins of the Roman Empire in the British Museum*, Vol. I, Trustees of the British Museum, London, 1965.
Sear = Sear, D. A., *Roman Coins and Their Values*, B. A. Seaby Ltd., London, 1964.
S = Seaby, H. A., *Roman Coins and Their Values*, B. A. Seaby Ltd., London, 1954.
H = Hill, G. F., *Notes on the Ancient Coinage of Hispania Citerior*, The Amer. Numis. Soc., New York, 1931.
Sim. = Similar to
Mun. Ital. = Municipium Italica

† Density of pure Cu is 8.96 g/cm³

§A = Augustus

‖T = Tiberius; T(A) = struck under Tiberius, but portrait of Augustus; Dr = Drusus.

** AE 25 = AE means copperbased coin; 25 means 25 mm in diameter; denomination uncertain.

††Ag = Agrippa

§§Grose: S. W. Grose, "The Catalogue of the McClean Collection of Greek Coins," Cambridge.

‖‖ Lac. = Lacaedemon; Thes. = Thesalonica; Perg. = Pergamum; Com. = Commagene; all these are ancient mints.

8.5a
Obverse of *As* minted
in Spain (R522) (2X).

8.5b
Reverse of *As* minted in
Spain (R522) (2X).

8.6a
Obverse of *As* minted
in Spain (R280) (2X).

8.6b
Reverse of *As* minted in
Spain (R280) (2X).

8.7a
Obverse of copper-
based coin minted in
Nemausus (R178) (2X).

8.7b
Reverse of copper-
based coin minted in
Nemausus (R178) (2X).

8.8a
Obverse of AE-17
minted in Phillippi
(R-526) (2X).

8.8b
Reverse of AE-17 minted
in Phillippi (R-526)
(2X).

8.9a
Obverse of AE-30
minted in Commagene
(30 mm diam) (R458).

8.9b
Reverse of AE-30 minted
in Commagene (30 mm
diam) (R458).

8.10a
Obverse of AE-25
minted at Antioch by
Augustus or Tiberius
(25 mm diam) (R530).

8.10b
Reverse of AE-25 minted
at Antioch (R530).

8.11a
Obverse of AE-25
minted at Antioch
(25 mm diam) (R316)

8.11b
Reverse of AE-25 minted
at Antioch (R316).

8.12a
Obverse of "Imitation"
As made at unknown
mint (R516).

8.12b
Reverse of "Imitation"
As made at unknown
mint (R516).

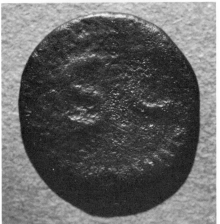

8.13a
Obverse of "Imitation" *As* made at unknown mint (R476).

8.13b
Reverse of "Imitation" *As* made at unknown mint (R476).

8.14a
Obverse of probable overstrike on Republican *As* by Augustus (R601).

8.14b
Reverse of probable overstrike on Republivan As by Augustus (R601).

8.15a
Obverse of unknown Spanish coin (R174).

8.15b
Reverse of unknown Spanish coin (R174).

8.16a
Obverse of coin probably minted at Lacaedemon (R126).

8.16b
Reverse of coin probably minted at Lacaedemon (R126).

Compositions of Some Copper-Based Coins of Augustus and Tiberius
120

tertius'' produced at Rome. Figures 8.3 to 8.11 represent various colonial coins, and Figures 8.12 to 8.16 illustrate unusual or unidentified coins.

Analytical Results

X-Ray fluorescence frequently has been discussed as a method for analyzing ancient coins and other archaeological objects (References 3 to 10). Consequently there is no need to repeat a detailed description of the method. A General Electric XRD-5 was used. An aluminum specimen holder confined the area of each coin irradiated by X-rays to approximately 1 cm². Other specific operating conditions are in Table 8.2. It is, however, important to discuss here the precision and accuracies of determinations of elements in ancient coins carried out by X-ray fluorescence. The most important factors affecting precision comprise the following: (1) counting statistics, (2) reproducibility of counting rate, and (3) surface roughness of the coin. The main factors affecting accuracy are (1) surface preparation, (2) homogeneity of metal, and (3) composition (and accuracy of composition) of standards.

In general the precision of X-ray fluorescence determinations of various elements in coins exceeds the accuracy at concentrations above 0.1 percent. Liebhafsky and others (Reference 11) have shown that for N, the total number of counts observed in a determination by X-ray fluorescence, the Standard Counting error, SC, is $\pm\sqrt{N}$. Table 8.3 shows hypothetical counts of Pb in 10 seconds at various concentrations and the calculated standard counting error as a function of concentration. Of the 10 elements determined in this study, only As has a lower precision than Pb.

The counting rate is reproducible in a given period except shortly after the instrument has been turned on. After 5 minutes of operation, the variation is less than one part in 40, and even this shift was largely corrected for by measuring the counting rate at the beginning, middle, and end of a run. Then an average counting rate is used, and the error in reproducibility of counting rate is less than ±1.5 parts per 100. This error is small compared with the overall standard deviations of the analyses.

Table 8.2
X-Ray Fluorescence: Analytical Conditions

Element	Target in X-Ray Tube	Counter	Crystal	Helium	Typical Counts for 1.0% of Element§
Fe	W*	Scin.†	LiF	No	17,500
Co	W	Scin.	LiF	No	19,000
Ni	W	Scin.	LiF	No	16,000
Cu	W	Scin.	LiF	No	260,000‖
Zn	W	Scin.	Topaz	No	3,100
As	W	Scin.	LiF	No	2,100
Ag	W	Scin.	LiF	No	15,500
Sn	Cr*	Flow†	LiF	Yes	4,100
Sb	Cr	Flow	LiF	Yes	4,200
Pb	W	Scin.	LiF	No	2,600

*W = Tungsten target; Cr = Chromium target.

†Scin. = Scintillation counter; Flow = Flow Counter # SPG-4.

§Counts in a 10 second period (used in all determinations).

‖Counts for 100% Cu (8.5 mA current at 50 kV used; 39.5 mA for all other elements).

Table 8.3
Counting Rate and Standard Counting Error for Lead Versus Concentration

Concentration (wt. % Pb)	Total Counts (in 10 sec)	Standard Counting Error (wt. % Pb)
100	260,000	0.3*
10	26,000	0.09†
1	2,600	0.03§
0.1	260	0.02‖
0.01	26	0.01‖

* Background = 550 counts/10 sec (negligible); standard of 100% Pb: 260,000 counts above background/10 sec. Calculated according to Liebhafsky (Reference 11).

† Background = 550 counts/10 sec; standard of 10% Pb: 26000 counts above background/10 sec.

§ Background = 550 counts/10 sec; standard of 1.0% Pb: 2600 counts above background/10 sec.

‖ Background = 550 counts/10 sec; standard of 0.10% Pb: 260 counts above background/10 sec.

Flat surfaces give reproducible and usually maximum counting rates obtainable for a given element in a given specimen. Any roughening of the surface usually decreases the counting rate. This presents a problem in coin analysis because the surfaces of coins vary widely in roughness and in relief. Relief depends on factors such as amount of wear experienced by the coin, the sharpness and relief of the original dies used, and the skill with which the coin was produced. Roughness is frequently a result of the amount of corrosion occurring on an individual coin. Roughness and relief can cause a decrease in the counting rate up to 20 percent.

Relief and roughness affect the counting rates of all elements although lighter elements having high X-ray absorptivities are affected about twice as much as heavier elements. The relief and roughness factor was corrected in the present determinations by comparing counting rates for various elements on several coin surfaces compared with the reverses of the coins filed flat and smooth. All the determinations for ten elements are summed up and then corrected by making the sum arbitrarily equal to 99.7 percent (arbitrarily allowing 0.3 percent for other elements such as Si and P). These corrections usually affect only the elements that are reported to one part in a hundred. Over 100 coins were analyzed for 25 elements, and in every case the 10 elements determined in the analyses reported here accounted for over 99.5 percent of the material in the coins.

The variation caused by roughness and relief is estimated to be less than ±1 to 5 parts per 100. At concentrations of 0.1 percent or less the statistical variation in counting rate affects the precision greater than both of the other factors. Reproducibility of several determinations of the same coin and of determinations of different coins minted at about the same time confirm that the precision is satisfactory for obtaining necessary information for drawing many conclusions useful to archaeologists and numismatists.

Accuracy

In X-ray fluorescence, concentrations of elements are determined in a thin surface layer, usually less than 0.0005 cm. If the composition of the surface layer is different from that of the interior, misleading results will be obtained by X-ray fluorescence. Indeed, Hall has shown that this occurs for late Roman denarii, Ag coins containing several percent Cu (References 7 to 10).

If the surfaces are not properly prepared, then all coins comprising two-phase systems (e.g. Ag-Cu, Cu-Pb, Cu-Sn, Cu-Sb provided at least 1 percent of both elements are present) will show a surface depletion of the more electropositive metal. The author has theorized that whenever a coin comprises two metallic phases, the more electropositive phase corrodes preferentially until all of that phase exposed at the surface is depleted (Reference 4). Consequently X-ray fluorescence will give misleading results unless a thin layer of metal is removed from the surface by electropolishing or abrading. A useful method for the latter is abrading with aluminum oxide powder (−325 mesh) carried in a stream of air. When 0.001 to 0.003 cm is removed, the X-ray fluorescence analysis of the coin surface is essentially identical with that of the coin interior obtained by filing the coin (References 3 and 4). The only apparent exception is copper coins containing over 10 percent lead. A thicker surface layer needs to be removed from these coins probably because of the large size of Pb particles corroded from the surface.

The second main factor affecting accuracy of X-ray fluorescence analyses is the homogeneity of the coins. Obviously if the coins are grossly inhomogeneous, inaccurate analyses will be obtained by X-ray fluorescence. Most Roman coins are homogeneous since the interiors of filed coins usually have essentially the same compositions as the coin surfaces (References 3 and 4). The only general exceptions are the orichalcum (brass) coins where the zinc content varies throughout the coins as a result of the method of manufacture of the alloy: a high-temperature diffusion process involving solid copper. As Caley has found, occasionally large chunks of copper-rich alloy occur in orichalcum coins (Reference 2). However, in X-ray fluorescence one determines the average zinc content in a thin surface layer over an area of about 1 cm²; unless there is an obvious copper-rich particle in this area, the determination of zinc is accurate to ±1 part in 20. By usual standards this is not very accurate, but it is sufficiently accurate to obtain useful conclusions in most coin analyses. Occasionally corrosion occurs preferentially at grain boundaries, causing the ratios of metals present to change somewhat. However, the cross-sectional area of grain boundaries relative to the exposed area of grains is very small, so no measurable effect results on determinations by X-ray fluorescence. It is concluded that inhomogeneity is relatively unimportant: when it occurs, it is present in highly alloyed coins and can be seen visually in most instances.

One of the most important factors in obtaining accurate X-ray fluorescence analyses is the accuracy of standards and the use of standards fairly close in composition to the unknown. Fortunately a number of brass and copper alloys of certified compositions are available from the National Bureau of Standards. Eleven of

Table 8.4
Compositions of
Standards

Standard No.	Analyst	Fe	Co	Ni	Cu	Zn	As	Ag	Sn	Sb	Pb	Other
62d	NBS*	0.86	—†	0.28	59.07	37.14	—	—	0.38	—	0.23	0.66 Mn 0.075 Si 1.23 Al
63c	NBS	0.0013	—	0.32	80.48	0.093	0.023	—	9.03	0.52	9.35	0.06 S 0.145 P
157a	NBS	0.174	0.022	11.82	58.61	29.09	—	—	0.021	—	0.034	0.174 Mn 0.009 P
158a	NBS	1.23	—	0.001	90.93	2.08	—	—	0.96	—	0.097	1.11 Mn 0.026 P 3.03 Si 0.46 Al
C1100	NBS	0.072	—	0.052	67.4	32.2	—	—	0.055	—	0.106	0.01 P 0.01 Si 0.003 Mn
C1102	NBS	0.011	—	0.005	72.8	27.1	—	—	0.006	—	0.020	.004 Mn .006 P .002 Si
C1109	NBS	0.053	—	0.10	82.2	17.4	—	—	0.10	—	0.075	P-Trace
C1111	NBS	0.010	—	0.022	87.1	12.81	—	—	0.019	—	0.013	P-Trace
C1112	NBS	0.07	—	0.10	93.4	6.3	—	—	0.12	—	0.057	.009 P
C1115	NBS	0.13	—	0.074	88.0	11.7	—	—	0.10	—	0.013	.005 P
C1120	NBS	0.015	—	—	80.1	18.1	Trace	—	—	—	0.105	1.46 Al .018 P
132	Com.*	0.01	0.067	0.14	77.4	—	0.66	0.11	3.26	1.41	18.0	
235	Com.	0.06	<0.02	0.02	99.6	—	<0.01	0.03	<0.02	0.08	0.08	
335	Com.	0.15	0.013	0.02	96.3	3.40	—	0.08	0.03	0.04	0.05	
435	Com.	0.12	<0.02	0.04	98.6	<0.01	—	0.05	0.85	0.15	0.16	
535	Com.	0.006	0.016	0.06	95.2	—	<0.01	2.20	1.75	0.08	1.38	
635	Com.	0.18	0.004	0.04	97.3	1.34	—	0.03	0.95	—	0.10	

* NBS = National Bureau of Standards; Com. = Commercial Analyst.

† Dash means element not present in detectable amounts.

Table 8.5

Estimated Accuracies of X-Ray Fluorescence Analyses of Coins

Approximate Concn. (wt. %)	Fe	Co	Ni	Cu	Zn	As	Ag	Sn	Sb	Pb
100	—*	—	—	1†	—	—	—	—	—	—
10	—	—	—	—	5	—	2.5	2.5	—	10
1	5	—	3	—	5	10	10	10	10	10
0.1	20	10	10	—	20	50	35	25	25	20
0.01	100§	20	35	—	100	>100	>100	50	50	>100

* A dash means that this element is never found at this concentration level in Roman copper-based coins.

† Estimated accuracy: twice standard deviation expressed as parts per hundred.

§ 100 = limit of detection.

these standards have been used in addition to pure metals. Six additional standards were prepared by melting and re-melting alloys having approximately the same compositions as certain coins. These standards were analyzed by three commercial firms and then were used in this work. Table 8.4 contains the compositions of all the standards used in this work. In most cases these standards are satisfactory for calculating the contents of important elements in ancient coins. Inter-element effects on absorption or emission, such as the increased counting rate of nickel in the presence of zinc, are included in the calculations for the determinations of various elements.

Undoubtedly better standards (closer in composition to the coins studied) would enable an improvement in accuracy of some determinations such as As and Sb. Present estimates of accuracy take the standards into account as well as background, surface preparation, and homogeneity. (Surface depletion and inhomogeneity reduce the accuracies of lead and zinc determinations respectively when these elements are present in concentrations above 5 percent.) Estimated accuracies appear in Table 8.5.

Coins Minted in Rome

Thirty to thirty-two coins analyzed in this study were minted in Rome from about 23 B.C. to A.D. 37 (see Table 8.6). These coins may be separated into at least ten compositional groups:

A. Coins R-281, 257, 259; 23 B.C.; features: moderately high Fe, high Ni, high Ag, moderate Sn, high Sb, high Pb.[1]

B. Coins R-262, 78, 261; 23 to 17 B.C.; features: high Fe, very low Ni, high Zn, high Ag in two coins, high Sn in one coin, low Sb in two coins, high Pb in one coin.

C. Coins R-298 and R-297; ca. 13 B.C.; features: moderate Fe, moderate Sn, low Sb, moderate Pb.

D. Coins R-253 and 254; ca. 13 B.C.; features: moderately high Fe, low Sn, low Sb.

E. Coin R-600; ca. 13 B.C.; features: unusually high Fe, high Co, moderately high Ni, high Pb.

F. Coin R-80; ca. 5 B.C.; features: no Ni, low Ag, low Sn, average Sb and Pb.

G. Coins R-245 and 258; ca. A.D. 15–16; features: no Ni, low Ag, low Sn, no or low Sb, no Pb.

H. Coins R-299, 60, 249, 250, 251, 605, 252, 96; A.D. 22–28; features: variable (low to moderate) Fe, Co, very high Ni, low Ag, low Sn, no Sb except possibly in one coin, no Pb in most coins.

I. Coins R-97, 256, 79, 260, 518, 606, 95, and 63; A.D. 34–37; features: variable (low to high) Fe, no Co, no Ni, moderate Ag, very low Sn, moderate Sb, moderate Pb.

J. Coins R-476 and 516; imitations—probably dating from A.D. 30 to 45; features: very low Fe, no Co, no Ni, low to very low Sn, Sb, and Pb.

Not all of the categories are proved as compositional groups since some "groups" contain only one or two coins. Others, such as Group B, include specimens having somewhat different compositions, and further analyses may show three or more groups for coins placed in B. However, it is noteworthy that most coins tend to fall into well-defined compositional groups. For instance, three coins in Group A have similar and unique compositions. High Ag, Ni, and Sb are typical of these early coins. Group B is unusual in its low Ni contents and the relatively high Ag contents of two coins in Group B indicates a close relationship to the early coins in Group A. Groups C and D are unusual in that these are the purest Roman copper coins prepared until this time. It is rather surprising that R-254 and R-297, both having the same catalog number, fall into two slightly different groups.

Coin R-600 is unique in its high Fe content—this is probably a contaminant. It also has high Co and the highest Pb content of any coin minted in Rome and

[1]Note: throughout this chapter the terms "high," "moderate," or "low" are relative to the average concentrations of elements in coins minted in Rome between 23 B.C. and A.D. 37.

Table 8.6
Compositions of
Coins Minted in
Rome

Coin No.	Date	Fe*	Co	Ni	Cu	Zn	As	Ag	Sn	Sb	Pb	Arbitrary Composition Group
	B.C.											
R-281	23	0.18	N†	0.24	98.7	0.01	0.02	0.12	0.07	0.25	0.12	A
R-257	23	0.16	N	0.20	98.8	N	0.05	0.13	0.015	0.35	N§	A
R-259	23	0.24	N	0.22	98.4	N	0.03	0.27	0.03	0.51	0.15	A
R-262	23–17	0.15	N	0.005	81.8	17.5	N	0.07	0.02	0.01	0.06	B
R-78	21	0.38	N	0.015	78.8	21.1	N	0.18	0.03	0.08	0.12	B
R-261	17	0.33	0.005	0.02	81.7	17.2	0.15	0.12	0.15	0.015	N§	B
R-298	ca. 13	0.07	N	0.04	99.4	N	0.03	0.08	0.06	0.01	0.03	C
R-297	ca. 13	0.085	N	0.07	99.3	N	0.02	0.09	0.05	0.015	0.08	C
R-254	ca. 13	0.19	N	0.025	99.4	N	N	0.06	0.015	0.01	N	D
R-253	ca. 13	0.11	0.005	0.06	99.4	N	0.02	0.07	0.015	0.015	0.05	D
	B.C.											
R-600		1.48	0.03	0.10	97.9	0.04	0.03	0.08	0.03	0.015	0.19	E
R-80	ca. 5	0.05	N	N	99.6	N	N	0.04	0.01	0.03	0.04	F
R-516	?	0.005	N	N	99.4	0.13	0.02	0.07	0.02	0.01	0.02	J
	A.D.											
R-245	ca. 15–16	0.065	N	N	99.6	N	N	0.03	0.015	N	N	G
R-258	ca. 15–16	0.12	N	N	99.5	N	0.03	0.03	0.01	0.01	N	G
R-299	22–3	0.24	0.025	0.32	99.0	N	0.03	0.04	0.04	N	0.02	H
R-60	22–3	0.09	0.015	0.28	99.3	N	N	0.01	0.01	N	N	H
R-249	22–3	0.015	0.005	0.28	99.4	N	N	0.03	0.01	N	N	H
R-250	22–3	0.03	0.01	0.28	99.3	N	N	0.03	0.015	N	N	H
R-251	22–3	0.03	0.005	0.25	99.4	N	N	0.01	0.01	N	N	H
R-605	22–8	0.10	0.01	0.30	99.3	N	N	0.03	0.015	0.01	0.04	H
R-252	22–8	0.03	0.025	0.31	99.3	N	N	0.04	0.01	N	0.02	H
R-96	22–8	0.085	0.015	0.27	99.3	N	N	0.02	0.01	N	N	H
R-476	?	T‡	N	N	99.7	N	0.04	0.08	0.04	0.03	0.01	J
	A.D.											
R-97	34–5	0.25	N	N	99.3	N	N	0.06	0.01	0.03	0.06	I
R-256	34–6	0.12	N	N	99.4	N	0.02	0.05	0.01	0.08	0.05	I
R-79	ca. 34–7	0.22	N	N	99.3	N	N	0.09	0.01	0.03	0.05	I
R-260	ca. 34–7	0.08	N	N	99.4	N	N	0.09	0.01	0.04	0.11	I
R-518	ca. 34–7	0.085	N	N	99.4	N	0.03	0.09	0.02	0.06	0.03	I
R-606	ca. 34–7	0.08	N	N	94.4	N	N	0.09	0.015	0.08	0.07	I
R-95	ca. 34–7	0.03	N	N	99.5	N	0.02	0.05	0.01	0.04	0.06	I
R-63	ca. 34–7	0.14	N	N	99.3	N	0.02	0.07	0.01	0.06	0.08	I

* All determinations are percent by weight.

† N = None detected: usually less than 0.005%.

§ Corrected for As concentration.

‡ = Trace detected: less than 0.01%.

analyzed in this study. Coin R-80 starts a long unique period from 5 B.C. to A.D. 37 in which no Ni was detected in the coins except for the period from A.D. 22 to 28 when an unusually high Ni content is present. Coin R-80 is different from Group G, coins minted in about A.D. 15–16, only in having average Sb and Pb whereas group G coins have little or no Sb and Pb present.

Group H is truly remarkable in that all eight coins have very high Ni and some Co. Nearly all these coins contain very little Sn, Sb, and Pb. There is no doubt that all these coins belong to the same period of time. The British Museum Catalog lists some of these coins as undated, but Sutherland later dated them from A.D. 22 to 28 because of die links found with coins known to have been minted in this period (Reference 12). Obviously the ore was from a different source during A.D. 22 to 28 than at any other period. Why this should be so can perhaps be explained by historians. It certainly was a period of intrigue, but that can be said of most of Roman history.

Group I coins, minted from A.D. 34 to 37, also have no Ni present. This is most definitely a distinct compositional group. The low Sn and moderate Ag, Sb, and Pb are characteristic of this group.

Group J consists of two coins that are known as "imitations". These are coins having inferior workmanship to the ones minted in Rome. It is not known where they were minted nor by whom. The imitations reached their peak during the reign of Claudius in about A.D. 41–45. It is possible that the two imitations in Group J were also minted in this period. It is most interesting that coin R-476, which is an imitation of R-605, has a composition which indicates it was made at a different period and/or place from R-605 and the others in Group H.

Further analyses of coins, particularly those minted from 17 to 13 and 7 to 4 B.C., should differentiate additional compositional groups. Coins minted in different periods of time in the early Empire do indeed have identifiably different compositions from each other. It is concluded from the above results that X-ray fluorescence is an extremely useful tool for obtaining compositional data on large numbers of ancient coins.

The densities of 27 copper coins minted in Rome vary from 8.85 to 8.96 g/cm³ compared with a density of 8.96 g/cm³ for pure Cu. These measurements show that the coins are not porous. The densities of the three brass coins vary from 8.58 to 8.62 g/cm³, well below the range of densities of pure copper coins.

Coins Minted in Lugdunum

Lugdunum, which is now Lyons, France, was a mint of special importance to the first several Roman emperors. At Lugdunum large quantities of silver and gold coins were produced, and these were made under the specific control of the emperor. It has been disputed how much the emperor controlled the Roman copper coinage as opposed to control by the Roman senate.

The Lugdunum coins of this study are moderately different in style from each other. Therefore it is not surprising that the compositions vary moderately (see Table 8.7). Seven of the coins were minted in about 10 to 6 B.C. Coin R-94 has a composition different from all the others and similar to that of Group A minted in Rome: high Sb, Ni, and Ag and moderately high Sn and Pb contents compared with coins minted in Rome. In general the early Lugdunum coins had high but varying contents of Sb. Silver tends to be higher than found in coins minted during the lifetime of Christ. Lead and tin contents are nearly always higher than found in coins minted in Rome at the same time.

Coins R-517, 255, and 233 are similar enough in composition to be classified in the same group. Coins R-171 and 179 are very similar in composition. Coin R-602 is somewhat similar to R-171 and 179. Apparently there are at least three and possibly more distinct compositional groups of Lugdunum coins minted in *ca.* 10 to 6 B.C.

Table 8.7
Compositions of Coins Minted in Lugdunum

Coin No.	Date	Fe	Co	Ni	Cu	Zn	As	Ag	Sn	Sb	Pb
	B.C.										
R-94	10–6	0.10	N	0.13	98.3	N	0.02	0.20	0.13	0.70	0.10
R-517	10–6	0.02	N	0.03	99.0	N	N	0.09	0.27	0.23	0.06
R-255	10–6	0.04	N	0.015	99.0	N	0.05	0.08	0.23	0.19	0.02*
R-233	10–6	0.025	N	0.03	98.9	N	N	0.04	0.24	0.31	0.08
R-171	10–6	0.045	N	0.015	99.0	N	0.04	0.09	0.07	0.31	0.14
R-179	10–6	0.08	N	0.01	99.0	N	0.07	0.09	0.09	0.30	0.04*
R-602	10–6	0.03	N	0.035	99.2	N	N	0.06	0.04	0.17	0.15
	A.D.										
R-604	12–14	T	N	N	99.5	0.01	0.03	0.07	0.01	0.04	0.08
R-603	12–14	N	N	0.015	96.3	0.01	N	0.04	3.3	0.01	0.08
R-81	12–14	0.36	T	0.08	84.9	14.1	N	0.02	0.13	0.005	0.05

Compositions of Some Copper-Based Coins of Augustus and Tiberius

* Corrected for As (perhaps overcorrected).

Lugdunum coins minted in A.D. 12–14 are different from the earlier ones. R-604 is similar in composition to R-80, minted in Rome in *ca.* 5 B.C. R-603 is remarkable because it is the only Lugdunum coin containing high tin (3.3 percent). Otherwise this coin is similar to R-604. The R-81, an orichalcum coin, would be expected to have a relatively high Fe content, as almost all orichalcum coins do. Its Zn content is significantly lower than that of coins minted in Rome at about the same time (see also Reference 2). Its Ni content is higher than in most Lugdunum coins.

The densities of coins minted in Lugdunum on the average are slightly lower than those of coins made in Rome. In Lugdunum, as in Rome, copper coins of this period were made of essentially pure copper (>99 percent pure). Lugdunum is the only mint outside of Rome for which this is true. Obviously the compositions of coins minted at various places were controlled by at least general directives from Rome.

Coins Minted in Nemausus

Nemausus was another notable Gallic mint. From it came a great series having both Agrippa and Augustus face to face on the obverse with a crocodile chained to a tree on the reverse. These coins vary considerably in style and skill of manufacture.

All four coins are notable for their very low Fe (typical of Republican copper-based coins), high As, high Ag with little variation, high Sb, very high Sn, and generally high Pb (Table 8.8). Coins R-170 and 424 are similar in composition, whereas the other two coins are somewhat different. The densities reflect the ratio of tin to lead in these coins.

Some numismatists have argued that these coins were struck at Nemausus long after the death of Agrippa in 12 B.C. and even into the Christian era. However, the compositions (especially the relatively high Ag concentrations) of these four coins point to an early period for their manufacture—a date prior to 20 B.C. and most likely no later than Agrippa's death.

Coin R-601 is interesting in that apparently it is an overstrike of Augustus on the obverse and (probably) Agrippa on the reverse. Both the Sb and the Ag contents are much lower than in the Nemausus coins, while the Co concentration is very high (relatively), which is typical of Republican coins. Hence this coin is probably an earlier Republican coin overstruck by Augustus at an unknown mint.

Coins Minted in Spain

Many Spanish mints produced coins during the early part of the Empire. Almost all the Spanish coins contain several percent Sn (Table 8.9). This is not surprising because Spain was a prime source of Sn in this period. Most of the Spanish coins also contain high Pb, which further distinguishes them compositionally from coins minted in Rome or Lugdunum.

Three of the Spanish coins (R-522, 175, and 172) were probably made relatively early, judging from their high Sb and Ag contents. Both R-175 and 172 also have high Ni—in fact, R-172 has the remarkably high content of 1.0 percent. Those coins having low Sb contents also have

Table 8.8
Compositions of Coins Minted in Nemausus

Coin No.	Date	Fe	Co	Ni	Cu	Zn	As	Ag	Sn	Sb	Pb
R-170	After 27 B.C.	0.015	N	0.18	82.0	N	0.18	0.27	7.8	0.84	8.5
R-424	After 27 B.C.	0.02	N	0.12	82.3	N	0.15	0.30	10.6	1.1	5.0
R-178	After 27 B.C.	0.015	0.005	0.015	88.5	N	0.23	0.28	8.9	0.80	1.0
R-234	After 27 B.C.	0.005	N	0.02	87.5	N	0.05	0.31	6.4	0.53	4.9
R-601*	?	0.085	0.06	0.075	86.9	N	0.11	0.14	6.8	0.14	5.5

* Mint unknown

Table 8.9
Compositions of Coins Minted in Spain

Coin No.	Date	Fe	Co	Ni	Cu	Zn	As	Ag	Sn	Sb	Pb
	B.C.										
R-522	?	0.21	N	0.04	77.8	N	N	0.39	9.5	0.74	11.1
R-175	6	0.08	N	0.22	81.4	N	0.02	0.17	5.5	0.53	11.8
R-172	?	N	N	1.1	88.9	N	0.22	0.49	0.58	2.4	6.2
R-520	?	0.03	N	0.06	83.8	N	N	0.10	11.6	0.08	4.1
R-173	?	0.015	N	N	78.1	N	N	0.05	7.3	0.03	14.2
R-174	?	T	N	N	84.9	N	0.04	0.03	1.8	0.01	13.0
	A.D.										
R-521	14–37	0.025	N	N	92.1	N	0.03	0.10	7.2	0.09	0.15
R-280	14–37	0.005	N	N	77.0	N	0.03	0.10	7.3	0.04	15.2
R-523	14–37	0.01	N	N	90.5	N	0.05	0.10	6.9	0.09	2.1

low Ag. The absence of Ni and the low Ag and Sb in coins R-173 and 174 indicate that these coins were made later than the others, possibly in the era A.D. if one assumes that compositions of colonial coins parallel somewhat the compositions of coins made in Rome.

All three Spanish coins of Tiberius have moderately low Sb and moderately high Ag contents. As in coins minted in Rome, Ni is undetectable. Also, Fe is very low. All three coins are very similar except for their Pb concentrations, which vary greatly.

The R-280 is very similar to R-173, and R-523 is close to R-520. These similarities add further evidence that R-173, 520, and 174 were likely made after the birth of Christ. However, these coins were made in different mints, but this does not preclude identical sources of ores or perhaps even metal.

Many more Spanish coins must be analyzed before compositional groups can be established and correlated with both time and places of origin of the metals. X-Ray fluorescence should be a powerful tool in carrying out the needed investigations, which will probably add greatly to the information presently known about Roman coins minted in Spain.

Coins Minted in Greece

Only four colonial Greek coins were analyzed. None of these is similar to the others in composition (Table 8.10), and they are different from the coins discussed above. Coin R-126 is noteworthy because it is made of orichalcum, Roman brass. However, Sn and Pb are substituted for some of the zinc. The Fe is high as in most orichalcum coins. Coin R-526 is fairly pure since it only contains a total of about 1 percent Sn and Pb. It is the

purest coin in the present group minted outside of Rome and Lugdunum. Coin R-527 contains high Sb and moderately high Ag as well as several percent Zn. Also, it is high in both Sn and Pb. Coin R-528 contains a very high concentration of Pb and high Sn. The small amount of Zn may indicate a few brass coins or objects remelted in the batch of metal from which this coin was made.

Coin R-180 has high As, Ni, and Co as well as moderately high Sn and Pb (Table 8.10). Coin R-279 has very high Co, low Ni and Sb, and moderately low Pb. The only other Roman coins having as high Co as R-279 are early Republican coins. Perhaps there was a common ore source for the Republican coins and this coin. Republican coins probably were not melted down to make this coin because of the low Pb content.

The two Commagene coins are nearly the same in composition for the elements Sb, Sn, Ag, As, Zn, Co, and Fe; Coin R-458 contains relatively much more Pb and a little more Ni than R-459. It is interesting that the Ni contents of these Commagene coins, minted in A.D. 20–21, were much lower than in coins minted in Rome in A.D. 22–28.

Six coins minted in Antioch during the reigns of Augustus and Tiberius have very similar compositions (Table 8.11). These coins are essentially pure alloys of bronze (Cu-Sn). The very low Ni is typical of coins minted in Rome at this same time. The Sb and Pb are low or moderately low. Almost all Roman coins minted after A.D. 50 have higher Sb and Pb contents, as shown in other work (Reference 6).

This series of Cu coins minted at Antioch was very special. These coins were unique among coins minted outside of Rome in

Coins Minted in Miscellaneous Mints in the Near East

Coins Minted in Antioch

Table 8.10 Compositions of Coins Minted in Greece and the Near East

Coin No.	Date	Fe	Co	Ni	Cu	Zn	As	Ag	Sn	Sb	Pb
R-126	27 B.C.–A.D. 14	0.36	N	0.03	84.7	9.2	0.04	0.09	4.1	0.10	1.0
R-526	?	0.025	0.01	0.01	98.4	N	N	0.08	0.61	0.06	0.49
R-527	?	0.06	0.005	0.04	80.7	3.6	0.07	0.12	7.2	0.32	7.5
R-528	?	0.09	N	0.03	74.6	0.19	N	0.10	6.4	0.08	18.2
R-180	27 B.C.–A.D. 14	0.11	0.04	0.18	85.8	N	0.19	0.08	8.3	0.12	4.8
R-279	23 B.C.	0.04	0.10	0.01	92.6	N	0.10	0.08	6.6	0.015	0.11
R-458	20–1 A.D.	0.03	0.005	0.04	88.4	0.015	0.05	0.13	8.6	0.07	2.3
R-459	20–1 A.D.	0.005	N	N	89.8	N	0.05	0.15	9.6	0.03	0.06

Table 8.11 Compositions of Coins Minted in Antioch

Coin No.	Date	Fe	Co	Ni	Cu	Zn	As	Ag	Sn	Sb	Pb
R-534	23 B.C.–A.D. 14	0.005	N	T	91.8	N	0.03	0.06	7.7	0.03	0.09
R-530	?	0.01	N	N	90.0	N	N	0.11	9.6	0.03	0.07
R-525	A.D. 14–37	0.07	N	N	88.6	N	0.09	0.10	10.8	0.02	0.01*
R-536	A.D. 14–37	0.015	N	T	90.6	N	0.02	0.07	8.8	0.05	0.21
R-316	A.D. 33	0.01	N	0.01	91.2	N	0.06	0.09	8.2	0.05	0.02*
R-460	A.D. 33	0.02	N	N	91.7	N	N	0.10	8.8	0.02	0.08

* Corrected (perhaps overcorrected) for As.

that the reverse contains a large "SC," probably for *Senatus Consulto,* "by consent of the senate." Furthermore this series is unique in its longevity, for coins of this general type were minted at Antioch for over 200 years! The legends were in Latin until nearly A.D. 100. This was about the only eastern mint that did not use Greek legends.

Obviously Antioch was a mint of special importance to the emperor. This is reflected in the composition of the coins. Very likely there was a directive made by Augustus and continued by Tiberius to make these coins of a special alloy—a pure bronze of Cu and Sn only.

Conclusions

The above analyses are even more meaningful when they are placed in the context of compositions of copper-based Roman coins minted from 200 B.C. to A.D. 400. For instance, the extremely low Sb, Sn, Pb, and Ni are unique to the period of 20 B.C. to A.D. 37; the relatively high Ni is also unique to coins of 23 B.C. and to A.D. 22–28. The high purity of Cu coins is unique to the early Empire. The concentrations of Zn in orichalcum coins decrease in the time of Vespasian, never again to equal the high concentrations of the first 100 years of the empire.

Republican Cu coins were crude in style and impure. Augustus instituted radical changes in the styles, compositions, denominations, and policies of Roman coinage. These changes were all improvements. The coinage of Augustus must have given his regime a strong political lift because the people undoubtedly associated the improved coinage with the new government. Augustus' coinage helped create a favorable image for the newly formed Empire.

To Augustus and Tiberius, Lugdunum was the most important mint outside of Rome. Pure Cu coins were struck there, but the types were severely limited. Of all the other colonial mints, Antioch seems to have been the next most important one in the Empire. Here pure bronze coins of uniform composition were struck under both Augustus and Tiberius. All other colonial mints were probably instructed to strike coins using alloys of Cu, Sn, and Pb, but apparently the directives to these mints did not further specify compositions. In the colonies minting procedures were somewhat different from those in Rome.

The results reported above show that X-ray fluorescence is a most important method for analyzing ancient coins essentially nondestructively. The compositions of coins definitely may be correlated with time and mints; since coinage in the early Roman Empire was sporadic, individual groups of coins minted in 1 to 6 year periods indeed do have similar compositions and each group has a unique composition.

Contrary to the "SC" on the reverse of most copper-based coins minted in Rome, it was probably not the senate but rather the emperor who decided policies for the coinage of copper-based money. Very likely the senate was incapable of formulating such a brilliant system of copper-based coins. This system must be due to the genius and boldness of Augustus. Special mints and consistent, but different, compositions in mints of key importance indicate that the emperor was interested in copper coinage to the extent of specifying different compositions for the key mints.

The historical and numismatic implications of the above results will largely be left to archaeologists, historians, and numismatists. It is hoped that archaeologists and numismatists who have special problems to study and who have access to the supplies of coins needed for such studies will seek out the assistance of those who are able to analyze coins by X-ray fluorescence. Only after many of the vast number of ancient coins in existence today have been analyzed will the most useful information be disclosed in the study of ancient coins.

References

1.
Caley, E. R.

Analysis of Ancient Metals. Macmillan Co.,
New York, 1964.

2.
Caley, E. R.

"Orichalcum and Related Ancient Alloys,"
Amer. Numismatic Soc., New York, 1964.

3.
Carter, G. F.

Anal. Chem., **36,** 1264, 1964.

4.
Carter, G. F.

Archaeometry, **7,** 106, 1964.

5.
Carter, G. F.

Science, **151,** 196, 1966.

6.
Carter, G. F.

Chemistry, **39,** 14, Nov. 1966.

7.
Hall, E. T.

Archaeometry, **3,** 29, 1960.

8.
Hall, E. T.

Archaeometry, **4,** 62, 1961.

9.
Hall, E. T.

Endeavour, **18,** 83, 1959.

10.
Hall, E. T.

Recent Advances in Conservation, Butterworths, London, 1961, pp. 29–32.

11.
Liebhafsky, H. A.,
Pfeiffer, H. G.,
Winslow, E. H.,
and Zemany, P. D.

*X-Ray Absorption and Emission in Analyti-
cal Chemistry*, John Wiley & Sons, Inc.,
New York, 1960.

12.
Sutherland, C. H. V.

Coinage in Roman Imperial Policy—31
B.C. *to 68* A.D., Methuen & Co., Ltd.,
London, 1951.

Chapter 9

Trace Impurity Patterns in Copper Ores and Artifacts[1]

P. R. Fields, J. Milsted, E. Henrickson,[2] and R. Ramette[2]
Chemistry Division, Argonne National Laboratory

Copper, one of the earliest metals worked into tools, housewares, and the implements of war, undoubtedly played an important role in the ancient history of civilization. It is intriguing to ask whether the early artisans obtained their copper locally or by trading with distant suppliers and how the smelting and alloying techniques developed with time. If copper artifacts could be traced to their sources, ancient trade routes might be identified. One method of accomplishing this might be to determine the trace impurity patterns (or "fingerprint") present in a copper artifact from a known source and compare it with the impurity patterns in different copper sources. Several workers (References 2 and 5) have shown that such a technique should be applicable. Four different analytical approaches for determining the impurity "fingerprint" of copper ores and artifacts have been investigated. The techniques and their applications to various archaeological problems are reported in this paper.

Emission Spectroscopy

The first method investigated was high sensitivity optical spectroscopy. Approximately 350 ore samples from various parts of the world and 100 artifacts were analyzed. In addition, many of the ores were reduced to metallic copper by a primitive method (heating with carbon), and the resulting metal was also analyzed. The smelting approach not only revealed which impurities were the best indicators of the original ore type and were likely to be reliable tracers but also supported the contention that there was a relationship between the impurities in an artifact and those in the original ore.

The copper ores were divided into three groups depending on the type of chemical reaction required to produce metallic copper: (a) Naturally-occurring metallic copper (native copper), (b) "Oxidized ores" consisting of oxygen-bearing compounds of copper, such as oxides, and carbonates, and (c) "Reduced ores" consisting of sulfides and sulfosalts of copper.

Native copper metal was certainly used directly and was probably the first type of copper to be exploited by primitive people since it required no treatment, except perhaps heating as an aid to fabrication. The oxidized ores such as cuprite and malachite are brightly colored, readily identifiable as copper-bearing material, and easily reduced to copper by primitive means. These were probably the first ores to be converted into metallic copper by

smelting processes. Reduced ores usually require roasting to convert them to oxides before they can be reduced to the metal. They are not so easily identified as copper-bearing ores, and, because they require more elaborate processing, they were probably the last sources of copper to be developed.

From the spectrographic analyses of the metal produced by reducing various ores, it was found that silver, arsenic, bismuth, iron, antimony, and lead were the most abundant metallic impurities with tin and gold occasionally present in both the smelts and the ore from which it was derived. A relatively large fraction of these metal impurities (30–80 percent) is transferred from the ore to the metallic copper during the reduction process.

As a basis for comparison with the analyses of artifacts, probability distributions were calculated for each of these impurities in each of the three ore types. Tables 9.1, 9.2, 9.3, and 9.4 show these distributions for oxidized ores and smelts, reduced ores and smelts, native copper from Michigan, and native copper from other sources. In these Tables the following logarithmic concentration ranges were used:

Range Number	Concentration Range (percent)
1	100–3
2	3–0.3
3	0.3–0.03
4	0.03–0.003
5	<0.003

These rather broad ranges were dictated by the limited number of samples (~350 ores and smelts) and the large analytical errors. When more samples have been analyzed it may be possible to adopt narrower ranges.

The probability that a given artifact was derived from one or another of these ore types was determined by comparing its analysis with these impurity distributions. For each ore type the probability of observing a concentration of a given element similar to that observed in the artifact was determined from the distribution tables, and the probability that the artifact was derived from this ore type was assumed to be proportional to the product of these probabilities for the eight elements mentioned above. A more complete description of this statistical method is given in Reference 2.

[1] Based on work performed under the auspices of the U.S. Atomic Energy Commission.

[2] Present address; Carleton College, Northfield, Minnesota.

131

Table 9.1 Relative Probability of Occurrence of Impurities in Oxidized Ores and Smelts—Worldwide (135 Samples* measured by emission spectroscopy)

Concentration Range	Elements							
	Silver	Arsenic	Gold	Bismuth	Iron	Lead	Antimony	Tin
1	<0.001	0.007	<0.001	<0.001	0.10	0.01	0.004	<0.001
2	0.02	0.09	0.007	<0.001	0.25	0.04	0.01	<0.001
3	0.13	0.16	<0.001	0.02	0.20	0.19	0.03	<0.001
4	0.20	0.21	0.007	0.11	0.27	0.26	0.06	0.06
5	0.65	0.52	0.99	0.86	0.19	0.50	0.90	0.94

* 33 malachites; 22 cuprites; 15 chalcanthites; 42 azurites; 8 chrysocollas; 5 brochantites; and 10 all others.

Table 9.2 Relative Probability of Occurrence of Impurities in Reduced Ores and Smelts—Worldwide (50 Samples* measured by emission spectroscopy)

Concentration Range	Elements							
	Silver	Arsenic	Gold	Bismuth	Iron	Lead	Antimony	Tin
1	<0.001	0.02	<0.001	0.01	0.16	0.04	<0.001	<0.001
2	0.08	0.08	<0.001	0.03	0.30	0.04	0.04	0.02
3	0.52	0.16	<0.001	0.04	0.34	0.14	0.06	0.04
4	0.23	0.14	0.02	0.16	0.15	0.16	0.11	0.15
5	0.17	0.60	0.98	0.76	0.05	0.62	0.79	0.79

* 9 covellite samples and 41 chalcocite samples.

Table 9.3 Relative Probability of Occurrence of Impurities in Native Copper—Northern Michigan (82 Samples measured by emission spectroscopy)

Concentration Range	Elements							
	Silver	Arsenic	Gold	Bismuth	Iron	Lead	Antimony	Tin
1	<0.001	0.02	<0.001	<0.001	<0.001	<0.001	<0.001	<0.001
2	0.04	0.01	<0.001	<0.001	0.04	<0.001	<0.001	<0.001
3	0.59	0.10	<0.001	<0.001	0.11	<0.001	<0.001	<0.001
4	0.28	0.18	0.006	<0.001	0.48	<0.001	0.01	<0.001
5	0.10	0.69	0.99	1.00	0.37	1.00	0.99	1.00

Table 9.4 Relative Probability of Occurrence of Impurities in Native Copper—All Other Sources besides Northern Michigan (30 Samples measured by emission spectroscopy)

Concentration Range	Elements							
	Silver	Arsenic	Gold	Bismuth	Iron	Lead	Antimony	Tin
1	<0.001	<0.001	<0.001	<0.001	<0.001	<0.001	<0.001	<0.001
2	<0.001	<0.001	<0.001	<0.001	<0.001	<0.001	<0.001	<0.001
3	0.23	0.10	<0.001	<0.001	0.13	<0.001	<0.001	<0.001
4	0.38	0.20	<0.001	<0.001	0.42	<0.001	<0.001	<0.001
5	0.38	0.70	1.00	1.00	0.45	1.00	1.00	1.00

The spectroscopic analyses of ores, smelts, and artifacts already obtained indicate that significant correlations of artifacts with broad ore types can be observed by this method. However, the sensitivity and accuracy of the method appear to be inadequate for more specific correlations, such as the geographical origin of the ore from which a given artifact was derived.

Neutron Activation

From the results of emission spectroscopy, it was obvious, particularly for samples of native copper, that most metal impurities were present at levels below the spectroscopic detection limit. Because the success of the "fingerprint" concept depends on the number of impurities determined, neutron activation was explored. The principles of this method have repeatedly been explained in the literature (References 1, 3, 4, and 7) and will not be discussed here. Basically, the technique consists of irradiating a small sample of copper with thermal neutrons in a reactor, in this case the Argonne CP-5 reactor, for a few days, in which time nearly all impurities are partially converted to radioactive isotopes. The sample is allowed to decay for two weeks, and the emitted gamma radiation is then examined with a lithium-drifted germanium detector and a multichannel analyzer to identify and quantify the impurities present. The capabilities of this method are much broader than emission spectroscopy; both very high and very low concentrations of an impurity can be measured accurately.

Since neutron activation is a much more precise and sensitive technique than emission spectroscopy, the method will be described in greater detail and some of its limitations pointed out in the discussion which follows.

The Sample

Since samples vary in quantity, type, and composition, in some cases being metallic artifacts, various ores, or even such unusual samples as petrified trees, it is necessary to select a known portion in order to obtain quantitative results. Usually samples are obtained by drilling small holes into the specimen and collecting the chips that result. Other techniques can be used, such as scraping, or, in the case of ores that are usually abundant, chipping off a portion of the material. Experience has shown that drilling is a reliable technique and can even be done unobtrusively on a valuable museum object without noticeably damaging it in any way. Furthermore, tests have demonstrated that the drilling process does not introduce any apparent metallic impurities.

One of the good features of neutron activation analysis is that very small samples often suffice. To detect the more sensitive impurities at the parts per billion level only about 50 milligrams of sample are needed, although 1 mg samples can be used with loss of sensitivity and accuracy. A very small object might even be irradiated whole, and subsequently returned to the owner if he were willing to accept the presence of low-level, long-lived radioactivity in the object.

With geological specimens of large size, it is possible to drill at several locations, making a sample which is reasonably representative of the whole specimen. In dealing with artifacts and minute samples, however, it must be recognized that the trace impurities found may not give a fair picture of the specimen.

The Irradiation

The weighed samples are sealed in small quartz tubes which are placed in an aluminum can designed for insertion in the reactor. At the same time, other quartz tubes are included with known (microgram) quantities of elements (those which are expected as impurities in the samples) serving as standards. In this way one can avoid uncertainties caused by the composition of the neutron flux, precise location in the reactor, length of irradiation, etc. After three days, the tubes are removed from the reactor and allowed to decay for two weeks until they are ready for measurement.

The first major problem in this neutron activation analysis is that the copper matrix is inescapably included in the irradiation because it is not reasonable to separate the metal impurities first. Not only would there be uncertainty as to the

efficient separation of all desired impurities, but there would be the risk of gross contamination from impurities in the chemical reagents and also the need for extensive sample processing before it could be made ready for irradiation. Therefore, essentially the entire metallic content of the sample consists of copper, which is 69 percent ^{63}Cu and 31 percent ^{65}Cu. Both of these isotopes readily absorb neutrons, to become ^{64}Cu and ^{66}Cu, respectively, and typically the resultant gamma radiation from a sample is extremely high and hazardous upon removal from the reactor. Unfortunately, this precludes the immediate examination of the sample. The ^{66}Cu has a half-life of only 5.1 minutes and does not interfere after several hours of decay. However, a small amount of ^{67}Cu is formed by capturing two successive neutrons and its 61-hour half-life gives a persistent peak in the gamma spectrum. More serious is the high concentration of ^{64}Cu formed in the irradiation, because this isotope decays with a 12.9-hour half-life, and thus requires a lapse of about two weeks after irradiation before samples can be measured. In this time, trace impurities which form radioactive isotopes of relatively short half-life become undetectable through decay. Hence, neutron activation analysis for impurities in copper is limited to those which (a) have a large neutron cross section for the absorption of neutrons, (b) absorb neutrons to produce isotopes which are gamma emitters, and (c) yield gamma emitters which have half-lives of the order of two to three days or longer. As might be expected, these requirements decrease the number of elements which can be detected at trace levels.

Two other limitations should be mentioned, because they are peculiar to the irradiation of a copper matrix. First, during irradiation there is a buildup of ^{64}Cu which simultaneously decays by beta particle emission to form the stable isotope, ^{64}Zn. This in turn undergoes neutron capture, so that measurable amounts of ^{65}Zn, a long-lived gamma emitter, are formed. The higher the neutron flux, and the longer the irradiation the more serious this contamination becomes. The ^{65}Zn formed by this path is indistinguishable from the ^{65}Zn formed by the irradiation of whatever zinc might have been present in the original sample as a normal impurity. Under the conditions used (neutron flux about 5×10^{13}, three days of irradiation), the active zinc produced is equivalent to an impurity level of about 10 parts per million; hence we have an unfortunately high lower limit for the determination of zinc as an impurity.

The second special limitation arises because at any position in the reactor there will be some concentration of high-energy (fast) neutrons in the flux. Depending on

133

the neutron energy distribution, there will be more or less production of ^{60}Co by the process of capture by ^{63}Cu of a fast neutron, followed immediately by emission of an alpha particle. The ^{60}Co produced in this fashion is indistinguishable from that formed by thermal neutron capture by ordinary ^{59}Co present as an impurity. This problem can be minimized by selecting a location in the reactor which has a small fast neutron flux with a relatively high thermal flux. In the irradiation facilities available at the CP-5 reactor, the ^{60}Co contamination was kept down to the equivalent of a few parts per billion of impurity.

The Trace Impurities

Neutron absorption by the impurities proceeds independently of the matrix problems, and the production of radioactive isotopes during irradiation depends on several factors. First, of course, the quantity of active isotopes produced will be directly proportional to the quantity of impurity present in the sample.. At some point, depending on many factors, a given impurity will escape detection because its slight radioactivity is concealed by background interferences as will be shown later.

Second, the fraction of impurity which is activated will depend directly on the isotopic composition of the element. For example, gold occurs in nature entirely as ^{197}Au, and therefore all atoms present are available for conversion to ^{198}Au, a gamma emitter useful for activation analysis. By contrast, iron occurs as a mixture of stable isotopes and only one, ^{58}Fe, produces through neutron capture a long-lived gamma emitter, ^{59}Fe, but only 0.37 percent of iron exists as ^{58}Fe.

Third, the rate at which an isotope absorbs neutrons is dependent upon its nuclear properties, and the neutron capture cross section is a measure of absorption efficiency. A high value for the cross section can offset other limitations in some cases. For example, less than 1 percent of selenium exists as the ^{74}Se isotope. The cross section of ^{74}Se, however, is relatively large (17 barns) and therefore small amounts of selenium can be determined through observation of the ^{75}Se produced during the irradiation.

Fourth, as already mentioned, the long cooling period required for the decay of activated copper eliminates from consideration any elements which form only short half-life isotopes. Gold is an interesting exception. With the 2.7-day half-life of ^{198}Au, the induced activity falls to less than 3 percent of its value in the two-week cooling period. However, gold not only exists entirely as ^{197}Au but also has a very high cross section (98 barns) and therefore remains detectable for a sufficiently long time if it is present to the extent of parts per million or greater.

Fifth, the production of capture products depends both on the intensity of the neutron flux in the reactor and on the time allowed for irradiation. To avoid multiple neutron capture and neutron-alpha reaction, fluxes higher than 5×10^{13} were purposely avoided, and a standard three to four day irradiation period was selected.

Sixth, the number of characteristic gamma rays per disintegration varies considerably for the different radioactive isotopes produced. While this is not a factor governing the production of a radioactive isotope, it is very important in the detection of an isotope.

Finally, when large numbers of samples are to be analyzed it is impractical to carry out time-consuming chemical separations of the activities produced. The composite gamma spectrum of all the impurities in the sample must therefore be examined. It is useless to look for gamma emission of low energy less than 100 keV, for at the low energy end of the spectrum there are overwhelming contributions from both Compton scattering and X-rays. As a consequence, the low-energy gammas resulting from activated isotopes are obscured.

Had the standard sodium iodide crystal been the only gamma ray detector available, the work reported here would not have been attempted. It is only the very high resolution of the lithium-drifted germanium (Ge-Li) detector which allows the identification and counting of many gamma peaks in a single composite spectrum. As an illustration of this point, consider Figure 9.1 which shows the gamma spectrum for ^{110m}Ag as observed by both kinds of detectors. Obviously, many more gamma peaks can be resolved with the Ge-Li detector, and what is true for ^{110m}Ag applies to mixtures of different nuclides. Figure 9.1 also reveals a problem constantly faced in this work: Silver is usually the major impurity and the complicated spectrum of ^{110m}Ag spreads over the entire energy range and contributes heavily to the Compton scattering background.

The Detector and the Gamma Spectrum

Figure 9.2 shows a complete gamma spectrum for a sample of copper from Greece which contains several elements in measurable amounts. The procedure for calculating the amount of an impurity present in a sample consists simply of measuring the total number of counts in the characteristic peak (the counts per minute contained under the peak but above the background) and comparing this value with the value observed for the known quantity of the element in the standard which was simultaneously irradiated.

It is characteristic of all gamma detectors that gamma rays of higher energies are more likely to expend only part of their

9.1
A comparison of Ag[110m] gamma spectrum taken with a sodium iodide and a lithium drifted germanium crystal detector.

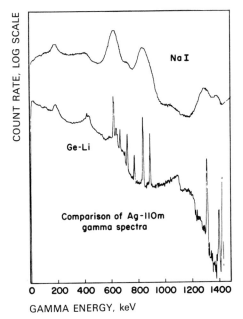

COUNT RATE, LOG SCALE

Na I

Ge-Li

Comparison of Ag-110m gamma spectra

GAMMA ENERGY, keV

9.2
A gamma spectrum of impurities in a copper artifact from Greece after neutron irradiation (Neutron flux = 5 × 10^{13}, time = 3 days, decay time = 2 weeks).

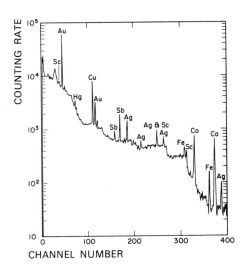

COUNTING RATE

Au
Sc
Cu
Hg
Au
Sb
Ag
Sb
Ag
Ag & Sc
Ag
Sc
Fe
Co
Co
Fe
Ag

CHANNEL NUMBER

energies in the crystal detector. This means that higher energy gammas are characterized by spectra which have relatively small photopeaks and larger Compton continua. Thus, isotopes emitting high-energy gamma rays such as zinc (1117 keV), iron (1290 keV), etc., have low detection efficiencies. With germanium detectors the efficiency of photopeak production is about 100 times smaller at 1000 keV than 100 keV. However, it is also true that the high-energy peaks, though small, appear in a part of the spectrum which is very low in background radiation, whether from cosmic rays or from Compton effects, and elements emitting high energy gamma rays can be determined easily. Therefore, these two effects counterbalance each other. When larger volume germanium crystals are used, the detection efficiency problem will be ameliorated.

Mercury is an important impurity in copper and is determined through the 279 keV gamma of ^{203}Hg. However, when the mercury level is very low, the 279 keV peak is sometimes obscured by the Compton background. In such cases the mercury can be isolated from the rest of the sample and counted separately. The irradiated sample, after composite counting, is placed in a quartz tube and heated to white heat. Mercury distills out and recondenses on the upper, cooler sides of the tube, which is then sealed and separated from the lower part.

Bismuth is the only impurity which is not detected by measuring a characteristic gamma ray. Bismuth, consisting of the single isotope ^{209}Bi, forms ^{210}Bi by neutron capture, which in turn decays to ^{210}Po, a 138-day alpha emitter. The bismuth is then determined by counting the ^{210}Po alpha particles. In three weeks about 95 percent of the ^{210}Bi has decayed into ^{210}Po.

In summary, then, the metal impurities that are determined in copper samples are the following:

1. antimony
2. bismuth
3. cerium
4. cesium
5. chromium
6. cobalt
7. gold
8. hafnium
9. indium
10. iridium
11. iron
12. mercury
13. scandium
14. selenium
15. silver

Table 9.5 lists pertinent nuclear properties and the relative sensitivity for detecting these elements, ignoring the problem of Compton background.

Approximately 350 ores and smelts and 220 artifacts were analyzed by neutron activation analysis. The results will be discussed later in the paper.

Mercury and Bismuth

135

Table 9.5
Relative Sensitivity*
of Detection of
Copper Impurities

Nuclide	Relative Sensitivity	Abundance of Parent Isotope (%)	Cross Section (σ_c barns)	Half-Life ($T_{1/2}$ days)
$_{79}Au^{197}$	1	100	98.8	2.7
$_{77}Ir^{191}$	5.82×10^{-2}	38.5	750	74.2
$_{58}Ce^{140}$	1.60×10^{-3}	88.48	0.6	32.5
$_{80}Hg^{202}$	1.13×10^{-3}	29.80	4	46.9
$_{21}Sc^{45}$	7.28×10^{-4}	100	13	83.9
$_{51}Sb^{123}$	3.41×10^{-4}	42.75	3.3	60.9
$_{72}Hf^{174}$	3.11×10^{-4}	0.163	400	70.0
$_{55}Cs^{133}$	2.84×10^{-4}	100	28	766
$_{34}Se^{74}$	2.80×10^{-4}	0.87	30	121
$_{49}In^{113}$	1.35×10^{-4}	4.23	8	50.0
$_{24}Cr^{50}$	1.05×10^{-4}	4.31	17	27.8
$_{27}Co^{59}$	2.86×10^{-5}	100	19	1910
$_{47}Ag^{109}$	2.25×10^{-5}	48.65	3	253
$_{83}Bi^{209}$	1.41×10^{-5}	100	0.015	138.4
$_{26}Fe^{58}$	1.05×10^{-7}	0.31	1.1	45.1

* Sensitivity factor $= \dfrac{\sigma_c \times \text{branching ratio} \times \text{isotopic abundance} \times \text{detector efficiency}}{T_{1/2}}$

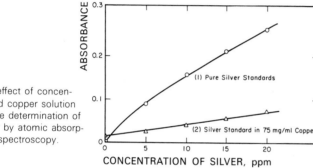

9.3
The effect of concentrated copper solution or the determination of silver by atomic absorption spectroscopy.

Atomic Absorption and Spark Source Mass Spectroscopy

Two other analytical techniques were briefly examined to determine their applicability to the copper problem. These were atomic absorption spectroscopy and spark source mass spectroscopy. The first method, atomic absorption spectroscopy, was investigated because in many samples several important metal impurities such as tin, lead, zinc, nickel, and arsenic were either too low in abundance to be observed by emission spectroscopy, or after neutron activation formed radioactive isotopes that were obscured by other radiations, or possessed too short a half-life to be observed after the two-week decay period. This technique should have been capable of detecting impurities in the range of parts per million or even lower, but various interferences were encountered which made it difficult to obtain reliable results.

Atomic absorption spectroscopy is a fairly simple technique in which an aqueous solution containing the material to be analyzed is aspirated into a hot flame where the atoms of solute are dispersed and partially dissociated. Light from a hollow cathode lamp containing one or more elements is passed through a monochromator and the characteristic line for a given element is selected and passed through the flame. If some of the atoms

in the flame are of the same species as the atoms excited in the lamp, they will absorb the characteristic wavelength light. The absorbance of light is calibrated with standard solutions and the concentration of an element in the aqueous solution is then determined by the absorption of a given frequency of light as compared to the known absorbance by a standard.

In order that impurity levels should not fall below the detection limit of the method, it was necessary to keep the copper concentration high. As a result, the increased viscosity and high salt concentration decreased the rate of atomization and reduced the amount of impurity atoms that reached the flame. This resulted in a considerable loss in sensitivity. Figure 9.3 illustrates this effect for silver, and a similar behavior was observed for zinc, lead, and nickel. To circumvent this difficulty various modifications were tried which did overcome the problem of high copper concentration, but they led to longer procedures and required much larger samples. Other problems such as inadequate resolution arose which were connected with limitations in the instrument. Improvements in instrumentation will undoubtedly overcome the resolution problem and this technique may yet make a valuable contribution to the study of copper archaeology.

Discussion

Since atomic absorption spectroscopy was not used to analyze many samples, further discussion of the method is not warranted here. The second method, spark source mass spectroscopy, holds great promise for the determination of larger numbers of metallic impurities, particularly those metals that cannot be detected by neutron activation analysis. Preliminary measurements on representative samples showed that more than 30 impurities could be detected. With proper modifications the technique can be made insensitive to the large amount of copper matrix present in almost all samples. The most recent models of this type of mass spectroscope can detect impurities in the parts per billion range and can handle very small samples. So far, this technique has been applied to a small number of specimens and further refinements will be made before it is applied on a more extensive scale.

In analyzing the data accumulated to date, a statistical approach similar to that used in the emission spectrographic work was employed. In the case of neutron activation, the sensitivity and precision were greater, and narrower concentration ranges were warranted. Therefore, the following scale was employed:

Unit	Range of Concentration (percent)
1	100 – 32
2	32 – 10
3	10 – 3.2
4	3.2 – 1
5	1 – 0.32
6	0.32 – 0.1
7	0.1 – 0.032
8	0.032 – 0.01
9	0.01 – 0.0032
10	0.0032 – 0.001
11	$10^{-3} - 3.2 \times 10^{-4}$
12	$3.2 \times 10^{-4} - 1.0 \times 10^{-4}$
13	$1 \times 10^{-4} - 3.2 \times 10^{-5}$
14	$3.2 \times 10^{-5} - 1.0 \times 10^{-5}$
15	$1.0 \times 10^{-5} - 3.2 \times 10^{-6}$
16	$3.2 \times 10^{-6} - 1.0 \times 10^{-6}$
17	$1.0 \times 10^{-6} - 3.2 \times 10^{-7}$
18	$3.2 \times 10^{-7} - 1.0 \times 10^{-7}$
19	$1.0 \times 10^{-7} - 3.2 \times 10^{-8}$
20	$3.2 \times 10^{-8} - 1.0 \times 10^{-8}$
21	$1.0 \times 10^{-8} - 3.2 \times 10^{-9}$

A computer program has been developed which can recall from storage the impurity composition of an ore, a smelt of an ore, or an artifact from any given region of the world. Because of sampling errors, inhomogeneity of the samples, and other sources of errors which have not been thoroughly evaluated, no overall error has been assigned to each analysis, but the relatively broad concentration ranges reported in the tables probably include the experimental errors. Additional refinements are being incorporated into the program as more data are accumulated.

At the present stage of the project, only 350 ores and smelts of the ores have

been analyzed by neutron activation. This is still too small a number of samples to obtain a statistically significant distribution of impurities for a type of ore from a particular area in the world. Therefore, the relative probabilities that elements will fall within a given concentration range are listed in Tables 9.6, 9.7, and 9.8 for worldwide samples only. In most cases, cesium was not detected and bismuth analyses were not done, so both elements were omitted from the tables. Typically, all native copper samples have silver and mercury, whereas the mineral ores frequently do not contain these impurities. Also, the iron and antimony content of the mineral ores is much greater than that found in native copper. If the emission spectroscopic results are also included, as they should be since the technique determined lead, tin, arsenic, and bismuth, one can clearly see that native copper is much lower in impurities than the oxidized or reduced ores. This characteristic is used to identify copper artifacts made from native copper.

Northern Michigan is the only local area in the world which has been adequately sampled for an ore (native copper), and a fairly good statistical distribution of impurities was obtained. Large numbers of samples were gathered from this area to study in depth the impurity patterns for a given mining region.

Additional studies are being carried out to improve the sampling techniques used for mineral ores and to prepare copper smelts of all the ores. The variation in impurity content of the smelts with temperature of reduction is also being investigated. It may well be that the impurities in the smelts are more reliable indicators for comparison with artifacts than the original ores. The analysis of a metal sample is more accurate and the sampling is more uniform.

The probabilities of occurrence of impurities in artifacts determined by neutron activation are summarized in Tables 9.9, 9.10, 9.11, and 9.12 in the usual statistical fashion. Table 9.12 hardly has any statistical significance since it is based on seven samples. However, it would be too laborious and would probably be a burden on the reader to list the impurity levels for each artifact. The distribution tables for artifacts are listed merely to provide average impurity concentrations observed in different regions for comparison purposes. In actual practice, the impurity fingerprint of each artifact will be compared to ore or smelt compositions in an attempt to determine the geographic origin of the copper used in the artifact. The computer program now compares an artifact not only with ores and smelts but also with other artifacts. Thus, the computer not only tries to locate the origin of the copper in the artifact but also determines if the particu-

137

Table 9.6
Relative Probability of Occurrence of Impurities in Oxidized Ores and Smelts— Worldwide (67 Samples measured by neutron activation)

Concentration Range	Elements												
	Silver	Mercury	Iron	Scandium	Cobalt	Antimony	Selenium	Gold	Cerium	Chromium	Hafnium	Indium	Iridium
1	—*	—	—	—	—	—	—	—	—	—	—	—	—
2	—	—	0.0895	—	—	—	—	—	—	—	—	—	—
3	—	—	0.0448	—	—	—	—	—	—	—	—	—	—
4	—	—	0.0895	—	—	—	—	—	—	—	—	—	—
5	—	—	0.179	—	—	—	0.0298	—	—	—	—	—	—
6	0.0747	—	0.164	—	—	0.0298	—	—	0.0149	—	—	0.0149	—
7	0.0597	—	0.104	0.0149	0.0298	0.0149	—	—	0.0747	—	—	0.0747	—
8	0.134	0.0448	0.0448	0.0298	0.0747	0.0448	0.0895	—	0.0747	—	0.0149	0.0597	—
9	0.104	0.0448	—	0.0747	0.0895	0.0895	0.0448	0.0149	0.0448	—	0.0298	0.0298	—
10	0.0895	0.0448	—	0.104	0.0747	0.209	0.0597	0.0149	0.0298	0.104	0.0747	0.0149	—
11	0.0895	0.209	—	0.0597	0.164	0.209	0.104	—	—	0.0597	0.0149	—	—
12	0.0597	0.194	—	0.104	0.164	0.104	0.0597	0.0149	—	0.119	0.0298	—	—
13	0.0149	0.0448	—	0.0895	0.0448	0.0747	0.0747	0.0448	—	0.0149	—	—	0.0149
14	—	0.0149	—	0.104	0.0298	—	0.0298	—	—	—	—	—	0.0149
15	—	—	—	0.134	—	—	—	0.0298	—	—	—	—	0.0895
16	—	—	—	0.0448	—	—	—	—	—	—	—	—	—
17	—	—	—	0.0149	—	—	—	—	—	—	—	—	0.0149
18	—	—	—	—	—	—	—	—	—	—	—	—	—
19	—	—	—	—	—	—	—	—	—	—	—	—	0.0149
20	—	—	—	—	—	—	—	—	—	—	—	—	—
21	—	—	—	—	—	—	—	—	—	—	—	—	—
22	—	—	—	—	—	—	—	—	—	—	—	—	—
Undetected	0.373	0.403	0.283	0.223	0.328	0.223	0.522	0.896	0.761	0.702	0.836	0.821	0.851

* No samples fell in this range.

Table 9.7
Relative Probability of Occurrence of Impurities in Reduced Ores and Smelts— Worldwide (17 Samples measured by neutron activation)

Concentration Range	Elements												
	Silver	Mercury	Iron	Scandium	Cobalt	Antimony	Selenium	Gold	Cerium	Chromium	Hafnium	Indium	Iridium
1	—*	—	—	—	—	—	—	—	—	—	—	—	—
2	—	—	0.118	—	—	—	—	—	—	—	—	—	—
3	—	—	0.235	—	—	—	—	—	—	—	—	—	—
4	—	—	0.118	—	—	—	0.0588	—	—	—	—	—	—
5	—	—	0.118	—	—	—	—	—	—	—	—	—	—
6	—	—	0.118	—	—	0.118	—	—	—	—	—	0.0588	—
7	0.176	—	0.0588	0.118	—	0.0588	0.0588	—	0.0588	—	—	0.118	—
8	0.353	0.118	—	0.0588	0.118	0.176	—	0.0588	0.0588	—	0.0588	0.0588	—
9	0.294	0.0588	—	0.0588	0.118	—	—	—	—	—	—	—	—
10	—	0.0588	—	0.118	—	0.235	0.0588	—	0.0588	—	—	—	—
11	—	0.235	—	0.0588	—	0.176	0.0588	—	—	0.0588	—	—	—
12	—	0.176	—	—	0.176	—	0.0588	—	—	0.0588	0.0588	—	—
13	—	—	—	0.235	0.0588	—	0.0588	—	—	—	—	—	—
14	—	—	—	0.0588	—	—	—	—	—	—	—	—	0.0588
15	—	—	—	0.0588	—	—	—	—	—	—	—	—	—
16	—	—	—	—	—	—	—	—	—	—	—	—	0.0588
17	—	—	—	—	—	—	—	—	—	—	—	—	—
18	—	—	—	—	—	—	—	—	—	—	—	—	—
19	—	—	—	—	—	—	—	—	—	—	—	—	—
20	—	—	—	—	—	—	—	—	—	—	—	—	—
21	—	—	—	—	—	—	—	—	—	—	—	—	—
22	—	—	—	—	—	—	—	—	—	—	—	—	—
Undetected	0.176	0.352	0.235	0.235	0.530	0.235	0.647	0.941	0.824	0.882	0.882	0.765	0.882

* No samples fell in this range.

Table 9.8
Relative Probability of Occurrence of Impurities in Native Copper—Worldwide (202 Samples measured by neutron activation)

Concentration Range	Elements												
	Silver	Mercury	Iron	Scandium	Cobalt	Antimony	Selenium	Gold	Cerium	Chromium	Hafnium	Indium	Iridium
1	—*	—	—	—	—	—	—	—	—	—	—	—	—
2	—	—	—	—	—	—	—	—	—	—	—	—	—
3	—	—	0.0050	—	—	—	—	—	—	—	—	—	—
4	0.0148	—	0.0254	—	—	—	—	—	—	—	—	—	—
5	0.0050	—	0.0346	—	—	—	—	—	—	—	—	—	—
6	0.0099	0.0050	0.0990	—	—	—	—	—	—	—	—	—	—
7	0.228	—	0.0842	—	—	0.0050	0.0099	—	—	—	—	—	—
8	0.555	0.0297	0.0500	—	—	—	0.0148	—	0.0050	—	—	—	—
9	0.104	0.0297	0.0500	—	—	—	0.0148	—	—	0.0254	—	—	—
10	0.0346	0.262	0.0842	0.0050	0.0099	0.0148	0.0745	—	0.0050	0.0198	—	—	—
11	0.0396	0.307	0.0446	0.0099	0.0050	0.0050	0.0941	—	0.0050	—	—	—	—
12	0.0050	0.178	0.0050	0.0396	0.0842	0.0346	0.114	—	—	0.0545	—	—	—
13	—	0.134	—	0.144	0.0842	0.0500	0.0198	—	—	0.0643	—	—	—
14	—	0.0198	—	0.193	0.0099	0.0198	—	—	—	0.0396	—	—	—
15	—	0.0050	—	0.154	0.0050	0.0254	—	0.0050	—	0.0050	—	—	—
16	—	0.0050	—	0.0892	—	0.0297	—	—	—	0.0050	—	—	—
17	—	—	—	0.0594	—	0.0050	—	—	—	—	—	—	—
18	—	—	—	0.0446	—	—	—	—	—	—	—	—	—
19	—	—	—	0.0148	—	—	—	—	—	—	—	—	—
20	—	—	—	—	—	—	—	—	—	—	—	—	—
21	—	—	—	—	—	—	—	—	—	—	—	—	—
22	—	—	—	—	—	—	—	—	—	—	—	—	—
Undetected	0.005	0.025	0.579	0.248	0.804	0.817	0.658	0.995	0.985	0.787	1.00	1.00	1.00

* No samples fell in this range.

Table 9.9
Relative Probability of Occurrence of Impurities in Artifacts—Middle East (32 Samples measured by neutron activation)

Concentration Range	Elements								
	Silver	Mercury	Iron	Scandium	Cobalt	Antimony	Gold	Selenium	Chromium
1	—*	—	—	—	—	—	—	—	—
2	—	—	0.031	—	—	—	—	—	—
3	—	—	0.188	—	—	0.031	—	—	—
4	—	—	0.094	—	—	—	—	—	—
5	0.031	—	0.125	—	—	—	—	0.031	—
6	—	—	0.219	—	—	0.031	—	—	—
7	0.250	—	—	—	—	0.125	—	—	—
8	0.375	0.094	—	—	0.188	0.125	—	0.156	—
9	0.281	0.375	—	—	0.469	0.344	—	0.312	0.031
10	—	0.250	—	—	0.156	0.160	0.094	0.156	0.094
11	0.031	0.031	—	—	0.063	0.125	0.031	0.125	0.062
12	—	0.062	—	0.125	0.031	0.031	0.031	—	0.062
13	—	—	—	0.219	—	—	—	—	—
14	—	—	—	0.125	—	—	0.031	—	—
15	—	—	—	—	—	—	—	—	—
16	—	—	—	—	—	—	—	—	—
17	—	—	—	—	—	—	—	—	—
18	—	—	—	—	—	—	—	—	—
19	—	—	—	—	—	—	—	—	—
20	—	—	—	—	—	—	—	—	—
Undetected	0.031	0.188	0.344	0.531	0.094	0.031	0.810	0.219	0.750

* No samples fell in this range.

Table 9.10
Relative Probability of Occurrence of Impurities in Artifacts—South America (56 Samples measured by neutron activation)

Concentration Range	Elements									
	Silver	Mercury	Iron	Scandium	Cobalt	Antimony	Gold	Selenium	Cerium	Chromium
1	—*	—	—	—	—	—	—	—	—	—
2	—	—	—	—	—	—	—	—	—	—
3	—	—	—	—	—	—	0.018	—	—	—
4	0.036	—	—	—	—	—	0.035	—	—	—
5	0.054	—	0.018	—	—	—	0.054	—	—	—
6	0.054	—	0.071	—	0.018	—	0.018	—	—	—
7	0.232	0.018	—	—	—	0.036	0.125	0.018	—	—
8	0.321	0.018	—	—	—	0.250	0.250	0.036	—	—
9	0.214	0.089	—	—	—	0.232	0.143	0.125	0.017	0.036
10	0.089	0.339	—	—	0.071	0.250	0.196	0.161	0.036	0.036
11	—	0.161	—	—	0.107	0.125	0.018	0.107	0.054	—
12	—	—	0.018	—	0.161	—	0.107	0.107	—	0.017
13	—	—	—	0.125	0.054	—	—	—	—	—
14	—	—	—	0.107	0.018	—	—	—	—	—
15	—	—	—	0.089	—	—	—	—	—	—
16	—	—	—	0.036	—	—	—	—	—	—
17	—	—	—	—	—	—	—	—	—	—
18	—	—	—	—	—	—	—	—	—	—
19	—	—	—	—	—	—	—	—	—	—
20	—	—	—	—	—	—	—	—	—	—
Undetected	0.00	0.375	0.893	0.643	0.571	0.107	0.036	0.446	0.893	0.910

* No samples fell in this range.

Table 9.11
Relative Probability of Occurrence of Impurities in Artifacts— Europe (57 Samples measured by neutron activation)

Concentration Range	Elements								
	Silver	Mercury	Iron	Scandium	Cobalt	Antimony	Gold	Selenium	Chromium
1	—*	—	—	—	—	—	—	—	—
2	—	—	—	—	—	—	—	—	—
3	—	—	—	—	—	—	—	—	—
4	—	—	0.018	—	—	—	—	—	—
5	—	—	0.035	—	—	—	—	—	—
6	—	—	0.070	—	0.070	0.018	—	0.018	—
7	0.158	0.018	0.176	—	0.053	0.105	—	—	0.018
8	0.526	—	—	—	0.298	0.474	0.017	—	—
9	0.193	—	—	—	0.298	0.140	0.140	0.053	0.018
10	0.035	0.053	—	—	0.123	0.193	0.544	0.386	—
11	0.018	0.018	—	—	0.088	0.018	0.122	0.158	0.018
12	—	0.035	—	—	0.018	—	0.070	0.035	0.035
13	—	—	—	0.053	—	—	0.035	—	—
14	—	—	—	0.053	—	—	—	—	—
15	—	—	—	—	—	—	0.018	—	—
16	—	—	—	—	—	—	—	—	—
17	—	—	—	0.018	—	—	—	—	—
18	—	—	—	—	—	—	—	—	—
19	—	—	—	—	—	—	—	—	—
20	—	—	—	—	—	—	—	—	—
Undetected	0.070	0.877	0.702	0.877	0.053	0.053	0.053	0.351	0.912

* No samples fell in this range.

Table 9.12
Relative Probability of Occurrence of Impurities in Artifacts— North America (7 Samples measured by neutron activation)

Concentration Range	Elements									
	Silver	Mercury	Iron	Scandium	Cobalt	Antimony	Gold	Selenium	Cerium	Indium
1	—*	—	—	—	—	—	—	—	—	—
2	—	—	—	—	—	—	—	—	—	—
3	—	—	—	—	—	—	—	—	—	—
4	—	—	0.30	—	—	—	—	—	—	—
5	—	—	0.30	—	—	—	—	—	—	—
6	—	—	—	—	—	—	—	—	—	—
7	0.14	—	0.14	—	—	—	—	—	—	—
8	0.57	—	—	—	—	—	—	—	—	0.14
9	0.30	—	—	—	0.14	—	—	—	0.29	—
10	—	0.86	—	—	—	—	—	0.14	0.14	0.29
11	—	0.14	—	—	0.14	0.14	—	0.14	—	—
12	—	—	—	0.14	0.29	0.29	0.14	—	—	—
13	—	—	—	0.29	0.14	0.14	0.14	—	—	—
14	—	—	—	—	—	—	—	—	—	—
15	—	—	—	—	—	—	—	—	—	—
16	—	—	—	—	—	—	—	—	—	—
17	—	—	—	—	—	—	—	—	—	—
18	—	—	—	—	—	—	—	—	—	—
19	—	—	—	—	—	—	—	—	—	—
20	—	—	—	—	—	—	—	—	—	—
Undetected	0.000	0.000	0.26	0.57	0.29	0.43	0.71	0.71	0.57	0.57

* No samples fell in this range.

lar artifact being considered resembles other artifacts from the same region or other areas in the world.

Until more samples are analyzed and a better fingerprint library is established, the best application of the techniques described is to study problems of a local character. As an example, a fairly complete set of samples of ore, slag, flux, ingot, and artifacts found by the Arabah expedition under Dr. B. Rothenberg (Reference 6) have been examined by emission spectroscopy and neutron activation. The impurity analyses indicate that the metallurgists of that day, 4000–5000 years ago, added a fluxing material to their smelting process. The iron content of the ores is fairly low, but the final copper smelts are quite high in iron. The iron contents of suspected flux materials were also very high. Such questions as whether all the copper artifacts found in a tomb came from the same location or were fabricated at about the same time can also be probed by these techniques.

In summary, four techniques have been applied to the problem of measuring the trace impurity fingerprints of copper ores, smelts, and artifacts. The most promising method appears to be neutron activation analysis, but there is hope that spark source mass spectrometry may prove to be a superior analytical tool. Many ores and artifacts were analyzed, but as yet an insufficient number to obtain a good fingerprint of ores and artifacts for different areas of the world. The techniques have been used with some success to investigate local problems such as smelting procedures, comparison of artifacts found in close proximity, and to determine from which type of ore an artifact was derived.

Acknowledgments

We would like to acknowledge the efforts and contributions of the following honors students: Mary Conway, Carleton College; Mark Kastner, University of Chicago; Ellen Kerman, Beloit College; Nancy Linder, Grinnell College; Marcia Rokus, Ripon College; A. Grant Mauk, Lawrence University; and Sue Potterton, Randolph-Macon College. We are also grateful to the operating personnel of the Argonne CP-5 reactor who were so cooperative in arranging for the irradiation of the samples. We would like to thank Dr. A. M. Friedman for his helpful discussions.

References

1.
Bowen, H. J. M., and
Gibbons, D.

Radioactivation Analysis, Clarendon Press,
Oxford, 1963.

2.
Friedman, A. M.,
Conway, M.,
Kastner M.,
Milsted, J.,
Metta, D.,
Fields, P. R.,
and Olsen, E.

"Copper Artifacts: Correlation with Source
Types of Copper Ores," *Science*, **152,**
1504, 1966.

3.
Lenihan, J. M. A.,
and Thompson, S. J.

Activation Analysis, Academic Press, New
York, 1965.

4.
Moses, A. J.

*Nuclear Techniques in Analytical Chemis-
try*, Macmillan Co., New York, 1964.

5.
(a) Nenninger, H.,
and Pittioni, P.;
(b) Pittioni, P.;
(c) Coughlan, H. H.

(a) "Jahressch. Salzburger Mus. Carolino
Augusteum" 1958; (b) *Archeol. Austriaca,*
26, 1959; (c) Viking Fund Publ., Antro-
pol. **28,** 1960.

6.
Rothenberg, B.,
and Lupu, A. N.

"Excavations at Timna (Arabah)," Museum Haaretz, Tel Aviv Bull. No. 7, 1965,
pp. 19–28.

7.
Taylor, D.

*Neutron Irradiation and Activation Analy-
sis*, G. Newnes Ltd., London, 1964.

Chapter 10

Rapid Nondestructive Activation Analysis of Silver in Coins

Adon A. Gordus
The University of Michigan

Introduction

Of all of the artifacts of ancient and medieval cultures that are extant today, coins are by far the most prevalent. They probably number in the tens of millions and, although this number is only a small fraction of the total amount minted, those coins that have survived through the ages are fairly representative of the types and denominations of coins that were in circulation. The high survival rate for coins, as compared for instance with written records or artifacts such as pottery and household items, is the result of a number of factors. A coin, or more specifically the metal of which the coin is made, has an intrinsic value in itself and would be saved for this reason. Coins are convenient in size and can be hoarded in inconspicuous places, to be recovered at a later time. Because of their metallic properties, gold and silver coins in particular are able to survive the ravages of time. As examples of works of art or simply because of interest in artifacts of previous cultures, coins have been collected and saved for a longer period of time than any other utilitarian object: we have historical evidence, for instance, that the Emperor Augustus collected Greek and old Roman coins that were especially beautiful and interesting and gave them as gifts to his friends. Finally, since the Renaissance and particularly since the eighteenth century, coins have been deliberately saved by collectors and museums because of their value in scholarly studies of past cultures.

In spite of the abundance of coins, historians have tended to neglect this source of data and rely almost completely on written records. This is not to imply that historians never use numismatic evidence in their research. Indeed, they do. But the numismatic studies have been limited to the examination of the designs, legends, mintmarks, dates, denominations, and weights of the coins. It is equally important to know what is in the coin, for the fineness of silver or gold in a coin, as well as its weight, determines its value as a monetary unit.

Understandably, until a few years ago, probably no more than about 2000 coin analyses had been performed, since a chemical analysis meant the destruction of at least a portion of the coin. Even the use of small scrapings for spectroscopic studies has been limited because of the reluctance of curators and collectors to allow any permanent damage to the coins.

Nondestructive Analysis Methods

A number of nondestructive methods of analysis of coins are available. The simplest method, the determination of the specific gravity of the coin, can be helpful in *estimating* the fineness of gold coins (Reference 6) since the density of gold (19.3 g/cm^3) is appreciably different from that of the more common alloying metals: silver (10.5), copper (8.9), and lead (11.3 g/cm^3). In estimating the fineness of silver coins, however, specific gravity measurements are not particularly useful since the densities of copper and lead bracket and are numerically similar to the value for silver.

X-Ray fluorescence analysis of coins can provide data on the composition of elements at the surface of a coin. But unless a coin is in mint condition, the immediate surface of the coin will be depleted in the more reactive elements because of corrosive oxidation. A reliable X-ray surface analysis will be obtained only if a thin outer layer of the surface is removed and studies have shown (Reference 8) that typically only 0.001 inch need be removed in order to obtain composition data representative of the coin as a whole. However, many curators are reluctant to permit such cleaning because they feel that the characteristic patina of old coins which is thus removed is an essential feature of the coin as an historical and artistic object. A special X-ray fluorescence analyser, the X-ray milliprobe, developed at the Research Laboratory for Archaeology and History of Art at Oxford University (Reference 4), partially circumvents this problem in that an area of only a few mm^2 need be cleaned.

A nondestructive analysis procedure that permits determining the internal composition of a coin is nuclear activation. Bombardment with nuclear particles, such as neutrons, which penetrate through the coin, results in the production of radioactivity characteristic of the elements in the coin. Measurement of the amounts of radioactivity produced permits determining the content of most elements in the irradiated coin.

This method of analysis has, in recent years, been utilized by a number of workers. One of the most extensive studies using reactor neutron activation analysis was performed at Oxford where 500 fifth century B.C. Greek silver coins were analysed for their copper and gold impurities (Reference 1); Wyttenbach and Herman (Reference 18) reported on the determination of the Cu and Ag contents of 400 fifteenth century Swiss coins. Other studies include Norman and Suebic gold coins (Reference 17), third to eighth century B.C. electrum coins from Lydia and Carthage (Reference 9), ancient Roman copper coins (Reference 19), fourth to sixth century B.C. Greek silver coins (Reference 5), and Roman silver coins of the period 27 B.C. to A.D. 275 (Reference 10). Kusaka used a low-intensity radium-beryllium neutron source to activate modern Japanese silver coins (Reference

14); using charged particle activation (52 MeV protons and 26 MeV deuterons) Meyers analysed Roman gold, silver, and copper coins (Reference 16).

Described in this paper is a method of neutron activation analysis of coins that differs in two important respects from the procedure used by others.

By using a relatively weak neutron source, we avoid producing any detectable amount of the 255-day half-life isotope of silver, ^{110m}Ag. Only short-lived isotopes of silver are observed and the induced activity decays in 10 to 20 minutes. This method of irradiation was deliberately chosen in order to satisfy a number of requirements. We considered it important to be able to assure those from whom coins were borrowed that there would be no residual activity in the metal. Even if the owners of the coins would be willing to permit a small amount of activity in each coin, we felt it undesirable since the accumulation of a very large number of mildly radioactive coins could pose a health hazard and we envision an increasing number of coins being subjected to this numismatic analysis. Lastly, it seemed to us that an atomic-age esthetic principal was involved; even though activation analysis would not alter the appearance of the coin, any residual activity still constitutes an internal alteration.

When a beam of neutrons or charged particles travels through an object, the intensity of the beam is decreased because of partial absorption as well as scattering of the nuclear particles. This decrease in intensity is dependent not only on the thickness but also on the composition of the object being irradiated. The usual activation analysis, whether it be using a reactor, a charged-particle accelerator, or a low-intensity neutron source, will result in reliable quantitative data only if the sample being irradiated is quite small, in which case very little variation in the beam intensity will occur. A typical coin is much too large and the calculated silver contents could be grossly in error. For example, by irradiating pre-1965 U.S. coins, all of which contain 90 percent silver, we could use data for a 10-cent piece to calibrate the irradiation-analysis procedure. Analysis of a 25-cent piece, a 50-cent piece, and a silver dollar in a typical irradiation might then indicate incorrect silver contents of 73 percent, 59 percent, and 43 percent, respectively.

Previous workers have prepared metal standards of the same composition and thickness as the coins in order to correct for this effect. We have devised a method of irradiation which compensates directly for such analysis errors and results in data that are independent of the thickness of the coin.

The irradiations described below were performed by placing the coin and a silver disk or an uncirculated (pre-1965, 90 percent silver) U.S. 10-cent piece (taped to the back of the coin) about 1.5 inches from a 5 curie Pu-Be neutron source (Figure 10.1) housed in a paraffin-filled Howitzer (Nuclear Chicago Corp., Model NH-3). At this position the thermal neutron flux was approximately 4×10^4 neutrons cm^{-2} sec^{-1} when the 1.5 inch space was filled with paraffin. The high-energy flux at this position was not measured but should have been much less than the thermal flux. The coin and silver disk were irradiated for 1.00 min, resulting in the formation of detectable amounts of 2.4 min ^{108}Ag and 24 sec ^{110}Ag.[1] For these irradiation conditions, it can be calculated that less than one in every 10^{17} silver atoms becomes activated—and eventually decays to cadmium.

A 1.00 min count was taken on each coin starting 25 sec after the end of the irradiation. The coin was counted using a 2 in $\times$ 2 in NaI(Tl) scintillation detector shielded by 1 cm of plastic to absorb beta radiation. The detector was coupled to a single-channel analyser with the detection level set so that all activity between 0.16 and 1.60 MeV was recorded. Under these conditions very little of the beta activity of ^{108}Ag and ^{110}Ag was detected and essentially only decay gamma rays were recorded. Scintillation detection was chosen because it was possible to detect gamma rays preferentially. If appreciable beta activity had been detected it would have been markedly dependent on the thickness of the coin because of beta-ray absorption within the coin. The silver disks or U.S. 10-cent pieces were uniform in size and thickness and were counted by placing them 1 cm from a 3.2 mg/cm^2 end-window beta counter. This type of detector was chosen since the background activity was approximately 50 times less than that recorded by the scintillation detector. Appreciable beta-ray self-absorption occurred in the disk or 10-cent pieces, but the uniformity of these silver backing pieces assured that the fractional self-absorption was constant in these two types of silver disks. A number of modern U.S. and European coins of known silver contents (see Table 10.1) were used in testing the validity of the method of analysis. The data reported for these standards represent averages of 10 or more determinations.

[1]The 65 hr ^{198}Au activity can also be formed but at a level less than 0.01 of the silver activity. Correction for the induced gold activity becomes important only in coins of very high gold content. Some ^{110m}Ag (255 day) activity, to be precise, is also formed, but in so small an amount (less than 10 counts/year) as to be considered nonexistent and certainly nondetectable.

Table 10.1

Analysis of the Silver Contents of Modern Coins

Coin	Thickness (cm)	Actual	Experimental* Eq. 1	Eq. 2	Eq. 3
			Percent Silver		
1961 Filed Mexican Peso	0.098	10.0	11.26	19.8	10.28
1961 Mexican Peso	0.198	10.0	9.76	23.7	10.25
1945 U.S. 5¢	0.173	35.0	34.4	33.1	33.4
1967 U.S. 50¢	0.175	40.0	32.9	44.7	39.2
1922 Filed British Half-Crown	0.097	50.0	52.8	37.0	47.4
1930 British 6 Pence	0.112	50.0	52.5	40.4	48.8
1929 British Florin	0.196	50.0	42.8	53.7	49.0
1925 Austrian Shilling	0.128	64.0	56.3	73.3	64.5
1944 Philippine 20 Cent	0.124	75.0	76.0	65.3	73.8
1951 Canadian 25¢	0.142	80.0	76.7	70.5	79.4
1886 Swiss Franc	0.122	83.5	84.6	81.9	83.7
1964 Filed U.S. 25¢	0.051	90.0	86.9	107.5	88.6
1964 Filed U.S. 25¢	0.074	90.0	91.5	104.0	93.2
1964 Filed U.S. 25¢	0.099	90.0	86.5	90.5	89.8
1908 U.S. 25¢	0.127	90.0	90.8	89.0	93.2
1944 U.S. 50¢	0.183	90.0	90.9	88.2	91.8
1882 U.S. $1.00	0.234	90.0	83.0	93.8	92.1
1918 Canadian 25¢	0.130	92.5	97.1	81.4	92.7
Pure Silver	0.0084	100.0	70.8	49.0	63.9
Pure Silver	0.017	100.0	86.1	62.1	77.7
Pure Silver	0.025	100.0	89.4	121.2	87.3
Average % Deviation†			8.0%	23.7%§	2.1%

* Experimental values for each coin were calculated using the parameters of Eqs. 1–3 as given in Figures 10.1 to 10.3 by the best fits of the composite data for all coins. Each value here and each data point in Figures 1–3 is based on the average of 10 or more individual analyses.

† Pure silver data were omitted in calculating the average. Percent deviation of a coin = 100 × absolute value of the difference between the actual and the experimentally determined silver content, divided by the actual silver content.

§ Average % deviation = 12% if Mexican peso data are omitted.

As noted earlier, the observed activity per gram of silver in the coin is markedly dependent upon the thickness of the coin. This is illustrated graphically in Figure 10.2. The linear relationship implied by these data involves a quadratic expression in the percent silver P in the coin and is given by the equation,

$$StmP^2 + ImP = C \qquad (1)$$

where S and I are the slope and linear-extrapolated intercept as determined from Figure 10.2, where t is the thickness, m is the mass, and C the observed silver radioactivity of the coin. This method of analysis is very similar to that described by Wyttenbach and Herman (Reference 18). Since ancient and medieval coins are very irregular in thickness, this method, which depends markedly on the thickness, could result in calculated silver contents that are grossly in error (Reference 12).

A mathematically simpler relationship is implied by the data obtained for the shielded disk or 10-cent piece (Figure 10.3). The disks serve in a manner analogous to that of a photocell in a spectrophotometer and the activity induced in the disks is a measure of the number of neutrons that are not absorbed by the coin and, hence, related to the silver absorption (or silver content) of the coin. The equation of Figure 10.3 is

$$\log \frac{I}{C} = -StP \qquad (2)$$

As in Equation 1, this relationship also indicates a strong dependence of P on the thickness of the coin and can lead to widely variant data.

However, we were able to formulate an empirical relationship that was independent of t over a wide range of thicknesses, as is shown in Figure 10.4. The equation in the range where the data are thickness independent is

$$P = \frac{C_c}{C_d mE} \qquad (3)$$

where C_c and C_d are the observed counts in the coin and disk (or 10-cent piece), respectively, and E is the empirically determined constant which, for the data of Figure 10.4, is equal to 0.371.

As indicated in Table 10.1, silver contents based on Equation 3 are more accurate than those based on Equation 1 or 2 even though modern coins are relatively uniform in thickness.

147

10.1
The coin and a U.S. 10-cent piece or silver disk taped to the coin are irradiated with neutrons emitted from a Pu-Be source.

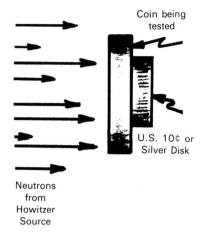

Coin being tested

U.S. 10¢ or Silver Disk

Neutrons from Howitzer Source

10.2
Activity per gram of silver in the coin as a function of thickness X% silver in the coin. Each data point is an average of approximately 10 determinations.

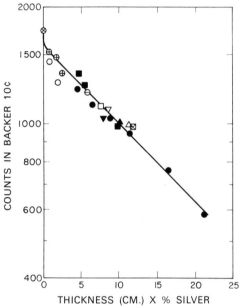

⊕ 100 % Silver
⊠ 92.5 % Canadian
● 90 % U.S.A.
▲ 83.5 % Swiss
△ 80 % Canadian
▽ 75 % Philippine
▼ 64 % Austrian
■ 50 % British
□ 40 % U.S.A.
⊖ 35 % U.S.A.
○ 10 % Mexican

THICKNESS (CM.) X % SILVER

10.3
Activity in the U.S. 10-cent backer disks as a function of the thickness X% silver in the front coin. Refer to Figure 10.2 for identification of data. Point at zero thickness is for an unshielded 10-cent piece.

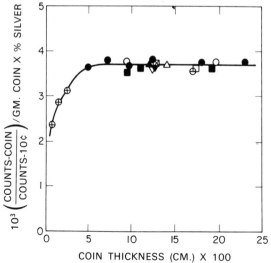

COUNTS IN BACKER 10¢

THICKNESS (CM.) X % SILVER

10.4
Ratio of the activity per gram of silver in the coin to the activity in the 10-cent backer disk as a function of the coin thickness. Data identification given in Figure 10.2.

$10^3 \left(\frac{COUNTS\text{-}COIN}{COUNTS\text{-}10¢} \right) / GM.\ COIN\ X\ \%\ SILVER$

COIN THICKNESS (CM.) X 100

To date we have analysed over 3500 coins using the method of Equation 3, usually obtaining an average silver content for a coin based on seven or eight replicate determinations. About 50 to 100 irradiations and analyses were usually performed in sequence with every seventh coin irradiated being one of the modern coin standards listed in Table 10.1. The data based on standards from a sequence of analyses were used to calculate the (average) value of the constant E for the group of analyses. In general, the average value of E obtained in a set of irradiations had a standard deviation of ± 1 to 2 percent of E.

As an independent verification of this method, the silver contents of four Islamic coins were also determined chemically; the two analyses were shown to be in agreement (Reference 14).

As indicated in Table 10.1, the method of analysis based on Equation 3 results in data valid to about ± 1 to 2 percent. A separate study, using this method to determine the silver contents of 48 pre-1965 (90 percent silver) U.S. 10-cent and 25-cent coins resulted in data that average 89.9 ± 0.8 percent.

Historical Studies

Exact knowledge of the silver content of coins provides the economic historian with unbiased information about the economic conditions of ancient and medieval cultures. If written records are available, the historian is able to determine the validity of those documents which deal with the economic history of the period. If no written records are extant, the historian can use the coin analysis data to establish the time and extent of debasement as well as reform of the coinage. Economic history is crucial to the study of any past civilization since the fluctuations in a money economy are the clearest and most sensitive indicators of changes in a society, whether social, political, demographic, or environmental.

Sasanian Persia (A.D. 224–651) is an example of a society which, despite its high development, is known to us only through very unsatisfactory sources. The only Sasanian sources (excluding coins and objets d'art) are inscriptions. The literary evidence is peripheral to Persia itself since it is composed of Roman and Byzantine contemporary chronicles and later Arab histories.

No previous analyses of Sasanian coins had been made, and it was generally assumed that all coins (Figure 10.5) from this society contained 90 to 100 percent silver. Preliminary data based on the analysis of over 300 Sasanian silver coins are given in Figure 10.6. Unfortunately, only the coins minted after approximately A.D. 450 bear mintmarks and dates. However, the coins can be grouped according to

the reigning monarchs whose names and portraits appear on the coins. In some cases it is possible, on the basis of other numismatic studies, to divide the coins into subgroups which can be classified as early or late issues of a particular reign. The open circles in Figure 10.6 represent the average silver contents of groups of coins at which the data are concentrated whereas the solid curve above A.D. 500 indicates the approximate variation in silver content of the dated coins.

Each of the five solid circles in Figure 10.6 represents a single coin. These data were not included among those data clusters joined by a solid curve since the silver contents for these five coins appear abnormally low compared with other coins from the same reigns. It may be that these five coins are ancient counterfeits, although another explanation could hold for the two coins of 21 percent and 31 percent silver from the reign of Shapur I (A.D. 240 to 272). It has been noted (Reference 11) that Shapur I acquired Roman flans during his Syrian campaigns and used these flans for his own coinage. Analysis of Roman coins of this period (Reference 10) indicate that the silver contents were being decreased from about 38 percent to about 5 percent and it is possible that these two Sasanian coins are authentic and were struck on the Roman flans.

These data of Figure 10.6 indicate that a number of periods were characterized by marked debasement and subsequent monetary reform. It is during these periods of debasement that the historian might expect to find that the Sasanians were at war or experiencing a famine or internal strife. In a few instances where intense Sasanian military activity is noted in Roman chronicles (as in the late third century) debasement invariably occurred even though some of the Sasanian military campaigns were successful. Apparently the sovereigns were forced to debase their currency in order to meet the increased expenses of the war (Reference 16).

Additional historical studies of a more subtle nature can be made by determining the changes in silver contents of coins issued from various mints. For instance, data on Islamic coins from the period A.D. 700–740 show an increase in silver content from about 90 to 95 percent for all mints except Al Andalus, the present-day city of Cordoba, Spain. Data for some of these mints are given in Figure 10.7 and are seen to be in agreement with the chemical analysis data of Caley (Reference 7), which are represented by solid circles. The decreasing silver content of the coinage from the Spanish mint is probably caused by a number of factors, but certainly one of the important reasons must be related to the geographic displacement of Al Andalus from the center of the Islamic Empire.

149

Analysis for Other Elements

In order to utilize coins as a source of historical data it is necessary to be able to determine which, if any, of the coins being examined are modern forgeries. Unfortunately, one of the factors that has assisted in retaining the coins for posterity, the desire of individuals to acquire and collect coins, has, in the last 100–200 years, given rise to other groups of individuals who have been only too willing to assist in satisfying this demand.

If coins are known to be part of an excavated hoard, this is usually a sufficient indication of the authenticity of the coins. Individual coins can usually be authenticated by a professional numismatist, although modern methods of forgery are becoming extremely sophisticated. Some of the fake coins can be detected by the fact that they were prepared from casts rather than being die struck—which is the method normally used by the ancient mints. Other fakes can only be distinguished by subtle errors in design. But it seemed to us that many modern fakes also might be detected by the fact that the level of trace impurities in the metal could differ markedly from that in an authentic ancient coin.

An analysis of the trace elements in ancient coins can also provide additional data relevant to historical research. For example, it may be possible to distinguish various sources of silver, each having different levels of trace impurities. From an indication of the amount of each type of silver used at each mint, it would then be possible to suggest the manner and extent to which the raw silver was transported and distributed throughout a kingdom.

Since we did not wish to irradiate a coin in the reactor, for reasons given in the first section of this article, we instead used a method devised by Dr. E. Sayre of Brookhaven National Laboratory for analysing metallic works of art. First, a small portion on the edge of the coin was lightly cleaned by stroking a few times with fine-grain emery paper to remove about 0.001 in. of the oxidized surface. Then about 0.0001 g of the coin was transferred by streaking the fresh coin surface on an aqua regia cleaned piece of etched quartz (Figure 10.8).

This piece of streaked quartz was sealed in polyethylene tubing and irradiated for two hours in the high-intensity neutron flux (2×10^{13} neutron-cm^{-2}-sec^{-1}) of the University of Michigan reactor. Enough radioactive gold, copper, arsenic, and antimony—as well as silver—was produced to permit detecting these isotopes using gamma-ray spectrometry[2] and determining the relative amounts of these activities at a common reference time. Data are obtained and are reported throughout this paper as *radioactivity ratios*. Streaks of gold-silver standards irradiated and analysed under the same conditions as the coins indicate that the Au/Ag radioactivity ratio = approximately 5000 × (percent Au/percent Ag). Usually three streaks were taken, each from a different part of the edge of the coin. The Au/Ag radioactivity ratios for these three streaks were found to agree within 10 percent. This variation of 10 percent is in accord with the estimated uncertainties of the radioactivity measurements. However, the Cu/Ag radioactivity ratios, on occasion, would differ by as much as 30 percent. This is understandable. The gold is an impurity associated primarily with the silver whereas the copper was added to produce the particular coin alloy. Unless the copper and silver had been thoroughly mixed when the alloy was prepared, localized copper-silver inhomogeneities could have resulted.

Among the 175 Sasanian coins that were analysed by the coin-streak method (Figure 10.9) were six that were cast[3] rather than die-struck. These modern forgeries, depicted by closed squares in Figure 10.9, all have low gold contents indicating that they were made of silver more highly refined than the silver used in a typical Sasanian coin. Modern silver is highly purified and most European coins for the past century have Au/Ag of less than 1.0; present-day coins have an even lower and almost undetectable level of gold impurity.[4] On the other hand, the ancients, in all probability, did not even know that the silver they were using contained small amounts of gold. On the basis of these data it is possible that the one coin at A.D. 585 having Au/Ag = 0.8 is also a modern forgery. Silver content data for these seven coins were excluded from Figure 10.6.

The gold-silver ratio data for the authentic coins suggest that it may be possible to group the coins according to these ratio values and that each grouping may corre-

---

[2] A 10 cc Ge (Li) detector was used, coupled to a Northern Scientific 2048-channel (Model 615) pulse-height analyser.

[3] We appreciate the assistance given us by Prof. T. V. Buttrey who examined the various coins to determine which were made by casting.

[4] It should be noted, however, that some of the silver sources available to the ancients had very little gold impurity. Data from Oxford University (Reference 1), for instance, indicate that silver in fourth to fifth century B.C. Athenian coins, which was obtained from the local mines at Laurium, would result in Au/Ag ratios of 0.2 to 2. Thus, a low gold content in an ancient silver coin is, in itself, an insufficient indication of the coin being a fake and the Au/Ag ratio is meaningful only in comparison with similar data from a group of authentic coins of the same type. Thus, for example, based on the Oxford data we are able to label as fakes three "fourth century B.C." Athenian coins we analysed that had Au/Ag ratios of 25–30.

10.5
Examples of Sasanian coins. (1 and 2) Modern fakes of Ardashir I (A.D. 224–240), both coins are from the same casting. (3–10) Authentic coins. (3) Early Ardashir I. (4) Late-issue Ardashir I. (5) Shapur I (A.D. 240–272) late issue. (6) Bahram II (A.D. 276–293). (7) Shapur II (A.D. 309–379). (8) Peroz (A.D. 459–484). (9) Khosro I (A.D. 531–579). (10) Khosro II (A.D. 591–628).

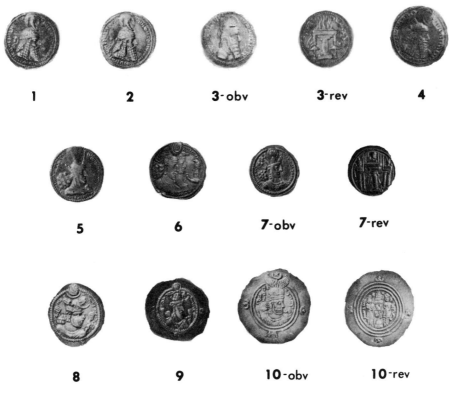

1   **2**   **3-obv**   **3-rev**   **4**

5   **6**   **7-obv**   **7-rev**

8   **9**   **10-obv**   **10-rev**

10.6
Silver contents of Sasanian coins. Open circles indicate values at which data cluster. Closed circles are data for single coins that may be ancient counterfeits; refer to text.

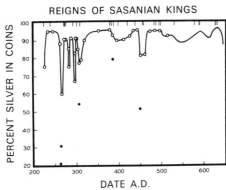

REIGNS OF SASANIAN KINGS

PERCENT SILVER IN COINS

DATE A.D.

UMAYYAD DIRHEMS

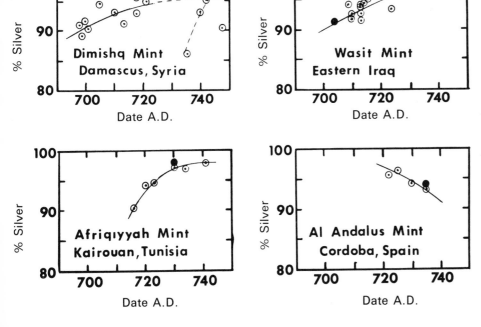

% Silver — **Dimishq Mint Damascus, Syria** — Date A.D.

% Silver — **Wasit Mint Eastern Iraq** — Date A.D.

% Silver — **Afriqiyyah Mint Kairouan, Tunisia** — Date A.D.

% Silver — **Al Andalus Mint Cordoba, Spain** — Date A.D.

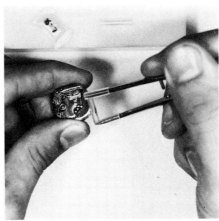

10.7
Silver contents for single Umayyad dirhems struck at various Islamic mints during the period A.D. 700–740.

10.8
About 0.0001 g of a coin is transferred by streaking a fresh surface of the coin on a piece of etched quartz.

10.9
Gold-silver radioactivity
ratios for Sasanian
coins. Solid squares are
modern fake Sasanian
coins.

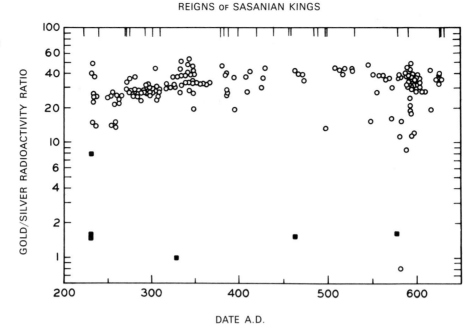

10.10
Gold-silver radioactivity
ratios for streaks taken
from 20 Sasanian art
objects.

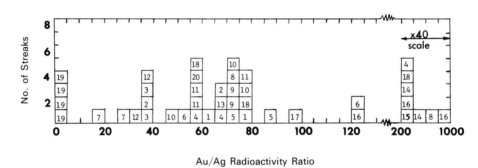

spond to a different source of silver ore. From the preliminary data of Figure 10.9, certain patterns are already becoming evident: (a) It appears that one source of silver ore having Au/Ag of approximately 15 and another source having a ratio of about 25 were used for most of the coins from the period A.D. 224–272. Additional data from a hoard of 35 coins[5] from the reign of Ardashir I (A.D. 224–240) also indicate a radioactivity ratio of about 15 for all but two of the coins. These two have ratios of 25 and 32. (b) All but two of the later issue coins which bear mintmarks (A.D. 500–651) and have Au/Ag ratios of less than 20 were probably minted in Zarang,[6] the most eastern of the Sasanian mints. Apparently a separate and distinct source of silver was used for this mint. (c) The remaining data suggest the possibility of utilization of additional silver sources having Au/Ag ratios of approximately 27, 32, 38, and 45.[7]

Metallic Art Objects

We were permitted to take a total of 43 streaks from 20 Sasanian silver art objects owned by the Metropolitan Museum of Art and by two private dealers in New York City. These art objects are mainly plates and bowls identified as Sasanian art. They are purported to have been excavated in Iran and, in a number of cases, have the figure of a king (frequently on horseback) wearing a crown similar in style to those that appear on Sasanian coins. Some of these plates were constructed by joining together separately fabricated subunits. Many of the objects were partially gilded.

The Au/Ag radioactivity ratios for these 20 objects (Figure 10.10) are most interesting in view of the data for Sasanian coins (Figure 10.9), which exhibit a range of 9 to 52. What is surprising is that only nine of the 43 streaks from the art ob-

[5] These coins (owned by Yale University) were made of a mixture called potin and were found to contain 15–17 percent silver. Data for these coins have not been included in Figures 10.6 or 10.9.

[6] The identification of Sasanian mints is a subject of controversy and the location given here is based on the latest study of Göbl (Reference 11, p. 85), who identifies the mint as being near the border of present-day Afghanistan.

[7] It should be stressed that this study is the first attempt to utilize Au/Ag ratio data to assist in the identification of silver sources and only tentative conclusions are proposed. Various factors, such as the simultaneous use of silver from a number of sources, a variation in the Au/Ag content of a given source, or the extensive reuse of old silver (coins or artifacts) in the minting of coins in ancient times, could limit the utility of these Au/Ag ratio data. However, based on our determination of the Au/Ag ratios of over 600 ancient and medieval coins, we feel that these data will be of at least partial utility. In all cases where groups of coins from a given country and time period were analysed, certain characteristic Au/Ag groupings become apparent.

jects are in the range of values found for Sasanian coins. These nine streaks were obtained from four objects, numbered 2, 3, 7, and 12. However, another streak from a separately fabricated section of Object No. 2 had a higher ratio of 70. Thus, only three of the 20 objects resulted in Au/Ag ratios that agreed with the coin data.

Object No. 19 was an item about which the dealer had doubts as to its Sasanian origin, postulating that it had been fabricated within the last 250 years. His suspicions apparently are confirmed in that all four streaks from the object have Au/Ag ratios of only about 2.5.

But what explanation can be given for streaks having Au/Ag ratios in excess of 55? The temperatures used in gilding permit some of the gold to diffuse into the silver (Reference 15), and it is possible that the samples were taken from areas that had been gilded even though we were careful to avoid all such regions. However, in gilding, the penetration of gold is very slight (Reference 15), and we always cleaned the surface prior to streaking the object, as we had done prior to streaking a coin.

We offer instead the following possible explanations. The 10 streaks having Au/Ag ratios in excess of 120 correspond to gold contents that range between 2 and 15 percent gold. Of the 600 ancient and medieval coins we have examined, none has a Au/Ag radioactivity ratio in excess of 100. Therefore, these very high Au/Ag ratios for the art objects could be the result of the deliberate addition of gold.

On the other hand, we do have some coin-streak data, based on eleventh century Mediterranean coins, that indicate Au/Ag radioactivity ratios in the range of 55 to 80. Thus, in the eleventh century and possibly even earlier at least one silver source having a high gold content was being utilized.

Prof. Oleg Grabar, in discussing Sasanian silver from an art-historical view, has suggested that much of what is called Sasanian is in fact probably post-Sasanian and may have been fabricated in the seventh or eighth centuries and, in some cases, perhaps as late as the eleventh century (Reference 13).

Our data also suggest that some, and perhaps many, of these art objects are not of the Sasanian period. Therefore, we plan to examine various seventh to eleventh century coins minted in the region that is present-day Iran, in order to determine if any of these coins were made of silver that would have Au/Ag ratios in excess of 55. Our expectations are that we will find coins of this type.

These various data, taken together, support the view (Reference 13) that some of what is called Sasanian art is Sasanian only in style rather than in period of manufacture. The mystique associated with this dynasty, about which little is known, results at least partially from an "emotional allegiance" to a past heritage. "In this Islamic context Sasanian Iran appeared indeed as a sort of heroic and brilliant past, part legend and part history, which served for centuries as a symbolic model for high Islamic culture . . ." (Reference 13).

Sasanian metalwork is not the only art about which questions have been raised concerning the period and provenance of manufacture. All great styles of art have been copied, imitated—and also forged. Although this study represents the first attempt to correlate the compositional data from coins with similar data from metallic art objects, we feel that these correlations are valid and will prove to be a valuable aid in understanding the arts and artifacts of the past.

Other Studies

The data reported in this paper represent only a small fraction of the total analyses we have performed. In addition to these studies, we also have determined the silver contents of 250 Parthian coins (second century B.C.–A.D. 224, ancient Iran), over 100 post-Sasanian coins, 158 Mamlūk dirhems (Reference 2) issued by the rulers of Egypt and Syria (A.D. 1250–1517), 100 ancient Greek coins as well as 50 modern fakes (both silver and gold), 500 ancient Roman coins, a hoard of 198 Ilkhanid coins (Turkey, A.D. 1310–1314), and various eleventh to thirteenth century coins from Greece and Cyprus. Data based on these studies will be reported in separate publications.

Acknowledgments

This study would not have been possible without the assistance of a number of individuals and institutions. Most of the coins were loaned to us by the American Numismatic Society and by Princeton University. Miss Kate Lefferts of the Metropolitan Museum of Art arranged for Mrs. Meryl Johnson (Conservator in Art at the University of Michigan) to take streaks of the Metropolitan's Sasanian silver art objects. Prof. Jere L. Bacharach, of the Department of History at the University of Washington, first suggested to the author the need for a reliable nondestructive method of analysis of silver coins, and he has cooperated in the study and identification of many of the Sasanian and post-Sasanian Islamic coins. A number of students at Michigan assisted in the actual analyses; appreciation is particularly extended to Ron Krapp, Mark DeNies, Bob Heinonen, Horst Hübel, and Andrew Osei-Boateng, who worked on the Sasanian coins and streaks. And lastly, we gratefully acknowledge the financial assistance of the University of Michigan-Phoenix Project and the U.S. Atomic Energy Commission, Division of Research. This is publication COO-912-15.

References

1.
(a) Aitken, M. J.,
Emeleus, V. M.,
Hall, E. T., and
Kraay, C. M.;
(b) Emeleus, V. M.;
(c) Kraay, C. M.,
(d) Thompson, M.;
(e) Kraay, C. M. and
Emeleus, V. M.

(a) "Conf. Radioisotopes in the Physical Sciences and Industry," Vol. 2, 263. Intl. Atomic Energy Agency, Vienna 1962; (b) *Archaeometry*, **1,** 6, 1958; (c) *Archaeometry*, **2,** 1, 1959; (d) *Archaeometry*, **3,** 10, 1960; (e) "The Composition of Greek Silver Coins," Ashmolean Museum Monograph, 1962.

(a) *Archaeometry*, **9,** 139, 1966; (b) *Helv. Chim. Acta.*, **49,** 2555, 1966.

18.
(a) Wyttenbach, A.,
and Hermann, H.;
(b) Wyttenbach, A.

(a) Atomic Energy Comm., Istanbul, Report No. CNAEM-21, part 1 (1965), CNAEM-35, part 2 (1966); (b) *Archaeometry*, **6,** 46, 1963; (c) *Archaeometry*, **4,** 56, 1961.

19.
(a) Zuber, I. K.;
(b) Ravetz, A.;
(c) Sutherland, C.H.V.

2.
Bacharach, J. L.,
and Gordus, A. A.

J. Econ. Soc. Hist. Orient, 11, part 3, 298, 1968.

3.
Bacharach, J. L.,
and Gordus, A. A.

J. Oriental Studies, to be published.

4.
Banks, M., and
Hall, E. T.

Archaeometry, **6,** 31, 1963.

5.
Bluyssen, H., and
Smith, P. B.

Archaeometry, **5,** 113, 1962.

6.
Caley, E. R.,

Ind. Eng. Chem., **24,** 676, 1952; *Ohio J. Sci.*, **XLIX,** No. 2, 73, 1949.

7.
Caley, E. R.

Am. Numismatic Soc. Notes, **7,** 211, 1957.

8.
Carter, G. F.

Archaeometry, **7,** 106, 1964.

9.
Das, H. A., and
Zonderhuis, J.

Archaeometry, **7,** 90, 1964; *Chem. Weekblad*, **61,** 18, 215, 1965.

10.
Gibbons, D., and
Lawson, D.

"Proc. 1968 Intl. Conf. Mod. Trends in Act. Anal.", Nat. Bur. Stnds. Spec. Pub. 312, Vol. I, p. 226.

11.
Göbl, R.

Sasanidische Numismatik, Klinkhardt and Biermann, Braunschweig, 1968, p. 25.

12.
Gordus, A. A.

Archaeometry, **10,** 78, 1967.

13.
Grabar, O.

"An Introduction to the Art of Sasanian Silver", in the catalog of the exhibit of Sasanian Silver, University of Michigan Museum of Art, 1967.

14.
Husaka, Y.

Japan Analyst, **8,** 111, 1959.

15.
Lechtman, H. N.

Chapter 1, this volume.

16.
Meyers, P.

"Proc. 1968 Intl. Conf. Mod. Trends in Act. Anal.", Nat. Bur. Stnds. Spec. Pub. 312, Vol. I, p. 230.

17.
Meloni, S., and
Maxia, V.

Gazz. Chim. Ital., **92,** 1432, 1962.

Chapter 11

Two Examples of the Use of Chemical Analysis in the Solution of Archaeological Problems

E. T. Hall
Oxford University

A wide selection of more or less nondestructive methods of chemical analysis have been employed in our Oxford laboratory and elsewhere for the examination of archaeological objects and works of art. In our experience we have found that only three of these methods are of general importance in fitting most of the required criteria for this type of work. These criteria can be summarized as follows:

1. Speed. In attempting to solve almost any problem many samples have to be analyzed.

2. Damage. Only small samples must be used and in many instances no removal of sample is permissible.

3. Range of elements. In most instances several (up to 20) elements should be estimated.

4. Size of object. In those cases where sample removal is not permissible and the object is large, the apparatus must be able to accommodate the specimen.

We have found in practice with the above criteria in mind that three methods of analysis are important: optical emission spectrometry, X-ray fluorescence spectrometry, and neutron activation analysis. Other chapters in this book are concerned with neutron activation, and so I intend to mention two projects as illustrations of the other two techniques. From the scientific point of view, there is no novelty involved, but they may serve to demonstrate to archaeologists the types of problems which may be tackled.

Optical Emission Spectrometry

Pottery Composition Types in the Aegean Area in Mycenaean Times

When we first started this type of analysis on ceramics some twelve years ago, we wondered which elements would be significant when trying to find unique characteristics of a given site. We thought that the most likely elements would be those that occurred at the lowest concentration measurable. In our case these concentrations were in the 1 to 20 ppm range. To our surprise we found that generally speaking these elements were very randomly distributed at a given site and no definite pattern could be built up.

However those elements which appeared in concentrations from 100 ppm to 20 percent gave us much more meaningful results. In particular, the analyses within an archaeological group were more consistent. The elements which we finally settled on for our analyses were nickel, chromium, manganese, titanium, magnesium, calcium, sodium, iron and aluminum. As mentioned later only germanium of the rarer elements proved to be of importance in typifying a source group, at least

among the sherds we have studied so far.

The method used is to obtain a 20 mg sample by either breaking off a small piece of sherd and grinding it or by using a tungsten carbide drill. The 20 mg of powder is mixed with 5 mg of pure lithium carbonate as an internal standard. This mixture is arced under controlled conditions in a Hilger large quartz spectrometer with the plate holder set to obtain a spectrum between the limits 2445 Å and 3500 Å. The resulting plate is measured in a microdensitometer, and the results reduced to percentages by reference to standard curves obtained by analysis of controls of well-known composition. This technique is laborious compared with modern direct reading instruments, and there is no doubt that such equipment would greatly speed our output of results.

Early work using this technique showed its potential. For example, it proved possible to identify the source of manufacture of various types of Romano-British pottery, in particular the rough mortaria ware widely found throughout Britain (Reference 7). The Palestinian origin of pottery found at Tell el 'Amarna in Egypt is another example (Reference 2). It was soon after this early work that Palmer made his well-known attack on the veracity of Sir Arthur Evans, the archaeologist who first excavated the royal palace at Knossos in Crete (References 4 and 5). (See Figure 11.1.)

In this paper it would be impossible to examine at all thoroughly the arguments put forward by either side in the controversy which followed Palmer's bombshell. Suffice it to say that the complexity of the arguments was nearly as great as the ferocity with which the protagonists assaulted each other. It was to help elucidate some of the problems involved that we undertook certain analyses of the Knossian pottery. This initial project resulted in a program of analysis of over 1000 sherds from some 50 sites.

Among the thousands of sherds found in the ruins of the palace—its first destruction from great magnificence took place somewhere between 1400 and 1250 B.C.—some were undoubtedly of Mycenaean origin rather than of local manufacture. Since there were extensive cultural exchanges between the Peloponnesian mainland area of Mycenae and Knossos, much of the pottery is indistinguishable both in style and appearance of the fabric. The question was, could we determine, using analytical criteria, whether a particular sherd was of local or Mycenaean origin? Figure 11.2 shows the results of analyses of more than 50 sherds of pottery which was obviously Mycenaean and

11.1
Aegean analysis sites.

11.2
Composition patterns of
pottery from Mycenae
and Knossos. (Approxi-
mately 50 sherds in
each group.)

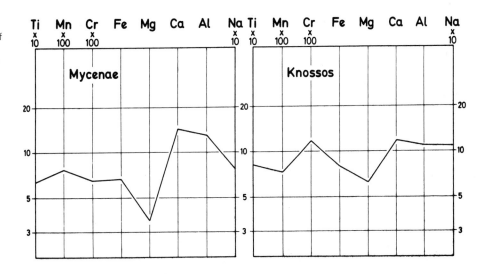

a similar number of sherds which were definitely Knossian. The analyses are plotted for each element on a logarithmic scale and the points joined up; we call these "constituent patterns." As may be seen from Figure 11.2, the analyses for the two series are quite different, and the two composition types should enable unknown sherds to be identified.

Encouraged by this success, we proceeded to tackle a more important problem associated with the Palmer controversy. One of the cardinal points in Palmer's argument was concerned with the Theban stirrup jars (Figure 11.3).

These 25 jars are of a rare type seldom found elsewhere in the Mycenaean world,[1] and they are peculiar in that many are inscribed with Linear B symbols. Palmer, professor of Philology at Oxford, noticed that two of these words which occurred on several of the Theban pots also occurred consecutively on one of the Linear B tablets found at Knossos. These words (translatable thanks to Ventris and Chadwick) were place names presumably in Crete. Hence Palmer suggested these pots must have been made in Crete presumably at Knossos. Their date was thought to be *post* the destruction of Knossos; it is, however, most unlikely that such high-class pottery could have been made by a "squatter community" supposed by Evans to have occupied Knossos after the destruction of the palace. Palmer's supposition is therefore that it was not a squatter community but a thriving one which occupied the site of Knossos after the destruction. The protectors of Evans's original theory claim that the Theban jars were not made at Knossos but either near Thebes or on the Peloponnesian peninsula.

To throw light on this problem we had to attempt to verify whether we could differentiate Theban pottery from Mycenaean and Knossian. Figure 11.4 shows that this proved difficult. The limits of Type B (Knossian) pottery overlapped, in all elements, the composition of Theban sherds. (In these preliminary trials we used Theban material other than the stirrup jars.) It looked as if our efforts were to be confounded. However after very careful reexamination of the spectrographic plates it was found that *all* the Theban samples contained a small amount of germanium (1 to 5 ppm) whereas *none* of the Knossian spectra contained germanium. This rare element was, therefore, in this case vital.

The stirrup jars could now be tackled. We

were most fortunate in getting permission from the Greek authorities to sample these valuable pots, and we are most grateful for their permission. The method of sampling is to use a small (2 mm diameter) tungsten carbide drill driven by a miniature high-speed drill. If such a hole about 5 mm deep is made in the base of the pot (it may be filled after removal of the sample) the appearance of the pot is in no way impaired, and its importance as an archaeological specimen is in no way affected.

The results of the analyses were somewhat unexpected. The majority, it would appear, were not made in Thebes, Mycenae, and its neighborhood, or in Knossos. Their compositions fell into two groups (Type F and Type O in our classification) which were quite different from the compositions of these three sources. It so happens that these two compositions, Types F and O, are also found in east Crete at Zakro and Palaikastro, respectively, and at no other source found so far. This is illustrated in Figure 11.5a and b. It would seem a reasonable conclusion that the majority of the Theban jars came from east Crete.

This result does not fully answer the problem set; that is, were the Minoans at Knossos still producing high-class pottery after the palace destruction? What is reasonably certain is the fact that another settlement in the vicinity of Zakro and Palaikastro in east Crete was trading vigorously with Thebes and if east Crete was so doing, why not Knossos, which was likely to be closely associated?

Incidental to the Thebes–Crete controversy, the work undertaken during this project has thrown considerable light on other problems associated with these sites in Crete in the Mycenaean period.

As has been stated earlier, ceramic samples from some 50 sites have been analyzed and some 20 different composition types established. These analyses can form background controls for a number of future problems associated with trade in the Mycenaean period. In fact the elucidation of some of these problems is being attempted at the present time. At the same time, we wonder whether the basis of these differentiations could be broadened by using more sensitive analytical techniques. Although we found the 1 to 20 ppm range discouraging, I wonder whether the range *below* 1 ppm might be more rewarding. Optical emission techniques would not be sensitive enough, but perhaps neutron activation or mass-spectrographic methods might be the answer at least for certain elements. Unfortunately this brings complications since the important advantages of the present method are twofold: a single exposure gives quantitative information on nearly all

Future Possibilities in Spectrographic Analysis

[1] The reason why the greater proportion of all stirrup jars were found at Thebes is baffling. A large horde of rare cylinder seals with cuneiform inscriptions were found in the same area. Could it be that there was a keen collector active in Thebes?

11.3
Theban stirrup jar.

11.4
Composition patterns of
pottery from Thebes
and Knossos.

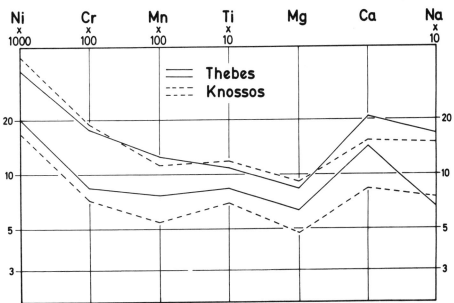

159

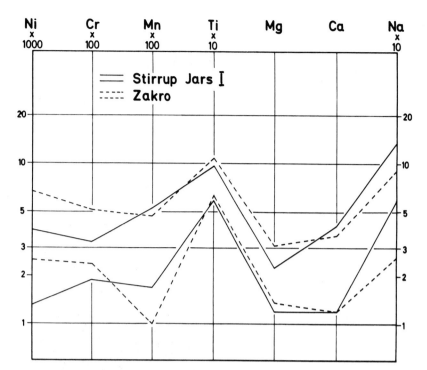

11.5a
Composition patterns of
stirrup jars Type I and
pottery from Zakro.

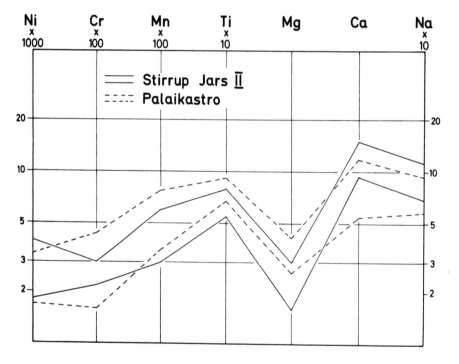

11.5b
Composition patterns of
stirrup jars Type II and
pottery from Palaikastro.

Table 11.1
Results of Magnetic
Separation

	Mg	Ca	Al	Fe	Na	Ti	Cr	Mn	Ni
Mycenae	2.2	31	12	2.4	1.5	0.19	0.036	0.046	0.006
Berbati	1.4	7.3	11	1.5	2.0	0.36	0.037	0.012	0.003
Knossos	1.0	2.3	1.8	1.2	1.5	0.52	0.062	n.d. *	n.d.

* n.d. = none detected

Two Examples of the
Use of Chemical
Analysis in the
Solution of
Archaeological Problems

elements; moreover the apparatus is inexpensive and may be used by semiskilled operators. The other two techniques do not have the same ease of operation.

Mineral Separation

Associated with our program of thermoluminescent dating of ceramics, we need to separate the various crystal forms contained in ceramic samples. One of the techniques used is the magnetic separator. Grains with varying magnetic susceptibilities are separated into different fractions. It occurred to us that these fractions might show increased regional differences when chemically analyzed. Table 11.1 shows the results of such separation of 3 nonmagnetic crystalline extracts from Knossos, Mycenae, and Berbati (a neighboring site to Mycenae). Much wider differences in chemical composition, over the untreated ceramic samples, have resulted. Not only is Mycenaean pottery more different from Knossian but it is also differentiated from Berbati material which previously gave very similar results. More work is needed to verify this result. Among the factors still to be investigated is the extent to which magnetic separability is dependent upon the firing conditions employed in making the pottery.

Analysis of Raw Clays

Attempts have been made in the past to correlate chemical analyses of bronze artifacts with their mother ores. Not surprisingly this has met with little success. The ore goes through many processes before it appears as molten metal and the fate of the impurities is uncertain and variable; moreover the added complication of remelting exists. In contrast little attempt has been made to date to trace ceramic compositions back to their clay sources. This would seem a much more reasonable project, since, in the first place, it is very seldom that reuse occurs. Moreover, we have shown that the composition of a raw clay is very similar to that found after firing the same clay; it follows that no corrections are required for the two analyses.

The determination of typical compositions of clays (or locally manufactured bricks, pottery, or tiles) over the Aegean area would be well while and would increase the value of the one-thousand-odd analyses of Aegean pottery we already have in our files.

X-Ray Spectrometry: Analysis of Dark Age Gold and Silver Coins

Quantitative analysis by X-ray fluorescence using conventional equipment is beset by difficulties. The sample chamber may not be large enough, the sample may be too small, insufficient flat surface may be available at the point where analysis is required, or the object is inhomogeneous and X-ray analysis will only estimate the composition of the surface rather than the whole object. The use of the Milliprobe (Reference 1) (Figure 11.6) developed in our laboratory obviates some or all of these objections. The sample may be of infinite size, although the area of analysis

may be as small as 100μ; this small analysis area may mean that surface-enriched specimens can be inconspicuously "rubbed down" to a more representative interior region. The fact that the analysis is only of the surface has in the past limited quantitative work to such archaeological materials as glass and ceramic glazes, whereas the analysis of coins has been the province of neutron activation. It is the purpose of this part of the paper to describe some work where X-ray fluorescence has been successfully used in the analyses of precious coins.

The Coins

(See Figures 11.7a and b). It has long been realized that debasement of the gold coinage of Europe took place gradually after the loss of influence of the Byzantine empire. This decline of the coinage took place in Britain during the seventh century, but the precise moment and the stages of debasement have not been clear. "Good" gold in numismatic terms may mean anything from 100 percent to 70 percent gold, whereas "pale" gold may vary from 70 percent to 30 percent gold. Moreover, the surface color gives little idea of the true gold content because of the variable amounts of alloying elements silver and copper and impurities such as iron.

The coins of the period are very rare and so a destructive method of analysis would not be permissible. However, since we only require a representative surface of about $\frac{1}{2}$ mm², this may be obtained by careful treatment with emery paper removing the first 100μ of surface which might be unrepresentative.

Analysis

The coins are carefully positioned in front of the aperture of the spectrometer and irradiated by a Machlett OEG 50 tungsten target X-ray tube operating at 50 kV 40 mA. The secondary X-rays are allowed to pass through a thin pinhole "Mylar" window and are analyzed by a linear bent crystal (LiF) spectrometer using a sealed beryllium window xenon-filled counter. The spectrometer is of special design to obviate the necessity for a pivot point at the point of analysis. The spectrometer can operate with Bragg angles between 9° and 70°, so enabling all elements above potassium in the periodic table to be estimated.

A series of Bragg angles corresponding to the elements required to be analyzed may be set on front panel dials, and these angles are set in turn in the spectrometer by a synchro servosystem to an accuracy better than $\frac{1}{2}$ minute of arc.

The X-rays registered by the xenon counter are pulse-height analyzed and recorded by a print-out system or on a special drum recorder, the paper of which is printed in terms of Bragg angle along one axis. This drum recorder is used for draw-

11.6
Milliprobe X-ray spectro-
meter.

11.7a
Dark Age gold coins.

Two Examples of the
Use of Chemical
Analysis in the
Solution of
Archaeological Problems
162

Table 11.2
X-Ray Spectrometry
Analysis Results

Gold Siliquae	7	6	5	4	3	2	1	0
Postulated Percent	100	85.7	71.4	57.1	42.9	28.6	14.3	0
Actual Mean Percent	95	81.5	71.6	57.2	43.4	28.2	13	2
No. of Coins	9	2	10	11	7	5	1	18

ing out spectra when the elements present are unknown.

Results

Table 11.2 gives a summary of the results of the analyses, but requires some explanation. The standard weight of this type of coin was 7 siliquae[2] (from the Byzantine standard), and it might seem likely that if they were to "devalue" they might do this in seventh parts. The evidence for this is given by the analyses of the coins; it can be seen that their compositions "cluster" around those compositions which are equivalent to 4, 3, and 2 siliquae of gold, the balance being silver. These compositions have definite gaps between them. There are sufficient analyses of these gold coins to make the results statistically most convincing, and it would appear likely that the devaluation took place in discrete steps of one seventh. This is a result which was in no way suspected before the analyses had been carried out.

Other analyses of later dark age silver coins (Figure 11.7b) have recently been undertaken. Here we find much the same story as for the gold coins, certainly during the early period of the use of silver. The silver is debased with copper in sevenths from fine silver to six-sevenths and five-sevenths. After this, chaos set in as far as the economy was concerned and no systematic debasement appears to have occurred since the silver content becomes very variable or nonexistent.

Perhaps it is noteworthy that when Britain again devalued in 1967, they also did so in sevenths, or 14.3 percent.

Acknowledgments

The optical emission spectrographic analyses have largely been undertaken by Mrs. Millett, while those using X-ray fluorescence have been undertaken by Mrs. J. Stern and Miss J. Hamblin; this paper would have been impossible without their collaboration, for which I am most grateful. Much of the work has been published in *Archaeometry*, the journal of our laboratory.

[2]There is some evidence to show that this was equal to 21 (barley-) grains and the coins do in fact weigh about 21 modern grains. This would mean that 1 siliqua was equal to 3 grains.

References

Archaeometry, **6**, 31, 1964.

1.
Banks, M. and Hall, E. T.

Archaeometry, **6**, 1963, pp. 10–17.

2.
Hennessy, J. B., and Millett, A.

Archaeometry, **10**, 76, 1967.

3.
Millett, A., and Catling, H. W.

The Observer, 3rd August, 1960.

4.
Palmer, L. R.

Mycenaeans and Minoans, London, 1961.

5.
Palmer, L. R.

Archaeometry, **2**, 1959, pp. 23–31.

6.
Richards, E. E.

Archaeometry, **3**, 1960, pp. 25–28.

7.
Richards, E. E.

Chapter 12

High-Resolution Gamma Ray Spectroscopic Analyses of Mayan Fine Orange Pottery[1]

Appendix

Edward V. Sayre and Lui-Heung Chan
Brookhaven National Laboratory

Jeremy A. Sabloff
Peabody Museum, Harvard University

Fine Orange ware is a very distinctive pottery found generally, but in relatively small abundance, at Mayan sites in Mesoamerica. The ware tends to be in the form of very elegant, thin-walled vessels with surfaces covered in elaborate relief decoration. It is clearly a luxury ware, contrasting greatly in style with the heavy utilitarian wares of the sites at which it is found. Another point of contrast with utilitarian ware is that true Fine Orange is made from an especially fine-grained, homogeneous clay without temper while Mayan pottery generally is tempered. When fired under oxidative conditions, the paste becomes a bright orange. Some similar vessels of a fine-grained, untempered grey paste, so-called Fine Grey ware, might differ from Fine Orange only in having been fired in a reducing atmosphere. Representative specimens of Fine Orange sherds and of utilitarian ware sherds from Altar de Sacrificios are shown in Figures 12.1 and 12.2, respectively.

Fine Orange ware can be divided into at least five main stylistic types which have been designated in chronological order, Z, Y, X, V, and U (Reference 3). The Z and Y types relate to the Terminal Late Classic Mayan period of the ninth and tenth centuries A.D.; the X type is thought to have been produced in the early post-classic period, perhaps well into the eleventh and twelfth centuries; the V and U types are correspondingly more recent in date with the U pottery having been produced as late as the period of the Spanish conquest.

Some years ago Professor Linton Satterswaithe of the University Museum, Philadelphia, was kind enough to furnish some Type Y Fine Orange and utilitarian sherds from Kixpek and Piedras Negras for one of our first investigations of ancient artifacts by means of neutron activation. In this initial investigation it was found that Fine Orange ware from Kixpek and Piedras Negras, two well-separated Mayan sites in Guatemala, were very similar in the trace impurity concentrations measured but that they differed significantly in this respect with the utilitarian ware found at Piedras Negras. Not long ago Professor Gordon Willey and Mr. Jeremy Sabloff of the Peabody Museum, Harvard University, suggested a continuation in greater depth of this investigation. We were indeed interested in pursuing further this worthwhile problem, particularly as the new high-resolution gamma ray detectors would

permit the determination of a greater number of trace elements within the specimens. (Reference 2.) Willey and Sabloff first furnished for this new study an extensive group of sherds from the Peabody Museum excavations at Seibal and Altar de Sacrificios, sites in the Peten Province of Guatemala. Within the groups from each site there were included Type Z and Type Y Fine Orange, Tres Naciones Fine Grey, and utilitarian specimens. Together with this basic group of specimens, we included, with Professor Satterswaithe's permission, specimens that had been saved of the Fine Orange bowl from Kixpek and the Fine Orange and utilitarian sherds from Piedras Negras. Willey and Sabloff further obtained two specimens of Y Fine Orange and one of X Fine Orange from the Carnegie Institution of Washington excavations at Uaxactun in northeastern Guatemala. This provided representation of five important excavation sites geographically rather broadly distributed from central through northern Guatemala. From outside of Guatemala to the east, single specimens of Y Fine Orange were obtained from two excavations in British Columbia, El Cayo, and San Jose. From locations much further to the northwest near the coast of the state of Tabasco in Mexico, a specimen of Fine Grey was provided from the Carlos Greene site near Comalcalco, a specimen of Fine Orange from each of two as yet unnamed nearby sites, and two Fine Orange specimens from Cintla, near the mouth of the Usumacinta River. A Fine Orange figurine was provided from Jonuta, which is on the lower Usumacinta, and from Nueva Esperenza, further up this river but still within Tabasco, two pairs of sherds of local manufacture, one calcite tempered and one covered with a red slip, were obtained for comparison with the Fine Orange specimens. Finally, a group of three sherds of the somewhat later Type X were obtained from the Carnegie Institution excavations at Chichen Itza. The individual collections to which we are indebted for each of these groups of specimens are acknowledged in the comments on the archaeological background and implications of these analyses which Mr. Sabloff has kindly prepared as an appendix to this paper. In all, the sites from which the specimens have come spread moderately well over the geographical area associated with the late classical and early past classical Mayan culture. Their locations are shown in Figure 12.3.

There are a number of interesting questions which the analysis of these specimens might help answer. Among them

[1] Research carried out under the auspices of the U.S. Atomic Energy Commission.

165

12.1
Some Type *Y* Fine Orange sherds from Altar de Sacrificios. See Table 12.3 for accession numbers and analyses of these specimens.

12.2
Some utilitarian ware sherds from Altar de Sacrificios. See Table 12.12 for accession numbers and analyses.

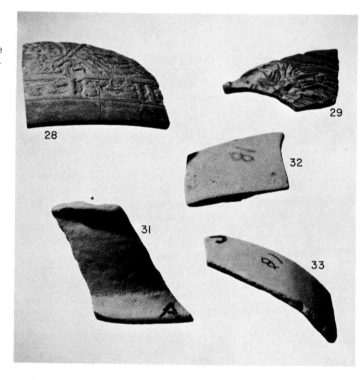

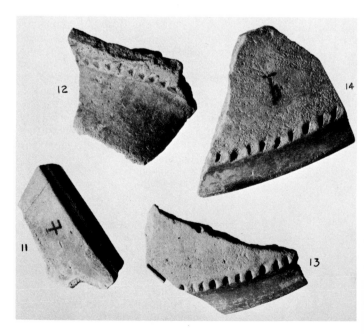

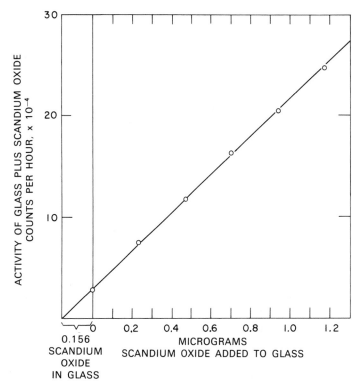

12.4
Calibration curve for the determination of scandium oxide in the standard glass.

ACTIVITY OF GLASS PLUS SCANDIUM OXIDE COUNTS PER HOUR, x 10⁻⁴

30

20

10

0.156 SCANDIUM OXIDE IN GLASS

0   0.2   0.4   0.6   0.8   1.0   1.2

MICROGRAMS
SCANDIUM OXIDE ADDED TO GLASS

12.3
Excavation sites from which specimens analyzed in this study were obtained.

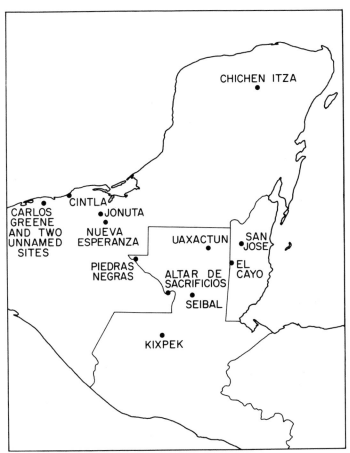

CHICHEN ITZA

CINTLA

CARLOS
GREENE
AND TWO
UNNAMED
SITES

JONUTA

NUEVA
ESPERANZA

UAXACTUN

SAN
JOSE

PIEDRAS
NEGRAS

ALTAR DE
SACRIFICIOS

EL
CAYO

SEIBAL

KIXPEK

are whether Fine Orange ware was an item of commerce originating from one or a few geographic regions instead of being made locally. Did such regions of manufacture remain constant with time, that is, had the Z, Y, and X types common origins? Were the Fine Orange and Fine Grey pastes indeed alike except for state of oxidation? Could the same clay have been used in utilitarian ware that was used to produce Fine Orange, and is there any evidence of commerce in utilitarian ware?

Experimental Procedure

Slices of the firm interior portions of the sherds were used as samples for activation. These sample plates were approximate squares of about a centimeter on a side and about one millimeter thickness which were cut from the sherds by means of a carborundum-impregnated disk saw. All surface material was cut from them by this saw or by means of a carbide rotating burr, and they were leached in distilled water for 24 hours and dried before activation. Leaching was decided upon because the pottery is somewhat porous and there is the possibility that ground water could have leached salts from or deposited them in the sherds. At least controlled leaching would tend to bring the specimens to a similar condition with respect to water soluble components. The samples that had been retained from earlier studies, i.e., specimens from Kixpek and Piedras Negras, were powders which had been removed from the interior of the specimens by means of a tungsten carbide stylus. In this instance only 20 to 40 milligram samples had been retained.

Squares of a standard glass, essentially identical in dimension to the pottery plate samples were used for flux monitors. These glass squares which are cut from a single box of microscope slides were found to be uniform in composition and to contain all of the elements determined in concentration adequate to produce photopeaks following activation. Hence, each of the photopeaks measured in the specimens was monitored by the same photopeak of the same element in the standard glass, and variations in activation conditions within the reactor or changes in the response of the detector with gamma ray energy could be cancelled out. Difficulty was encountered in measuring the manganese peak in the standard glass with adequate accuracy because of an intense accompanying sodium activity; therefore, U.S. Geological Survey standard rock specimens AGV1, BCR1, GSP1, and G2 were run together with the pottery specimens during the short activation for standardization of manganese.

The concentrations of measured elements in the standard glass were determined by adding by means of a micropipet increasing increments of standard solutions of an element to one of a pair of standard glass plates. The solution was dried and the residue covered with the second plate. These pairs of glass plates had been carefully selected to form matched sets of pairs that closely agreed with each other in total weight. The "sandwiches" were then activated together and counted. The straight line plate of resultant activity versus the amount of element added, as shown in Figure 12.4 for scandium, permit the determination of the concentration in the glass itself and confirms the compositional uniformity of the glass pairs used in the calibration and the overall linearity of our measurements.[2]

Manganese was determined by a short activation, ten seconds at a flux of 4.4 x 10^{12} neutrons/cm^2 sec in the PN4 tube of the Brookhaven Graphite Reactor. Solid samples were enclosed in polyethylene vials and powdered samples sealed in heat-sealing Mylar envelopes. Interference of the 847-keV photopeak of manganese-56 by short-lived magnesium activity, the 837-keV peak of magnesium-27 which occurred in most utilitarian specimens but not appreciably in Fine Orange specimens, required that counting be delayed until about an hour after activation. Sodium could easily have been counted along with manganese, but deliberately none of the alkali metals were determined because of the uncertainty of the extent to which their concentrations might have been affected during burial. Also aluminum could have been measured with short activation but was not for practical reasons.

Longer lived activities were measured after a 24-hour irradiation in the North 8 Facility of the Brookhaven Graphite Reactor at a flux of 1.0 x 10^{13} neutrons/cm^2 sec. The counting of samples was started eight days after activation. However, as in the case of manganese, it was found that it was often necessary to wait for longer periods before some isotopes could be counted free of interference. The half-lives of the photopeaks were all measured as a criterion for a safe counting period. Table 12.1 lists the photopeaks counted. The measured activities of manganese-56 and chromium-51 contained interfering components arising from n,p and n,α reactions with the relatively high concentrations of iron present in the sherds, i.e., the Fe^{56} $(n,p)Mn^{56}$ and Fe^{54} $(n,\alpha)Cr^{51}$ reactions. Corrections for these interferences were calculated from the measured iron concentrations.

[2]Subsequent to the original calibration, the concentrations in the standard glass were compared to U.S. Geological Survey standard rock specimens AGV1, BCR1, GSP1, G2 by Dr. Pieter Meyers, and small corrections in concentrations were made to bring our absolute calibrations into agreement with these widely used standards. See Gordon, et al., *Geochimica et Cosmochimica Acta* 32, 1968, pp. 369 to 396, for resume of data for the standard samples.

Table 12.1
Isotopes Measured
Following Neutron
Activation

Element	Isotope Measured	Energy of γ-Ray Chosen (keV)	Half-Life	Time of Measurement After Activation
Manganese	Mn-56	847	2.58 hours	1 hour
Lanthanum	La-140	1596	40.2 hours	8 days
Thorium	Pa-233	312	27.4 days	26 days
Chromium	Cr-51	320	27.8 days	26 days
Cerium	Ce-141	145	32.5 days	26 days
Iron	Fe-59	1291	45 days	35 days
Scandium	Sc-46	889	84 days	8 days
Cobalt	Co-60	1173	5.27 years	35 days
Europium	Eu-152	122	13 years	26 days

12.5
Comparison of the concentration of various oxides in a Fine Orange bowl from Kixpek (o) and the standard deviation ranges of concentrations of Fine Orange ware from Piedras Negras (◇), Seibal (□), Altar de Sacrificios (◆), Uaxactun (■) and Chichen Itza (+).

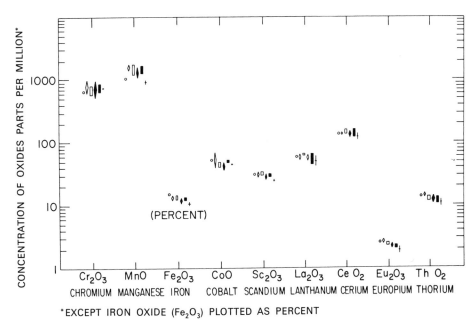

12.6
Some Type *X* Fine Orange sherds from Chichen Itza. See Table 12.7 for accession numbers and analyses.

12.7
Ratios of concentrations in specimens from British Honduras to mean concentrations in all matching Fine Orange specimens.

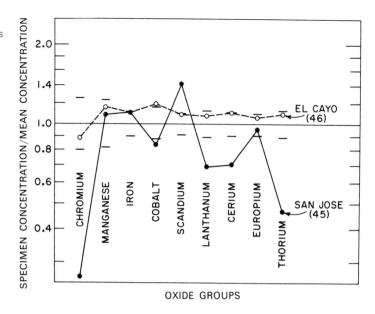

Table 12.2
Fine Orange Ware From Seibal (Concentration in parts per million of oxide*)

12.8
Ratios of concentrations in matching Fine Orange specimens from Tabasco to mean concentrations in all matching Fine Orange specimens.

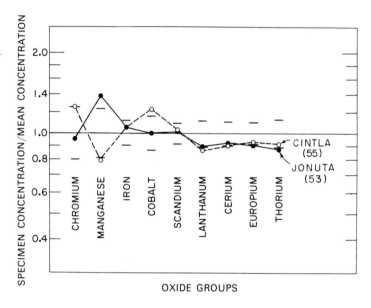

Table 12.3
Fine Orange Ware from Altar De Sacrificios (Concentration in parts per million of oxide*)

12.9
Ratios of concentrations in nonmatching Fine Orange specimens from Tabasco to mean concentrations in all matching Fine Orange specimens.

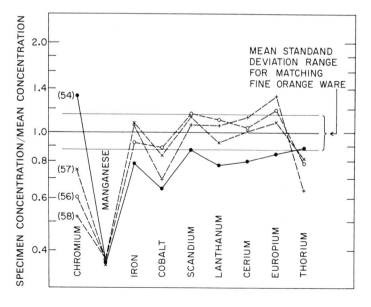

Table 12.4
Fine Orange Ware From Kixpek (Concentration in parts per million of oxide*)

Sample No.	Field Catalog No.	Type	Chromium Cr$_2$O$_3$	Manganese MnO	Iron Fe$_2$O$_3$*	Cobalt CoO	Scandium Sc$_2$O$_3$	Lanthanum La$_2$O$_3$	Cerium CeO$_2$	Europium Eu$_2$O$_3$	Thorium ThO$_2$
(15)	S-205	Y	610	1770	8.1	36	32	65	104	2.05	14.0
(16)	S-861	Y	620	1610	8.2	39	34	59	99	2.14	14.8
(17)	S-920	Y	660	869	8.2	33	32	60	107	1.97	15.3
(18)	S-70	Y	770	669	7.0	33	28	55	90	1.97	13.3
(19)	S-90	Y	770	763	7.4	36	30	58	98	1.88	14.4
(20)	S-90	Y	650	1400	8.2	38	32	60	95	2.05	13.6
(23)	S-891	Y	760	1210	8.8	37	33	59	103	1.97	15.1
(24)	S-738	Y	830	1010	8.4	38	27	58	96	2.05	16.1
(25)	S-974	Y	860	1230	7.9	40	30	61	103	2.05	13.9
(21)	S-128	Z	810	1410	7.8	37	31	58	92	2.05	12.5
(22)	S-415	Z	590	1410	8.9	46	31	61	103	2.28	15.7
(26)	S-139	Grey	540	1290	6.9	40	30	61	84	1.97	14.5
(27)	S-1077	Grey	910	1010	8.2	35	31	59	91	2.14	15.1
Mean			720	1060	7.9	38	31	60	97	2.04	14.5
Standard Deviation Range			610–840	867–1550	7.4–8.6	34–41	29–33	57–62	91–104	1.94–2.14	13.4–15.5
Standard Deviation as Percent of Mean			17.8%	33.7%	8.0%	9.3%	5.9%	4.0%	7.4%	5.0%	7.3%

* Except Fe$_2$O$_3$ reported as percent.

Sample No.	Accession No.	Type	Chromium Cr$_2$O$_3$	Manganese MnO	Iron Fe$_2$O$_3$*	Cobalt CoO	Scandium Sc$_2$O$_3$	Lanthanum La$_2$O$_3$	Cerium CeO$_2$	Europium Eu$_2$O$_3$	Thorium ThO$_2$
(28)	58-38-20/21773	Y	920	1480	7.5	38	29	58	103	2.05	17.5
(29)	58-38-20/21773	Y	710	1460	7.3	36	30	53	84	1.88	14.7
(30)	58-38-20/21771	Y	560	2110	7.0	36	28	54	91	1.97	12.1
(31)	58-38-20/21771 (33)	Y	1290	1120	6.3	40	25	50	82	1.88	12.9
(32)	58-38-20/21771 (33)	Y	1050	869	7.5	36	27	57	101	1.97	16.4
(33)	58-38-20/21771 (33)	Y	440	657	6.2	24	26	43	73	1.54	12.3
(35)	58-38-20/21774	Y	870	1760	7.0	38	30	59	122	2.05	14.3
(36)	58-38-20/22811	Y	600	1590	7.6	38	30	45	91	1.88	12.1
(37)	58-38-20/21777	Y	920	1300	6.3	33	28	58	85	1.97	14.4
(38)	58-38-20/21777	Y	870	1750	6.4	34	26	57	93	1.88	15.2
(47)	58-38-20/21771 (43-K-1)	Y	560	1010	7.1	38	26	52	88	1.97	13.4
(48)	58-38-20/21771	Y	780	1160	6.9	35	25	54	86	1.88	15.4
(34)	58-38-20/21769 (43)	Z	900	1220	7.6	35	29	55	91	1.97	15.7
(39)	58-38-20/21729	Grey	820	1190	7.1	38	27	54	87	2.05	15.9
(40)	58-38-20/21736	Grey	480	1230	7.1	39	25	49	83	1.88	12.5
(41)	58-38-20/21772	Grey	730	1170	7.0	36	26	54	88	1.80	14.4
(49)	58-38-20/21772	Grey	530	1070	6.5	33	25	47	82	1.80	11.1
Mean			730	1260	6.9	36	27	53	89	1.90	14.0
Standard Deviation Range			550–990	953–1670	6.5–7.5	32–40	25–29	48–58	80–100	1.80–2.00	12.3–16.0
Standard Deviation as Percent of Mean			34.8%	32.4%	7.4%	12.3%	7.0%	9.6%	12.0%	7.1%	13.6%

* Except Fe$_2$O$_3$ reported as percent.

Sample No.	Identification No.	Type	Chromium Cr$_2$O$_3$	Manganese MnO	Iron Fe$_2$O$_3$*	Cobalt CoO	Scandium Sc$_2$O$_3$	Lanthanum La$_2$O$_3$	Cerium CeO$_2$	Europium Eu$_2$O$_3$	Thorium ThO$_2$
K1	Na-11606	Y	690	869	8.9	43.3	33	54	91	2.14	15.9

* Except Fe$_2$O$_3$ reported as percent

Results

The most significant and striking aspect of the analytical data on these specimens is the close similarity of composition of Fine Orange and Fine Grey ware from Mayan sites widely spread throughout the central region of Mayan culture. The analyses of Fine Orange specimens from five Guatemalan sites, Seibal, Altar de Sacrificios, Kixpek, Piedras Negras, and Uaxactun are listed in Tables 12.2 through 12.6, respectively. The statistical summaries of these tables show that the concentrations of the oxide of iron, cobalt, scandium, lanthanum, cerium, europium, and thorium in this fine ware from any one site are consistent with a standard deviation of about ten percent. The concentrations of chromium and manganese are somewhat less consistent but still are grouped with standard deviations of only twenty to thirty percent. It should perhaps be made clear that these are the standard deviations of the groups of determinations themselves and not deviations of the means of the groups. As is common practice in the field of forensic trace impurity analysis, the component concentrations have been assumed to be logarithmically rather than linearly distributed. The means and standard deviations have been calculated accordingly, that is, they are arithmetical means and standard deviations of the logarithms of concentrations. When these arithmetic means and standard deviations of logarithms are converted back to concentrations, they become the geometric means of the concentrations and factors of variation by which one multiplies and divides the geometric mean to express a standard deviation range. The deviation of these factors from 1 is what we have listed in our tables as standard deviation expressed as percent of mean. A standard deviation factor of 1.10, therefore, would be recorded as a deviation of ten percent of the mean.

The close agreement between the Fine Orange specimens from the different sites is shown in Figure 12.5, in which the length of the diamonds plotted indicate the extent of one standard deviation range for a group. Clearly the means for each of the groups generally agree within average standard deviations for the groups, and there is no indication that a Fine Orange specimen from one of these sites would exhibit significant differences from similar specimens from another site. The combined specimens of these groups include twenty seven *Y*, three *Z* and one *X* Fine Orange, and eight Fine Grey specimens. Thus within the extent of this sampling, we observe no chronological change in concentrations and no significant compositional differences between the Fine Orange and Fine Grey objects.

A light sampling of sites somewhat peripheral to the central region of Mayan settlement has indicated that some of the Fine Orange pieces at these more outlying locations are consistent in composition with the main body of Fine Orange ware and some are significantly different from it. A group of three of the somewhat more recent Type *X* sherds from Chichen Itza (Table 12.7 and Figure 12.6) were all essentially consistent with the earlier Fine Orange from the Peten. Except for chromium, however, their concentrations were all a little below average, and it is possible that a more extensive sampling of Chichen Itza Fine Orange might establish that some small compositional differences are characteristic of it. The means for these three specimens are also plotted in Figure 12.5.

From the more eastern region of present-day British Honduras, we received a Fine Orange specimen from San Jose and one from El Cayo. Their analyses are listed in Tables 12.8 and 12.9, respectively. The San Jose sherd was compositionally quite different from the usual Fine Orange ware, having only about one-third as much chromium and half as much thorium. On the other hand, the sherd from El Cayo agreed reasonably with the usual Fine Orange pattern of composition. The ratios of the concentration of oxides in these specimens to the mean concentrations of the corresponding oxides in the large group of matching Fine Orange specimens are shown in Figure 12.7. The horizontal lines equally spaced above and below the unity ratio line are the single standard deviation range limits for the matching Fine Orange data in this and following similar figures.

From the more northwestern region of the Mexican state of Tabasco, we have received Fine Orange or Fine Grey specimens from five sites: Jonuta, Cintla, Carlos Greene, and the as yet unnamed sites near Carlos Greene. In this more outlying region one again finds some matching and some nonmatching specimens (Table 12.10). A comparison of the matching specimens, one from Jonuta and one from Cintla, to the means of the large group of matching Fine Orange is shown in Figure 12.8. A similar comparison of these specimens which do not agree in composition with the matching Fine Orange is shown in Figure 12.9. Here it is apparent that specimens 56, 57, and 58 from Carlos Greene and the nearby unnamed site all deviated from the basic Fine Orange in a similar manner which, of course, suggests that they might have been made of the same local clay. Again for this new type of clay, there seemed to be no significant compositional difference between a Fine Grey specimen 56 and related Fine Orange specimens 57 and 58. The other nonmatching sherd, specimen 54, from Cintla, is like them in having relatively low manganese, but on the whole is independently different.

All in all we have analyzed 45 Fine Orange or Fine Grey sherds which match

Table 12.5
Fine Orange Ware From Piedras Negras (Concentration in parts per million of oxide*)

Table 12.6
Fine Orange Ware From Uaxactun (Concentration in parts per million of oxide*)

Table 12.7
Fine Orange Ware From Chichen Itza (Concentration in parts per million of oxide*)

Table 12.8
Fine Orange Ware From El Cayo, British Honduras (Concentration in parts per million of oxide*)

Table 12.9
Fine Orange Ware From San Jose, British Honduras (Concentration in parts per million of oxide*)

Table 12.10
Fine Orange Ware From Tabasco (Concentration in parts per million of oxide*)

Sample No.	Identification No.	Type	Chromium Cr$_2$O$_3$	Manganese MnO	Iron Fe$_2$O$_3$*	Cobalt CoO	Scandium Sc$_2$O$_3$	Lanthanum La$_2$O$_3$	Cerium CeO$_2$	Europium Eu$_2$O$_3$	Thorium ThO$_2$
PN1	L-88-42	Y	530	1240	8.5	37	32	63	92	2.48	16.6
PN2	L-88-55	Y	870	1130	7.5	39	28	57	92	2.14	15.6
PN3	L-88-40	Y	950	1010	6.8	38	26	49	86	2.05	14.9
PN4	L-88-41	Grey	930	1370	8.5	58	31	52	94	2.14	16.8
PN5	L-88-46	Grey	900	1500	8.2	59	32	54	94	2.31	18.4
Mean			810	1240	7.9	45	30	55	92	2.22	16.3
Standard Deviation Range			640–1040	1060–1550	7.2–8.6	36–57	27–32	50–60	88–95	2.06–2.39	15.2–17.7
Standard Deviation as Percent of Mean			27.4%	16.8%	10.0%	26.7%	8.9%	10.0%	3.8%	7.9%	8.4%

* Except Fe$_2$O$_3$ reported as percent.

Sample No.	Accession No.	Type	Chromium Cr$_2$O$_3$	Manganese MnO	Iron Fe$_2$O$_3$*	Cobalt CoO	Scandium Sc$_2$O$_3$	Lanthanum La$_2$O$_3$	Cerium CeO$_2$	Europium Eu$_2$O$_3$	Thorium ThO$_2$
(42)	33-99-20/3191(893)	Y	730	1220	7.4	40	30	53	88	1.88	15.2
(43)	34-108-20/2893	Y	920	786	7.8	44	29	61	106	1.88	14.4
(44)	24-108-20/3778	X	730	962	7.1	43	28	42	83	1.80	12.3

* Except Fe$_2$O$_3$ reported as percent.

Sample No.	Accession No.	Type	Chromium Cr$_2$O$_3$	Manganese MnO	Iron Fe$_2$O$_3$*	Cobalt CoO	Scandium Sc$_2$O$_3$	Lanthanum La$_2$O$_3$	Cerium CeO$_2$	Europium Eu$_2$O$_3$	Thorium ThO$_2$
(50)	52-33-20/19324(17)	X	770	669	5.9	38	23	44	76	1.61	11.6
(51)	52-33-20/19324(17–11)	X	790	798	6.5	38	24	39	75	1.53	13.0
(52)	52-33-20/19324(17)	X	770	704	6.5	38	24	58	93	1.80	12.6

* Except Fe$_2$O$_3$ reported as percent.

Sample No.	Accession No.	Type	Chromium Cr$_2$O$_3$	Manganese MnO	Iron Fe$_2$O$_3$*	Cobalt CoO	Scandium Sc$_2$O$_3$	Lanthanum La$_2$O$_3$	Cerium CeO$_2$	Europium Eu$_2$O$_3$	Thorium ThO$_2$
(46)	34-138-20/3707 (B-C IV)	Y	650	1200	8.2	46	31	58	101	2.05	15.6

* Except Fe$_2$O$_3$ reported as percent.

Sample No.	Accession No.	Type	Chromium Cr$_2$O$_3$	Manganese MnO	Iron Fe$_2$O$_3$*	Cobalt CoO	Scandium Sc$_2$O$_3$	Lanthanum La$_2$O$_3$	Cerium CeO$_2$	Europium Eu$_2$O$_3$	Thorium ThO$_2$
(45)	38-7-20/6355 (SJV)	Y	200	1170	8.2	32	41	38	68	1.88	6.7

* Except Fe$_2$O$_3$ reported as percent.

Sample No.	Identification No.	Site	Chromium Cr$_2$O$_3$	Manganese MnO	Iron Fe$_2$O$_3$*	Cobalt CoO	Scandium Sc$_2$O$_3$	Lanthanum La$_2$O$_3$	Cerium CeO$_2$	Europium Eu$_2$O$_3$	Thorium ThO$_2$
(53)	C/2593	Jonuta	720	1580	7.8	38	25	49	85	1.80	12.5
(54)	4827	Cintla	990	434	5.8	25	22	42	73	1.65	12.5
(55)	4825	Cintla	940	904	7.8	47	26	47	84	1.80	13.0
(56)†		Carlos Greene	450	446	6.8	34	28	60	95	2.28	11.3
(57)		Unnamed	560	434	7.9	32	28	49	92	2.14	11.7
(58)		Unnamed	390	434	7.8	27	26	58	103	2.62	9.2

* Except Fe$_2$O$_3$ reported as percent.
† Fine Grey specimen, sample number 56.

sufficiently closely for us to regard them as belonging to a single group. The overall statistics for this group are presented in Table 12.11. All of our specimens of Fine Orange from the central Mayan region have belonged to this group and about half of those found at more outlying sites. When specimens disagree with the main group in composition, the differences they exhibit tend to be quite pronounced and definite.

The utilitarian ware contrasts greatly with the Fine Orange in showing relatively little compositional uniformity. For example, in Table 12.12 which contains analyses of utilitarian ware from Altar de Sacrificios, differences as great as a factor of ten in the concentration of some elements occur with differences as great as a factor of two occurring for virtually all elements. Figure 12.10 compares the compositions of three of these specimens to the means of the matching Fine Orange group. The most immediate aspect of the chart is the disparity between the specimens. It is interesting to ask, in comparing these specimens to the Fine Orange, whether they could have been made of the same clay as the Fine Orange. The differences between them and Fine Orange might have arisen, of course, simply because of temper having been added to the utilitarian but not to the Fine Orange pottery. The temper in much of the utilitarian ware appears to have been a sand that one generally would have expected to have been a more pure material than clay. The addition of it probably would have resulted in a diluting down of the concentrations of the measured elements in the pottery matrix. Indeed most of the concentrations of oxides in the utilitarian specimens are lower than in the Fine Orange. However in utilitarian specimens 11 and 12, the concentrations of some elements, chromium, manganese, and cobalt, are so much below their concentrations in Fine Orange that these specimens could not possibly have been made with Fine Orange clay. These concentrations are in some instances only a tenth of the concentrations in Fine Orange, hence even if these elements were virtually absent in the temper and Fine Orange clay were used, nine parts of temper would have had to have been added to one part of clay to achieve this degree of dilution. Some pottery does contain a great deal of temper, but 90 percent does seem to be too high a proportion of temper to produce an acceptably strong pottery.

On the other hand, the concentrations in specimen 10 are remarkably parallel to the concentrations in Fine Orange except that they are lower by a reasonably constant factor of about one-fourth. Truly this specimen could have been made of Fine Orange clay. In fact in the accompanying paper in this symposium by Olin and Sayre on the analysis of American Colonial

and British North Devon pottery (see Reference 1) it is noted that in terms of the elements determined the North Devon gravel ware, which contains a sandy temper, is different from the North Devon fine ware in only being diluted approximately by about fifteen percent. Of course this simple relation between untempered and tempered pottery of the same regions will not always exist, but one can hope that when the source of the matching Fine Orange is located not only will fired clay from the region have the matching Fine Orange composition but that much of the local utilitarian ware will parallel the Fine Orange in composition. Whether specimen 10 was made from Fine Orange clay or not, it is still nearly unique among our utilitarian specimens in being so similar to Fine Orange. Only from Nueva Esperanza have there been other utilitarian specimens that are like Fine Orange except for a factor and their agreement to Fine Orange is not as close as is that of specimen 10.

Among the utilitarian specimens from Seibal (Table 12.13), there has also been a variety of compositions, but from this site there has been a small subgroup of specimens that are quite similar to each other in composition. The utilitarian specimens from Piedras Negras (Table 12.14) and from Nueva Esperanza (Table 12.15) introduced still more compositional variety. As has already been pointed out, there is some parallel between the Nueva Esperenza red slipped specimens and this matching group of Fine Orange. These particular specimens were selected to test the possibility that the matching Fine Orange might have originated in this region. At present our data allow this as a possibility but provide no strong evidence of its probability.

Table 12.11
Mean Concentration of 45 Matching Fine Orange Specimens (Concentration in parts per million of oxide*)

Table 12.12
Utilitarian Ware From Altar de Sacrificios (Concentration in parts per million of oxide*)

Table 12.13
Utilitarian Ware From Seibal (Concentration in parts per million of oxide*)

Table 12.14
Utilitarian Ware From Piedras Negras (Concentration in parts per million of oxide*)

Table 12.15
Utilitarian Ware From Nueva Esperenza (Concentration in parts per million of oxide*)

	Chromium Cr$_2$O$_3$	Manganese MnO	Iron Fe$_2$O$_3$*	Cobalt CoO	Scandium Sc$_2$O$_3$	Lanthanum La$_2$O$_3$	Cerium CeO$_2$	Europium Eu$_2$O$_3$	Thorium ThO$_2$
Mean	750	1150	7.4	38	29	54	92	1.97	14.3
Standard Deviation Range	600–930	869–1530	6.6–8.2	33–44	26–31	49–61	83–101	1.80–2.14	12.8–16.0
Standard Deviation as Percent of Mean	25.0%	33.0%	11.1%	15.3%	10.0%	12.0%	10.7%	9.9%	12.2%

* Except Fe$_2$O$_3$ reported as percent.

Sample No.	Accession No.	Chromium Cr$_2$O$_3$	Manganese MnO	Iron Fe$_2$O$_3$*	Cobalt CoO	Scandium Sc$_2$O$_3$	Lanthanum La$_2$O$_3$	Cerium CeO$_2$	Europium Eu$_2$O$_3$	Thorium ThO$_2$
(10)		660	681	4.7	36	19.4	39	63	1.30	10.5
(11)	58-38-20/21780 43 (E) 1	90	143	3.1	3.6	13.9	17.6	26	0.72	4.4
(12)	58-38-20/21745	70	505	5.8	8.6	23	33	56	1.06	17.6
(13)	63-33-20/22767 43 (E) 1	660	481	4.1	14.7	12.9	33	56	0.84	13.7
(14)	63-33-20/22767 43 (E) 1	500	340	3.6	8.8	12.2	27	44	0.85	12.3

* Except Fe$_2$O$_3$ reported as percent.

Specimen No.	Field Catalog No.	Chromium Cr$_2$O$_3$	Manganese MnO	Iron Fe$_2$O$_3$*	Cobalt CoO	Scandium Sc$_2$O$_3$	Lanthanum La$_2$O$_3$	Cerium CeO$_2$	Europium Eu$_2$O$_3$	Thorium ThO$_2$
(1)	S-173	100	126	2.3	7.3	18.9	24.3	46	0.95	5.4
(3)	S-470	380	128	2.9	5.7	16.1	7.1	16.6	0.31	3.9
(4)	S-961	260	88	1.6	7.6	15.6	49	67	1.97	5.2
(7)	S-393	43	182	1.4	3.7	11.7	18.1	28	0.59	3.7
Subgroup of Specimens with Similar Composition										
(2)	S-192	138	110	1.3	4.6	10.8	11.7	16.0	0.54	3.9
(5)	S-1098	215	117	2.1	8.2	15.3	21.5	41	0.95	4.4
(6)	S-63	141	122	2.8	7.0	13.3	20.6	26	0.84	4.9
(8)	S-571	370	211	2.6	6.8	12.7	22.5	37	0.67	6.1
(9)	S-89	198	154	2.7	4.7	13.4	14.0	24	0.54	4.1
Mean of Subgroup		198.0	138	2.2	6.1	13.0	17.4	28	0.68	4.6
Standard Deviation Range		133–290	106–181	1.6–3.1	4.7–7.9	11.4–14.9	13.0–23.5	19.3–40	0.54–0.88	3.9–5.5
Standard Deviation as Percent of Mean		49.2%	30.6%	37.9%	30.0%	13.5%	34.1%	45.8%	28.7%	18.6%

* Except Fe$_2$O$_3$ reported as percent.

Sample No.	Chromium Cr$_2$O$_3$	Manganese MnO	Iron Fe$_2$O$_3$*	Cobalt CoO	Scandium Sc$_2$O$_3$	Lanthanum La$_2$O$_3$	Cerium CeO$_2$	Europium Eu$_2$O$_3$	Thorium ThO$_2$
PN6	78	72	3.5	6.5	16.3	19.7	41	0.93	5.6
PN8	68	106	3.0	5.2	14.9	22.5	39	1.09	6.1
Mean	73	87	3.2	5.8	15.6	21.5	40	1.01	5.9
Standard Deviation Range	66–80	67–115	2.9–3.5	4.9–6.8	14.7–16.6	19.7–22.5	39–41	0.91–1.13	5.5–6.2
Standard Deviation Range as Percent of Mean	9.7%	31.7%	10.1%	18.1%	6.2%	8.5%	4.3%	11.8%	6.4%

* Except Fe$_2$O$_3$ reported as percent.

Sample No.	Type	Chromium Cr$_2$O$_3$	Manganese MnO	Iron Fe$_2$O$_3$*	Cobalt CoO	Scandium Sc$_2$O$_3$	Lanthanum La$_2$O$_3$	Cerium CeO$_2$	Europium Eu$_2$O$_3$	Thorium ThO$_2$
(59)	Red Slipped	430	563	4.5	20	18.3	43	65	1.37	12.3
(60)	Red Slipped	890	505	3.6	15	14.6	38	59	1.25	14.2
(61)	Calcium Carbonate Tempered	470	340	3.1	17	11.6	22.5	38	0.88	6.8
(62)	Calcium Carbonate Tempered	820	183	3.4	17	20.8	21.5	41	0.84	8.2

* Except Fe$_2$O$_3$ reported as percent

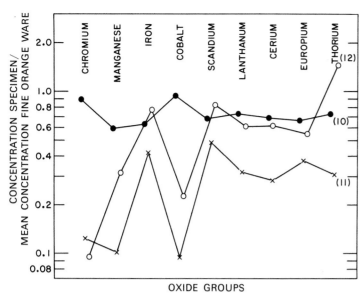

12.10
Ratios of concentrations
in some utilitarian ware
from Altar de Sacrificios
to mean concentrations
in the matching Fine
Orange ware.

High-Resolution Gamma
Ray Spectroscopic
Analyses of Mayan
Fine Orange Pottery

Concluding Resume

It is the contrast between the disparity of composition among the utilitarian specimens and the uniformity among the main body of Fine Orange specimens, along with the fact that not all Fine Orange specimens are matching in composition, that gives credence to the conclusion that the observed uniformity must be significant. By far the most simple logical explanation of the compositional uniformity of the matching Fine Orange specimens is that they were all made from the same clay, and hence were distributed through an extensive commerce from a single source. The use of a common clay in the fabrication of the matching subgroup of Seibal utilitarian specimens is likewise indicated. Here, since the compositional pattern appears to be a relatively unique local one, the use of a local clay is indicated.

Most of the Fine Orange specimens analyzed were Type Y, but the few specimens of Type Z and Type X that were included were not compositionally different from these Type Y specimens. This, of course, indicates the continuation of the tradition of Fine Orange manufacture at its primary site of origin for at least several centuries. There was also always a close consistency between Fine Orange and related Fine Grey specimens which suggests that they were indeed manufactured together.

Little evidence indicating a commerce in utilitarian pottery appears in our data, but the general inconsistency of its composition at individual sites greatly complicates any conclusions concerning its origins. In many instances, however, it can be concluded that the utilitarian pottery could not have been made from the same clay as the matching Fine Orange pottery.

Mr. Sabloff very kindly has been willing to comment upon the historical significance of our data and we are pleased to have his permission to append his comments to this paper. We are also very gratified that Professor Willey and Mr. Sabloff have agreed to continue to supply specimens which one hopes might eventually provide indications of the origin of the matching Fine Orange.

Acknowledgments

We wish to thank Professors Gordon Willey and Linton Satterswaithe and Mr. Jeremy Sabloff for the assemblage of this significant group of sherds and for their advice and encouragement. Particular thanks are also due to Dr. Pieter Meyers for reestablishing the calibration of our standard monitoring glass and to Mrs. Patricia Donnelly who was of continuous helpful assistance in activation and counting.

References

1.
Olin, J. S., and
Sayre, E. V.

"Compositional Categories of Some English and American Pottery of the American
Colonial Period." Chapter 14, this volume.

2.
Sayre, E. V.

"Refinement in Methods of Neutron Activation Analysis of Ancient Glass through
the Use of Lithium Drifted Germanium
Diode Counters." *Proceedings of the VIIth
International Congress on Glass,* Paper
220, Brussels, 1965.

3.
Smith, R. E.

"The Place of Fine Orange Pottery in
Mesoamerican Archaeology." *Amer.
Antiquity* **24,** 1958, 151–160.

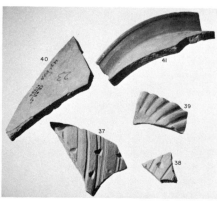

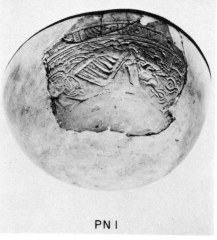

KI

PN I

A.1
Type *Y* Fine Orange
specimens from Seibal.
See Table 12.2.

A.2
Type *Z* (21 and 22),
Type *Y* (23, 24 and 25)
Fine Orange and Tres
Naciones Fine Grey (26
and 27) specimens
from Seibal. See Table
12.2.

A.3
Type 2 (34) and Type *Y*
(30 and 35) Fine Or-
ange specimens from
Altar de Sacrificios. See
Table 12.3.

A.4
Type *Y* Fine Orange (47
and 48) and a Tres Na-
ciones Fine Grey (49)
Specimen from Altar de
Sacrificios. See Table
12.3.

A.5
Type *Y* Fine Orange (37
and 38) and Tres Na-
ciones Fine Grey (39,
40 and 41) specimens
from Altar de Sacri-
ficios. See Table 12.3.

A.6
Type *Y* Fine Orange
bowls from Kixpek (K1)
and from Piedras Negras
(PN1). See Tables 12.4
and 12.5.

A.7
Type *Y* Fine Orange
(PN2 and PN3) and
some Fine Grey (PN4
and PN5) specimens
from Piedras Negras.
See Table 12.5.

A.8
Type *Y* (42 and 43)
and Type *X* (44) Fine
Orange specimens from
Uaxactun. See Table
12.6.

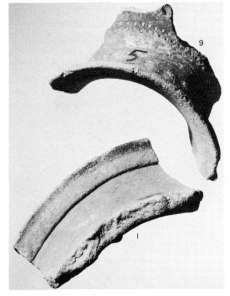

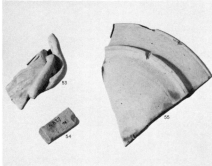

A.9
Type *Y* Fine Orange
specimens from San
Jose (45) and El Cayo
(46). See Tables 12.8
and 12.9.

A.10
Fine Orange specimens
from Jonuta (53) and
Cintla (54 and 55). See
Table 12.10.

A.11
A Fine Grey specimen
(56) from the Carlos
Greene site and two
Fine Orange specimens
(57 and 58) from
nearby unnamed sites.
See Table 12.10.

A.12
A utilitarian specimen
from Altar de Sacri-
ficios. See Table 12.12.

A.13
Utilitarian specimens
from Seibal. See Table
12.13.

A.14
Utilitarian specimens
from Seibal. See Table
12.13.

A.15
Utilitarian specimens
from Seibal. See Table
12.13.

A.16
Utilitarian specimens
from Piedras Negras.
See Table 12.14.

A.17
Sherds of probably lo-
cally made ware from
Nueva Esperenza. Red
slipped specimens (59
and 60) and calcite
tempered specimens
(61 and 62). See Table
12.15.

Appendix:

Comments on the Archaeological Background and Implications of the Neutron Activation Analyses of Fine Paste Pottery

The Brookhaven National Laboratory neutron activation study of Fine Orange and other pottery has, to date, been concerned with Fine Paste and non-Fine Paste material from fourteen different Southern Mesoamerican sites. The data which the study has so far uncovered are of much interest to the archaeologist and are quite relevent to any reconstruction of the cultures of the Terminal Classic and Early Postclassic Periods in southern Mesoamerica and their interrelationships (see Reference A2).

The results of the Brookhaven analyses indicate that the following were all made from the same clays: the Altar group Fine Orange pottery from Seibal (Peabody Museum excavations), Altar de Sacrificios (Peabody Museum excavations), Piedras Negras (University Museum excavations), Kixpek (University Museum excavations), Uaxactun (Carnegie Institution of Washington excavations), and El Cayo (Lundell collections). They further indicate that the following also were made from the same clays as the Altar group Fine Orange: the Balancan group Fine Orange and Tres Naciones group Fine Grey from Seibal and Altar de Sacrificios, the Silho group Fine Orange from Uaxactun, a Fine Orange figurine censer from Jonuta (Maler collection), and a plate from Cintla (Berendt collection). Finally, it points to the probability that the Silho group Fine Orange from Chichen Itza was also made from the same clays.

On the other hand, the results show that the monochrome and unslipped tempered sherds from Seibal and Altar de Sacrificios were made from different clays than the Fine Paste pottery, although there is some internal consistency among the non-Fine Paste sherds and even a small amount of intersite consistency in clays. However, the percentages of trace elements in one sherd of the Cambio unslipped type from Altar de Sacrificios seemed to differ from the Fine Orange percentages by only a constant factor. The non-Fine Paste sherds from Nueva Esperanza also differed from Fine Paste sherds, although two sherds only differed by a constant factor (but not as clearly as in the case of the Altar de Sacrificios sherd). In addition, the Altar group Fine Orange sherd from San Jose, one Late Postclassic Fine Orange sherd from Cintla, and the three Fine Paste sherds from sites near Comalcalco all differed from the other Fine Paste sherds. (Figures A.1 to A.17 are photographs of those analyzed specimens that have not appeared in the figures in the text of this chapter.)

What inferences can be drawn from these data? First of all, the sites of Seibal, Altar de Sacrificios, Piedras Negras, Kixpek, Uaxactun, and a site near El Cayo, which all have Altar group Fine Orange made from the same clays, were all connected during Terminal Late Classic times (A.D. 800–950) by trade or movements of people or both. It is possible that the Fine Orange pottery was traded to these sites from a single source. Yet, the Fine Orange appears in contexts at Seibal and Altar de Sacrificios which suggest that it was carried and made by nonclassic Maya peoples who took over these sites in the ninth century A.D. (see References A1 and A2). In addition, the Fine Paste pottery appears in collections at Piedras Negras and Uaxactun which date to the approximate abandonment of these sites. At the former, there was destruction of some monuments at this time, while at the later, a major building was left in a half-completed state. Sabloff and Willey (Reference A2) have hypothesized that the collapse of classic Maya civilization in the southern lowlands was specifically caused in part by an invasion of peoples from the gulf coast (Tabasco-Campeche) who were related to or in contact with the Toltecs of central Mexico and who also invaded northern Yucatan. These peoples may also have entered the Guatemalan highlands (where Kixpek is located) at this time. In light of this broad hypothesis, the findings of the neutron activation analyses and, specifically, the new analyses of the Silho group Fine Orange from Chichen Itza are of much interest. Silho group Fine Orange, which differs in style and form from Altar group Fine Orange, has been considered the ceramic marker for the Toltec takeover of Chichen Itza, although the exact date of the takeover is a matter of dispute. The identity of the clays of Fine Orange sherds from the southern lowlands and northern Yucatan is obviously quite suggestive.

It is possible that the clays themselves were traded over great distances, although there is no ethnohistorical or ethnographic evidence to back up such an hypothesis. But whether it was the clays or finished pots which were traded or carried by invaders, it is of much importance to try to find the source area of the Fine Paste clay. Before the neutron activation study began, it was generally believed that the Tabasco lowlands were the source of

Balancan group Fine Orange, the Cam-
peche lowlands were the source of Silho
group Fine Orange, and that the periphery
of the Peten might be the source of Altar
group Fine Orange (Reference A4). The
neutron activation analyses have not completely clarified the situation to date, although they have indicated that Fine
Paste pottery found in the Maya lowlands
might have one instead of three sources.
It will probably be necessary to wait for
the results of future analyses of clays from
the Pasión area and clays and pottery
from the gulf coast lowlands before more
can be said about source areas.

It is of some interest to note, however,
that there are indications that the composition of Fine Orange sherds may differ
within the Tabasco region itself and that
there may have been more than one center of manufacture. On the basis of the
analysis of the material from the Carlos
Greene site and the two nearby unnamed
sites, it would appear that there was a
pottery center(s) which did not draw on
the same clays as did the one which supplied the Fine Orange pottery for Yucatan
and the Peten. Did the former center(s)
draw on clays from the Grijalva and its
tributaries and supply the Fine Orange for
Chiapas? And did the latter center draw
on clays from the Usumacinta? If so,
where is the center located? Apparently, it
was not at Nueva Esperanza, and the data
from Cintla are somewhat ambiguous and
do not help at the present moment. Or,
the question might be asked, was Fine
Paste pottery locally made at a number of
gulf coast sites but imported only from
one? More work is needed before these
questions can be answered.

Finally, it should be noted that the data
from San Jose are quite puzzling and do
not fit any hypothesis at the present time.

All in all, the neutron activation analyses
have so far connected the Fine Paste pottery from a number of far-flung sites and
have not been at all inconsistent with the
hypothesis of "Mexican" incursions in the
southern and northern Maya lowlands at
the end of the classic period. When the
study is completed, we should be in a
good position to formulate some tight
hypotheses about the Fine Paste situation
from the neutron activation data (instead
of the random kind of questions asked
here) and to formulate strategies for testing them.

References

The Ceramics of Altar de Sacrificios.
Papers of the Peabody Museum, Harvard
University. In press, 1968.

A1.
Adams, Richard E. W.

"The Collapse of Maya Civilization in the
Southern Lowlands: A Consideration of
History and Process". *Southwestern Journal of Anthropology*, Albuquerque, Vol.
23, No. 4, 1967, pp. 311–336.

A2.
Sabloff, Jeremy A.,
and Willey, Gordon R.

"Type Descriptions of the Fine Paste
Ceramics of the Bayal Boca Complex,
Seibal, Peten, Guatemala". In press,
1968.

A3.
Sabloff, Jeremy Arac

"The Place of Fine Orange Pottery in
Mesoamerican Archaeology". *American
Antiquity*, Salt Lake City, Vol. 24, No. 2,
1968, pp. 151–160.

A4.
Smith, Robert E.

Chapter 13   **Pottery Analysis by Neutron Activation**[1]   **I. Perlman and Frank Asaro**
University of California, Berkeley

Introduction

Archaeologists have long been concerned with the provenance of pottery and have evolved elaborate systems of classification based largely upon form and decorative style. In more recent years such deductions have been supplemented by examination of the fabric, in particular the identification of the minerals that appear in the fired clay. (See Reference 1.) Such studies bear the implicit assumption that pottery produced in a particular area will carry a specific geochemical fingerprint. Another form of chemical fingerprinting considers the elemental composition of the pottery. For reasons which will become clear, the only feasible techniques for this type of analysis are those which can determine many elements simultaneously and those which are sensitive to the minor components. Two such techniques have been exploited: emission spectroscopy (Reference 2) and neutron activation (Reference 3). Of these two, neutron activation is capable of measuring a considerable number of trace elements down into the parts-per-million range.

The present study is a detailed evaluation of the accuracy attainable by neutron activation analysis employing a germanium gamma-ray spectrometer. (Reference 4.) When pottery samples are irradiated with neutrons, many radioactive species are formed and the mixture produces very complex gamma-ray spectra. Analysis of a spectrum gives information which can be converted to the abundances of those elements measured. For a large number of analyses, the data processing becomes so tedious that the use of a computer is virtually mandatory.

Addressed to problems in archaeology, there were no a priori guidelines for the accuracy required or the number and kinds of elements for which data would be useful. The questions so posed are still not completely answered. However, the initial premise—that the highest possible accuracy on the largest number of elements is desirable—seems borne out. Even so, some compromises were necessary in order to economize on time and equipment utilization.

Method of Analysis

After cleaning a small area of the potsherd with a sapphire scraper, a powder sample is taken with a drill fashioned from a rod of synthetic sapphire whose base could be placed in the chuck of an ordinary hand drill. Approximately 100 mg of powder is mixed with 50 mg of cellulose and compacted into a pill (1 cm $\times$ 1.5 mm) using a hand-operated hydraulic press. After wrapping in pure aluminum foil, the sample is ready for irradiation. Each batch

of aluminum foil must be irradiated before use so that corrections may be applied for impurities present.

The pills are placed in a cylindrical capsule fitted with a jig which holds the pills on edge in a radial array. Twelve pills fit on one tier and two tiers fit in a capsule. Along with ten specimens to be analyzed, two pills made of a standard are placed in each tier. (The preparation and calibration of a proper standard was a central issue in this study and will be described in the next section.) The sealed capsule is suspended by a wire in the central thimble of the Berkeley Triga Reactor and rotated during irradiation. The rotation of the pills ensures that each sees the same radial neutron flux pattern and all pills in each tier have virtually identical vertical positioning.

Our equipment for gamma-ray analysis consists of a germanium detector ($\sim$5 cm^3 volume) and a 1600-channel analyzer. This assembly gives gamma-ray peak half-widths of about 2.1 keV under ideal operating conditions but about 2.8 keV at 1 MeV energy under the actual conditions employed in pottery analysis. The loss of resolution comes from compressing the spectrum to about 1 keV per channel and operating at counting rates up to 10,000 counts per second. The stored data are placed on magnetic tape for computer analysis, and we also print out the actual numbers on paper tape and obtain an automatically printed graph of the spectrum either from the analyzer storage or from the magnetic tape. The data processing will be described separately.

The employment of standard pill size assures a constant solid angle for the counting of the gamma rays, and the rotating assembly during irradiation assures that the specimens and standards are exposed to the identical neutron environment. Tests have shown that the entire analytical process is reproducible with a standard error of 0.4 percent, and this spread includes inhomogeneities in the composition of our standard material.

The recipe we have employed for irradiation, cooling, and counting was devised to optimize the accuracy in determining the maximum number of useful elements. Each batch is subjected to two irradiations: the first for six minutes at a flux of about 1.7×10^{12} neutrons/cm^2 sec and the second for eight hours at a flux of 2×10^{13}. Two hours after the short irradiation, gamma-ray analysis is begun and each sample is counted for 15 min. The elements determined here are Mn, Na, K, Eu, Ba, Sr, Cu, In, and Ga, but only Mn and Na are measured with high precision. Two of these, Eu and Ba, are

[1]This work was performed under the auspices of the U.S. Atomic Energy Commission.

measured with better accuracy in the long irradiation; K is simply insensitive to neutron activation; In, Cu, and Ga, although sensitive, are usually found in ceramics in very low amounts.

The pills are encapsulated again and eight days after the 8-hr irradiation are again placed on the analyzer, this time for counting periods of 50 min each. This regime is aimed at those radioactive species with half-lives in the range 1-10 days and the 8-day cooling period is employed to permit decay of the intense radiation from Na^{24} which has a 15-hr half-life. For many elements, the accuracy attainable depends upon the Compton background to which Na^{24} would be the heaviest contributor at earlier times. The elements measured in the 50-min counts are U, Sm, Lu, Ti, Ca, Yb, La, As, Br, and Sb. The attainable accuracies differ considerably as will be shown in Table 13.3.

After the 50-min counts, the pills are cooled for another two weeks after which they are counted for periods of three hours or more. This cooling period effects considerable diminution in background and permits better accuracy in the determination of the longer-lived species. The elements programmed for these "long runs" are Fe, Sc, Ta, Eu, Zn, Co, Cs, Sb, Cr, Hf, Th, Ba, Ni, Rb, and Yb. This list includes a number of the most accurately determined elements.

Standardization and the Analysis of Errors

Counting Statistics and Other Sources of Error

The statistics of counting radioactive events determines one of the errors of neutron activation analysis. The contribution to the standard error of a determination from this source is given by the square root of all of the counts used in measuring a particular element. For a strongly activated element such as scandium, this may amount to only a fraction of a percent; for others, the errors may be so large as to make the analysis of doubtful value. Obviously, there is advantage in counting the radioactivity with high efficiency and for as long a period of time as practicable.

Other errors have to do with the reproducibility of all conditions of the neutron irradiation and the measuring instruments. Errors of this kind are controllable. A third category, which we shall call the "background error," is more subtle and will be discussed separately.

Neutron Monitoring

A major concern is the proper monitoring of the neutrons to which the specimens are exposed. Neutrons within a reactor are not monoenergetic and the response (cross-section) for absorbing neutrons is an energy-distribution function which can be quite different for different isotopes. Furthermore, even within a particular reactor the energy profile can be different in different positions and change as the reactor is loaded differently and as fuel burns. Finally, neutron capture cross-sections are in general not well known. The only safe way of handling this problem if accuracy is demanded is to have present standard amounts of each of the elements for which the specimens are to be analyzed. For the present problem in which many elements are determined simultaneously, it is not practicable to have separate monitors for each element so a composite material is much preferred. This requirement has led to the preparation and calibration of "Standard Pottery." If the standards and the specimens are maintained in the same time-averaged neutron environment, the analytical results become independent of uncertainties in numbers of neutrons or their energy distribution.

In addition to problems of neutron monitoring, other important difficulties are overcome in using a composite standard. It should be remembered that each gamma-ray peak in the specimen has its identical counterpart in the standard. The conversion of raw gamma-ray data to abundances of activated elements demands implicitly that one determine or know (1) the efficiency of gamma-ray detection (energy dependent), (2) the absolute gamma-ray intensity of each decay event, (3) the half-lives of the radioactive species, and (4) the neutron flux history throughout irradiation period. All of these are measured quantities with inherent errors, not always well known. With a calibrated composite standard, none of these need be determined because they cancel, except for half-life inaccuracies as they accrue for the relatively short period of time between the analyses of the standards and the samples. It is now possible even to change detectors without going through the tedious process of calibrating counting efficiencies and, by the same token, to compare results from different laboratories using a similar system.

A more subtle issue about which this form of monitoring proves beneficial concerns the computer data processing. In our analyzing equipment, a spectrum is stored in 1600 channels corresponding with that many small energy intervals, slightly more than 1 keV per channel. The counts in each peak are integrated by instructions specifying which channels are to be summed. Even with stabilized electronics, the peak widths are not strictly the same from day to day so it is possible that the number of counts summed are not strictly comparable. Such shifts in resolution will also apply to the standards and hence are compensated.

Appreciable peak broadening also results when the total number of counts going into the analyzer becomes large. This effect is corrected separately by empirically determined factors tabulated according to counting rate.

Reproducibility of Gamma-Ray Counting

183

It should be clear that in activation analysis, as in others, the accuracy of analysis for each element cannot be better than that for the particular element in the standard. This would suggest that in constructing a composite standard, the typically weak peaks of pottery should be enhanced in the standard whereas each strong peak should be minimized to a level which still gives good counting statistics. (The overall gamma-ray intensity should be kept to a minimum because the Compton distributions from all gamma rays contribute to the background under the peaks and this is a major source of error for many elements.) In principle, these objectives could be reached by formulating a completely synthetic standard from appropriate compounds. This approach was rejected because of the anticipated difficulty of homogenizing the material and keeping it so. If we consider standards weighing 100 mg with some elements present to less than 1 ppm, this means that 0.1 microgram of that element must be dispersed in a statistically satisfactory number of particles, say 10,000 or more. There seemed to be no method of accomplishing this and knowing that it had been accomplished other than by trial and error. Since the calibration of the standard was expected to take at least six months, we were not encouraged to pursue a trial-and-error approach.

Since fine pottery clay is already a highly dispersed system presumably containing the elements of interest, it was decided to start with this as the basis for the standard. A clay was selected and found (fortunately) to contain a number of the weakly activated elements in amounts more than normal and such strongly activated elements as manganese, sodium, and iron in low amounts. Its single largest drawback was the presence of scandium in "normal" amount, which is more than necessary. As expected of any particular clay, it was undesirably deficient in a few elements, a problem to be handled separately.

The clay was first ground wet in a ball mill for 40 hours. Then the wet mix was put through a 60-mesh screen and dried. The clay was broken up, ground wet for ten hours, and then spiked with a water solution containing desired amounts of cobalt, nickel, bromine, and arsenic. The original clay was deficient in these substances, and it was thought that by adding them in this fashion, they would be uniformly dispersed by coating the large surface area of the clay particles. The "doped" clay was then ground wet for 26 hours, strained with a 120-mesh screen, cast into convenient shapes, dried and fired to 705°C for one-half hour. The fired ceramic was ground in the ball mill for nine hours yielding a final product of about 2 kg of fine powder.

Before undertaking the laborious task of calibration, eight random samples were pressed into standard pills, irradiated, and analyzed for uniformity. Each of several radioactive species agreed virtually within counting statistics so the pottery was considered suitable for calibration and use as a standard.

For calibrating the standard pottery, known quantities of chemicals representing each of 38 elements were separately pressed into pills and irradiated with the standard pottery. At least two independent sources of each compound were employed and where attested primary standards were not available, conventional chemical analysis was employed to establish the absolute content of the element. This turned out to be a long process because most compounds are not stoichiometric with the nominal formula, and many preparations and irradiations were required.

During the course of these calibrations, there was ample opportunity to test the *reproducibility* of the entire analytical process quite aside from the absolute accuracy. If one chooses gamma-ray peaks that give good counting statistics, all other factors causing variations in analysis become lumped together in the scatter of the values. Included, of course, is the lack of uniformity of the standard pottery. As already mentioned, the reproducibility was found to be about 0.4 percent, a value low enough to permit concentration on the assessment of other errors and, finally, the real differences between potteries. For many of the elements, the apparent reproducibility will not be this good because the limiting errors are set by the statistics of counting.

Tables 13.1, 13.2, and 13.3 give the composition of the standard pottery in terms of the elements detected by neutron activation analysis as well as constituents determined by other means. It is important to make clear the nature of the errors shown for the absolute abundances, because it often appears that agreements between potteries are better than these errors would indicate. The errors shown include those of radioactive counting and calibration, but in addition are often dominated by the "background error" to be explained presently. As an example, the value given for cesium in Table 13.3 is 8.31 ± 0.55 ppm, an error of 6.6 percent. This is an expression of how well we think we know the cesium content of our standard pottery should one wish to analyze it by *any* method. Relative to the standard pottery, however, the cesium content of another ceramic can be determined more precisely as will now be explained.

From the data presented in graphical form in Figure 13.1, one can show that the

Table 13.1

Composition of Major Components in Standard Pottery

Element	Composition Element (%)	Composition Oxide (%)	
SiO_2		60.4 ± 0.3	(SiO_2)
Al	15.3 ± 0.2	28.9	(Al_2O_3)
K	1.35 ± 0.04	1.9	(K_2O)
Fe	1.02 ± 0.01	1.5	(Fe_2O_3)
Ti	0.79 ± 0.03	1.3	(TiO_2)
Mg	0.5 ± 0.2	0.8	(MgO)
Na	0.26 ± 0.1	0.3	(Na_2O)
Ba	0.072 ± 0.003	0.08	(BaO)
$\sum$ Trace Elements		0.1	
Volatile Components		3.99 ± 0.10	
Total Components		99.3	

Table 13.2

Composition of Volatile Components in Standard Pottery

Element	Composition Element (%)	Composition Oxide (%)
C	0.03 ± 0.03	$0.11 \{0.13 \pm 0.07\}$*
H	$0.54 {}^{+0.00}_{-0.05}$	4.7
Total		4.8

* Measured directly.

counting error for the cesium peak at 796 keV is 1.2 percent, and this includes the counting statistics of both the peak and the background. However, the cesium content in the standard pottery was calibrated with pure cesium sources which give essentially no background so the question concerns the absolute reliability of background counts in the pottery. If the background chosen in this case is off by 2 percent, this would make an error of 7 percent in the absolute abundance of cesium in the pottery.

For the central issue of archaeological studies, the comparison of potteries, the errors involved need not be as great as the errors shown for the absolute abundances. Using a pottery standard to analyze pottery, the makeup of the background will not be as different as that between pottery and the separate pure substances used for calibration. Furthermore, the closer in composition two pieces of pottery are to each other, the more nearly identical will be the backgrounds, so, for relative comparisons, the errors should converge on what we term the *precision of measurement*. Examples will be given to show that this situation actually occurs. The difficulty that arises is in comparing abundance profiles of pottery analyzed in different laboratories using different methods of standardization or different methods of analysis. Where this applies, it would be prudent to use the more liberal errors.

One element for which analyses are carried out, calcium, has only a limit in Table 13.3. Calcium is very insensitive toward neutron activation so that very large amounts of a calcium compound would have had to be added to the standard pottery (approximately 20 percent by weight) in order to obtain an internal standard which would surpass in accuracy alternative ways of handling this problem. Addition of such a large amount of material as a separate solid was considered too risky. The analysis for calcium is accomplished indirectly by using an iron peak for reference. Indirect comparisons of this kind can be made for any element provided one is willing to accept the errors that result from changes in neutron energy distribution as they effect the two elements differently. For an element such as calcium which is determined with poor precision, the added error from this effect is not considered serious. The interest in calcium determination, albeit with large error, is twofold: (1) It varies tremendously between different sources of pottery, so even a rough value is of diagnostic value; and (2) In some potteries it is a major constituent and, if arising from added temper, variations could effectively produce different dilution factors for all of the elements determined.

It will be recalled that bromine (as KBr solution) was added to our clay before firing. It turned out that most of the bromine was lost during firing. We had already noted in analysis of pottery from a single site that the bromine content was often extremely variable and had suspected that its presence is sensitive to firing conditions. In confirmation, a sample of clay from the Nile Valley was analyzed before and after firing in an electric furnace at 800°C, and 90 percent of the bromine disappeared. The amount as shown in Table 13.3 is too small to be used as an internal standard. The interest in continuing to analyze bromine in pottery lies not in fingerprinting but conceivably in obtaining information as to firing conditions. Since our standard pottery does not contain usable amounts of bromine, this element, like calcium, must be analyzed in terms of another element.

Finally, in order to characterize our standard pottery more completely, we attempted to obtain a material balance of the major constituents. This information is shown in Tables 13.1 and 13.2. All components were determined by neutron activation analysis except for the volatile fraction, SiO_2, CO_2, and Ca. As already mentioned, our standard pottery is atypical in its low values for Na, Fe, and Ca.

Absent from this report is the necessarily detailed description of which gamma-ray peak is chosen for analysis of each element, the corrections which are applied for interferences by other elements, and the recipe for determining the background for each peak. After examining the spectrum obtained by irradiating each pure element, we could determine the amount of

13.1

Gamma-ray spectrum of
long-lived radioactivities
in standard pottery.
Only those peaks used
in the analysis are identified. Symbols in paren-
theses indicate the ele-
ments for which the iso-
topic symbols above
provide gamma-rays for
analysis. Note the loga-
rithmic ordinate scale.
This particular spectrum
was taken on a
101.5-mg sample for a
counting period of 642
min, 25.2 days after an
8-hr irradiation at a flux
of $\sim 2 \times 10^{13}$ n/cm^2
sec.

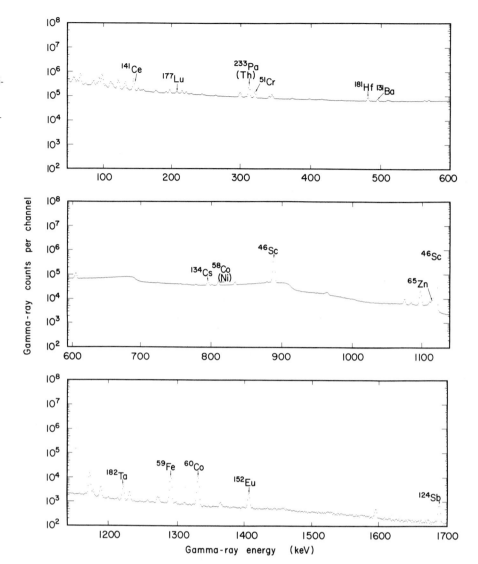

Table 13.3
Composition* of
Standard Pottery

Element	Species Studied	Technique†	Composition Diff. Techniques	Best Value	Chemical Symbol
Aluminum	^{28}Al	neut act 1		$(15.3 \pm 0.2) \times 10^{-2}$	Al
Antimony	^{122}Sb	neut act 3	$(1.66 \pm 0.12) \times 10^{-6}$		
	^{124}Sb	neut act 4	$(1.73 \pm 0.06) \times 10^{-6}$	$(1.71 \pm 0.05) \times 10^{-6}$	Sb
Arsenic	^{76}As	neut act 3		$(3.08 \pm 0.22) \times 10^{-5}$	As
Barium	^{139}Ba	neut act 2	$(7.13 \pm 0.32) \times 10^{-4}$		
	^{131}Ba	neut act 4	$(7.0 \pm 1.1) \times 10^{-4}$	$(7.12 \pm 0.32) \times 10^{-4}$	Ba
Bromine	^{82}Br	neut act 3		$(2.3 \pm 0.9) \times 10^{-6}$	Br
Calcium	^{47}Ca	neut act 3	$< 1 \times 10^{-2}$		
		opt spec	$< 1 \times 10^{-3}$		
		wet chem	$< 2 \times 10^{-4}$	$< 2 \times 10^{-4}$	Ca
Carbon	CO_2	C-H anal		$(3 \pm 3) \times 10^{-4}$	C
Cerium	^{141}Ce	neut act 4		$(8.03 \pm 0.39) \times 10^{-5}$	Ce
Cesium	^{134}Cs	neut act 4		$(8.31 \pm 0.55) \times 10^{-6}$	Cs
Chlorine	^{38}Cl	neut act 1		$< 1.3 \times 10^{-4}$	Cl
Chromium	^{51}Cr	neut act 4		$(1.151 \pm 0.038) \times 10^{-4}$	Cr
Cobalt	^{60}Co	neut act 4		$(1.406 \pm 0.015) \times 10^{-5}$	Co
Copper	^{64}Cu	neut act 2	$(6.0 \pm 0.8) \times 10^{-5}$		
	Cu	wet chem	$(5.8 \pm 0.5) \times 10^{-5}$	$(5.9 \pm 0.5) \times 10^{-5}$	Cu
Dysprosium	^{165}Dy	neut act 2		$(4.79 \pm 0.19) \times 10^{-6}$	Dy
Europium	^{152m1}Eu	neut act 2	$(1.286 \pm 0.048) \times 10^{-6}$		
	^{152}Eu	neut act 4	$(1.296 \pm 0.047) \times 10^{-6}$	$(1.291 \pm 0.034) \times 10^{-6}$	Eu
Gallium	^{72}Ga	neut act 2		$(4.44 \pm 0.46) \times 10^{-5}$	Ga
Gold	^{198}Au	neut act 3		$\leq 1 \times 10^{-8}$	Au
Hafnium	^{181}Hf	neut act 4		$(6.23 \pm 0.44) \times 10^{-6}$	Hf
Hydrogen	H_2O	C-H anal		$\left(5.4 \begin{array}{c} +0.0 \\ -0.5 \end{array}\right) \times 10^{-3}$	H
Indium	^{116m1}In	neut act 2		$(1.09 \pm 0.08) \times 10^{-7}$	In
Iron	^{59}Fe	neut act 4		$(1.017 \pm 0.012) \times 10^{-2}$	Fe
Lanthanum	^{140}La	neut act 3		$(4.490 \pm 0.045) \times 10^{-5}$	La
Lutetium	^{177}Lu	neut act 3		$(4.02 \pm 0.36) \times 10^{-7}$	Lu
Magnesium	^{27}Mg	neut act 1	$(5 \pm 2) \times 10^{-3}$		
		opt spec	$(7 \pm 2) \times 10^{-3}$	$(5 \pm 2) \times 10^{-3}$	Mg
Manganese	^{56}Mn	neut act 2		$(4.09 \pm 0.05) \times 10^{-5}$	Mn
Nickel	^{58}Co	neut act 4		$(2.79 \pm 0.20) \times 10^{-4}$	Ni
Potassium	^{42}K	neut act 2		$(1.35 \pm 0.04) \times 10^{-2}$	K
Rubidium	^{86}Rb	neut act 4		$(7.00 \pm 0.63) \times 10^{-5}$	Rb
Samarium	^{153}Sm	neut act 3		$(5.78 \pm 0.12) \times 10^{-6}$	Sm
Scandium	^{46}Sc	neut act 4		$(2.055 \pm 0.033) \times 10^{-5}$	Sc
Silicon dioxide	SiO_2	wet chem		$(6.04 \pm 0.03) \times 10^{-1}$	SiO_2
Sodium	^{24}Na	neut act 2		$(2.58 \pm 0.04) \times 10^{-3}$	Na
Strontium	^{87m}Sr	neut act 2		$(1.45 \pm 0.22) \times 10^{-4}$	Sr
Tantalum	^{182}Ta	neut act 4		$(1.550 \pm 0.044) \times 10^{-6}$	Ta
Thorium	^{233}Pa	neut act 4		$(1.396 \pm 0.039) \times 10^{-5}$	Th
Titanium	^{47}Sc	neut act 3		$(7.82 \pm 0.34) \times 10^{-3}$	Ti
Uranium	^{239}Np	neut act 3		$(4.82 \pm 0.44) \times 10^{-6}$	U
Ytterbium	^{175}Yb	neut act 3		$(2.80 \pm 0.36) \times 10^{-6}$	Yb
Zinc	^{65}Zn	neut act 5		$(5.9 \pm 0.8) \times 10^{-5}$	Zn

* These compositions and all others in this paper refer to the elements unless otherwise noted.

†The entries in this column have the following meanings: *neut act 1*, neutron activation measurement with special irradiations for very short half-lives; *neut act 2*, usual neutron activation measurement for half-lives less than 1 day; *neut act 3*, usual neutron activation measurement for half-lives from 1 to 6 days; *neut act 4*, usual neutron activation measurement for half-lives longer than 6 days; *neut act 5*, special neutron activation measurement about 8 months after irradiation; *opt spec*, measurement with optical spectrograph; *wet chem*, measurement by wet chemical analysis; *C-H anal*, measurement of carbon and hydrogen by combustion analysis.

each of its gamma rays relative to the peak selected for analysis which we may term the *reference peak*. The counts from these gamma rays which fall within the channels used for analysis of other elements are subtracted by applying appropriate factors to the reference peak. The computer analysis includes instructions for these and other corrections.

One of the special instructions has to do with the determination of the zinc peak which, as shown in Figure 13.1, lies close to the very intense scandium peak. The problem here is that a slight change in the peak width for scandium will add or remove substantial numbers of counts under the zinc peak. The computer determines the width of the scandium peak and applies corrections to the zinc channels which were obtained empirically by varying peak widths in a sample of pure irradiated scandium. The analysis for zinc seems to be quite satisfactory.

As already mentioned, the errors shown in Table 13.3 include the estimated background errors which are often dominant. The errors which define the precision of the measurements in typical potteries will be found in the illustrative data of the final section.

Grouping of Analytical Data

Sensitivity of the Method

In a number of instances during the course of our analysis of many sherds and vessels, two independent drillings were taken from the same piece. Thus far the agreement has been better between such duplicates than has been encountered between any two different pots of the same archaeological grouping. The inferences to be drawn are several: (1) the potter's lump of clay from which the vessel was made had been well homogenized; (2) we have not yet encountered more than one vessel made from the same lump; (3) local clay sources have a certain variation in composition; and, of course, (4) the method of analysis is sensitive enough to make these distinctions.

In a few instances, pairs of separately marked sherds agreed in composition within the experimental error and upon careful examination proved to have come from the same pot. The results from one such pair is shown in Table 13.4. Abundances of 20 elements are listed along with errors due only to the statistics of gamma-ray counting. Two-thirds of the elements should agree within one unit of the standard error and, in this case, 15 of the 20 elements do so.

Also shown in Table 13.4 are results from two different pots which we classify within a group. These come from the same general area as the other pot. Even a cursory examination shows that they agree better with each other than they do with the "twins" but show internal discrepancy beyond the counting errors.

We should not leave the impression that we have proved that all clays prepared by the potter will be uniform toward this form of chemical analysis. Quite obviously, ceramics are not homogeneous; and when small samplings are taken, they must in some degree differ from the body as a whole. It seems, however, that in the limited number of tests we have made, either we have obtained representative amounts of both clay mineral and temper, or the temper did not differ in composition from the clay sufficiently to show up strongly as a "sampling error." We have not yet had the opportunity to follow up on some fragmentary evidence for substantial difficulties of the type just alluded to. We suspect, but have not proved, that one of our sources of pottery has temper consisting in part of high concentrations of certain elements present in clays to a much lower degree.

Analyses from about 1000 sherds from many different sites have shown that there is no difficulty in distinguishing these. It has been possible to show in many instances that pieces which are stylistically different are all local in the sense that they have a common origin of source materials. Also pieces have turned up which must clearly be labeled imports both on stylistic and chemical grounds. Nevertheless, difficulties in interpretation do exist and these are both challenging and sobering.

In most instances in which a sizable number of sherds from one site have been analyzed, the results have been quite complex. Although the whole array may look like nothing yet seen elsewhere, they may divide into two or more distinct groups. Often these groups will not differ grossly in composition and lead one to suspect that they are all *local* but that somewhat different clay sources were used in a single settlement. In other cases, they may be quite different in composition. These too could well be local, because it should not be surprising that in some areas there can be clay beds with distinctly different geochemical history. The sobering aspect of the situation just outlined is the realization that a large number of analyses must be made to establish which pottery is local to a particular site because there are few apparent independent guidelines. It is always tempting to exploit a technical method for all it can tell, and this now appears to be a formidable task.

With this background, it is obvious that the first task is to establish pottery groups from sherds found at a site whatever might be the archaeological story behind the groupings. It is also clear that some quantitative index of chemical similarity must be devised. A system of statistical analysis will be presented which is not entirely satisfying but perhaps as good as our present state of knowledge permits. It

Establishment of Pottery Groups

Table 13.4
Analyses on Two Sherds from Same Pot and Two Pots from Same Group.*

	AYA1	AYA3	ACU6	ACU7		AYA1	AYA3	ACU6	ACU7
Mn	597 ± 14	560 ± 12	652 ± 11	738 ± 12	Co	8.79 ± .13	8.66 ± .13	7.14 ± .11	8.68 ± .11
Na (%)	0.952 ± .015	0.958 ± .015	1.268 ± .015	1.051 ± .012	Ta	0.868 ± .031	0.846 ± .031	1.663 ± .039	1.654 ± .028
U	5.56 ± .13	5.67 ± .13	5.97 ± .12	5.45 ± .12	Cs	13.95 ± .19	13.54 ± .19	10.96 ± .17	8.86 ± .15
Lu	0.356 ± .012	0.340 ± .012	0.271 ± .010	0.285 ± .012	Cr	24.65 ± .59	24.76 ± .70	26.76 ± .70	34.04 ± .70
La	36.53 ± .37	35.33 ± .37	23.59 ± .30	25.63 ± .31	Hf	6.52 ± .12	6.68 ± .12	4.05 ± .10	3.84 ± .10
Ti (%)	0.435 ± .010	0.422 ± .010	0.314 ± .017	0.387 ± .014	Th	18.44 ± .06	18.37 ± .06	14.93 ± .06	14.10 ± .06
Sb	2.39 ± .05	2.26 ± .05	1.33 ± .03	1.15 ± .03	Ba	466 ± 22	442 ± 22	564 ± 24	735 ± 27
As	22.63 ± .65	20.85 ± .67	8.66 ± .38	14.55 ± .43	Rb	157 ± 6	158 ± 6	168 ± 7	156 ± 7
Fe (%)	3.10 ± .03	3.06 ± .03	2.34 ± .03	2.58 ± .03	Zn	131 ± 5	135 ± 5	105 ± 5	122 ± 5
Sc	11.36 ± .04	11.34 ± .04	9.19 ± .04	10.32 ± .04	Ca (%)	1.6 ± .8	1.8 ± .8	3.7 ± .8	3.0 ± .8

* We are indebted to Professor John Rowe, Dr. Dorothy Menzel, and Mrs. Betty Holtzman for the Peruvian pottery from whose analyses these illustrative data are taken. All sherds are from the region of Ayacucho, Peru. AYA1 and AYA3 are two sherds of the Ocros style which proved to come from the same vessel. ACU6 and ACU7 belong to a group of chemical composition embracing at least five different styles. These particular two sherds are classed Regular Chakipampa. Errors shown following each value are the standard errors of radioactive counting. The abundance of elements are in parts-per-million except for those designated (%).

Table 13.5
Pottery Groups from Ballas*

	Mn	U	Lu	La	Fe (%)	Sc	Co	Cs	Hf	Th
BAL 1	1151 ± 18	1.84 ± .15	0.502 ± .016	32.86 ± .37	6.51 ± .06	22.38 ± .04	33.09 ± .39	1.00 ± .22	7.95 ± .19	6.80 ± .06
BAL 2	1269 ± 19	2.03 ± .13	0.513 ± .016	31.33 ± .34	6.12 ± .06	21.11 ± .04	30.25 ± .38	1.07 ± .22	11.15 ± .21	6.65 ± .06
BAL 3	1209 ± 18	2.52 ± .15	0.555 ± .016	33.28 ± .36	6.96 ± .06	23.59 ± .04	34.81 ± .41	1.21 ± .22	9.22 ± .19	8.20 ± .06
BAL 6	1178 ± 18	1.81 ± .15	0.525 ± .017	30.90 ± .36	6.60 ± .06	22.61 ± .06	33.89 ± .45	0.84 ± .26	9.53 ± .23	6.49 ± .07
BAL 7	1250 ± 18	1.66 ± .15	0.534 ± .017	32.96 ± .36	6.81 ± .06	22.96 ± .06	35.06 ± .42	1.44 ± .22	9.61 ± .21	6.91 ± .06
BAL 8	1228 ± 17	1.87 ± .15	0.521 ± .016	33.52 ± .36	6.95 ± .06	23.92 ± .06	35.44 ± .42	1.45 ± .22	8.59 ± .19	7.60 ± .07
BAL 9	1059 ± 15	2.32 ± .13	0.489 ± .016	31.54 ± .34	6.73 ± .06	22.85 ± .06	33.62 ± .41	1.04 ± .22	8.76 ± .19	6.79 ± .07
BAL 10	1154 ± 16	2.30 ± .13	0.511 ± .016	35.66 ± .36	6.34 ± .06	22.28 ± .04	30.42 ± .38	1.71 ± .22	7.72 ± .19	7.72 ± .07
Mean	(1187 ± 77)	(2.04 ± .37)	(0.519 ± .022)	(32.76 ± 1.67)	(6.63 ± .35)	(22.71 ± .92)	(33.32 ± 2.30)	(1.22 ± .35)	(9.07 ± 1.20)	(7.15 ± .77)
BAL 12	350 ± 7	5.23 ± .15	0.362 ± .014	37.69 ± .37	4.59 ± .04	16.51 ± .04	17.03 ± .25	2.88 ± .20	5.92 ± .15	9.90 ± .05
BAL 17	365 ± 5	4.36 ± .13	0.334 ± .013	35.33 ± .33	4.41 ± .04	16.27 ± .04	17.30 ± .28	2.18 ± .22	4.75 ± .15	8.86 ± .06
BAL 18	387 ± 5	4.42 ± .14	0.334 ± .013	38.32 ± .36	4.18 ± .04	15.66 ± .04	15.75 ± .25	3.12 ± .20	5.54 ± .15	10.08 ± .06
BAL 20	410 ± 5	4.43 ± .15	0.325 ± .013	38.95 ± .37	4.55 ± .04	17.23 ± .04	19.31 ± .27	2.97 ± .20	5.21 ± .12	9.70 ± .06
BAL 21	372 ± 5	4.52 ± .15	0.389 ± .014	40.27 ± .39	4.62 ± .04	18.13 ± .04	17.61 ± .24	2.80 ± .18	5.56 ± .12	10.18 ± .05
BAL 22	335 ± 4	4.75 ± .15	0.378 ± .013	40.61 ± .39	4.58 ± .04	17.85 ± .04	17.07 ± .25	3.24 ± .21	5.62 ± .15	10.04 ± .06
BAL 24	454 ± 7	4.16 ± .14	0.379 ± .014	37.48 ± .36	4.71 ± .04	17.56 ± .05	17.49 ± .31	2.72 ± .24	6.14 ± .17	9.32 ± .07
Mean	(382 ± 45)	(4.55 ± .37)	(0.357 ± .033)	(38.38 ± 1.99)	(4.52 ± .19)	(17.03 ± 1.22)	(17.37 ± .98)	(2.84 ± .35)	(5.53 ± .47)	(9.73 ± .55)

* The upper series is made up of representative pots from a larger group made of a clay which we term "Nile mud." The lower series is taken from another group made of a calcareous clay. This group is one of several distinct groups of the same general type found in this region.

The 36 elements for which analyses are made are reduced to 20 for diagnostic purposes, and 10 of these are shown in this table. All abundances are in parts-per-million except for Fe which is in percent.

lacks some rigor in statistical formulation and includes some intuitive bias developed in examining large numbers of results.

The basis of the method is to treat the various elements analyzed as independent variables, a supposition which is by no means obviously true. If it should turn out that the proportions of certain elements are always constant, it would be incorrect to attach statistical significance to the behavior of more than one of these. As an example, we determine seven rare earth elements and, although their ratios do change in different potteries, there is still a high level of coherence in their variance. In selecting a group of elements for diagnostic purposes, we have included only lanthanum and lutetium, which do seem to vary with respect to each other as much as most other elements. The examination of large numbers of data has led us to use 20 elements. Aside from an effort to eliminate redundancies, we have not included a number of other elements, because they are determined with poor accuracy—and one element, bromine, because its abundance seems to be sensitive to the firing temperature of the pottery. It will be noted that some families of the periodic system are represented by more than one element. In all cases the geochemical processes leading to clay formation apparently do not see these elements as similar.

The first step in handling the data is to create a *trial pottery group* by visual determination of chemical similarity. A computer program has been written to calculate the mean value and standard deviation for each of the 20 elements in this pottery group. If we have chosen a statistically valid array, one might expect a normal distribution of values for each element whose spread is characterized by the standard deviation. Now any sherd, within or outside of the trial group, may be tested for agreement with the group on the basis of this single element. If it lies at two standard deviations from the mean for example, the odds are about 20 to 1 that it does not belong. Now if all of the other elements may be treated as independent variables, the odds become the product of the odds for each element. It may readily be visualized that this treatment is extremely sensitive and that numbers of astronomical magnitude appear when pottery compositions are appreciably different for a large number of elements.

If the 20 elements were to constitute a perfect statistical array, we can now write down a quantitative *index of disagreement* for any sherd we wish to compare with the group. Comparison is made element by element. The deviation d between the element's value in the sherd and the mean value in the group is divided by the standard deviation for the group σ. We call this ratio X. To each of these values of X,

one can assign the odds, found in standard statistical tables, that the sherd does not belong. The odds that the sherd does not belong based on all of the elements is the product of the individual odds.

At this point, we depart from rigorous statistical practice. For a number of reasons, we assign odds of 1 for any value of d that lies *within* 0.675σ, the point of equal odds. If now the other members of the array are given their statistical odds, the product will be a large number even if the distribution is normal. From the 20 elements, we next throw out the four with greatest disagreements. If the distribution were normal, this would simply involve the elimination of four members from the tail of the distribution and not otherwise change the interpretation. The objective, however, is to be sure to eliminate occasional values which may be wild for reasons having little or nothing to do with the normal distribution. The remaining 16 elements are then treated as described earlier.

The subjective choice to be made is the cutoff value for the index of disagreement beyond which we say that the pot does not belong to the group. We have tentatively chosen the number 1000. Examples will be given which are taken from actual analytical data, and then the matter will be discussed further.

As already mentioned, 2 sherds shown in Table 13.4 (ACU 6 and ACU 7) are members of a chemical pottery group. This group, comprising several stylistic types, is made up of 12 sherds so far. If each of these 2 sherds is compared with its group through the statistical analysis just mentioned, the index numbers found are 4.6 and 30.3 for ACU 6 and ACU 7, respectively. The number for acceptability in the group, it will be recalled, is 1000. The differences between these numbers and 1000 are not as dramatic as it may seem because of the extreme sensitivity which ensues when so many elements are involved.

Examination of the data in Table 13.4 shows that AYA 1 is perceptibly different from ACU 6 and ACU 7, but one must compare it with the actual spread in values for the group to which these sherds belong in order to be convinced that AYA 1 does not belong to the group. Using the same analysis which gave index numbers of 4.6 and 30.3 for ACU 6 and ACU 7, sherd AYA 1 gave 6.8×10^{20}. This should give adequate demonstration that there is no problem in distinguishing potteries which differ even less than the example given here.

The larger difficulty is what to do with the inevitable borderline cases which might arise for archaeologically insignificant reasons. Suppose, for example, that quartz temper were used in this pottery and that ACU 6 had additional quartz to the extent of 5 percent of the pottery weight. Quartz is quite free of elements analyzed by neutron activation, therefore it acts as a simple diluent. The effect can be simulated by revising downward by 5 percent each value for ACU 6 in Table 13.4. When the diluted ACU 6 is now compared with the group, the index number has changed from 4.3 to 460: It would still have been retained in the group but not by a large margin. A program has been devised to normalize the abundances of elements by applying a specific "dilution factor" for a particular sherd. If the elements vary randomly because of the inhomogeneity of the paste, it would, of course, not be possible to bring about better agreement by this means. So far this has been applied to a single group of 13 sherds, but the results have been rather interesting. Before normalizing the abundances, the average of the standard deviations for 15 elements was 7.1 percent. This value reflects a fairly close-knit group, but it became even tighter when the computer analysis threw out 3 pots, keeping ten. After normalizing, the average standard deviation was 5.1 percent and the analysis kept all 13 pots. This is remarkable agreement within a group, particularly when it is recognized that there is an average standard deviation of 2.6 percent simply from the counting statistics of the elements chosen. The 3 pots were discarded before normalizing, because they differed in a systematic fashion and failed the statistical analysis badly (because the standard deviations for many of the elements were small).

It is worth re-emphasizing that the criterion adopted for judging whether or not a sherd belongs to a group is rather arbitrary. We strongly suspect that some of the basic assumptions that would make possible rigorous statistical treatment are not strictly valid. For example, the index number 4.6 found in comparing ACU 6 with its group is smaller than would be expected from a normal array. This might mean that there is a small level of coherence in the variation of the elements so that a sherd with a few of its elements near the median of the group will have a larger number of elements brought near the median. Conversely, one might expect to find valid members of the group with rather large index numbers. Despite the obvious shortcomings of this system for data interpretation, it must be emphasized that our uncertainties arise from very fine distinctions. Further experience may dictate that other methods are more realistic and rigorous, but in the meantime we feel that the method can yield useful information.

The labor of forming pottery groups and testing agreement is considerable if handled manually. A computer program has been devised which makes all of the statistical computations pertinent to the trial group. It then tests successively each member of the group for agreement with the group by the preset value for the odds, say 1000. When it comes to a pot that falls outside this value, it discards the pot, recomputes the statistical parameters for the new group, and then starts over. Only when the sherds remaining all fit does the iterative process stop. Needless to say, any pot not in the original test group may be tested in like manner. The amount of computer time required for these operations is trivial, but not so the amount of printing generated.

It is not possible within the confines of this report to give an account of the archaeological problems to which the methodology described here has been directed. The following paragraphs are aimed only at displaying representative data and to convey some feeling for how archaeological problems might be attacked.

A rather large number of analyses have been made on materials from three early cemeteries within a small area of Upper Egypt: Nag ed Deir, Ballas, El Ahaiwah. A complex picture of pottery compositions is emerging. For the present purposes, we are showing analytical results on two groups simply to give the reader a view of how an array of compositions appears (see Table 13.5). All three cemeteries contained a chemical pottery type that we ascribe to Nile mud. Stylistically these appear as (1) burnished red-slip ware, (2) black-top ware, and (3) coarse ware. The first group shown pertains to these wares. Pottery was also made from calcareous clays brought in from regions away from the river. A considerable number of distinct groups have been characterized, one of which is shown as the second group of analyses. Wavy-handled pottery, decorated ware, and drab wares were made from these clay types. Occasionally, a red-slip jar is found from these calcareous clays, and these vessels look superficially like the dominant redware made of Nile mud.

The errors shown for the individual numbers are simply the statistical errors of counting the radioactivity and are a reflection of how accurate the analyses could be done if the calibrations were carried out meticulously and if great pain were taken to control background errors. The numbers in parentheses are the mean values for the group and the *standard deviations*. The latter indicate the spread encountered for the various elements in these particular groups and are used in the statistical analysis to determine if any vessel belongs to a particular group. It will be noted that the standard deviations (if expressed as percentages of the mean values) vary considerably from element to element. An element which has a small spread in one pottery group is not neces-

Pottery Groups from Upper Egypt

sarily a well-behaved element in another group.

Each of the pottery pieces shown here belongs to its respective group according to the statistical analysis described in previous sections. Examination of the individual numbers reveals that now and again a wild value appears. The statistical analysis discards such data as described in the previous section.

Table 13.5 provides some support for the supposition that the elements selected may be treated as independent variables. Note for example that the rare earth Lu is higher in the top group whereas La is higher in the lower group. Similarly, hafnium and thorium (which share some common chemical properties) show this inverse relationship. In another pottery group selected at random, the La and Lu are somewhat like the upper group in Table 13.5 but the Hf/Th ratio is 2.77 instead of 0.79.

Relation of Clay to Finished Pottery

The pottery analysis could, in principle, be related to actual clay beds establishing provenance in an absolute manner. Important as this approach may be, it is unfortunately not one which can be employed generally. Even if it were possible to obtain clay samples from each site under consideration, it is by no means possible to know that these are the sources used by the ancient potters. Furthermore, there will usually be uncertainties as to how the potters treated the clays before fabrication. At present, the relation between clay sources and ceramics from an area appears to be a separate and difficult problem, albeit an important one and susceptible to experimental attack. Some exploratory investigations are underway in our laboratory aimed at coming to grips with this problem.

Under uncomplicated circumstances, the relation between pottery and clay can be simple, as illustrated in Table 13.6. Among the jars from Upper Egypt which we analyzed, a few were sealed with clay plugs, and there is every reason to believe that these were inserted between the times the jars were fabricated and placed in the burials. A sample of one of these plugs was fired, and analysis shows that it fits well with the "Nile mud" pottery. For contrast, analysis is also shown for the jar in which it was found. This jar was made from one of the clays which appears in pottery of this area.

Imports; Example of an Unfinished Problem

In the development of the current methodology, there was little to tell us what to expect from archaeological material; hence, the selection was often purely exploratory. Experience has indicated that exploratory examination of a limited number of sherds may often be an efficient prelude to the design of a more ambitious archaeological problem. The examples presented here aim to illustrate this point. It will be seen that the sherds are too few in number to define pottery groups as well as one would like, but they do permit one to define problems and to set up sampling schedules accordingly.

We are concerned here with two sites in Israel: One, Tell Ashdod, is a large habitation site in the southern coastal region, and the other, Tell Eitun, represents tomb finds in a region inland from Ashdod. The dominant pottery style in both places was Philistine (or earlier local types) and a few pieces of Cypriote and Mycenaean styles were included. (All of these are, of course, not of the same age.)

The results used for illustration are shown in Table 13.7. There are five sherds in each of the two groups of "local" pottery displayed in Columns 1 and 2. Statistical analysis shows that these two groups are indistinguishable and likely came from the same place, Ashdod. In order to be certain of this deduction, one would need a larger sampling from Ashdod to establish better its composition as well as sampling from other coastal sites to make certain that these are distinguishable from Ashdod.

Column 3 gives the analysis of a single "Mycenaean style" vessel from Eitun. It appears to be very much like the two other groups, but statistical analysis reveals that it does not belong. This deduction should be viewed with caution, because it could turn out that a more adequate sampling from Ashdod would broaden the present group to include this piece. The other possibility, of course, is that this vessel came from another site in the vicinity yet to be revealed. It seems fairly unlikely that it is an import from some distance.

The Cypriote piece (Column 4) is distinctly different. Fifteen of the 20 elements differ from those of the groups by more than two standard deviations; some differ hugely. Note, for example, the high values for La, Sc, Cs, and Cr, and the low value for Hf. Clearly this is an import, but at present we have no library of information on Cypriote ware to tell from where.

The next column (Column 5) pertains to a Mycenaean piece from Ashdod. It again is distinctly different. Although it is clearly not from the exact source as the Eitun Cypriote piece, there are some intriguing resemblances. Note for example that they are both very high in Cs and Rb, and low in Hf. We have some fragmentary information that compositions of this general type are characteristic of the Greek mainland and islands. Of course, the objective of this work is to pinpoint places of origin and not to delineate general areas.

Finally, a Cypriote sherd from Ashdod is shown in Column 6. This is completely

Table 13.6
Comparison of Fired
Clay and Pottery of
Same Provenance*

	"Nile Mud" Ware 32 Sherds (mean values)	BAL38F	BAL14
Mn	1204 ± 68	1277	421
Na (%)	1.335 ± .215	1.271	0.500
U	2.26 ± .41	2.05	3.70
Lu	0.512 ± .027	0.520	0.319
La	32.77 ± 1.20	33.92	32.93
Ti (%)	0.996 ± .049	1.037	0.433
Sb	0.29 ± .07	0.29	0.70
As	0.88 ± 1.14	1.42	4.58
Fe (%)	6.82 ± .24	7.33	4.00
Sc	23.11 ± .96	25.46	14.78
Co	34.96 ± 1.60	39.64	16.13
Ta	1.445 ± .106	1.372	0.89
Cs	1.39 ± .21	1.66	2.86
Cr	180.8 ± 15.6	194.5	156.8
Hf	8.67 ± .75	8.66	5.56
Th	6.94 ± .49	6.76	8.19
Ba	493 ± 74	475	320
Rb	61 ± 7	51	47

* The "Nile mud" group is made up of 32 sherds from three neighboring cemeteries in upper Egypt. The clay plug after firing at 900°C (BAL38F) fits in this group. Twelve of the 18 elements should lie within one standard deviation and exactly that number do. The jar BAL14 is the vessel in which the clay plug was found. It was made from quite a different type of clay as shown by the analysis.

Table 13.7
Local Ware and
Imports (Tell Ashdod
and Tell Eitun)*

	(1) Ashdod Philistine 5 Pieces (mean values)	(2) Eitun Philistine 5 Pieces (mean values)	(3) Eitun Mycenaean	(4) Eitun Cypriote	(5) Ashdod Mycenaean	(6) Ashdod Cypriote
Mn	779 ± 76	733 ± 48	795	874	958	776
Na (%)	0.668 ± 0.026	0.707 ± 0.088	0.873	0.687	0.587	1.163
U	2.48 ± 0.17	2.30 ± 0.10	2.54	3.30	2.58	1.34
Lu	0.464 ± 0.033	0.448 ± 0.024	0.514	0.444	0.392	0.378
La	29.22 ± 1.50	27.92 ± 1.14	31.65	42.93	31.57	9.05
Ti (%)	0.665 ± 0.078	0.628 ± 0.027	0.655	0.504	0.444	0.342
Sb	0.398 ± 0.061	0.338 ± 0.076	0.446	0.713	0.880	0.229
As	4.45 ± 0.58	4.92 ± 2.27	3.77	8.27	2.31	1.28
Fe (%)	3.86 ± 0.07	3.70 ± 0.07	3.95	4.79	5.28	6.26
Sc	12.84 ± 0.36	12.98 ± 0.18	13.69	18.84	21.37	36.68
Co	18.95 ± 0.93	17.02 ± 1.15	17.80	22.64	29.33	34.33
Ta	1.198 ± 0.040	1.138 ± 0.048	1.125	1.311	0.817	0.356
Cs	1.62 ± 0.13	1.56 ± 0.28	1.83	7.94	9.17	0.68
Cr	126.2 ± 5.8	116.7 ± 1.7	126.5	154.4	251.4	185.7
Hf	13.40 ± 2.38	11.56 ± 0.73	10.54	5.21	3.92	2.24
Th	7.98 ± 0.83	7.29 ± 0.53	7.83	13.75	11.23	2.51
Ba	387 ± 122	557 ± 209	366	383	375	145
Rb	53 ± 5	53 ± 2	51	154	158	31
Zn	142 ± 6	140 ± 5	212	209	292	262
Ca (%)	6.2 ± 2.3	7.0 ± 1.5	10.1	3.6	10.6	4.4

* Analytical results are expressed in parts-per-million for the respective elements except those designated by the % sign. The ± limits denote standard deviations for the elements within the pottery group for which mean values are given. The single sherds have the analytical figures without error limits. The experimental errors on these numbers are almost always smaller than the spread of values encountered in a group.

different from any of the others, but at this point our repertory of local potteries is too limited even to guess at its provenance.

The purpose of displaying these fragmentary results is to illustrate how they might be the basis for a series of archaeological problems. Among the questions which come to mind and the materials necessary for their answers are the following:

1. A better sampling is needed to establish the characteristics of Ashdod Philistine ware, and this should be expanded to include other coastal sites.

2. The diffusion of such ware to inland sites such as Eitun can then be tested more meaningfully.

3. The determination of the provenance of the imported Cypriote and Mycenaean wares demands a systematic examination of pottery from suspected sites of origin and a more comprehensive sampling of suspected imported ware at the sites in Israel.

Acknowledgments

We are greatly indebted to many individuals for their expert handling of important aspects of this long and detailed study. This study would not have been possible without the contribution of Mr. Duane Mosier in setting up the electronic pulse-height analyzer and the interface equipment which permits computer processing of the data. Our assistant, Mrs. Helen V. Michel, gave her usual skilled and painstaking performance in participating in almost all phases of this work. For the demanding task of computer programming and key-punch operation, we owe thanks to Miss Susanne Halvorsen. We also gratefully acknowledge the cooperation of the staffs of the Berkeley Research Reactor under the direction of Professor Lawrence Ruby and Dr. Leonel Stollar and the Lawrence Radiation Laboratory Computer Center.

In the work, part of which is described here, it was necessary to operate our equipment around the clock and seven days a week. In relieving us of the off-hours task of changing samples and recording data, we wish to thank the staff of the Safety Services' Operation's Group who are present in the Laboratory at all times. We also wish to thank the members of the Analytical Group, Dr. Eugene Huffman, Mr. Robert Giauque, Mrs. Ursula Abed, and Mr. Ray G. Clem for their valuable assistance.

Finally, special thanks are due to Drs. F. S. Goulding and Richard Pehl for preparing the excellent germanium detector which was the foundation for the gamma-ray analyses.

References

1.
(a) Shepard, A. O.;
(b) Farnsworth, M.;
(c) Shepard, A. O.,
and Matson, F.

For information on this technique, see (a) *Ceramics for the Archaeologist* Carnegie Institute of Washington, Publication 609, 1965; (b) "Greek Pottery: A Mineralogical Study," *Am. J. Archaeology,* **68,** No. 3, pp. 221–228, 1964; and (c) contributions to this volume by A. O. Shepard and F. R. Matson.

2.
(a) Catling, H. W.,
Blin-Stoyle, A. E.,
and Richards, E. E.;
(b) Millet, A., and
Catling, H.;
(c) Hall, E. T.

(a) *Annual of the British School of Athens,* Vol. 58, p. 94, 1963; (b) *Archaeometry,* **9,** p. 92, 1966; and (c) the contribution to this volume by E. T. Hall.

3.
(a) Perlman, I., and
Asaro, Frank;
(b) Al Kital, R. A.,
Chan, Lui-Heung,
Sayre, Edward V.;
(c) Gordon, Glen E.
et al.;
(d) Sayre, E. V.; and
Chan, L.-H.; and
Olin, J. S., and
Sayre, E. V.

For recent accounts of neutron activation analyses on kindred problems with high-resolution analyzing equipment, see: (a) University of California Report UCRL-17937, October 1967; (b) Brookhaven National Laboratory Report BNL 11563; (c) *Geochim. Cosmochim. Acta,* **32,** p. 369, 1968; and (d) contributions to this symposium by E. V. Sayre and L.-H. Chan, and by J. S. Olin and E. V. Sayre.

4.
Hollander, J. M.,
and Perlman, I.

For a popular account of semiconductor counters and their applications, see: *Science,* **154,** p. 3745, 1966.

Chapter 14

Compositional Categories of Some English and American Pottery of the American Colonial Period,[12]

Jacqueline S. Olin[3] and Edward V. Sayre
Brookhaven National Laboratory

As students of maritime enterprise are aware, there are some curious gaps in the story of one of the most famous exploits in English history—Sir Francis Drake's circumnavigation of the globe. Drake's ships left England on the 13th of December 1577 from Plymouth, England which is on the southwestern coast between Cornwall and Devonshire. Drake is reported to have arrived at the coast of Brazil on the 6th of April 1578 and to have made a landing on the coast of California in July 1579. He returned to England on September 26, 1580. Evidence in the form of artifacts would be expected to be unlikely in connection with historical questions such as those involved here. Nevertheless, there might be such evidence, and excavations have taken place in the area of Drake's Bay, California. Among the artifacts which have been found there are two earthenware potsherds which in some aspects of appearance resemble Devonshire pottery of the time of Drake. These sherds have been examined as possible artifact evidence of the landing of one or more of Drake's ships at Drake's Bay. In the course of the investigation it was necessary to look in comparison at the compositional categories of some English and American pottery of the American Colonial period.

As early as the first half of the sixteenth century, there was an important center of earthenware manufacture in north Devon, England. (See Reference 1.) Clay for the potters working there at Bideford and Barnstaple came from three similar deep clay deposits in a valley running parallel with a river called the River Taw and lying between the two towns. (See Reference 3.) The potters of north Devon made several types of wares; "coarse" or common earthenware comprised the bulk of their product. They also made a sgraffito ware. An example of each of these is shown in Figures 14.1 and 14.2. The potsherds excavated at Drake's Bay are examples of a tempered coarse ware (Figure 14.3). In view of the close geographic association of Plymouth and the north Devon pottery manufacturing centers and the fact that a coarse earthenware was made by the north Devon potters, a possibility did exist that the potsherds found at Drake's Bay had been made in north Devon.

[1] Research carried out under contract with the U.S. Atomic Energy Commission.

[2] Subsequent to the original calibration, the concentrations in the standard glass were compared to U.S. Geological Survey standard rock specimens AGV-1, BCR-1, GSP-1, and G-2 by Dr. Pieter Meyers and small corrections in concentrations were made to bring our absolute calibrations into agreement with these widely used standards. See Gordan et al, *Geochimica et Cosmochimica Acta,* **32,** 1968, pp. 369–396 for resumé of data for these standard samples.

Numerous methods of physical or chemical analysis could be used in studying this question and further investigation would be reasonable and useful. The method we have worked with to date is that of neutron activation analysis with high-resolution gamma-ray spectroscopy obtained through the use of lithium drifted germanium diode detectors. This is a technique which has been applied to groups of archaeological artifacts from a given site with the objective of deriving internal correlations on the basis of the concentrations of the elements present. (See Reference 2.)

To our knowledge, no analytical data on north Devon pottery had been collected before this time. We began therefore by collecting together a group of pieces of north Devon pottery. Ten such pieces were available. These specimens, which we will describe in greater detail later, included seven sherds which are described as fine ware and three which are gravel-tempered ware. The data which have been collected on these ten specimens will now be available for future comparisons to other sherds in addition to the two from Drake's Bay. We have begun to make some of these comparisons on specimens from colonial American sites which are evidence of a trade between the potteries of north Devon and the colonies during the seventeenth century. (See Reference 4.)

The sherds from north Devon included the following (the number used is that which was assigned during analysis.):

1. Sherd from the Northwalk pottery site, Barnstaple, North Devon.

2. Tile from Bideford thought to have been made in Barnstaple.

3. Sgraffito sherd found in Bideford.

4. Sgraffito sherd found in Bideford.

5. Sgraffito sherd found in Bideford.

6. Sgraffito sherd found in Bideford.

7. Sgraffito sherd found in Bideford.

8. Gravel-tempered sherd from Bodmin Moor, Cornwall.

9. Piece of pottery oven from Bideford.

17. Gravel-tempered pan from Bideford, probably of nineteenth century origin.

In the case of the pottery sherds from colonial American sites which are believed to have come from north Devon, the artifact evidence preceded the historical evidence. The evidence which has been un-

[3] Research Collaborator from the Smithsonian Institution, Washington, D.C.

14.1
Gravel-tempered pan
from Bideford, probably
of nineteenth-century
origin.

14.2
North Devon harvest jug used in Sussex County, Delaware. This jug, 11 inches high and dated 1698, is in the collection of the Winterthur Museum. The inscription reads: "Kind Sʳ: i com to Gratifiey your Kindness Love and Courtisy and Sarve youre table with Strong beare for this intent i was sent heare: or if you pleas i will supply youre workmen when in harvist dry when they doe labour hard and swear good drinke is better far then Meat."

14.3
Samples from potsherds excavated at Drake's Bay, California. The gravel temper appears as white areas within the sample.

covered to show that there was a large and important commerce in north Devon earthenware between Bideford and Barnstaple and the colonies remained unnoticed until the pottery sherds found in the colonial sites at Jamestown, as well as elsewhere, prompted investigation. Since the first discovery of the two types of pottery, a sgraffito ware and a gravel-tempered ware at Jamestown, examples have been uncovered revealing widespread distribution. Numerous examples of sgraffito ware and gravel-tempered ware have been included in our studies. These have come from Virginia, Maryland, Maine, and Massachusetts:

10. Gravel-ware pan section excavated at Jamestown by the National Park Service, 1934–1935.

11. Gravel-ware sherd from Angelica Knoll, Maryland.

12. Gravel-ware sherd from the site of a house at Plymouth, Massachusetts. The site is referred to as the "R. M." site.

13. Sgraffito sherd excavated at Jamestown by the National Park Service, 1934–1935.

14. Sgraffito sherd found near the shore of Kent Island, Maryland. The sherd is one of a small collection of late seventeenth century and early eighteenth century material which was given to the United States National Museum.

18. Gravel-ware pan rim excavated at Pemaquid, Maine (from a site antedating 1676).

19. Slip-coated pan rim excavated at Pemaquid, Maine (from a site antedating 1676).

20. Sherd of sgraffito ware excavated at Jamestown by the National Park Service in 1956.

The two specimens from Drake's Bay, California were as follows:

15. Gravel-ware sherd, Drakes Bay, California.

16. Gravel-ware sherd, Drake's Bay, California.

We considered it necessary to look at specimens from colonial sites at Jamestown which on the basis of comparison to yellow-glazed sgraffito ware or gravel-tempered ware did not appear to have come from north Devon to ascertain that in such pottery one would not encounter an accidental agreement in composition with north Devon ware. Eleven sherds of this nature were analyzed. In addition we analyzed one specimen from a kiln site in Massachusetts which again is not considered to have come from North Devon:

22. Thumb-impressed rim sherd from a jar, excavated at Jamestown from a supposed kiln site.

23. Foot of a three-footed cooking pot excavated at Jamestown from a supposed kiln site.

24. Sherd of a pot lid excavated at Jamestown.

25. Sherd excavated at Jamestown.

26. Sherd excavated at Jamestown.

27. Sherd from the Bayley kiln site at Newburyport, Massachusetts. This site is dated 1750–1790.

29. Sherd from site of Green Spring Plantation, James City County, Virginia.

30. Sherd from site of Green Spring Plantation, James City County, Virginia.

31. Sherd from site of Green Spring Plantation, James City County, Virginia.

32. Sherd from site of Green Spring Plantation, James City County, Virginia.

33. Sherd from site of Green Spring Plantation, James City County, Virginia.

34. Sherd from site of Green Spring Plantation, James City County, Virginia.

The experimental procedures used in this research were essentially those described in some detail in Chapter 12 of this volume on the activation analysis of Mayan pottery by Sayre and Chan with the exception that only the longer lived activities were measured in this instance. Rather than repeat these details, we shall only summarize our methods here.

In brief, therefore, small plates cut from the interior of our pottery specimens, approximately 1 cm² in area and 1mm thick, were leached overnight in distilled water, dried, wrapped in aluminum foil and exposed to a flux of neutrons, 1.0×10^{13} n/cm² sec, for a period of 24 hours. These samples were accompanied in activation by similar plates of a standard glass which contained previously determined quantities of all of the elements measured and permitted an element by element flux monitoring of the neutron exposure and subsequent counting. The induced activities were counted by lithium drifted germanium detectors at times from 8 to 35 days after activation. Half-life measurements confirmed that at the times of counting interfering activities were insignificant.

The individual photopeaks measured were the 1600-keV gamma of lanthanum-140, the 890-keV gamma of scandium-46, the 1172-keV gamma of cobalt-60, the 1290-keV gamma of iron-59, the 122-keV gamma of europium-152, the 144-keV gamma of cerium-141, the 312-keV gamma of the protactinium-233 daughter of thorium-233, and the 321-keV gamma of chromium-51. The chromium-51 activity was corrected for the component within it arising from the n, α reaction of iron-54.

Interpretation of Data

The data presented in Tables 14.1 and 14.2 include the results of analysis of the ten north Devon specimens. In the north Devon fine ware, the evidence that the standard deviation is a relatively small percent of the mean in every case has led to the conclusion that this can be taken as a group. The mean values have all been calculated as geometric means. The evidence that led to the decision to calculate a geometric mean was gained in the analytical study of ancient glass. This evidence showed that the deviations from the mean concentration values for a group of related archaeological specimens tends to be of a fractional rather than an absolute amount, because it was observed that the distributions of concentrations of a group shows a normal chance, i.e., Gaussian distribution when the occurrence of specimens is plotted against the logarithm of concentration rather than against concentration itself.

The results of the analysis of the north Devon gravel ware show a somewhat higher coefficient of variation, but the specimens still form a related group for which the mean concentration for each element is approximately 0.85 of that in the north Devon fine ware. This strongly indicates that the north Devon gravel ware was made using the same clay as that used for the north Devon fine ware and contains in addition a temper which contains relatively little of the elements being analyzed. It would appear that the addition of temper approximately just diluted the pottery in the concentrations of the elements measured. Figure 14.4 graphically illustrates this point. The relationship of the concentrations of all the elements in the gravel ware to those in the fine ware can be seen to be approximately the same.

If a specimen has indeed been diluted with a relatively pure material so that the concentrations of many of its components all have been reduced to the same fraction f of the values they otherwise would have had, it is obvious that division by this fraction f would correct the measured concentrations to what they would have been had the dilution not occurred. The extent of relative dilution between one specimen and another or between a specimen and a group for which means have been determined can be estimated by some reasonable mean of the ratios of the individual elements. The best dilution fraction to use if N separate elements are being determined is the Nth root of the product of the N individual ratios. At least division by this fraction brings the individ-

ual concentrations of the specimen being corrected into an overall least squares closest agreement with the data to which it is being compared. This process has been called *obtaining the best relative fit* between specimens.

The values in Table 14.3 result from first obtaining a best relative fit concentration using the means of the north Devon fine ware for each concentration value for the north Devon gravel ware. The best fit values for the three gravel-ware specimens and the actual concentration values for the seven fine-ware specimens were then used to obtain a set of geometric means. Since best fit concentration values were obtained because of the presence of a gravel temper and since the fine ware itself appears to have some silica inclusions on visual examination, it was decided to use the geometric mean concentrations which were obtained for the ten north Devon sherds to obtain concentrations that best fit these means for every specimen in the group. These are given in Table 14.3. Also given in Table 14.3 are the ratios of the best fit concentrations to the mean concentrations and a set of 95 percent confidence limits for these ratios for each element of the total north Devon group. In all instances, statistical confidence limits have been estimated by means of "Student's" distributions for small numbers of samples. Figure 14.5 shows the 95 percent confidence limits for the ratios and the values for the ten specimens of north Devon ware. With one exception the plotted values lie within the confidence limits. The exception is not unexpected as this probability does exist.

Our specimens include one other related group of sherds. This is a group of six specimens (Figure 14.6) from a kiln site at Green Spring Plantation, James City County, Virginia. The data for these sherds are given in Table 14.4. The differences between the geometric means of the two groups, north Devon fine ware and the specimens from the Green Spring Plantation, appear to be great enough to distinguish the two groups. This was tested statistically by performing a t test of significance between the two sample geometric means for the logarithms of the concentrations of each element. The values obtained for t were as follows: Sc_2O_3, 4.64; La_2O_3, 12.43; Eu_2O_3, 12.04; CeO_2, 3.20; ThO_2, 0.30; Cr_2O_3, 3.27; Fe_2O_3, 5.50; CoO, 6.02. The value of t for $N_1 + N_2 - 2$ degrees of freedom when $N_1 + N_2 - 2$ is equal to 11 is 2.201 at a 95 percent confidence level. All of the values of t calculated are greater than 2.201 except ThO_2, hence the differences can be stated as significant for all other elements.

A second t test was performed to test the significance of the resolution of the groups. This enables one to determine the extent to which the separation of the geometric means for each element of the

Table 14.1
North Devon Fine Ware (Concentration in percent of oxide)

Table 14.2
North Devon Gravel Ware (Concentration in percent of oxide)

Table 14.3
North Devon Ware (Concentration in percent of oxide)

Analytical Specimen No.	Scandium Sc_2O_3	Lanthanum La_2O_3	Europium Eu_2O_3	Cerium CeO_2	Thorium ThO_2	Chromium Cr_2O_3	Iron Fe_2O_3	Cobalt CoO
1	0.0025	0.0035	0.000118	0.0056	0.00098	0.0116	5.6	0.00190
2	0.0024	0.0036	0.000107	0.0057	0.00100	0.0073	5.2	0.00179
3	0.0027	0.0040	0.000123	0.0053	0.00079	0.0097	6.1	0.00200
4	0.0025	0.0040	0.000127	0.0055	0.00084	0.0108	6.1	0.00220
5	0.0028	0.0037	0.000123	0.0056	0.00070	0.0109	6.2	0.00204
6	0.0024	0.0038	0.000117	0.0053	0.00076	0.0082	5.5	0.00191
7	0.0029	0.0043	0.000132	0.0060	0.00126	0.0148	6.2	0.00221
Mean of Group	0.0026	0.0038	0.000121	0.0055	0.00089	0.0102	5.8	0.00200
Standard Deviation as Percent of Mean	8.2	7.1	7.1	4.8	22.0	26.5	7.5	8.1

Analytical Specimen No.	Scandium Sc_2O_3	Lanthanum La_2O_3	Europium Eu_2O_3	Cerium CeO_2	Thorium ThO_2	Chromium Cr_2O_3	Iron Fe_2O_3	Cobalt CoO
8	0.0022	0.0030	0.000093	0.0043	0.00095	0.0086	6.3	0.00156
9	0.0023	0.0035	0.000111	0.0055	0.00075	0.0105	5.4	0.00178
17	0.0019	0.0035	0.000087	0.0040	0.00064	0.0081	4.6	0.00165
Mean of Group	0.0021	0.0034	0.000097	0.0046	0.00077	0.0091	5.4	0.00166
Standard Deviation as Percent of Mean	11.1	10.0	13.0	18.0	22.0	14.6	17.2	7.0
Ratio of Gravel-Ware Mean to Fine-Ware Mean	0.80	0.88	0.80	0.82	0.87	0.89	0.92	0.83
Average Ratio	0.85							

Analytical Specimen No.	Scandium Sc_2O_3	Lanthanum La_2O_3	Europium Eu_2O_3	Cerium CeO_2	Thorium ThO_2	Chromium Cr_2O_3	Iron Fe_2O_3	Cobalt CoO
1	0.0025	0.0035	0.000118	0.0056	0.00098	0.0116	5.34	0.0019
2	0.0026	0.0039	0.000117	0.0062	0.00109	0.0079	5.33	0.0019
3	0.0027	0.0040	0.000124	0.0053	0.00080	0.0098	5.79	0.0020
4	0.0024	0.0039	0.000124	0.0054	0.00082	0.0106	5.59	0.0022
5	0.0028	0.0037	0.000123	0.0056	0.00070	0.0109	5.90	0.0021
6	0.0026	0.0041	0.000126	0.0057	0.00083	0.0089	5.67	0.0021
7	0.0025	0.0037	0.000113	0.0051	0.00108	0.0126	5.02	0.0019
8	0.0025	0.0034	0.000108	0.0050	0.00111	0.0100	6.91	0.0018
9	0.0025	0.0038	0.000120	0.0060	0.00082	0.0114	5.54	0.0019
17	0.0024	0.0046	0.000113	0.0051	0.00083	0.0105	5.61	0.0026
Fitted Means of Group	0.00256	0.00384	0.000119	0.00550	0.000895	0.01035	5.65	0.00200

Ratios of Best Fit North Devon Ware Concentrations to Fitted Means of Total North Devon Ware

	Scandium	Lanthanum	Europium	Cerium	Thorium	Chromium	Iron	Cobalt
1	0.98	0.91	1.00	1.02	1.09	1.12	0.94	0.96
2	1.02	1.02	0.98	1.13	1.22	0.77	0.94	0.98
3	1.07	1.04	1.05	0.97	0.90	0.95	1.02	1.02
4	0.95	1.01	1.05	0.99	0.92	1.02	0.99	1.08
5	1.10	0.95	1.04	1.02	0.79	1.06	1.04	1.03
6	1.01	1.08	1.07	1.04	0.92	0.86	1.00	1.04
7	0.97	0.95	0.95	0.93	1.20	1.22	0.89	0.95
8	0.99	0.90	0.91	0.91	1.24	0.97	1.22	0.91
9	0.97	0.99	1.01	1.08	0.91	1.10	0.98	0.97
17	0.95	1.18	0.95	0.94	0.93	1.01	0.99	1.07
σ Range	1.051–0.952	1.085–0.922	1.053–0.950	1.071–0.933	1.172–0.853	1.145–0.874	1.088–0.919	1.058–0.945
95% Confidence Limits	1.118–0.894	1.203–0.832	1.123–0.891	1.168–0.856	1.432–0.698	1.357–0.737	1.211–0.826	1.137–0.880

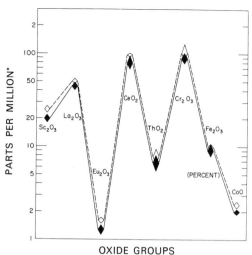

14.4
Comparison of mean
concentrations in north
Devon fine ware (◇)
and north Devon gravel
ware (◆)

14.5
Ratios of best fit north
Devon ware concentra-
tions to fitted means of
total north Devon ware

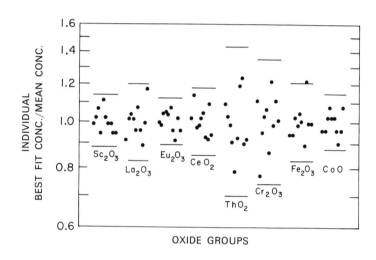

14.6
Sherds from kiln site at
Green Spring Plantation,
James City County,
Virginia. (Specimens
29–34)

Compositional Categories
of Some English and
American Pottery of the
American Colonial Period

14.7
Sgraffito sherd exca-
vated at Jamestown
by the National Park
Service, 1934–1935.
(Specimen 13)

14.8
Sgraffito sherd found
near the shore of Kent
Island, Maryland. (Speci-
men 14)

14.9
Slip-coated pan rim ex-
cavated at Pemaquid,
Maine from a site ante-
dating 1676. (Specimen
19)

14.10
Sherd of sgraffito ware
excavated at Jamestown
by the National Park
Service in 1956. (Speci-
men 20)

14.11
Gravel-ware pan section
excavated at Jamestown
by the National Park
Service, 1934–1935.
(Specimen 10)

14.12
Gravel-ware sherd from
Angelica Knoll, Mary-
land. (Specimen 11)

14.13
Gravel-ware pan exca-
vated at Pemaquid,
Maine from a site ante-
dating 1676.

14.14
Ratios of best fit con-
centrations to the fitted
means of total north
Devon ware for gravel
ware from American
sites.

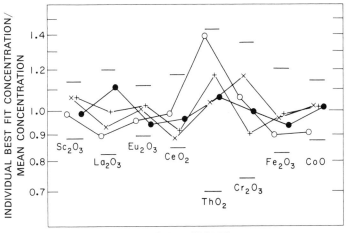

groups is significant with respect to the standard deviation of the groups. In this case the values obtained for t were: Sc_2O_3, 1.81; La_2O_3, 4.91; Eu_2O_3, 4.82; Ce_2O_3, 1.23; ThO_2, 0.12; Cr_2O_3, 1.32; Fe_2O_3, 2.16; and CoO, 2.39. In the cases of La_2O_3, Eu_2O_3, Eu_2O_3, and CoO the value calculated for t is greater than 2.201. One would say therefore that upon the basis of these three elements one could identify a given sample with one group or the other.

Ten of the sherds which were analyzed were for comparison to the north Devon group. These included four sherds (Figures 14.7 to 14.10) which had been found at colonial American sites on the eastern coast and were stylistically comparable to the sgraffito ware of north Devon. Four other sherds (three are shown in Figures 14.11 to 14.13), from similar American sites, are examples of gravel ware which could be from north Devon. The last two are the two specimens from Drake's Bay, California. These are also gravel-ware sherds. All concentration values have been adjusted to best relative fit to the north Devon ware.

The data in Table 14.5 for the four specimens which are stylistically comparable to north Devon fine ware contain some interesting information. Specimens 13 and 14 each have one ratio value lying just outside the north Devon confidence limits. In Table 14.5, and the following tables, ratios equal to or exceeding the confidence limits for north Devon ware have been underlined. It is obvious that if a number of elements are being determined (although there is only a 5 percent anticipation that any specific element will exceed a 95 percent confidence limit of deviation from the mean of a related group of specimens) there is a considerably greater probability that one element unspecified among the number determined might exceed the confidence limit. In fact if twenty elements are determined, one would intuitively expect one out of the twenty to be at or beyond a 95 percent confidence limit. It has seemed reasonable to us that if M independent elements have been determined the probability that the concentrations of any N of them might equal or exceed a deviation limit which includes $0.X$ fraction of the determinations could be estimated by $P_M^N (0.X)^{M-N} (1 - 0.X)^N$ in which P_M^N is the number of permutations of the N exceeding values among the M elements determined. Upon the basis of such an estimate, one concludes that the concentrations of at least two elements out of eight should exceed a 95 percent confidence limit before the overall deviation should be considered truly significant. If only one out of the eight elements exhibits a marked deviation, it should exceed a 99 percent confidence limit if the group of analyses is to be considered nonmatching. Specimen

20, however, has four elements for which the values of the ratios lie outside the confidence limits. This specimen is very probably not from north Devon and the specimen, as shown in Figure 14.10, is an example of sgraffito ware that does not look like the north Devon sgraffito ware.

In Table 14.6 the values are given for the four pieces of gravel ware from colonial American sites on the eastern coast. All of the ratios fall within the 95 percent confidence limits of the north Devon ware. Figure 14.14 is a plot of the values for these four specimens. Both the stylistic and analytical evidence indicates north Devon to be a likely source for these specimens.

Table 14.7 gives the values for a set of miscellaneous sherds (Figures 14.15 to 14.19). Five of these sherds come from Jamestown and the sixth is from a site of Daniel Bayley pottery, Newburyport, Massachusetts (1764–1799). (See Reference 5.) In order to compare these specimens to the north Devon group, the concentrations for each specimen were adjusted to a best relative fit to the north Devon mean concentrations and a set of ratios to the north Devon mean concentrations was calculated. None fit the north Devon mean closely but only specimens 24, 25, and 26 could be definitely excluded from the north Devon group on the basis of these data. Specimen 27 is of special interest since it is known to be from a source other than north Devon. The value of the ratio of only one element falls outside the confidence limits of the north Devon group.

Table 14.8 gives the data for the two specimens from Drake's Bay, California and the ratio values are plotted in Figure 14.20. As a better test of the comparability of the concentrations to those of north Devon gravel ware, best relative fit concentrations were again calculated. As can be readily seen from Figure 14.20, these specimens do not fall within the limits of the north Devon ware. For Specimen 15 there are six values which lie outside, and for Specimen 16 there are four. It is probable that Specimens 15 and 16 do not come from north Devon, and that they do not both come from the same pottery group. The data we have obtained to date have been, in a sense, only preliminary. We have not identified the source of the sherds from Drake's Bay; we have only presented evidence that they do not appear to belong to the group of north Devon ware which we have analyzed.

We have employed a number of steps in our investigation which are of some significance, however. We have looked further at the problems presented by the presence of temper in a piece of pottery and found further evidence that in some cases of pottery there are elements whose con-

Analytical Specimen No.	Scandium Sc_2O_3	Lanthanum La_2O_3	Europium Eu_2O_3	Cerium CeO_2	Thorium ThO_2	Chromium Cr_2O_3	Iron Fe_2O_3	Cobalt CoO
29	0.0029	0.0059	0.000165	0.0062	0.00090	0.0067	7.0	0.0023
30	0.0030	0.0069	0.00018	0.0072	0.00138	0.0071	6.8	0.0025
31	0.0028	0.0057	0.00018	0.0061	0.00079	0.0059	7.0	0.0024
32	0.0032	0.0060	0.00019	0.0057	0.00089	0.0079	8.0	0.0027
33	0.0035	0.0060	0.00018	0.0060	0.00085	0.0079	6.9	0.0026
34	0.0027	0.0060	0.00019	0.0064	0.00082	0.0081	7.8	0.0028
Mean of Group	0.0030	0.0060	0.00018	0.0062	0.00092	0.0073	7.2	0.00254
Standard Deviation as Percent of Mean	10.1	6.7	6.7	9.2	22.4	13.1	7.3	6.5

Analytical Specimen No.	Site	Scandium Sc_2O_3	Lanthanum La_2O_3	Europium Eu_2O_3	Cerium CeO_2	Thorium ThO_2	Chromium Cr_2O_3	Iron Fe_2O_3	Cobalt CoO
13	Jamestown	0.0025	0.0041	0.000122	0.0049	0.00085	0.0127	4.8	0.00198
14	Kent Island, Md.	0.0026	0.0040	0.001256	0.0058	0.00126	0.0142	5.1	0.00196
19	Pemaquid, Maine	0.0023	0.0040	0.000120	0.0038	0.00068	0.0093	6.1	0.00213
20	Jamestown	0.0027	0.0037	0.000103	0.0046	0.00056	0.0109	6.1	0.00160

Best Fit Concentrations Adjusted to Fitted Means of Total North Devon Ware

13		0.0025	0.0041	0.000123	0.0049	0.00085	0.0128	4.53	0.00199
14		0.0024	0.0037	0.000114	0.0053	0.00115	0.0129	4.41	0.00178
19		0.0025	0.0043	0.000131	0.0041	0.00074	0.0101	6.27	0.00231
20		0.0028	0.0039	0.000108	0.0048	0.00459	0.0177	6.31	0.00167

Ratios of Best Fit Concentrations to the Fitted Means of Total North Devon Ware

13		1.06	1.08	1.03	0.89	0.96	1.24	0.80	1.00
14		1.00	0.96	0.97	0.96	1.29	1.25	0.78	0.90
19		1.06	1.12	1.10	0.74	0.82	0.97	1.11	1.16
20		1.19	1.01	0.91	0.88	0.66	1.71	1.12	0.84

Analytical Specimen No.	Site	Scandium Sc_2O_3	Lanthanum La_2O_3	Europium Eu_2O_3	Cerium CeO_2	Thorium ThO_2	Chromium Cr_2O_3	Iron Fe_2O_3	Cobalt CoO
10	Jamestown	0.0022	0.0033	0.000108	0.0051	0.00108	0.0104	4.8	0.00168
11	Angelica Knoll, Md.	0.0021	0.0031	0.000102	0.0042	0.00079	0.0103	4.7	0.00170
12	Plymouth, Mass.	0.0018	0.0028	0.000089	0.0040	0.00077	0.0068	4.1	0.00143
18	Pemaquid, Maine	0.0022	0.0040	0.000105	0.0050	0.00091	0.0098	5.0	0.00188

Best Fit Concentrations Adjusted to Fitted Means of Total North Devon Ware

10		0.0023	0.0034	0.000114	0.0054	0.00125	0.0111	5.1	0.00178
11		0.0025	0.0036	0.000119	0.0049	0.00093	0.0121	5.4	0.00199
12		0.0025	0.0038	0.000122	0.0050	0.00105	0.0093	5.6	0.00195
18		0.0023	0.0043	0.000111	0.0053	0.00097	0.0103	5.3	0.00199

Ratios of Best Fit Concentrations to the Fitted Means of Total North Devon Ware

10		0.99	0.90	0.96	0.99	1.40	1.06	0.89	0.89
11		1.05	0.93	1.00	0.88	1.04	1.16	0.97	1.00
12		1.05	1.00	1.03	0.91	1.17	0.90	0.99	0.98
18		0.99	1.11	0.94	0.97	1.07	1.00	0.94	1.00

Table 14.7
Sherds Which Are
Stylistically Unlike
North Devon Sgraffito
Ware or Gravel Ware
(Concentration in
percent of oxide)

Analytical Specimen No.	Site	Scandium Sc_2O_3	Lanthanum La_2O_3	Europium Eu_2O_3	Cerium CeO_2	Thorium ThO_2	Chromium Cr_2O_3	Iron Fe_2O_3	Cobalt CoO
22	Jamestown	0.0024	0.0047	0.000141	0.0064	0.00078	0.0098	6.8	0.0031
23	Jamestown	0.0020	0.0040	0.000117	0.0052	0.00068	0.0071	4.4	0.0018
24	Jamestown	0.0020	0.0050	0.000132	0.0057	0.00074	0.0077	3.2	0.0075
25	Jamestown	0.0022	0.0044	0.000124	0.0052	0.00086	0.0081	4.1	0.0018
26	Jamestown	0.0023	0.0044	0.000121	0.0066	0.00107	0.0113	3.9	0.0019
27	Bayley Kiln Site, Newburyport, Mass.	0.0019	0.0045	0.000129	0.0060	0.00107	0.0093	5.0	0.0018

Best Fit Concentrations Adjusted to Fitted Means of Total North Devon Ware

22		0.0021	0.0042	0.000126	0.0057	0.00070	0.0087	5.7	0.0028
23		0.0023	0.0047	0.000135	0.0061	0.00079	0.0082	5.2	0.0021
24		0.0025	0.0063	0.000165	0.0071	0.00092	0.0096	3.9	0.0009
25		0.0024	0.0047	0.000135	0.0057	0.00094	0.0088	4.4	0.0019
26		0.0023	0.0043	0.000119	0.0065	0.00105	0.0111	3.9	0.0018
27		0.0019	0.0045	0.000130	0.0061	0.00108	0.0094	5.1	0.0018

Ratios of Best Fit Concentrations to the Fitted Means of Total North Devon Ware

22		0.91	1.10	1.06	1.03	0.78	0.84	1.01	1.38
23		0.99	1.20	1.14	1.10	0.88	0.79	0.92	1.04
24		1.07	1.63	1.39	1.28	1.03	0.93	0.70	0.48
25		1.02	1.24	1.14	1.03	1.05	0.86	0.78	0.95
26		0.96	1.11	1.00	1.17	1.17	1.07	0.68	0.94
27		0.82	1.18	1.10	1.10	1.20	0.90	0.89	0.89

Table 14.8
Sherds From Drake's
Bay, California (Con-
centration in percent
of oxide)

Analytical Specimen No.	Scandium Sc_2O_3	Lanthanum La_2O_3	Europium Eu_2O_3	Cerium CeO_2	Thorium ThO_2	Chromium Cr_2O_3	Iron Fe_2O_3	Cobalt CoO
15	0.0023	0.0023	0.000090	0.0035	0.00093	0.0014	6.6	0.00200
16	0.0018	0.0034	0.000077	0.0054	0.00129	0.0076	2.9	0.00139

Best Fit Concentrations Adjusted to Fitted Means of Total North Devon Ware

15	0.0035	0.0034	0.000134	0.0052	0.00138	0.0020	9.8	0.00297
16	0.0023	0.0043	0.000097	0.0068	0.00163	0.0096	3.6	0.00177

Ratios of Best Fit Concentrations to the Fitted Means of Total North Devon Ware

15	1.45	0.88	1.13	0.95	1.54	0.196	1.63	1.49
16	0.98	1.11	0.82	1.24	1.82	0.927	0.61	0.89

Compositional Categories
of Some English and
American Pottery of the
American Colonial Period
206

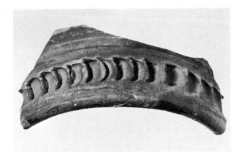

14.18
Sherd excavated at Jamestown. (Specimen 26)

14.19
Sherd from Bayley kiln site at Newburyport, Massachusetts. This site is dated 1750–1790. (Specimen 27)

14.15
Thumb impressed rim sherd from a jar excavated at Jamestown from a supposed kiln site. (Specimen 22)

14.16
Foot of a three-footed cooking pot excavated at Jamestown from a supposed kiln site and another sherd excavated at Jamestown. (Specimens 23 and 25)

14.17
Sherd of a pot lid excavated at Jamestown. (Specimen 24)

14.20
Ratios of best fit concentrations to the fitted means of total north Devon ware for Specimens 15 (o) and 16 (x) from Drake's Bay, California.

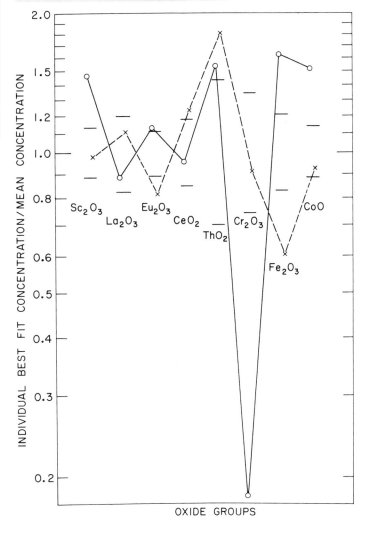

centration in the clay decisively predominate over those in the temper. We have also shown that it is possible to identify pieces of pottery with their source of origin despite the fact that they have been buried for several hundred years. This is the case with the sgraffito ware and gravel temper ware found in colonial American sites for which there is strong historical evidence that they did come from North Devon. We have also shown that for some elements one could clearly distinguish in the case of the north Devon fine ware and the specimens from the kiln site at Green Springs, Virginia, to which group an unknown specimen appears to have belonged. We have not developed compositional categories for any but two groups of pottery, but this work will be continued to that end.

We wish to thank C. Malcolm Watkins of the Museum of History and Technology, the Smithsonian Institution, for his generosity in obtaining the specimens for analysis and his encouragement of our study. We also thank Patricia Donnelly who made many of the measurements of the activities.

Acknowledgments

Compositional Categories
of Some English and
American Pottery of the
American Colonial Period
208

References

1.
Hall, T. M.

Report and Transactions of the Devonshire Association for the Advancement of Science, Literature, and Art, Devon, **22,** 317, 1890.

2.
Al Kital, R. A., Chan, L-H., and Sayre, E. V.

"Neutron Activation Analysis of Pottery Sherds from Hajar bin Humeid and Related Areas." Appendix to Van Beek, G. W., *Hajar bin Humeid, an Archaeological Investigation of a Pre-Islamic Town in South Arabia*, Johns Hopkins University Press, Baltimore, 1968.

3.
Maw, G.

Quarterly Journal of the Geological Society of London, **20,** 445, 1864.

4.
Watkins, C. M.

United States National Museum Bulletin, 225, 17, 1960.

5.
Watkins, L. W.

Early New England Potters and Their Wares, Harvard University Press, Cambridge, 1950.

Chapter 15

Analysis of American Obsidians by X-Ray Fluorescence and Neutron Activation Analysis

F. H. Stross, D. P. Stevenson, J. R. Weaver, and G. Wyld
Shell Development Company, Emeryville, California

In recent years several studies have been published that were aimed at characterizing obsidian by analyzing for elements present in small or trace quantities. If obsidian rock thus can be characterized according to source, the correlation of an artifact made of obsidian with its source becomes possible. Mediterranean and Afro-Asian obsidians were studied by Castiglioni and Renfrew and their associates (Reference 1), New Zealand obsidians by Green et al (Reference 2) and a corresponding study of American obsidians also has been made (Reference 3). The present paper is a continuation of the latter project.

Experimental

The samples were analyzed by X-ray fluorescence except for manganese, which was analyzed by neutron activation analysis, because the X-ray instrument was not equipped for a satisfactory analysis of this metal during the earlier stages of this study. The X-ray values are in terms of counts-per-second over background and have no absolute quantitative significance; the manganese values are given in parts per million by weight.

Aluminum, a major component, was not included in our measurements, because the grinding device used to powder the samples was made of alumina and unquestionably contaminated the samples with this metal during the grinding operation. The chromium values also were disregarded, because the chromium target (the only one available during most of the time when the analyses were made) gave a very high background for this metal.

In the measurements made by X-ray fluorescence, there are several sources of error: (1) It is not possible to reproduce the total alignment (optical and electronic) of the instrument exactly from day to day. This introduces an error difficult to avoid. (2) At low angles of scattering, the signal-to-noise ratio is less favorable than at higher angles, and therefore the heavier elements cannot be determined as precisely at low concentrations as those determined at more favorable angles. (3) The condition of the surface also has a considerable effect on the results. Two methods are ordinarily used to make the surface presented to the X-ray beam as homogeneous and repeatable as possible: One may pulverize the sample and pack the special sample holders to the top of the rim, and then confine the powder by means of a thin Mylar cover; alternatively, one may cut a thin slab of suitable size from the specimen by means of a diamond saw, which will assure that a flat smooth surface is obtained. Sometimes, however, nondestructive analysis is required, and therefore some experiments

were made to compare powdered samples and solid artifacts such as spear- and arrowheads, so as to evaluate the effect of differences in surface geometry. The results of these experiments, given in Table 15.1, show that the range of several determinations of the elements examined in powdered specimens is on the order of 10 percent; the range of the determinations on the solid artifacts is somewhat higher. This is consistent with expectations.

The error caused by variation of the surface geometry of the sample can be minimized by using ratios of elements rather than the values of the elements themselves. In essence, this procedure has been used in interpreting all the results in this paper.

Two techniques were used for making the X-ray fluorescence determinations during this study. That used in making the survey analysis (Figures 15.2, 15.3, and 15.4) and described in our earlier study (Reference 3) is quite adequate for this purpose. It can, however, be improved significantly at the cost of considerably longer analysis time by certain procedures developed in the course of this study. Aside from the preparation of homogeneous surfaces by pulverizing or cutting the specimen, one should, for getting the best results, align the instrument daily in a standardized manner (this ought always to be done by the same person) and take actual counts over a suitable period of time instead of reading the chart record, if possible one should standardize every day any element against the same element in a known standard consisting of the same type of material. This will minimize instrument as well as matrix errors. The optimizing procedure was used in obtaining data for Tables 15.1 and 15.2 and for Figures 15.1 and 15.5, and the error estimates indicated in these tables and figures are fairly firm. Because of the difference in these procedures, data in Tables 15.1 and 15.2 are not directly comparable with those illustrated in Figure 15.2. The complete data for the analyses are given elsewhere (Reference 3). To illustrate these data, Table 15.3 shows the results of the analyses of the unworked samples from the five deposits studied. The data for copper given in Reference 3 are not reliable because of excessive background under the conditions of the analysis, and there is no entry for this element in Table 15.3 for this reason.

The variability of the material within one source locality compared to the variation of average values among different sources is a crucial question. The presumption is that each "locality" represents a single

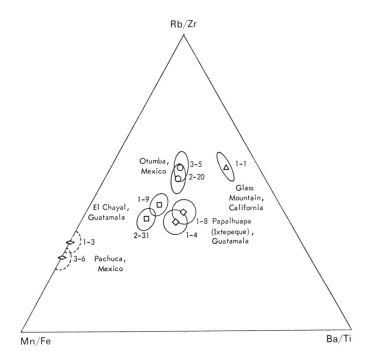

15.1
Classification of obsidian sources by element ratios.

15.3
Normalized ratios of Zr-Sr-Rb.

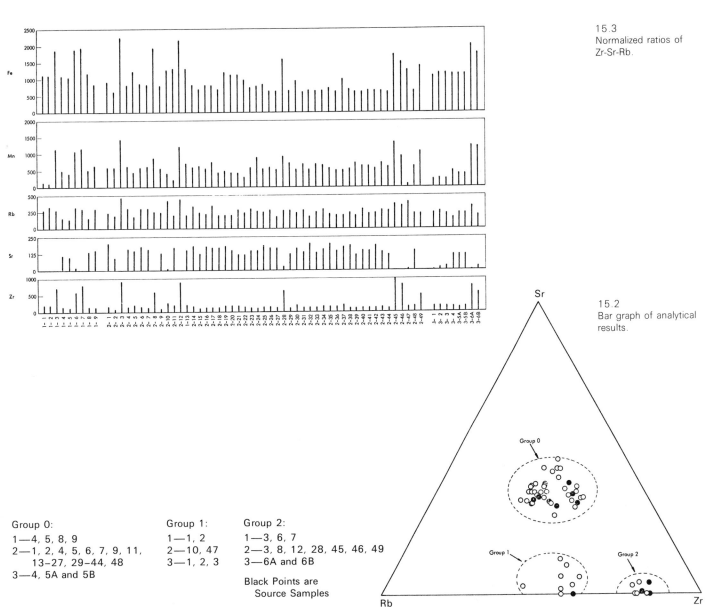

15.2
Bar graph of analytical results.

Group 0:
1—4, 5, 8, 9
2—1, 2, 4, 5, 6, 7, 9, 11,
    13–27, 29–44, 48
3—4, 5A and 5B

Group 1:
1—1, 2
2—10, 47
3—1, 2, 3

Group 2:
1—3, 6, 7
2—3, 8, 12, 28, 45, 46, 49
3—6A and 6B

Black Points are
Source Samples

Target	El Chayal, 1–9 Powder	Pieces†	Glass Mountain, Napa Co. Calif. Powder	§	Pieces	§	Papalhuapa 1–4 Powder	Pieces†	Otumba 3–5† Powder	Pieces†
W-target										
Zr (+SrK$_\beta$)·	70	77	146 ± 9	(5)	130 ± 20	(7)	115	115	98	90
Sr	82	82	15 ± 10	(5)	10 ± 5	(7)	84	67	80	70
Rb	80	69	89 ± 13	(5)	100 ± 10	(7)	56	42	65	58
Fe	1400	1480	2240 ± 108	(4)	2180 ± 240	(8)	2280	2330	2450	2300
Mn	96	96	28 ± 1	(5)	26 ± 5	(8)	74	64	70	70
Cr-target										
Fe	534	474	855 ± 82	(3)	877 ± 65	(6)	786	765	870	800
Ti	147	146	98 ± 10	(4)	100 ± 13	(8)	265	245	230	204
Ba (L$_\alpha$)	53	53	27 ± 2	(4)	28 ± 3	(8)	68	65	75	60
Ca	645	663	230 ± 19	(4)	252 ± 35	(8)	830	785	805	740
K (K$_\beta$)		292	336 ± 31	(4)	410	(1)	335	330	353	330

* All determinations used K$_\alpha$ lines except where otherwise noted.   § Numbers in parentheses are numbers of determinations made in each category.

† Average of only two or three determinations.

	Glass Mountain, Calif.* Average Counts per Second	n	σ (%)	Mt. Konocti, California† Average Counts per Second	n	σ (%)
Target						
Fe, (K$_\alpha$) (Cr-target)	898	15	9.7	948	12	13.4
Fe, (K$_\alpha$) (W-target)	2285	15	7.6	2472	10	9.6
Ratios of Elements	Ratio of Counts			Ratio of Counts		
Cr-target: Ti/Fe	0.126	15	4.9	0.359	12	4.1
Ca/K	0.784	10	5.2	2.14	12	17.5
Ba/Ti§	0.271	17	10.7	0.136	12	12.0
W-target: Mn/Fe	0.0119	15	10.0	0.0136	12	8.0
Zr/Fe	0.0578	10	10.4	0.0423	6	17.5
Rb/Zr	0.723	10	14.4	0.878	6	13.4
Sr/Rb	≤0.1‖	10	—	0.488	6	4.9

* Six unworked pieces, one arrowhead.   † Seven unworked pieces.

§ Ti signal at Ba L$_\alpha$ is 1.4% of Ti signal. Limit of detection of Ba set by Ti so that Ba/Ti > 0.05.

‖ Sr at the limit of detection.

Sample	Si	Cl	K	Ca	Ba	Ti	Fe	Co	Ni	Zn	Rb	Sr	Zr	Nb	Mn(ppm)†
1-1	1480	10	2400	320	32	75	1130	0	18	25	140	0	210	30	150
3	1360	20	2350	130	0	140	1880	0	25	78	140	0	720	85	1150
4	1440	9	2300	900	65	170	1080	0	15	15	80	110	160	0	500
8	1460	4	2500	970	65	160	1180	15	20	20	80	140	150	0	510
9	1320	8	2200	730	45	100	880	5	20	35	130	150	160	0	650
2-20	1240	5	2100	790	55	160	1140	10	15	25	120	150	160	15	440
2-31	1200	10	2050	720	45	90	610	10	25	25	140	140	140	15	700
3-5A	1220	5	1900	720	55	160	1160	5	12	20	120	120	140	10	400
5B	1200	0	1850	700	50	165	1160	0	10	30	120	120	160	10	400
6A	1220	20	2000	80	10	195	2020	10	25	70	170	10	770	80	1250
6B	1160	16	2150	140	10	190	1780	20	25	55	100	30	580	50	1220

* Data for the full set of 66 analyses appear in Reference 3.

† The values for manganese were obtained by neutron activation analysis and are given in parts per million.

Results

lava flow, which in turn might be presumed to be well mixed in a volcanic eruption.

The variability of composition of a given source was studied by making a number of measurements over a period of time on a number of unworked obsidian samples and on an occasional artifact from the same source. Table 15.2 shows such a tabulation of ratios of different elements of diagnostic value, the number of independent measurements n, the total number of samples examined from each source, and the relative standard deviation σ. The latter is seen to vary from approximately 5 to 15 percent. The estimated error in each case is indicated by the size of the symbols used in the plots of ratios of elements shown in Figures 15.1 and 15.5. We see that the variability between all the sources is such that in one or the other plot it almost always considerably exceeds the variability within a given source and that from the measuring error. The elements at present considered most likely to show significant variation in conveniently measurable concentrations are Mn, Fe, Ti, Ba, Ca; also, Sr, Rb, and Zr are suitable and have been used for the purpose in this study, but because their response lies in the low-angle region, the experimental error in the case of these last elements is greater, as indicated above.

For the neutron activation determination of manganese, 20-mg samples were irradiated for 30 minutes in a thermal neutron flux of 10^{11} neutrons/cm²/sec in the Aerojet-General Nucleonics Industrial Reactor in San Ramon, California. Ten micrograms of gold was added to each sample and standard as an internal standard to compensate for flux variations. Gamma-ray spectra were recorded by means of a solid, 3-inch sodium iodide detector and a Nuclear Data 512-channel analyzer. The only interference under these irradiation conditions was sodium. A computer program was used to remove the sodium interference by means of differences in the gamma-ray spectra and half-lives.

Artifacts from Mexico, Guatemala, Honduras, and some from California and Nevada were analyzed. The results of some survey analyses are shown in Table 15.3; the sample descriptions are given in Table 15.4. The data for Fe, Mn, Rb, Sr, and Zr are displayed in a bar-graph (Figure 15.2), and in two ternary plots (Zr-Sr-Rb and Mn-Sr-Rb, Figures 15.3 and 15.4). Figure 15.5 shows a plot of the ratio Ca/K against Ti/Fe.

The results shown in Figures 15.2, 15.3, and 15.4 were obtained without attempting to optimize the measurements as described above. We see that the plots enable us to classify the samples into several groups.

Group O in Figures 15.2 and 15.3, which comprises the greater part of source and site samples, is the group that clusters around the center of both the ternary plots, and thus is characterized by fairly constant ratios of strontium, rubidium, zirconium, and manganese concentrations.

Group 2 also is a fairly tight group, distinguished by a very low value for strontium, a high Zr/Rb ratio (4 to 6), and a high value for manganese. This group includes all the "green" obsidians in the collection of samples analyzed. The only Mexican source represented in this group is the Pachuca deposit (1–3, 3–6A, and 3–6B), which is well known for its green obsidian, and which is thought to have supplied the raw material for all the green artifacts found in Central America. A series of artifacts found in Lovelock Cave, Nevada (including sample 2–49) also gave values that placed them in Group 2; these specimens also appeared to have a slight greenish tinge (see Figure 15.6). Some artifacts from Buck Brush Springs, Nevada, located less than 100 miles from Lovelock Cave, were analyzed by the Department of Geology of the University of California (R. N. Jack, private communication) and were found to have characteristics of composition similar to those of 2-49, and a common source of the obsidian is suggested. No deposit with the composition typical of these artifacts is known to exist in the vicinity, and it will be of interest to find the source from which the Lovelock-type obsidian was obtained. (See also Figure 15.7.)

The representation of the remaining samples on Figures 15.2 and 15.3 illustrate an important feature in this type of analysis. In Figure 15.3, in which the normalized Sr, Rb, and Zr values are plotted, these samples form a single group, in which the relative concentrations do not show variations significantly greater than the experimental error. In Figure 15.4, however, where we have replaced Zr by Mn as one of the variables, two groups can be distinguished on the basis of a variation of their manganese concentration. The entire Group 1 has in common a low strontium content, and a much lower Zr/Rb ratio than Group 2 (approximately 1). In Figure 15.4, we see that the very low manganese concentration of samples 1-1, 1-2, and 2-47 places them apart from samples 3-1, 3-2, 3-3, and 2-10, which have a manganese content intermediate between Subgroup 1-A and Group O; they are designated as Subgroup 1-B.

Figure 15.1, which was used to illustrate our representation of the repeatability of analysis by the size of the symbol used, also shows how we can, with this type of plot, use six elements in the classification of the samples. The three ratios Rb/Zr, Mn/Fe, and Ba/Ti, normalized, do sepa-

213

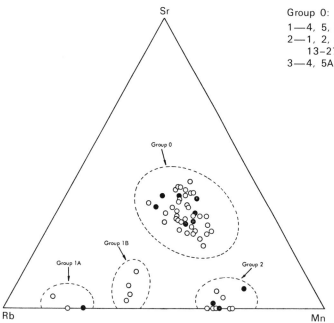

Sr

Rb

Mn

Group 0:
1—4, 5, 8, 9
2—1, 2, 4, 5, 6, 7, 9, 11,
    13–27, 29–44, 48
3—4, 5A and 5B

Group 1:
Subgroup 1A:
1—1, 2
2—47
Subgroup 1B:
2—10
3—1, 2, 3

Group 2:
1—3, 6, 7
2—3, 8, 12, 28, 45, 46, 49
3—6A and 6B

Black Points are
Source Samples

15.4
Normalized ratios of
Mn-Sr-Rb.

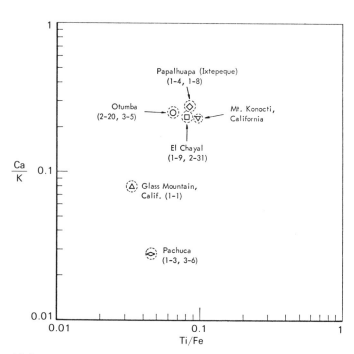

15.5
Element ratios of source
samples.

15.6
Green obsidian arrow-
heads, Lovelock Cave,
Churchill City, Nevada;
University of California,
Berkeley, Lowie Mu-
seum collection. Our
number 2-49.

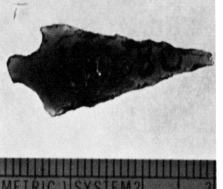

15.7
Green obsidian flake
blade, Kaminalhuyu,
Guatemala. Our number
2-45.

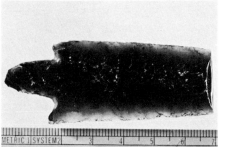

Analysis of American
Obsidians by X-Ray
Fluorescence and
Neutron Activation
Analysis

Table 15.4	Sample No.	Source Locality	Probable Source
Sample Identification* (Obsidians are black or gray unless otherwise noted)	1–1	Glass Mt., near St. Helena, Napa Co., Calif. Sample from quarry. Collected by R. F. Heizer, 1959.	—
	1–2	Site CA-Sol-2, Solano Co., Calif. Artifact in Lowie Museum of Anthropology.	1–1 Glass Mt. Napa Co.
	1–3	Green obsidian. Pachuca, Hidalgo, Mex. Sample from quarry. Collected by W. H. Holmes.	—
	1–4	Papalhuapa, Depto. Jutiapa, Guatemala. Sample from quarry. Collected by H. Williams, J. Graham, R. Heizer, 1964.	—
	1–5	Copán. Artifact in Peabody Museum Collection, Harvard University.	1–4, Papalhuapa
	1–6	Green obsidian. Teotihuacán, Mex. Surface artifact.	1–3, Pachuca
	1–7	Green obsidian. La Venta, Tab. Surface artifact.	1–3, Pachuca
	1–8	Red obsidian. Papalhuapa, Depto. Jutiapa, Guatemala. Sample from quarry.	—
	1–9	El Chayal, Depto. Guatemala, Guatemala. Sample from quarry.	—
	2–1	La Venta, Tab. Surface artifact.	1–9, El Chayal
	2–2	La Venta, Tab. Surface artifact.	1–9, El Chayal
	2–3	Green obsidian. Texcoco, Valley of Mexico, Los Melones Md. Artifact in Peabody Museum Collection, Harvard University.	1–3, Pachuca
	2–4	Yaxun, Lower Lacantun R., Chiapas, Boco or Jimba Phase. Artifact in Peabody Museum Collection, Harvard University.	1–9, El Chayal
	2–5	Cave of Loltun, Yucatan. Entrance to Chamber 1. Artifact (c/1998) in Peabody Museum Collection, Harvard University.	1–4, Papalhuapa
	2–6	Cave of Loltun, Yucatan, Sec. 1, Chamber 3. Artifact (c/2023) in Peabody Museum Collection, Harvard University.	1–4, Papalhuapa
	2–7	Labna, Yucatan, Md. 6 Late Classic Period. Artifact (c/2262) in Peabody Museum Collection, Harvard University.	1–4, Papalhuapa (?)
	2–8	Green obsidian, Mitla, Oaxaca. Artifact (c/5917) in Peabody Museum Collection, Harvard University.	1–3, Pachuca
	2–9	San Lorenzo, Lacantun R., Chiapas. Artifact in Peabody Museum Collection, Harvard University.	1–9, El Chayal
	2–10	Cuicuilco, D.F., Mexico. Tlalpan Phase (field cat. 769). University of California Collection.	2–20, Otumba
	2–11	"El Salvado." Artifact (30.0/2863) in Amer. Mus. Nat. Hist. Collection.	1–4, Papalhuapa
	2–12	Green obsidian, Tula, Hidalgo. Mexico. Surface artifact. Artifact in Amer. Mus. Nat. Hist. Collection.	1–3, Pachuca
	2–13	Copán, Honduras. Artifact in Peabody Museum Collection, Harvard University.	1–4, Papalhuapa (?)
	2–14	Uaxaxtun, Depto. Petén, Guatemala. Stela A-7 cache, Late Classic Period. Artifact (33-99-20/3393) in Peabody Museum Collection, Harvard University.	1–9, El Chayal
	2–15	Benque Viejo, British Honduras. Artifact in Peabody Museum Collection, Harvard University.	1–9, El Chayal
	2–16	Seibal, Depto. Petén, Guatemala. Collected by J. Graham, 1965.	1–9, El Chayal

Table 15.4
Sample Identification*
(Obsidians are black
or gray unless other-
wise noted) (Continued)

Sample No.	Source Locality	Probable Source
2–17	Iximche, Late Post Classic. Depto. Chimaltenango. Surface artifact collected by J. Graham and R. Heizer, 1965.	1–9, El Chayal
2–18	Nohoch Ek, Cayo Dist., British Honduras, Periods 4 and 5. Artifact in Peabody Museum Collection, Harvard University.	1–4, Papalhuapa
2–19	Weston site 6, near Belize, British Honduras. Terminal Classic. Artifact (3-20232) in Peabody Museum Collection, Harvard University.	1–4, Papalhuapa
2–20	Obsidian source locality ("Mine") 2 km. NE of San Marcos, near Otumba, Estado de México. Collected by M. Spence, 1966.	—
2–21	Teotihuacán, Tlamimilolpa Phase. Site sector 21E:N5W1. Collected by J. Bennyhoff.	2–20 Otumba
2–22	Teotihuacán, Tzacualli phase, Zona 5-9, Calle de los Muertos 0.199. Collected by Florencia Muller.	2–20, Otumba
2–23	Tikal, Depto. Petén, Guatemala, Early Classic. Artifact (12C-408/29) in Univ. of Pennsylvania Museum Collection.	1–9, El Chayal
2–24	Tikal, Depto, Petén, Guatemala, Early Classic. Artifact (12K-164-18) in Univ. of Pennsylvania Museum Collection.	1–9, El Chayal
2–25	Tikal, Depto, Petén, Guatemala, Late Preclassic. Artifact (12P-167/89) in University of Pennsylvania Museum Collection.	1–4, Papalhuapa
2–26	Tikal, Depto. Petén, Guatemala, Late Preclassic. Artifact (12P/138) in University of Pennsylvania Museum Collection.	1–9, El Chayal
2–27	Tikal, Depto. Petén, Guatemala, Middle Preclassic. Artifact (12P/152) in University of Pennsylvania Museum Collection.	1–9, El Chayal
2–28	Tikal, Depto. Petén, Guatemala, Early Classic. Artifact (127/226C/33) in University of Pennsylvania Museum Collection.	1–3, Pachuca
2–29	Tikal, Depto. Petén, Guatemala, Late Classic. Artifact (41F/2) in University of Pennsylvania Museum Collection.	1–9, El Chayal
2–30	Tikal, Depto. Petén, Guatemala, Early Post Classic. Artifact (98L/10) in University of Pennsylvania Museum, Collection.	1–9, El Chayal
2–31	El Chayal, Depto. Guatemala, Guatemala. Sample from quarry.	—
2–32	Bilbao (Sta. Lucia Colzumahualpa), Depto. Escuintla, Guatemala. Surface artifact collection by Graham, Heizer & Williams, 1965.	1–9, El Chayal (?)
2–33	Uaxactun, Tepeu phase, Depto. Petén, Guatemala. Artifact in Guatemala Museum of Archaeology Collection.	1–9, El Chayal
2–34	Uaxactun, Tepeu phase, Depto. Petén, Guatemala. Artifact in Guatemala Museum of Archaeology Collection.	1–9, El Chayal
2–35	Zacualpa, Depto. Quicha, Guatemala, Post Classic Period. Artifact in Peabody Museum Collection, Harvard University.	1–9, El Chayal
2–36	Zacualpa, Depto. Quiche, Guatemala, Post Classic Period. Artifact in Guatemala Museum of Archaeology Collection.	1–9, El Chayal (?)
2–37	Poptun, Depto. Petén, Guatemala. Late Classic Period. Artifact in Guatemala Museum of Archaeology Collection.	1–4, Papalhuapa

Analysis of American
Obsidians by X-Ray
Fluorescence and
Neutron Activation
Analysis
216

Table 15.4
Sample Identification*
(Obsidians are black
or gray unless other-
wise noted) (Continued)

Sample No.	Source Locality	Probable Source
2–38	Utatlan, Depto. Quiche, Guatemala. Classic Period. Artifact in Peabody Museum Collection, Harvard University.	1–9, El Chayal
2–39	Nebaj, Depto. Quiche, Guatemala. Classic Period. Artifact in Peabody Museum Collection, Harvard University.	1–9, El Chayal
2–40	Altar de Sacrificios, Depto. Petén, Guatemala. Artifact in Guatemala Museum of Archaeology Collection.	1–9, El Chayal
2–41	Piedras Negras, Depto. Petén, Guatemala. Classic Period. Artifact in Guatemala Museum of Archaeology Collection.	1–9, El Chayal
2–42	Agua Escondida, near lake, Depto. Solola, Guatemala. Artifact in Guatemala Museum of Archaeology Collection.	1–9, El Chayal
2–43	Kaminaljuyu, Depto. Guatemala, Guatemala. Artifact collected by R. Heizer and J. Graham, 1966.	1–4, Papalhuapa
2–44	Kaminaljuyu, Depto. Guatemala, Guatemala.	1–4, Papalhuapa
2–45	Green obsidian, Kaminaljuyu, Depto. Guatemala, Guatemala. Early Classic (Tomb A-V). Artifact in Guatemala Museum of Archaeology Collection.	1–3, Pachuca
2–46	Green obsidian, Chichén Itzá, Yucatan, Mexico. Artifact (c/5042) in Peabody Museum Collection, Harvard University.	1–3, Pachuca
2–47	Chichén Itzá, Yucatan, Mexico. Artifact (c/5038) in Peabody Museum Collection, Harvard University.	Unknown
2–48	Chichén Itzá, Yucatan, Mexico. Artifact (c/4919) in Peabody Museum Collection, Harvard University.	1–4, Papalhuapa
2–49	Green obsidian, Lovelock Cave, Churchill Co., Nevada. Artifact (1-19208) in Univ. Calif. Lowie Museum Collection.	Unknown Calif. Lowie
3–1	Tres Zapotes, Veracruz, Mexico. Preclassic Period (?) (sub-ash cultural level Trench 26). Collected by P. Drucker and R. Heizer, 1967.	2–20, Otumba (?)
3–2	Site buried in sand dune near Roca Partida, Tuxtla Mts., Veracruz, Mexico. Probably Preclassic. Collected by J. Graham, R. Heizer, H. Williams, 1967.	2–20, Otumba (?)
3–3	Eroded site on beach near Punta Roca Partida, Tuxtla Mts., Veracruz, Mexico. Probably Preclassic.	2–20, Otumba (?)
3–4	Copán, Honduras. Classic Period. Surface artifact collected by R. Heizer, J. Graham, H. Williams, Feb. 1967.	1–4, Papalhuapa
3–5A	Otumba, Estado de México, Mexico. Mine No. 1. Collected by Michael Spence, 1965.	—
3–5B	Otumba, Estado de México, Mexico. Mine No. 1. Collected by Michael Spence, 1965.	—
3–6A	Green obsidian, "Pachuca Mine No. 2," near Huasca, Hidalgo, Mexico. Collected by Michael Spence, 1965.	—
3-6B	Green obsidian, "Pachuca Mine No. 2," near Huasca, Hidalgo, Mexico. Collected by Michael Spence, 1965.	—

* We wish to thank the following persons for supplying obsidian samples: Drs. W. R. Coe and H. Moholy-Nagy of the University of Pennsylvania Museum (Samples 2-23/2-30); Dr. Harry Pollock, Peabody Museum, Harvard University (Samples 1-5, 2-3/2-9, 2-13/2-15, 2-18, 2-19); Dr. Gordon Ekholm, American Museum of Natural History (Samples 2-11, 2-12); Sr. Gustavo Espinosa, Guatemala Museum of Archaeology (Samples 2-33, 2-34, 2-36, 2-37, 2-40, 2-41, 2-45); Drs. J. A. Bennyhoff and Michael Spence, and Dra. Florencia Muller, Proyecto Teotihuacán (Samples 2-20/2-22, 3-5A/3-6B); and Dr. Clifford Evans, U.S. National Museum (Samples 1-3).

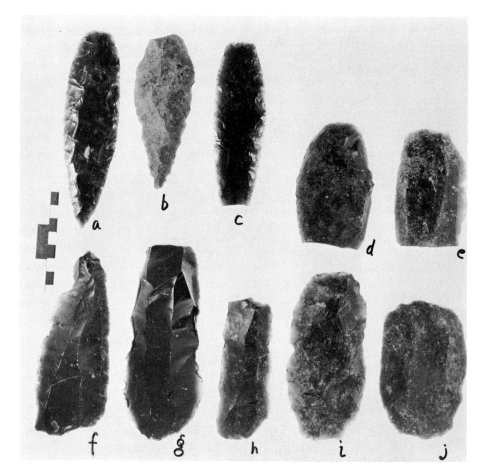

Analysis of American
Obsidians by X-Ray
Fluorescence and
Neutron Activation
Analysis
218

15.9
Prismatic blades, Papalhuapa, Guatemala.

a   b   c

15.10 (a and b)
Profile and flat platform base of large blade core, Papalhuapa, Guatemala.

rate the five sources as shown, although the separation, especially of the Papalhuapa (Guatemala) and the Otumba (Mexico) sources are not quite as good as we might desire. Figure 15.5 shows the values of the Ca/K ratios plotted against those for Ti/Fe for the 5 sources, and for an additional source, Mount Konocti (Lake County, Calif). The dimensions of the symbols again reflect the errors of the determination. This representation also separates the sources (which include several specimens in each case), but barely.

Conclusions

This study serves mainly to underscore the desirability of carrying out large-scale studies of this kind, which have been made possible by the efficient (but not inexpensive) techniques developed in recent years. However, in the case of the American obsidians, at least, we may have to do considerably more precise and careful work than is warranted in routine analysis, if we wish to distinguish individual lava flows and materials which, by some geological accident, resemble each other closely in composition, even in the concentration of the minor elements. (Figures 15.8, 15.9, and 15.10 show more of the obsidian artifacts analyzed and described in this chapter.)

In order, then, to classify an artifact approximately, we suggest making a ''survey'' analysis by X-ray fluorescence, particularly of the elements Fe, Mn, Ti, Ba, Ca, Sr, Rb, and Zr. The results of this preliminary analysis may in themselves suffice to assign the object to a distinctive class, such as the Pachuca source, on the basis of our present knowledge. If further work is indicated, it will be desirable to use our best technique: provide a flat surface or pulverize the sample, carefully align the instrument, use conditions that have been standardized for the instrument, and calibrate daily the values obtained for an element against those obtained for a known obsidian specimen. Ratios of pairs of elements are then plotted against another such pair of the series mentioned, and the point thus obtained compared with data on other specimens already available. If a series of such comparisons, using the analytical data available, cannot distinguish the sample under study from another, or from a group of other specimens, it may be considered evidence that it came from the same lava flow as the specimens used for comparison.

The question concerning the divergence from source to source and the homogeneity within one source has not been resolved completely. It has been our experience (Table 15.2, Figure 15.1) and that of others (Reference 4) that in most individual localities samples, even those taken relatively far apart and having different visual characteristics (color, transparency) have very similar compositions. However, in one or two cases, notably some un-worked samples from Lake County, California that were collected not very far apart on one ''locality,'' showed differences that exceeded experimental error. Whether this represents different lava flows, differences in weathering, or heterogeneity within one flow, we cannot at this time decide. Perhaps a greater effort in sampling the deposits may help in answering the question.

Calculations made after the verbal presentation of the paper allowed us, by plotting the data on the graph shown in Figure 15.1, to assign probable sources to most of the artifacts analyzed. These assignments are shown under the appropriate column in Table 15.4, and represent the conclusions of archaeological interest in this work. In most cases, the analyses placed the artifacts surprisingly well within the zone of error assigned to the individual sources. The relatively few cases in which there was real ambiguity are designated by a question mark. The analysis of one sample, 2–47, was so distinctly different from any of the sources known to us that we must assume the existence of at least one source for manufacture of artifacts that is at present not known to us.

Note Added During Preparation of the Final Manuscript:

References

1.
(a) Castiglioni, O. C., Fussi, F., and D'Agnolo, G.; (b) Renfrew, Colin, Dixon, J. E., and Cann, J. R.; (c) Cann, J. R., and Renfrew, Colin.

(a) Atti della Societa Italiana di Scienze Naturali, Milano, CII, No. 3, 1963; (b) *Proc. Prehistoric Society* **32,** 30, 1966, (c) *Proc. Prehistoric Soc.* **30,** 111, 1964.

2.
Green, R. C., Brooks, R. R., and Reeves, R. D.

New Zealand J. Science **10,** 675, 1967.

3.
(a) Heizer, R. F., Williams, Howel, and Graham, J. A.; Weaver, J. R. and Stross, F. H.; (b) Stross, F. H., Weaver, J. R., Wyld, G. E. A., Heizer, R. F., and Graham, J. A.

(a) *Contrib. Univ. of California Archaeol. Res. Facility* No. 1, **89,** 98, 1965. Some portions of the present paper and more detailed sample identifications appear in: (b) *ibid.,* No. 5, July, 1968, pp. 59–79.

4.
Jack, R. N., Le Joie, K. R., Carmichael, I. S. E.

Geol. Soc. Meeting, New Orleans, 1967.

Supplementary Bibliography

Azurdia, Carlos Enrique
"Las Ruinas de Papalhuapa," *Anales de la Sociedad de Geografía e Historia,* **4,** 1, 1927, pp. 65–70.

Breton, A.
"Some Obsidian Workings in Mexico." 13th Intern. Cong. Amer., New York, 1902, pp. 265–268.

Coe, M. D., and Flannery, K. V.
"The Pre-Columbian Obsidian Industry of El Chayal, Guatemala," *American Antiquity,* **30;** 1964, pp. 43–49.

Dixon, J. E., Cann, J. R., and Renfrew, C.
"Obsidian and the Origins of Trade," *Scientific American,* 218, 3, 1968, pp. 38–46.

Drucker, Philip
"La Venta, Tabasco. A Study of Olmec Ceramics and Art," Bureau American Ethnology, Bulletin 153, Washington, D.C., 1952.

Gordus, A. A., Wright, G. A., Griffin, J. B.
"Obsidian Sources Characterized by Neutron Activation Analysis," *Science,* 161, 1968, pp. 382–384. *See also* their paper in this volume (Chapter 10).

Holmes, W. H.
"The Obsidian Mines of Hidalgo, Mexico," *American Anthropologist,* **2,** 3, 1900, pp. 405–416.

Holmes, W. H.
Handbook of Aboriginal American Antiquities. Bureau American Ethnology, Bulletin 60, Washington, D. C., 1919.

Lunardi, Federico
Honduras Maya: Etnología y Arqueología de Honduras, Tegucigalpa, Honduras, 1948.

Parks, George A. and Tieh, T. T.
"Identifying the Geographical Source of Artifact Obsidian," *Nature,* No. 5046, 1966, pp. 289–290.

Renfrew, Colin, Cann, J. R., and Dixon, J. E.
"Obsidian in the Aegean," *The Annual of the British School of Archaeology at Athens,* **60,** Oxford, 1965, pp. 225–247.

Spence, Michael W.
"The Obsidian Industry of Teotihuacán," *American Antiquity,* **32,** 4, 1967, pp. 507–514.

Spence, Michael and Parsons, J.
"Prehispanic Obsidian Mines in Southern Hidalgo," *American Antiquity,* **32,** 4, 1967, pp. 542–543.

Stephens, J. L.
Incidents of Travel in Yucatan, 2 vols., Norman, Oklahoma, 1962.

Stoll, Otto
Guatemala, Reisen und Schilderungen aus den Jahren 1878–1883, Leipzig, 1886.

Thompson, J. E. S.
Maya Archaeologist, Norman, Oklahoma, 1963.

Villacorta Calderón, J. A. and Villacorta, Carlos A.
Arqueología Guatemalteca, Guatemala, 1930.

Washington, H. S.
"Obsidian from Copán and Chichén Itzá," *J. Washington Acad. Sci.,* **11,** 1921, pp. 481–487.

Williams, H., McBirney, A. R., and Dengo, G.
"Geologic Reconnaissance of Southeastern Guatemala," Univ. Calif. Publs. Geol. Sci., Vol. 50, Berkeley, 1964.

Chapter 16

Activation Analysis Identification of the Geologic Origins of Prehistoric Obsidian Artifacts

Adon A. Gordus, James B. Griffin, and Gary A. Wright[1]
The University of Michigan

Introduction

A fundamental problem in the study of prehistoric trade routes and cultural contacts is the unambiguous identification of the sources of the raw materials used in the manufacture of the archaeological artifacts. For example, when E. G. Squier and E. H. Davis reported in 1848 that they found obsidian artifacts in the 2000-year old Ohio Hopewell burial mounds (Reference 13), they asked: "Whence was this singular product obtained?" The nearest geologic sources are 1,500 miles to the west. During the past 120 years Alaska, the Pacific Coast of the United States, Yellowstone National Park, New Mexico, Central Mesoamerica, and Peru were each suggested as the possible origin of the Hopewellian obsidian.

Described in this paper are analytical studies we have performed which permit us to identify the geologic origin of an obsidian artifact. Based on these analyses, we are able to answer questions such as the one posed by Squier and Davis. But we also obtain information on the variation in the utilization of different obsidian sources during prehistoric times and, hence, are able to describe the changes that occurred in the obsidian trade patterns. Last, the analytical data have a value in themselves in that information related to the geochemistry of obsidian is also obtained.

Obsidian is an ideal material to study in determining prehistoric trade routes. Being a volcanic material, only a limited number of geologic sources exist and need be examined. Since obsidian is formed by rapid cooling, the composition of obsidian in a single flow is relatively uniform (Reference 5), unlike flint for example, which is a sedimentary material. The construction of an obsidian artifact does not alter the composition of the geologic material; ceramic or metallic artifacts, on the other hand, are frequently made of mixtures of various raw materials. Last, except possibly for a very thin surface layer, the composition of the obsidian artifact is unaltered by centuries of weathering during the time it was buried; it is a hard, nonporous material and, unlike pottery, is resistant to the penetration of groundwater. Only by heating obsidian to high temperatures is it possible to alter the mineral; the glassy structure is destroyed, much of the water released, and the result is a porous matrix. Among the 2000 obsidian artifacts we have analysed, only one appeared as though it had been subjected to excessive heat; the analytical data for this sample deviated markedly from the data for all other obsidian samples.

In recent years there has been an increased interest in the determination of the geologic origins of obsidian artifacts. The problem was first rigorously approached by J. R. Cann and C. Renfrew (Reference 2). After an intensive examination of a number of characteristics of the appearance of obsidian samples from different flows (e.g. color, translucency, etc.), they concluded that individual obsidian flows could not be characterized on the basis of appearance alone (Reference 12). The most unambiguous identification, they found, was achieved by considering the elemental composition, which they determined by emission spectroscopy.

F. H. Stross has examined various North American obsidian samples using both X-ray fluorescence analysis (Reference 15) and neutron activation analysis (Reference 14). On a more limited scale, R. C. Green, R. R. Brooks, and R. D. Reeves, using emission spectroscopy, have analysed obsidian from seven New Zealand sources (Reference 6) and G. A. Parks and T. T. Tieh, using X-ray fluorescence, have analysed obsidian from three regions in California (Reference 10).

Described in this paper are studies we have performed during the past three years, using neutron activation analysis as a means of determining the elemental composition of obsidian samples. Both prehistoric obsidian artifact and geologic quarry-site obsidian samples from throughout the world are represented in the 4000 individual samples we have analyzed.

There are a number of reasons why we chose to use neutron activation analysis in these studies: (1) If necessary, the sensitivity of the method would permit us to work with samples as small as a milligram or less. (2) The analysis is nondestructive. (3) In some cases, the analysis procedure can be automated. (4) Samples can be reanalyzed by reirradiating the samples after the original activity decays. (5) The sensitivity of detection of elements is dependent upon nuclear properties. Thus, certain common elements such as oxygen, hydrogen, carbon, and nitrogen are not easily activated. It is usually the elements that are readily activated, many of which may be present only in trace quantities, which frequently provide the greatest amount of information.

Given in Table 16.1 are the gamma-ray radioactivity levels that would be observed if 10 mg of a typical obsidian sample were irradiated for one minute in a thermal neutron flux of 10^{12} neutrons $\times$ cm^{-2} $\times$ sec^{-1}. Most geologic samples of obsidian

Method of Analysis

[1]Present address: Department of Anthropology, Case-Western Reserve University, Cleveland, Ohio 44106

Table 16.1
Radioactivity Formed
in a 1.0-Minute
Irradiation of 10 mg
of Obsidian

Element	Chemical Weight (%)*	Isotope Formed	Half-Life	Gamma Rays Emitted per Minute	
				End of Irradiation	2 Hours Later
Oxygen	42	^{19}O	29.1 sec	2200	—
Silicon	41	^{31}Si	2.6 hr	90	53
Aluminum	7	^{28}Al	2.3 min	13,000,000	—
Potassium	3.4	^{42}K	12.4 hr	4600	4100
Sodium	3.0	^{24}Na	15.0 hr	370,000	336,000
Iron	2.2	^{59}Fe	45.6 day	9	9
Calcium	0.9	^{49}Ca	8.8 min	2200	—
Magnesium	0.3	^{27}Mg	9.5 min	18,000	3
Titanium	0.16	^{51}Ti	5.8 min	1900	—
Hydrogen	0.14	—	—	—	—
Phosphorus	0.06	^{32}P	14.3 day	—	—
Cobalt	0.04	^{60}Co	5.3 yr	—	—
Manganese	0.02	^{56}Mn	2.6 hr	1,600,000	940,000
Carbon	0.01	—	—	—	—
Antimony	0.003	^{124}Sb	60.4 day	—	—
Scandium	0.0015	^{46}Sc	83.9 day	30	30
Lanthanum	0.0011	^{140}La	40.2 hr	135	130

* Composition of a typical obsidian sample.

Table 16.2
Radioactivity Formed
in a 24-Hour
Irradiation of 10 mg
of Obsidian

Element	Chemical Weight (%)*	Isotope Formed	Half-Life	Gamma Rays Emitted per Minute	
				End of Irradiation	16 days later
O, Si, Al, Mg, Ti, Mn	—	—	—	large	—
Sodium	3.0	^{24}Na	15.0 hr	520,000,000	60
Iron	2.2	^{59}Fe	45.6 day	130,000	102,000
Zinc	0.06	^{65}Zn	245 day	18,200	18,000
Cobalt	0.04	^{60}Co	5.3 yr	5000	5000
Rubidium	0.02	^{86}Rb	18.7 day	317,000	175,000
Antimony	0.003	^{124}Sb	60.4 day	50,000	40,500
Cesium	0.003	^{134}Cs	2.1 yr	34,000	34,000
Ytterbium	0.003	^{175}Yb	4.2 day	560,000	40,000
Scandium	0.002	^{46}Sc	83.9 day	430,000	380,000
Samarium	0.002	^{153}Sm	46.8 hr	2,150,000	7500
Lanthanum	0.001	^{140}La	40.2 hr	190,000	24,000
Hafnium	0.001	^{175}Hf	70 day	35,000	30,000
Luthecium	0.0001	^{177}Lu	6.7 day	180,000	35,000
Iridium	0.000004	^{192}Ir	74.2 day	6500	5500

* Composition of a typical obsidian sample.

contain almost the same amounts of the major elements: O, Si, Al, K. The sodium content may vary by a factor of two between sources, but the other elements that are present in smaller concentrations frequently exhibit an even larger variation between sources. For example, we have found manganese to differ by over a factor of 10 (i.e., 1000 percent) between some geologic sources (Reference 5). On the other hand, the variation in the elemental composition of obsidian for each geologic flow appears to be less than 40 percent (Reference 5).

The data of Table 16.1, therefore, suggest one type of neutron activation analysis that can be performed: samples irradiated in a high-flux beam of neutrons can be analyzed two hours after the irradiation and more than 99 percent of the observed activity will be owing only to ^{24}Na and ^{56}Mn. Therefore, the analysis of these irradiated samples was relatively simple and it was possible to automate some steps in the analysis procedure.

If, instead, a typical obsidian sample were irradiated for 24 hours in a thermal neutron flux of 10^{13} neutrons $\times$ cm^{-2} $\times$ sec^{-1}, then various gamma-ray activities, including those listed in Table 16.2, would be observed. If the sample were analyzed 16 days after the irradiation, it would be possible to detect at least 10 to 15 different isotopes.

Our analysis procedure includes both a series of short-term (32 sec) and a long-term (24 hr) irradiation of obsidian.

Short-Term Irradiation

Obsidian samples of 30 mg average weight were individually sealed in polyethylene tubing. Then 90 samples and 10 NaNO$_3$-MnCO$_3$ chemical standards were packaged in two polyethylene "rabbits" (Figure 16.1) and each irradiated for 32 sec at a neutron flux of 2×10^{12} neutrons $\times$ cm^{-2} $\times$ sec^{-1} in a pneumatic-tube facility of the University of Michigan nuclear reactor.

The irradiated samples were analyzed automatically by taking a 1-min count every 2 hr and 25 min for a total of 10 counts per sample. A NaI(Tl) scintillation detector was coupled to a single-channel analyzer and only the 0.76–0.93 MeV radiation, which includes the principal ^{56}Mn peak, was recorded. Since more than 99 percent of the detected radioactivity was owing to ^{24}Na (15.0 hr) and ^{56}Mn (2.58 hr), it was possible, by computer analysis, to resolve these composite decay data into the two decay components (Figure 16.2). Using the data obtained from the chemical standards, the computer then calculated the sodium and manganese contents of the obsidian. This irradiation and computer analysis procedure is described in detail elsewhere (Reference 4).

Since the induced activity was almost completely decayed in a week to ten days, it was possible to reirradiate the samples and obtain replicate Na-Mn analyses of the same samples. Usually four or five such determinations were made for each sample. Typically, the standard deviations of the mean for the replicate Na and Mn assays are within about ±5 percent of the mean.

Separate irradiations of aluminum and iron samples indicated that negligible ^{24}Na and ^{56}Mn interference activities were produced by high-energy neutron reactions.

The sodium and manganese content analyses permitted grouping the artifacts according to the percent-Na, percent-Mn, and the ratio: percent-Na/percent-Mn. Comparison of these data with geologic-source samples of obsidian provided a means of eliminating most sources as possible quarry sites.

In order to identify which of the few sources having percent-Na and percent-Mn contents identical with an artifact was the true source, it was necessary to determine the percentage of additional elements. The obsidian samples and chemical standards were irradiated for 24 hours at a neutron flux of 2×10^{13} neutrons $\times$ cm^{-2} $\times$ sec^{-1}.

Besides the production of radioactive Al, Na, and Mn, detectable amounts of the longer lived isotopes ^{140}La, ^{59}Fe, ^{46}Sc, ^{86}Rb, and ^{153}Sm, as well as about ten other species, also were produced. Analysis for these elements was performed by pulse-height gamma-ray spectrometry with a 10 cc Ge(Li) detector having a full width at half maximum of 4 keV. Typical gamma-ray spectra are shown in Figure 16.3. Data from these analyses are valid to about ± 20 percent.

Since Cs, Ta, Tb, Ir, and Ba were not included in the chemical standards, we have reported data for these elements (and Sc where it is used in a ratio) as radioactivity ratios, corrected for decay to the end of the irradiation.

In order to determine the geologic source of an obsidian artifact, it was necessary first to ascertain if each separate obsidian flow could be uniquely characterized by its elemental composition. This was found to be the case (References 5, 16, 17, 19). Elements that have been particularly useful in differentiating between geologic sources include Mn, Sc, La, and Sm.

Samples from almost 100 obsidian flows throughout the world have been analyzed. Presented here, for purposes of illustration, are data based on samples from a single geographical locality: Yellowstone and Teton National Parks.

Long-Term Irradiation

Elemental Identification of Obsidian

16.1
Obsidian samples and Na-Mn chemical standards are sealed in polyethylene tubing and packaged in polyethylene "rabbits" prior to irradiating the samples for 32 sec in the reactor.

16.2
The composite decay data for an obsidian sample is resolved into its ^{24}Na and ^{56}Mn components.

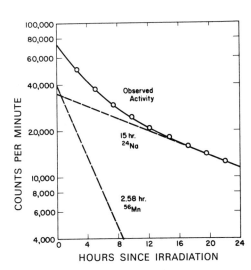

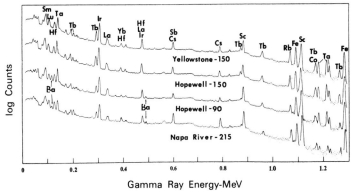

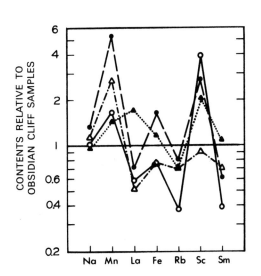

16.3
The gamma-ray spectra for obsidian samples indicate the presence of more than 15 radioactive isotopes.

16.4
Composition of various geologic obsidian samples relative to the average composition of 23 samples from Obsidian Cliff, Yellowstone National Park. Glass Butte, Ore., (5 samples): ○. Cerro de las Navajas, Mex., (10 samples): ●. Vias Mountain, New Mex., (5 samples): △. Powder River, Mont., (4 samples): ▲.

225

One of the major geographical areas of vulcanism having obsidian flows in the Rocky Mountain chain is the region of Yellowstone and Teton National Parks, and an exact count of the separate obsidian flows in this area has not been made. From the reports of J. P. Iddings (Reference 9) and F. R. Boyd (Reference 1), we have been able to itemize more than 20 "exposures" in Yellowstone. This does not include the region of the canyon of the Yellowstone River for which we were not able to obtain data. The United States Geological Survey (USGS) is conducting a new survey in Yellowstone Park, which includes the remapping of many of the obsidian flows, and Dr. B. Christiansen of the USGS will submit samples to us.

At this time, we have element composition data for 15 different exposures. They are listed in Tables 16.3 and 16.4. Most of the 15 localities were investigated by Iddings, and the samples from his survey were submitted for analysis by Dr. H. Banks, Smithsonian Institution. Dr. I. Friedman submitted the Teton Pass specimens, and G. A. Wright collected the Canyon Junction samples. The West Thumb and Norris Cut-Off specimens were in the collections of the University of Michigan Museum of Anthropology. A number of investigators are responsible for the Obsidian Cliff samples. Besides Iddings, they include Dr. E. W. Heinrich and Dr. J. B. Griffin. One exposure is represented by only one specimen (No. 528). It was received from the Field Museum of Natural History, Chicago, and was catalogued only as "Yellowstone." Hereafter, it will be referred to as Field Museum Yellowstone (FMY).

In terms of field geology and chemical analysis, Obsidian Cliff is one of the best studied obsidian flows in the world. Samples from this source have percent-Na/percent-Mn ratios which are approximately 150. This high ratio is a result largely of the extremely low Mn content in this flow, an average of about 2.1×10^{-2} percent

Specimens from two exposures in the Norris Basin (at Geyser Creek and on the east wall of Norris Geyser Basin) also have percent-Na/percent-Mn ratios of about 150. Based on the analysis data, these two exposures appear to belong to the same flow. They may be distinguished from Obsidian Cliff, however, by their lower Sc and La contents (Table 16.3). In addition, the Sc/Cs and Sc/Ta radioactivity ratios for the Norris Basin exposures are about one-half the value of the ratios for Obsidian Cliff.

The FMY sample has a percent-Na/percent-Mn ratio of approximately 90 and differs from West Thumb and Buffalo Lake samples on the basis of a higher Sc content. It also has a lower Tb/Cs radioactivity ratio than West Thumb,

and a slightly higher Fe content. Buffalo Lake seems to have both higher Na and Mn contents and, certainly, a higher Sc/Cs ratio in comparison to West Thumb.

The data of Tables 16.3 and 16.4 indicate that the various Yellowstone and Teton exposures may be readily differentiated in terms of their elemental content. In cases where two adjacent exposures appear chemically similar, they may in fact be from different exposures of the same flow. Only a more complete mapping of the volcanic features of this region will solve this part of the problem.

In summary, these and other data suggest that obsidian sources can be uniquely characterized on the basis of their elemental composition. One method of visually comparing these data is shown in Figure 16.4, where the composition of four North American sources is plotted relative to that of Obsidian Cliff. We will make use of this type of diagram in discussing the data for Hopewellian and Near Eastern obsidian artifacts.

Analysis of Obsidian Artifacts

In our studies of the geologic origins of obsidian artifacts, we have concentrated on two major areas: the middle-western United States (Reference 7) and the Near East (References 16, 17, 19). Data from some of these samples are summarized later. In addition, we have initiated a study of Mesoamerican obsidian and have analyzed over 1000 specimens from that region, but our data are not yet complete enough to permit a full description of the changing pattern of obsidian utilization in this area. This is primarily because we have not yet obtained adequate samples from the large number of potential sources.

Middle Woodland Obsidian

Although elemental analyses of obsidian from various geologic sources, including Yellowstone National Park, had been available since the late nineteenth century (Reference 9), no Hopewellian material had been tested until we began our studies in 1966.

We have tested 90 Hopewell obsidian artifacts for their Na and Mn contents[2] and found that the percent-Na/percent-Mn ratios of the samples fell into two groups[3] as seen in Table 16.5. One ranged from 132 to 170; this is our 150 Group. The second ranged from 84 to 101; this is our 90 Group.

[2]Most of these data are given in Reference 7.

[3]An obsidian group is defined here as a set of elemental-content data that form a cluster. We prefer to use the more neutral term, group, rather than source, since the sources for some of the Near East and Mesoamerican groups have not yet been identified. The code-numbering designations for the Near East obsidian groups are those used by Renfrew and his associates (References 2, 12); our data support his grouping of these samples.

Table 16.3
Yellowstone–Teton
Obsidian Analyses

Sample No.	Location	%-Na	%-Mn ×10²	%-La ×10²	%-Fe	%-Rb ×10²	%-Sc ×10⁴	%-Sm ×10³	%-Na %-Mn	Sc/Cs	Sc/Ta	Tb/Cs	Ir/Tb	Ir/Sc	Sc/Ba
Y-1†	Obsidian Cliff	3.59	2.41	1.2	1.3	2.3	1.8	1.6	149.5	—	—	—	—	—	—
Y-2	Obsidian Cliff	3.56	2.24	0.93	1.2	2.1	1.4	1.6	159.5	3.9	8.5	10.1	3.2	9.4	—
Y-3	Obsidian Cliff	3.39	2.24	0.97	1.2	1.8	1.5	1.8	152.4	—	—	—	—	—	—
Y-4	Obsidian Cliff	3.22	2.02	0.93	0.97	2.0	1.4	1.8	159.6	2.8	9.7	8.3	3.1	10.2	—
Y-5	Obsidian Cliff	3.35	2.18	1.0	1.3	2.0	1.7	1.8	153.7	3.3	8.2	9.7	3.3	9.5	23.5
Y-6	Obsidian Cliff	3.26	2.07	1.0	1.1	1.7	1.7	1.7	157.2	2.0	—	—	3.1	8.9	—
Y-7	Obsidian Cliff	3.54	2.30	0.93	1.1	2.1	1.4	1.6	154.2	2.7	7.1	7.4	2.7	7.4	17.7
Y-8	Obsidian Cliff	3.55	2.32	0.98	1.1	2.0	1.3	1.8	153.0	3.3	7.8	—	—	—	—
Y-10	Obsidian Cliff	3.25	2.00	1.0	1.1	2.0	1.5	1.5	162.5	2.8	9.0	7.9	3.3	9.5	—
Y-12	Obsidian Cliff	3.03	2.11	0.92	0.96	1.7	1.4	1.4	143.6	—	—	—	—	—	—
Y-16	Obsidian Cliff	3.42	2.22	1.0	1.2	1.8	1.5	1.7	153.7	3.0	7.6	9.2	3.3	9.8	
Y-19	Obsidian Cliff	3.11	2.13	0.97	1.1	1.8	1.3	1.9	146.1	—	—	—	—	—	
21	Obsidian Cliff	3.20	2.16	1.0	1.1	2.4	1.8	1.4	148.3	—	—	—	—	—	—
96	Obsidian Cliff	3.53	2.35	0.93	1.2	2.4	1.3	1.7	150.2	3.1	7.2	9.8	3.3	10.7	—
217	Obsidian Cliff	3.27	2.12	1.2	1.3	2.2	1.5	1.9	159.2	2.2	—	—	3.1	8.9	—
219	Obsidian Cliff	3.13	2.03	0.95	1.0	1.8	1.6	1.6	154.2	—	—	—	—	—	—
235	Obsidian Cliff	3.45	2.58	1.2	1.1	2.4	1.8	1.4	132.6	—	—	—	—	—	—
240	Obsidian Cliff	2.92	1.90	1.2	1.1	2.3	1.6	1.7	153.6	—	—	—	—	—	—
242	Obsidian Cliff	3.43	1.97	1.1	1.1	1.9	1.5	1.6	174.1	—	—	—	—	—	—
625	Obsidian Cliff	3.48	2.26	1.1	1.1	2.0	1.5	1.7	154.0	—	—	—	—	—	—
626	Obsidian Cliff	3.39	2.23	0.92	1.1	2.1	1.6	1.8	152.4	2.8	7.7	8.4	3.1	9.2	22.8
1343	Obsidian Cliff	3.08	2.14	0.98	1.3	1.8	1.5	1.5	144.0	3.2	10.0	8.9	3.1	8.7	—
1358	Obsidian Cliff	3.41	2.24	1.2	1.0	2.0	1.8	1.5	152.2	3.4	10.6	—	—	—	—
528	Yellow-stone	3.28	3.59	1.6	1.7	1.8	3.8	1.6	90.0	5.6	12.2	5.0	3.5	3.5	—
1284	Two Miles West of West Thumb	3.03	3.22	1.4	1.2	1.9	2.5	1.7	94.1	9.5	14.4	11.2	3.6	4.2	—
1067	2.6 Miles North of Canyon Junct.	2.63	2.50	0.73	0.89	1.3	4.4	0.93	104.9	—	—	—	—	—	—
1068	2.6 Miles North of Canyon Junct.	2.40	2.18	0.67	1.0	1.1	4.6	0.88	111.4	—	—	—	—	—	—
1095	2.6 Miles North of Canyon Junct.	2.86	2.42	0.74	0.85	0.92	4.3	1.1	118.2	—	—	—	—	—	—
1097	2.6 Miles North of Canyon Junct.	3.18	2.63	0.92	0.99	1.3	4.6	1.3	121.2	—	—	—	—	—	—
1333	North Side Lake of The Woods	3.68	2.52	1.0	1.3	3.1	1.8	1.7	146.0	2.6	8.2	7.8	3.2	9.5	—

Table 16.3
Yellowstone–Teton
Obsidian Analyses
(Continued)

Sample No.	Location	%-Na	%-Mn ×10²	%-La ×10²	%-Fe	%-Rb ×10²	%-Sc ×10⁴	%-Sm ×10³	%-Na %-Mn	Sc/Cs*	Sc/Ta*	Tb/Cs*	Ir/Tb*	Ir/Sc*	Sc/Ba*
1334	Plateau East of Willow Park	2.99	3.44	0.87	2.1	1.7	6.9	1.3	86.9	15.6	49.0	9.0	3.2	2.1	—
1335	Plateau East of Willow Park	2.81	3.05	0.95	2.3	1.8	7.0	1.4	92.1	15.5	47.5	10.4	3.2	2.0	—
1336	Plateau East of Willow Park	3.08	3.50	0.79	2.9	1.4	11.0	1.2	88.0	28.1	59.5	9.1	3.2	1.0	—
1337	Bluffs West of Falls of Boundary Creek	3.17	3.06	1.3	1.3	1.8	3.0	1.6	103.5	6.3	13.7	10.0	3.2	5.0	—
1339	West End of Madison Plateau	3.20	1.50	0.91	1.0	1.6	2.4	1.1	201.3	6.9	20.1	13.1	3.9	6.5	—
1340	West End of Madison Plateau	2.93	1.52	0.91	1.1	1.7	2.6	1.1	193.8	7.8	24.2	12.8	3.7	6.7	—
1344	Geyser Creek	3.19	2.09	0.72	1.1	2.4	1.1	1.6	152.6	1.6	4.6	8.7	3.1	13.0	—
1345	Geyser Creek	3.45	2.41	0.67	1.1	2.6	1.1	1.6	143.1	1.5	5.0	7.4	3.1	12.0	—
1346	East Wall Norris Geyser Basin	3.61	2.35	0.69	1.1	2.3	1.2	1.6	153.6	1.5	5.4	7.8	3.1	11.8	—
1347	East Wall Norris Geyser Basin	3.52	2.39	0.63	—	—	—	1.5	147.3	—	—	—	—	—	—
1348	Top of Mount Hancock	3.46	3.52	1.4	0.91	1.6	2.0	1.7	98.3	5.0	12.3	15.5	3.0	6.3	—
1349	NE. of Buffalo Lake	3.65	4.23	1.4	1.2	1.7	2.0	1.4	86.2	3.9	9.5	—	—	—	—
1350	5 Miles SE. of Kepler's Cascade	3.13	3.09	1.3	1.2	1.6	2.5	1.8	101.3	6.1	11.2	10.9	3.1	5.1	—
1352	North Branch Witch Creek	2.75	2.65	1.0	1.5	0.77	3.3	1.2	103.6	8.9	29.9	7.4	2.9	2.5	—
1353	North Branch Witch Creek	3.22	3.09	1.1	1.6	0.78	3.8	1.3	104.2	8.3	45.1	7.2	3.0	2.2	—
1354	North Branch Witch Creek	2.93	2.67	1.0	1.6	0.95	3.6	1.2	109.7	8.0	33.0	7.5	2.9	2.2	—
1355	Pelican Creek	3.52	3.07	1.2	1.2	2.2	2.0	1.7	114.7	3.5	9.4	9.1	3.1	4.6	—
1356	Pelican Creek	3.13	3.06	0.91	1.1	1.9	1.7	1.4	102.3	3.2	6.0	9.3	3.1	4.6	—
1357	Pelican Creek	3.32	2.92	1.4	—	—	—	2.0	113.7	—	—	10.2	2.9	—	—
1700	Teton Pass	3.48	4.60	0.47	1.1	0.93	3.1	0.72	75.7	—	—	—	—	—	—
1701	Teton Pass	3.53	4.53	0.50	1.1	0.83	3.0	0.71	77.9	—	—	—	—	—	—

* Data are given as radioactivity ratios.

† The Y samples are from a single 2″ × 2″ × 1″ piece from Yellowstone—Obsidian Cliff.

Table 16.4
The Na and Mn Data for Yellowstone Obsidian Samples Not Completely Covered in Table 16.3.

Origin		%-Na	%-Mn $\times 10^2$	%-Na / %-Mn
Obsidian Cliff	N	73	73	73
	Ave.	3.27	2.13	153
	Range	2.92–3.57	1.90–2.60	132–174
Canyon Junction	N	10	10	10
	Ave.	2.92	2.63	110
	Range	2.52–3.18	2.26–2.97	104–121
West Thumb	N	3	3	3
	Ave.	3.07	3.23	95
	Range	3.02–3.16	3.18–3.29	92–99
Norris Cut-Off	N	3	3	3
	Ave.	3.37	3.70	91
	Range	3.22–3.46	3.42–3.93	88–92
Lake of The Woods	N	3	3	3
	Ave.	3.56	2.43	147
	Range	3.45–3.68	2.36–2.52	146–149
Boundary Creek	N	2	2	2
	Ave.	3.20	2.93	109
	Range	3.11–3.22	2.80–3.06	104–115

Table 16.5
Middle-Woodland Obsidian Samples Tested by Neutron Activation Analysis

Locality	Number of Sites	Number of Samples		
		150 Group	90 Group	Total
Ohio	4	39	11	50
Illinois	19	27	5	32
Indiana	1	—	1	1
Michigan	2	3	—	3
Wisconsin	3	1	2	3
Ontario	1	1	—	1
Totals	30	71	19	90

Table 16.6
Analysis of Hopewellian Obsidian Artifacts

Sample No.	Location	%-Na	%-Mn $\times 10^2$	%-La $\times 10^2$	%-Fe	%-Rb $\times 10^2$	%-Sc $\times 10^4$	%-Sm $\times 10^3$	%-Na / %-Mn	Sc/Cs*	Sc/Ta*	Tb/Cs*	Ir/Tb*	Ir/Sc*
81	Ogden-Fettie Site, Ill.	3.35	2.13	0.97	1.1	2.4	1.8	1.9	158	2.8	7.1	8.9	3.4	10.8
85	Damiansville Site, Ill.	3.32	1.98	0.99	1.2	2.4	1.8	1.8	168	2.6	7.3	8.0	3.2	10.1
101	Russell-Brown Site, Ohio	3.02	2.03	0.95	0.97	1.7	1.4	1.6	149	2.8	6.9	8.7	3.1	9.5
92	Hopewell Site, Md. 11, Ohio	3.35	2.25	1.0	1.0	1.9	1.5	—	149	—	—	—	—	—
542	Hopewell Site Md. 11, Ohio	3.38	2.22	1.1	1.0	1.7	1.6	1.4	153	—	—	—	—	—
561	Naomikong Site, Mich.	3.31	2.33	0.95	1.3	1.9	1.8	1.6	143	—	—	—	—	—
1296	Trempealeau Lakes, Wis.	3.35	2.26	1.0	1.0	1.8	1.8	1.9	148	2.8	7.3	7.7	3.3	9.3
90	Snyders Site, Ill.	3.03	3.46	1.6	1.8	1.6	3.6	1.3	88	5.0	11.3	5.0	3.5	3.5
525	Hopewell Site, Md. 25, Ohio	3.34	4.01	1.3	1.7	2.0	4.3	1.4	83	—	—	—	—	—
1293	Mann Site, Ind.	3.19	3.76	1.1	1.6	1.4	3.4	1.3	85	6.5	12.1	6.3	3.7	3.5
1295	Schwert Mound Group, Wis.	3.25	3.58	1.4	1.6	1.8	3.8	1.3	91	6.7	14.2	6.2	3.5	3.3

* Data are given as radioactivity ratios.

The differences were due to a consistently lower Mn content in the 150 Group specimens. There were 71 specimens in the former group and 19 in the latter. Both groups contained well-made ceremonial objects (e.g., large projectile points, Figure 16.5, and bifacially worked blades), cores, and chipping debris. The Hopewellian sites represented in the recent obsidian study are identified in Figure 16.6.

A number of samples in each Na-Mn group were tested for additional elements, and we found that these additional analyses confirmed the separation into the two groups. For example, the 150 Group showed a range in Sc content of 1.3 to 1.8×10^{-4} percent, whereas the range for the 90 Group was 3.4 to 4.3×10^{-4} percent. Using gamma-ray spectral data for each sample, we computed various radioactivity ratios for the samples. The Tb/Cs ratio ranged from 7.4 to 9.7 for the 150 Group and 5.0 to 6.3 for the 90 Group. All of the data from the 12 elements studied left no doubt as to the validity of the two groups. Some of these data are given in Table 16.6 and depicted in Figure 16.7.

Next, these Hopewell obsidian data were compared with similar data complied in our laboratory on obsidian flows in Alaska, the Pacific Coast, Yellowstone National Park, New Mexico, and central Mexico. Our conclusion (Reference 7) is that the 150 Group corresponds to Obsidian Cliff in Yellowstone National Park and the 90 Group corresponds to the FMY sample. This correspondence of source and artifact data is clearly seen in Figure 16.7. Equally important, the lack of correspondence of the Hopewell obsidian data with other source data is seen when diagrams such as Figure 16.4 are compared with Figure 16.7.

Archaeologically, the Yellowstone and Teton areas are extremely important because they contain at least two major sources of obsidian utilized by prehistoric Indians, and possibly a third source (Reference 20).

The Obsidian Cliff and FMY were extensively exploited, and specimens matching these sources have been recovered from archaeological sites of various ages ranging from Idaho (Reference 20) to the Northern Plains in the Missouri Valley (Reference 3) and to the Hopewellian sites in the Ohio and upper Mississippi Valleys. Thus, there is a link between the Hopewellian sites and the Yellowstone sources, but these distributional data do not indicate transmission from group to group across the Northern Plains into the Mississippi Valley. Obsidian Cliff appears to have been *the* major source for these areas (Reference 3), and, if one can trust the obsidian-hydration dates, was apparently utilized in the Northern Plains for

nearly 10,000 years. There also are historical references to historic Indian groups collecting obsidian in Yellowstone National Park, but the quarries are never identified.

There are two major regions of vulcanism in the Near East which contain obsidian flows, the Nevşehir-Aksaray-Niğde area of Central Anatolia and the Lake Van region of eastern Turkey. Near Eastern obsidian artifacts were divided into groups according to their elemental composition, using the notation of Renfrew (References 2 and 12). Artifacts of group 1e-f (source: Acigol) and 2b (source: Çiftlik) derive from obsidian sources in central Anatolia (Reference 19) whereas those that form group 3a (source: Bayezid ?), 4c (source: Nemrut-Dağ B), and 1g (source: ?) appear to derive from sources near Lake Van. The location of these sources and the sites from which obsidian artifacts were obtained for testing are shown in Figure 16.8. It has become apparent from these studies that a preliminary identification may be made on the basis of the Na content. All of the obsidian samples from central Anatolian sources have less than 3.8 percent Na whereas Lake Van source groups have 3.95 percent Na or more. Other element contents, particularly Mn and Sc as determined by us and Ba and Zr as determined by Renfrew et al. (References 2 and 12), provide an unambiguous separation of the various groups (Reference 16). Some of these data are depicted in Figure 16.9.

We will discuss here the data for archaeological obsidian artifacts found in two areas: the Zagros-Taurus arc—southern Mesopotamia—and the Levant. Although the use of obsidian in the Near East begins prior to 7500 B.C. and extends later than 3500 B.C., we will limit our discussion to that 4000-year period. This time range roughly defines the appearance of early village farming communities up to the end of the Ubaid Phase.

In Figure 16.10, Na and Mn data are given for samples from seven prehistoric sites in the Zagros-Taurus arc predating the Hassuna Phase which began about 5800 B.C. Two major obsidian groups are represented: 4c and 1g. Further tests on additional elements in the samples have confirmed these group designations (References 16 and 17). One sample from Çayönü lies outside the range of either group and appears to derive from a source near the town of Bingol which is situated between Çayönü and the Nemrut Dağ source (References 16 and 17). The final sample which falls outside the 4c and 1g Na-Mn ranges is from Jarmo. It belongs to an unknown group.

In Figure 16.11 are presented Na and Mn data for 11 sites in the same area which date between 5800 and 3500 B.C. It is clear that there is a major change in

16.5
Obsidian spears and knives from the second "Altar" of Mound 25 of the Hopewell Group in Ross County, Ohio. These specimens are in the Field Museum of Natural History. University of Michigan Museum of Anthropology Neg. No. 92-2-1.

16.6
Hopewellian sites represented in the present obsidian study. Data in parenthesis are number of samples of 150 Group and 90 Group:

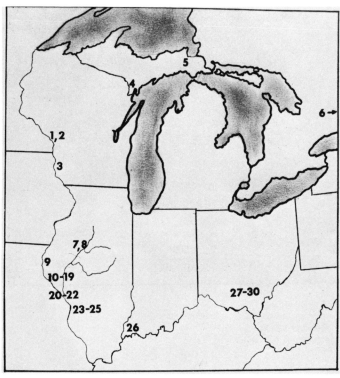

1. Trempealeau Md. Group(1,0)
2. Schwert Md. Group(0,1)
3. Sue Coulee Md. Group(0,1)
4. Menominee Cemetary(1,0)
5. Naomikong Point(2,0)
6. Long Sault Rapids (Ont.)(1,0)
7. Ogden Fettie(1,0)
8. Weaver(1,0)
9. Thien(1,0)
10. N. Edge of Meredosia(1,0)
11. 5 mi. E. of Meredosia(1,0)
12. Meredosia Md. Group(2,0)
13. Plum Creek(1,0)
14. Naples(0,2)
15. Bedford(1,0)
16. Manker(3,0)

17. Montezuma(1,0)
18. Mound House(3,0)
19. Apple Creek(4,0)
20. Knight(1,1)
21. Snyders(1,1)
22. Duncan Farm(0,1)
23. Kraske(2,0)
24. Damiansville(1,0)
25. North(2,0)
26. Mann(0,1)
27. Hopewell Md. 11(10,0)
    Hopewell Md. 25(27,10)
28. Mound City(1,0)
29. Seip(0,1)
30. Russell-Brown(1,0)

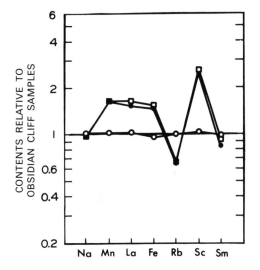

16.7
Composition of Hopewellian obsidian samples relative to the average composition of 23 samples from Obsidian Cliff, Yellowstone National Park. Seventeen Hopewell samples of the 150 Group: O. Nine Hopewell samples of the 90 Group: ●. Data for the FMY sample (No. 528): □.

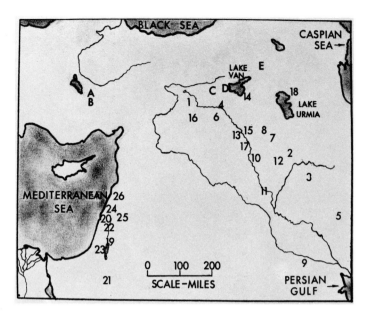

16.8
Location of archaeological sites and geologic obsidian sources discussed in this paper:

Geologic Sources
A- Acigol
B- Çiftlik
C- Bingol
D- Nemrut Dağ
E- Bayezid

Pre-Hassuna Sites
1. Cayonu
2. Jarmo
3. Sarab
4. Ayngerm
5. Ali Kosh
6. Tamerkhan
7. Tell Shemshara

Hassuna and Post-Hassuna Sites
8. Banahilk
9. Eridu-Ubaid
10. Arpachiyah
11. es Sawwan

12. Matarrah
13. Thalathat
14. Tilki Tepe
15. Tepe Gawra
16. Halaf
17. Hassuna
18. Yanik Tepe

Pre—7000–7200
B.C., Levant
19. Jericho (PPNA)
20. Nahal Oren

Post—7000–7200
B.C., Levant
19. Jericho (PPNB)
21. Beidha
22. Munhata
23. El Khiam
24. Beisamoun
25. Ramad
26. Byblos

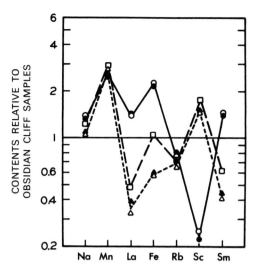

16.9
Composition of Near Eastern obsidian relative to the average composition of 23 samples from Obsidian Cliff, Yellowstone National Park. Three samples from Nemrut Dağ-B source (Group 4c): ○. Twenty-two artifacts (Groups 4c): ●. Two samples from Çiftlik source (Group 2b): △. Four artifacts (Group 2b): ▲. Four artifacts (Group 3a): □.

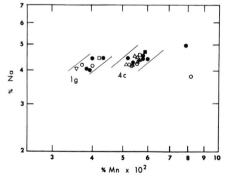

16.10
The Na and Mn contents of obsidian samples from archaeological sites that date to the Pre-Hassuna Phase: ● = Çayönü; ○ = Jarmo; □ = Sarab; ■ = Tamerkhan; △ = Anygerm; ▽ = Tell Shemshara; ▲ = Ali Kosh.

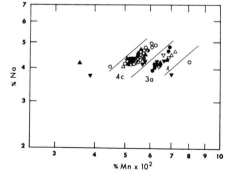

16.11
The Na and Mn contents of obsidian samples from archaeological sites that date to the Hassuna and Post-Hassuna Phases:
● = Banahilk; ○ = Eridu-Ubaid; ▲ = Arpachiyah; △ = es-Sawwan; □ = Matarrah; = Thalathat; ▼ = Tilki Tepe; ⊗ = Tepe Gawra; ■ = Halaf; ◑ = Hassuna; X = Yanik Tepe;

Activation Analysis Identification of the Geologic Origins of Prehistoric Obsidian Artifacts

232

source utilization, with 1g being replaced by 3a. Group 1g is found in the Zagros-Taurus arc—Southern Mesopotamia area during the 5800–3500 B.C. time period only at Arpachiyah where it is in association with both groups 3a and 1g.

The change in obsidian source exploitation by the end of the Hassuna Phase (ca 5200 B.C.) correlates closely with the initial settlement at the site of Tilki Tepe. This site is located on the eastern shore of Lake Van, near the major Eastern Anatolian obsidian sources. The excavator of the site recovered hundreds of large obsidian blades and more than 20 obsidian cores, one of which weighed more than 25 lb (Reference 11). The site has been functionally interpreted as an obsidian working and trading station because of its proximity to major obsidian sources, the presence of large blades and cores, and the absence of cores on most sites in the subarea (Reference 16).

In the Levant, prior to 7000 B.C., obsidian is known only from Pre-Pottery Neolithic-A sites (PPNA) at Jericho and Nahal Oren. These specimens all appear to derive from central Anatolia (group 2b) (Reference 11).

During the Pre-Pottery Neolithic B period (PPNB) (ca 7200 to 6250 B.C.), group 2b obsidian is known from Jericho and Beidha. There is an obsidian microblade from Munhata level 6 which seems to belong to group le-f, and a blade from level A at El Khiam for which the element data most closely approximate a minor central Anatolian source (Reference 18).

Obsidian from the Lake Van sources first reached the Levant during the PPNB. Group 4c obsidian is known from Beidha, Beisamoun, and Ramad (Reference 18).

By 4000 B.C. about one-half of the obsidian in the Levant was from Lake Van sources. Group lg, for example, did not reach the Levant until it was no longer utilized in the Zagros-Taurus arc. At one site, Byblos, five groups have been identified: le-f, lg, 2b, 3a, and 4c (Reference 16).

These obsidian data may be utilized to examine certain hypotheses about cultural development in the Near East. Earlier we mentioned that the obsidian data lend some support to the idea that Tilke Tepe was a manufacturing site for the preparation of obsidian for trade.

A second example concerns the domestication of wheat and its transferral out of its natural habitat zone to the rest of the Near East. J. R. Harlan and D. Zohary (Reference 8) have recently noted that there are two races of wild wheat: one located in the Zagros-Taurus arc and one south of the Syrian Saddle in the Jordan River watershed. Their studies suggest that "the present evidence indicates that most modern tetraploid cultivated wheat stemmed from the race now found in the upper Jordan watershed" (Reference 8). The crucial time period for the domestication of wheat and its spread is about 7500 to 6500 B.C. By 6500 B.C., it is known both at Beidha in Jordan and in the Zagros-Taurus arc. Lake Van obsidian is also known in the Levant at Beidha, Beisamoun (in the Jordan watershed), and at Ramad by 6500 B.C. These obsidian data clearly suggest contact between cultural groups in the Levant and the Zagros-Taurus arc during the crucial time period. The obsidian trade routes thus may have served as paths along which domesticated wheat moved from the Jordan Valley into the rest of the Levant, central Anatolia, and the Zagros-Taurus arc.

Related Studies

In addition to the extensive studies of obsidian sources, we have also initiated studies of flint, hematite, magnetite, and, in cooperation with Prof. Curt Beck of Vassar College, amber. The preliminary data for flint indicate that Na may be a particularly useful element to use in the identification of sources. Other elements which are activated and easily detected in flint include Mn, Fe, La, Sc, and As. The data from analyses of Mexican magnetite samples indicate that it may be possible to characterize each exposure by its Fe, Co, and Sc contents and by the presence or absence of a detectable level of Sm.

Acknowledgments

We gratefully appreciate the cooperation of the many individuals and museum curators who provided us with samples. Special thanks are extended to Mike Hill, Chuck Weibel, and Howard Backer for their assistance in performing various phases of the activation analyses. Funds for these studies were provided by the University of Michigan, Memorial Phoenix Project, the National Science Foundation (Grant GS-1196), and the U.S. Atomic Energy Commission, Division of Research. This is publication COO-912-16.

References

1.
Boyd, F. R.

Bull. Geo. Soc. Amer., **72**, 387, 1961.

2.
(a) Cann, J. R., and Renfrew, C.; (b) Renfrew, C., Dixon, J. E., and Cann, J. R.

(a) *Proc. Prehist. Soc.* **30**, 111, 1964; (b) *Proc. Prehist. Soc.*, **33**, 30, 1966.

3.
Frison, G. C., Wright, G. A., Griffin, J. B. and Gordus, A. A.

Plains Anthropologist, **13**, 209, 1968.

4.
Gordus, A. A.

Archaeometry, **10**, 87, 1967.

5.
Gordus, A. A., Wright, G. A., and Griffin, J. B.

Science, **161**, 382 1968.

6.
Green, R. C., Brooks, R. R., and Reeves, R. D.

New Zealand J. Sci., **10**, 675, 1967.

7.
Griffin, J. B., Gordus, A. A., and Wright, G. A.

Amer. Antiq., **34**, 1969, 1.

8.
Harlan, J. R., and Zohary, D.

Science, **153**, 1074, 1966.

9.
Iddings, J. P.

"The Rhyolites," in *The Geology of Yellowstone National Park, Part II*, U.S.G.S. Monograph, **32**, 356, 1899.

10.
Parks, G. A., and Tieh, T. T.

Nature, **211**, 289, 1966.

11.
Pfeiffer, R. H.

Bull. Amer. Sch. Orient. Res., **78**, 31, 1940.

12.
Renfrew, C., Cann, J. R., and Dixon, J. E.

Ann. Brit. Sch. Archaeol., Athens, **60**, 225, 1965.

13.
Squier, E. G., and Davis, E. H.

Smithsonian Contributions to Knowledge, Vol. 1, 1848.

14.
Stross, F. H., Weaver, J. R., Wyld. G. E. A. Heizer, R. F., and Graham, J. A.

Contrib. Univ. Cal. (Berkeley) Arch. Research Facility, No. 5, 59, 1968.

15.
Weaver, J. R., and Stross, F. H.

Contrib. Univ. Cal. (Berkeley) Arch. Research Facility, No. 1, 89, 1965.

16.
Wright, G. A.

"Obsidian Analyses and Early Trade in the Near East: 7500 to 3500 B.C.", University of Michigan, doctoral dissertation, available through University Microfilms, Ann Arbor, Michigan.

17.
Wright, G. A., and Gordus, A. A.

Am. J. Archaeology **73**, 75, 1969.

18.
Wright, G. A., and Gordus, A. A.

Israel Explor. J. **19**, No. 2, 79, 1969.

19.
Wright, G. A., Gordus, A. A., Benedict, P., and Özodogan, M.

Türk Tarih Kurumu Bulleten, in press.

20.
Wright, G. A., Griffin, J. B., and Gordus, A. A.

Tebiwa, **1**, 27, 1969.

Activation Analysis Identification of the Geologic Origins of Prehistoric Obsidian Artifacts

Chapter 17

Determination of the Origin of Greek Amber Artifacts by Computer-Classification of Infrared Spectra

Curt W. Beck, Audrey B. Adams, Gretchen C. Southard, and Constance Fellows
Vassar College

There are more than fifty named varieties of fossil resins in Europe which may be called amber. Predominant among them is Baltic amber, the succinite of mineralogists, of which the largest deposit on the Samland peninsula in the eastern Baltic has been estimated to contain ten billion pounds (Reference 20). However, the distribution of Baltic amber is not as narrow as the name suggests. Although this resin had its primary origin some sixty million years ago in a forest now covered by the Baltic Sea, later geological events, among them the land movements during the Ice Ages and the subsequent fluvial erosion, have spread succinite over much of northern and eastern Europe, from the east coast of England to the very shores of the Black Sea (References 12, 13, 17) (Figure 17.1).

The many lesser pockets of fossil resins outside this large area have not warranted commercial exploitation, and that may be the reason why they have had little attention from geologists, paleobotanists, and chemists. However, their existence raises an important question to archaeologists dealing with amber ornaments of prehistoric and early historic times which have been found outside the region where Baltic amber occurs naturally: Are these finds imports from the north or are they of more or less local origin? The question was raised as early as 1872 by Capellini, an Italian geologist and amateur archaeologist (Reference 6). The final answer, which has not yet been given, will affect our views of trade and cultural relations in early European archaeology.

Attempts to find that answer have been made repeatedly during the past hundred years. Outstanding among them is the extensive work of O. Helm (Reference 7) who believed that Baltic amber was uniquely distinguished by the substantial amounts of succinic acid which sublime when this resin is pyrolyzed. Historically, this stands as a milestone in the development of archaeometry. Methodologically, it suffers from a number of shortcomings which limit its usefulness quite severely. We have discussed these shortcomings in detail in the introduction to our studies of Minoan and Mycenaean amber artifacts (Reference 1). It is enough to repeat the central point here: While Helm was correct in claiming that all Baltic amber contains from three to eight percent of succinic acid, the corollary that all non-Baltic ambers contain less or no succinic acid does not hold. There are comparable amounts of succinic acid in ambers from Italy, France, Rumania, and Portugal (Reference 14). It follows that the analysis of an amber ornament by Helm's method

permits a firm conclusion only if no succinic acid is liberated; such a find cannot possibly be of Baltic amber. However, no positive identification can be made if succinic acid is formed; such an object *may* be of Baltic amber, but it may equally well have come from one of the four countries named.

Even on this conservative basis, the succinic acid method has given some support to Capellini's hypothesis: since a number of amber ornaments from early Italian sites were found to be free of succinic acid (References 15, 16) they must indeed be of some non-Baltic and presumably southern variety. The very few Greek amber artifacts which have been analyzed all gave direct or indirect evidence of containing succinic acid (References 8, 9) and hence their provenience remains an open question.

Even if the results of the succinic acid assay were more informative than they are, there is a second major disadvantage in that this test demands the pyrolytic destruction of more than a gram of amber. Its application has therefore been limited by the proper reluctance of archaeologists to sacrifice so much material to such uncertain ends.

The success of modern instrumental analysis to decide questions of archaeological provenience by means which are either nondestructive or which use very small samples has opened new approaches to the amber problem. Among the options, infrared spectroscopy has proven both decisive and convenient (References 3, 4). Infrared spectra do not distinguish unequivocally among all of the many non-Baltic European resins, probably because many of them have the same botanical sources. But they do permit the positive identification of Baltic amber and thus allow the direct recognition of imports from the north among the large number of amber finds in European, and particularly in Mediterranean, archaeology.

Infrared spectra of Baltic amber are characterized by their absorption pattern between 8 and 9μ (1250 and 1110 cm^{-1}). In well-preserved mineralogical specimens, this pattern begins with a perfectly horizontal, broad shoulder between 8.0 and 8.5μ (1250 and 1180 cm^{-1}), followed by a more or less intense peak centered at about 8.7μ (1150 cm^{-1}) as shown in Figure 17.2, Spectrum 74. Samples which have suffered atmospheric oxidation give somewhat altered spectra in which the horizontal shoulder assumes an increasingly negative slope. At the same time, an absorption peak at 11.3μ

(855 cm^{-1}), caused by a terminal alkene function, decreases in intensity. These changes are visible in Figure 17.2, Spectrum 179.

Archaeological amber finds have invariably undergone more extensive weathering than mineralogical samples. Their spectra only rarely show the unchanged absorption pattern of Baltic amber, and in many cases oxidative degradation has advanced so far that there is no longer any break between the shoulder and the peak (Figure 17.3, Spectrum 800). In addition, archaeological finds, precisely because they are usually brought to light in an oxidized, friable state, have commonly been treated in the field or in the museum laboratory with a view of consolidating them as well as to improve their appearance. These treatments may involve a coating of wax or of synthetic resins, both of which will penetrate deeply into the porous weathering crust. There is rarely a record of such conservation measures, and since the contaminants cannot be removed completely, they complicate the interpretation of the infrared spectra of archaeological amber artifacts still further by introducing extraneous absorption peaks in or near the range which is critical for the identification (Reference 5) of Baltic amber (Figure 17.3, Spectrum 784).

These two factors, oxidation and contamination, raise serious doubts about the reliability of visual interpretation of amber spectra. In order to eliminate the subjective element as far as possible from the process of classification, we have sought to express the characteristic properties of amber spectra in numerical terms which can then be compared objectively. Since each spectrum must be represented by a large number of readings, and since many spectra of archaeological and mineralogical amber samples must be compared, computer techniques were indicated. We will here briefly describe the program which has evolved and the results of its application to Greek amber artifacts from Mycenaean sites.

The computer storage and retrieval of infrared spectra is not new in itself, but past work has dealt with collections of spectra of organic compounds that differed in the major absorption bands caused by specific functional groups. The major bands of amber spectra are common to almost all varieties and have therefore very little diagnostic value. The subtle differences in the shapes of the absorption maxima in the range of 8 to 9μ (1250 to 1110 cm^{-1}), caused by variations in the molecular environment of carbon-oxygen single bonds, must serve as a basis of any classification. For Baltic amber the pattern in this range has been described earlier. Other varieties of amber have a number of different and more or less distinct patterns

(Figure 17.4). To encode these, we have used absolute absorbance readings at small wavelength intervals. The readings were first divided by the absorbance at 8.0μ (1250 cm^{-1}) to cancel out accidental fluctuations owing to differences in the concentration or thickness of the sample or in the zero point of the recorder.

Treating very short portions of the spectral curve as straight lines, the difference between any two neighboring reduced absorbances is proportional to the slope of the absorption curve. For an idealized spectrum of Baltic amber, the pattern could then be described by four slopes over four 0.2μ ranges (as shown in Figure 17.5a) and represented by the sequence o; o; $-$; $+$. For an idealized spectrum of Sicilian amber, or simetite, the sequence might be $-$; $+$; $-$; $+$, as shown in Figure 17.5b.

Using the signs of the slopes rather than their numerical values is crucial to the success of the scheme. No two amber spectra are quite identical. Not only do the absorbances vary over wide limits, but the wavelengths at which, for example, Baltic amber reaches its maximum absorption near 8.7μ (1150 cm^{-1}) may vary slightly in either direction. It is evident from Figure 17.5a that neither kind of variation will change the basic slope sequence o; o; $-$; $+$, although the numerical values of the negative and positive slopes would, of course, be different.

For oxidized Baltic amber, the first two slopes will no longer be zero, and the slope sequence will become $-$; $-$; $-$; $+$. As long as no other type of amber has either of the two Baltic sequences, they can serve as a sufficient criterion for the recognition of Baltic amber.

If one or more slope sequences can be found for each kind of amber which do not also describe any other kind, then every species of amber can be positively identified. This desirable state of affairs may be attainable or not. We think not, for if several geographically separate ambers, say those of Sicily and of Spain, happen to have the same botanical source, then they will have the same gross structures, the same infrared spectra, and also the same slope sequences. Before accepting this real possibility, there is nothing but to try to generate every conceivable type of slope sequence in the hope of finding those types which distinguish among as many varieties of amber as are, in fact, distinct. The computer is ideally suited to such a trial-and-error approach. While we are continuing to modify and extend our slope sequence programs, the seventh and latest program has proved useful for the classification of archaeological samples.

The computation part of the program re-

Determination of the
Origin of Greek Amber
Artifacts by Computer-
Classification of Infrared
Spectra
236

17.1
Amber in Europe.

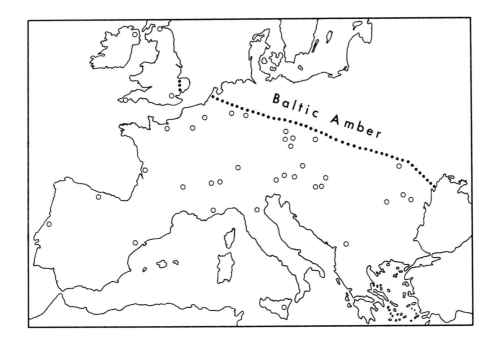

17.2
Baltic amber spectra;
mineralogical samples.

17.3
Baltic amber spectra;
archaeological samples.
(a) Weathered. (b) Con-
taminated with beeswax.

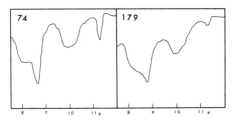

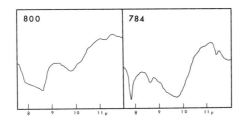

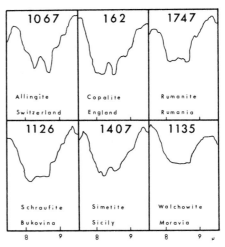

1067	162	1747
Allingite Switzerland	Copalite England	Rumanite Rumania
1126	1407	1135
Schraufite Bukovina	Simetite Sicily	Walchowite Moravia

17.4
Non-Baltic amber
spectra.

17.5
Slope sequences. (a)
Baltic amber. (b) Sicilian
amber.

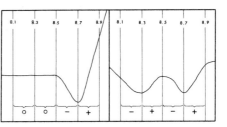

17.6
Computer classification
of amber spectra.

17.7
Spectra of Mycenean
amber from Tiryns.

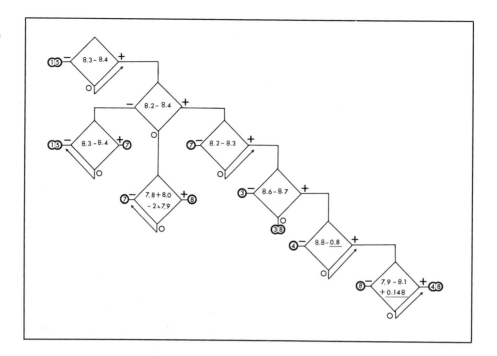

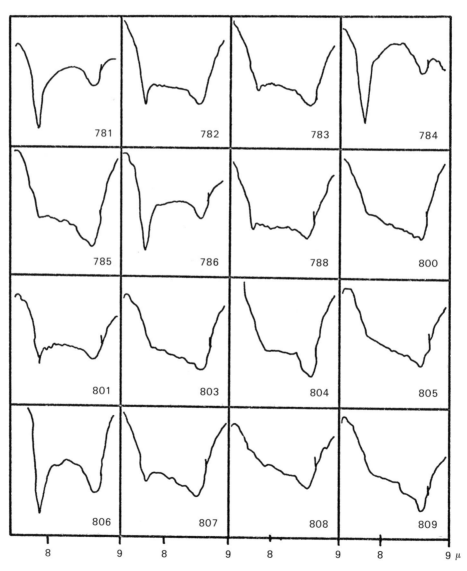

Determination of the
Origin of Greek Amber
Artifacts by Computer-
Classification of Infrared
Spectra
238

quires no explanation. The classification is done by a series of decision boxes which are shown schematically in Figure 17.6. The scheme covers Baltic amber or succinite coded as No. 1; Burmese amber or birmite coded as No. 3; Sicilian amber or simetite coded as No. 4; a variety of Baltic amber called beckerite, which has been regarded as contaminated succinite (References 19, 22) coded as No. 5; walchowite from Bohemia coded as No. 7; and schraufite, which occurs primarily in Rumania, coded as No. 8. The last decision box differs from the general method described in that the computer does not ask for the sign of the slope but whether or not it exceeds a given value, viz. − 0.148. In the last-but-one decision box no slope is used; the question is whether the reduced absorbance exceeds a given value, viz. + 0.800.

Succinite (No. 1) and beckerite (No. 5) are identified together in the first three decision boxes, thus confirming the identity of these two Baltic amber types. The other four varieties can be positively identified by one or more slope sequences, but there is one slope sequence which is common to birmite (No. 3) and schraufite (No. 8), and another which is common to simetite (No. 4) and schraufite (No. 8). These three resins can therefore be uniquely distinguished in some but not in all cases.

In a test of 118 randomly selected spectra of resins of known origin, the preogram identified all but three correctly as either Baltic or non-Baltic. The present approach is thus 97.5 percent successful in recognizing Baltic amber imports (Reference 2).

The first archaeological application of the program was to the gold-and-amber objects from the Late Mycenaean grave robbers' hoard known as the Tiryns Treasure (Reference 10). Nineteen spectra were prepared from sixteen separate amber beads or fragments. One spectrum of each sample is shown in Figure 17.7. It is evident that these spectra suffer both from oxidative degradation and from contamination. Only one spectrum (No. 804) is easily recognizable as that of pure, unweathered Baltic amber. However, the computer identified all 19 spectra as those of Baltic amber.

A larger group of Greek amber artifacts comes from Mycenae itself. From Schliemann's original excavation of the shaft graves of Grave Circle A within the citadel (References 11, 21) we have analyzed 33 samples of which the computer classified 28 as Baltic amber. From Wace's excavations of the chamber tombs at Kalkani Hill (Reference 23) we have analyzed 32 samples all of which are of Baltic amber by computer classification. The most recently dug amber beads come from Grave Omi-

cron of the Middle Helladic Grave Circle B which overlaps the so-called Tomb of Clytemnestra (Reference 18). Of 14 samples from this grave, 10 were recognized by the computer as being of Baltic amber.

Thus of 79 amber samples from Mycenae, dating from perhaps as early as 1650 B.C. to the end of the Mycenaean Era, 70 have been identified as Baltic amber from northern Europe. The other 9 could be of other resin deposits nearer to hand. More likely, they represent samples too deteriorated or too contaminated to be identifiable.

Since there are no earlier amber artifacts in Mycenaean Greece than those here listed, it is now established that Baltic amber reached the Aegean toward the end of the Middle Helladic period, and that Sicilian or Balkan ambers were not used for ornaments before the arrival of Baltic amber in mainland Greece.

Acknowledgments

This work has been supported by the U.S. National Science Foundation grants GS-739 (Anthropology) and GP-4729 (Geochemistry), as well as by travel grant No. 729 of the American Philosophical Society (Johnson Fund).

The collection of samples was made possible by the assistance and co-operation of Professor H. S. Robinson of the American School in Athens, Dr. J. Kontis of the Greek Archaeological Service, and Dr. V. Kallipolitis, Director of the Greek National Museum.

We thank Vassar College for the use of its IBM-360 Model 30 computer and Professor Winifred A. Asprey and her staff of the Vassar Computer Center for valuable advice.

References

1.
Beck, C. W.

Greek, Roman, and Byzantine Studies, **7,** 1966, pp. 191–211.

2.
Beck, C. W.

Paper read at 69th General Meeting of the Archaeological Institute of America, Boston, December 30, 1967; cf. abstract in *Amer. J. Arch.*, **72,** 1968 161.

3.
Beck, C. W., Wilbur, E., and Meret, S.

Nature, **201,** 1964, pp. 256–257.

4.
Beck, C. W., Wilbur, E., Meret, S., Kossove, D., and Kermani, K.

Archaeometry, **8,** 1965, pp. 96–109.

5.
Beck, C. W., Southard, G. C., and Adams, A. B.

Greek, Roman, and Byzantine Studies, **9,** 1968, pp. 5–19.

6.
Capellini, G.

Zeit. f. Ethnol., Verh., 1872, p. 198.

7.
Helm, O.

Arch. Pharm., [3] **11,** 1877, pp. 229–246.

8.
Helm, O.

Schrift. naturforsch. Ges. Danzig, N. F., **6,** No. 2, 1885, pp. 234–239.

9.
Jonas, R.

Schrift. phys.-ökon. Ges. Königsberg, **49,** 1908, pp. 351–368.

10.
Karo, G.

Athenische Mitt., **55,** 1930, pp. 119–140.

11.
Karo, G.

Die Schachtgräber von Mykenai, Berlin, 1930–1933.

12.
Köppen, F. T.

Ministerstvo narbdago provieshcheniia, Zhurnal, August 1893.

13.
Köppen, F. T.

Petermanns geograph. Mitt., **39,** 1893, pp. 249–253.

14.
LaBaume, W.

Schrift. naturforsch. Ges. Danzig, N. F., **20,** No. 1, 1935, pp. 5–48.

15.
Meyer, A. B.

Gurina im Obergailthal, Dresden, 1885.

16.
Meyer, A. B.

Abhandl. naturwiss. Ges. Isis, Dresden, 1892, pp. 49–53.

17.
Meyn, L.

Zeit. deutsche geol. Ges., **28,** 1876, pp. 171–198.

18.
Mylonas, G. E., and Papadimitriou, J. K.

Archaeology, **5,** 1952, pp. 194–200.

Tschermaks mineral. petrograph. Mitt., **3,** 1953, pp. 332–347.

19.
Paclt, J.

Zeitschrift für das Berg-, Hütten- und Salinenwesen im preussischen Staate, **16,** 1868, pp. 224–255.

20.
Runge, W.

Mycenae, New York, 1878.

21.
Schliemann, H.

Geol. Jahrb., Niedersächsisches Landesamt für Bodenforsch., Beiheft No. 45, Hannover, 1961.

22.
Schubert, K.

Archaeologia, **82,** 1932.

23.
Wace, A. J. B.

Part III   **Dating Techniques**

Chapter 18

Potential of Thermoluminescence Dating

Elizabeth K. Ralph and Mark C. Han
University of Pennsylvania

Introduction

Radiocarbon dating has provided one of the most important contributions from the physical sciences toward the development of chronologies in other fields of research. There continues to be a need, however, for other methods of dating. First of all, C-14 dating is confined to samples which contain carbon; but one of the most serious handicaps is the fact that the sample to be dated is usually related to the occupation level and its artifacts by association only. Here thermoluminescence has one obvious advantage—the pottery dated is itself an artifact.

Another fortunate circumstance for the application of thermoluminescence is that pottery was used universally throughout the ages back to about 7000 B.C. A minor point which might be mentioned too is that pottery is fragile so that there is less likelihood that the sample to be dated was used for many centuries prior to its final deposition. In contrast, in C-14 dating, when it is possible to date the artifact itself, it is usually a piece of a large beam of a structure, a plank of a ship, or similar material. Not only is there danger that the beam may have been reused, but it may have been originally a very large beam from which the outer growth layers, the ones contemporaneous with the time of construction, have disappeared.

Thermoluminescence dating, now in its infancy, has also inherent weaknesses and difficulties. Its potential is based upon the fact that it provides an entirely independent means of dating and that it is applicable to pottery and other fired ceramics—the objects found most commonly by archaeologists.

Development and Principles of the Method

The suggestion that thermoluminescence might provide a means of dating pottery was made by Farrington Daniels (Reference 2) and also by F. G. Houtermans (Reference 7) some years ago. The technique was investigated further by George Kennedy (Reference 8) and is now being engaged in actively at the Museum Applied Science Center for Archaeology (MASCA), University Museum, University of Pennsylvania, (Reference 5); the Research Laboratory for Archaeology and the History of Art, Oxford University, (Reference 1); the Institute of Geophysics and Planetary Physics, University of California at Los Angeles; the Departments of Anthropology and Physics, University of Wisconsin (Reference 10); and at Kyoto University in Japan.

Thermoluminescence in pottery results from the fact that radiations from the traces of radioactive elements in pottery bombard the other constituents of the clays and raise electrons to metastable levels. When the pottery is heated, such as in firing, enough additional energy is supplied to enable each electron to fall back to its stable position and to emit a photon of light. On being reheated, the amount of thermoluminescence observed is, therefore, representative of the accumulated radiation damage and hence of the time elapsed since the original firing of the pottery. Once an object has been heated to a temperature greater than 400°C and its electrons have emitted their thermoluminescent light, no further light may be obtained by reheating after a relatively short time. Consequently, recently fired ceramic ware or freshly cooled lava, both of which have all electrons in stable states, should show no thermoluminescence.

If all potsherds contained the same inherent radioactivities, were equally susceptible to radiation damage, and were homogeneous, then the amount of light emitted by a sample upon reheating would provide an age determination. The longer ago the sherd was fired, the greater would be the amount of light emission. Naturally, the situation is not so simple because the compositions of clays and other earth materials are extremely variable. For age determination, therefore, one must include at least two other factors.

The amount of metastable electron accumulation is dependent upon the rate of radioactive bombardment and upon the susceptibility of the pottery to this inherent irradiation. Also, we are concerned with a variety of types of particles and their effects in producing radiation damage may differ. In clays the predominant radioactive elements are normally uranium, thorium, and potassium. Each of the first two emits three different types of particles in its decay series—namely, alphas, betas, and gammas, while potassium-40 emits mostly betas plus a small fraction of gammas. The first question is: Which particles are most effective in creating radiation damage in clays?

From the known behavior of gamma, beta, and X-rays in producing ionization, one would expect the radiation damage from these three types to be similar, and our experimental evidence indicates that this is true for this relatively inhomogeneous pottery. Experiments with five different types of pottery (Nos. 1-A, 11, 12, 22, and 74) were carried out recently in our laboratory. Different portions of each sample were given doses of approximately 1000 rad of X-rays, gammas from Co[60], and betas from Sr[90], respectively. The resultant glow curves (x-y plots of light output versus temperature) were identical in shape. Their magnitudes (or peak heights) differed slightly because of the fact that the intensities of the doses were not exactly alike. These experiments indicate that the quantity of light emitted is directly proportional to the dose received below 1500 rad. In other words, within these comparatively low-level ranges, the response to increasing doses of artificial irradiation is linear. (See Figure 18.1.) This does not prove that the response from natural irradiation is linear, which is a necessary assumption for dating, but since 1000 rad is about the maximum dose received by normal pottery, it is an encouraging indication.

The shapes of the glow curves due to X-ray irradiation are shown in Figure 18.2, where one notes the increasing peak heights with increasing times of irradiation (at 30 kV and 12.7 mA). Also, one sees two discernible peaks at approximately 220°C and 320°C. It should be mentioned here that immediately after irradiation the lower temperature peak is very much larger than it appears in Figure 18.2 and usually masks the stable 320°C peak. After a waiting period of two weeks, however, the less stable lower peak decays sufficiently so that the higher temperature peak is discernible. As we shall see later (in Figure 18.4) the natural glow curve from ancient pottery contains only the stable 320°C peak because the unstable lower temperature peak or peaks have decayed.

We now know something about the effects of irradiation of pottery by X-rays, gammas, and betas, and we come to the problem of the alphas. Here we are dealing with very much heavier particles, some with energies of more than 4 MeV *but* with much less penetrating power. It has been estimated that the maximum range of these alphas is only 30 microns (Reference 4) less than the average grain size of pottery. Because of this limited range, it is more difficult to plan experiments to answer this question of the alphas, and to our knowledge this effect has not yet been determined quantitatively although we hope to do so in the near future. However, even though we have not succeeded in measuring the *effect* from alphas alone, we do know that the total natural irradiation in clays from traces of uranium and thorium is proportional to the alpha rate. This is somewhat fortuitous because for these very low-level natural radioactivities, the *rate* of alpha disintegration is the easiest to measure. Here we are dealing with the rate rather than the effect.

Not included in this alpha measurement is the contribution from the beta-emitting K^{40}. Its importance remains uncertain, until the comparative susceptibilities of clays from alpha and beta radiations are known. Measurements of the total potassium contents of sixteen different potsherds in our laboratory showed little variation

and had an average value of 2.5 percent. The K^{40} fraction of the total potassium is roughly 0.011 percent, and we estimate that this amount of K^{40} may contribute up to one quarter of the total radiation damage—but probably much less. However, since the potassium contents varied so little and since tentative correction factors based on these small variations did not improve the correspondence of these samples with their known ages, we have not been too concerned about this contribution in our present stage of experiments.

In regard to the rate of bombardment, there are other possible complications caused by the environment of the sample. There is the question of the contribution from radioactivities in the soil in which the sample has been buried. However, if alpha particles are essential in producing the radiation damage, this would be only a surface effect since the range of alphas in clays is very short. If a sample has not been buried very deeply, there is the possibility also of a contribution from exposure to cosmic rays. Fortunately, on the basis of our experiments made so far neither of these factors seems to make a significant contribution.

Another complicating factor is that the susceptibility of the pottery to radiation damage is dependent upon its composition and texture. Experiments have indicated that quartz is the component of clays which is most susceptible to radiation damage, and also that an excess of iron compounds tends to reduce the susceptibility (Reference 3). The grain size and homogeneity of the pottery influence the uniformity of radiation damage, since one would expect to find most of the inherent radioactivity in the nonquartz fraction. An attempt to isolate the different components by magnetic separation was made in our laboratory with pottery from Nigeria which contained large visible particles of quartz. Even though the separation of the nonmagnetic (the quartz) and the paramagnetic fractions seemed to be complete, the results were inconclusive. The peak height of the glow curve for the quartz component was almost four times as high as the whole sample, but its response to artificial irradiation was only 70 percent greater. More disturbing was the fact that both the natural and artificial glow curves of the whole sample and of the paramagnetic fraction (from which the quartz had supposedly been removed) were *identical* in amplitudes and shapes.

One of the difficulties is that actual behaviors cannot be predicted from theoretical considerations. In fact, even the basic mechanism by which this radiation damage is produced remains unclear.

A few other uncertainties should be mentioned before proceeding to the experi-

18.2
Artificial glow curves obtained after irradiation with X-rays for different lengths of time.

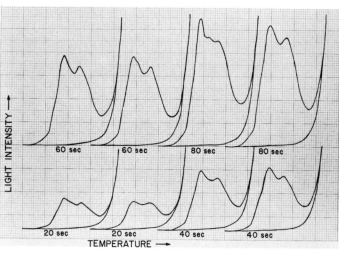

18.3
Block diagram of the glow curve apparatus.

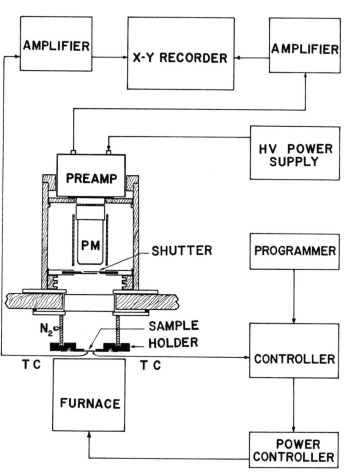

18.1
Plot of A-TL (Maximum light output at 320°C) versus various types of radiation dose received.

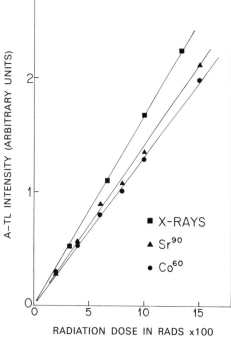

mental results. One is the possibility of the loss or decay of metastable electrons, especially from near the surface during the passage of time. This is a serious consideration for geological dating, but for the much shorter archaeological time scales, it does not appear to be a complicating factor. Another thought is the effect of the differing transparencies of clays upon the detection of the photons emitted when heated. Fortunately, the correction factor applied from the artificial irradiation tends also to correct for this variation. Third, one must consider the effect of grinding the pieces of pottery which is a necessary preliminary in the dating process. Experiments with prebaked samples indicate that negligible thermoluminescence is induced by our system of grinding.

Our first concern has been to assemble apparatus sufficiently sensitive and reliable to make a quantity of measurements. After initial feasibility experiments with borrowed equipment, our program has been supported by and appropriate components have been purchased with funds from the National Science Foundation.

Experimental Procedure

Samples of pottery are received usually in the form of fragments and are catalogued and washed. The grinding of each sample is done in the following fashion: Approximately 10 to 15 grams (a minimum of 3 grams is required) of clean potsherds are crushed to a size below 30 mesh (less than 600 microns) and are then placed in a small ball mill and ground to less than 200 mesh (or 75 microns).

A portion of the ground sample is used to measure its relative radioactivity. Since we have assumed that the major radiation damage is caused by α bombardment *or* is proportional to it, we have, therefore, constructed special low-background zinc sulfide screens and associated components for this low-level detection of α particles. The α emissions are counted in infinitely thick layers with the result that comparative values only are obtained.

For detection of the thermoluminescent photons emitted upon heating, our preliminary experiments indicated that rapid heating rates of thin layers of powdered potsherds were essential. Since the accumulation of metastable electrons is very small, high sensitivity is required to detect the light output which happens to be mostly in the visible range.

The apparatus for detection of the thermoluminescence is shown in Figure 18.3. Samples are mounted on a 7.6 by 7.6 cm square of heavy duty aluminum foil by means of the silk-screen technique. This is done by mixing a portion of the ground sample with a carrier, silicone oil,[1] which is both chemically and thermally stable up to 600°C, and which helps to produce a thin uniform layer on the foil. (By chance, the silicone oil inhibits any possible exposure effect of the finely ground potsherd to daylight.) The size of the sample deposited on the foil is 2 cm in diameter and it is approximately 0.13 mm thick. (This diameter was dictated by the area that can be heated uniformly by our particular furnace.) The foil on which the powdered pottery is mounted is pressed into the sample holder with the sample facing upward, and the back side of the foil is coated with a layer of graphite to obtain maximum heat absorption. The holder is then placed on the furnace, flushed with nitrogen, and it is heated linearly by means of a programmed control system from a starting temperature of 70° up to 450°C. Two thermocouples are located in direct contact under the back side of the foil: one for the purpose of recording the temperature and the other for the feedback to the control system. The light emitted during this process is detected by the photomultiplier tube. The signal from the photomultiplier and that from one of the thermocouples are fed into two separate amplifiers and are recorded on the x-y recorder. This produces the so-called "glow curve" which, in this case, is the natural thermoluminescence (N-TL) produced by the potsherd. About 20 replicate measurements are made for each potsherd in order to obtain a more representative result.

We have found that even though replicate samples were taken from a single piece of pottery that had been ground and mixed thoroughly, there were variations (standard statistical deviations) from ±5 to ±7 percent. This indicated that the corrections obtained by artificial bombardment should be applied to the identical samples that were measured for natural thermoluminescence. Fortunately, our mounting technique with silicone oil on aluminum foil allows this to be done easily. Therefore, each labeled sample is heated and measured for natural thermoluminescence, and it is then bombarded with X-rays (for 60 seconds at 30 kV and 12.7 mA). After this the artificial glow curve (A-TL) is obtained by reheating the sample. The peak height of this glow curve is used as a correction factor for each individual measurement. (We have found that the peak heights of replicate runs are more consistent than the total areas of the glow curves; also, that there is negligible annealing effect from repeated heatings of samples.) The standard statistical deviation of the ratio is reduced to less than ±5 percent. Examples of the natural thermoluminescence and artificial thermoluminescence glow curves are shown in Figure 18.4.

[1] A type of silicone oil that we have found suitable is Duxe Silicone (500 centistokes) made by Duxe Products, Cincinnati, Ohio.

18.4
Examples of the N-TL
and A-TL glow curves
obtained from measure-
ments of Sample P-T-5A.

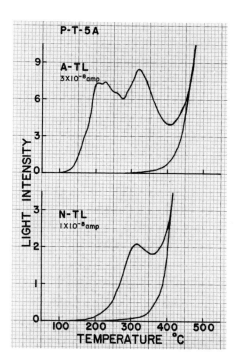

18.5
Plot of the specific thermoluminescence versus
known-age samples:

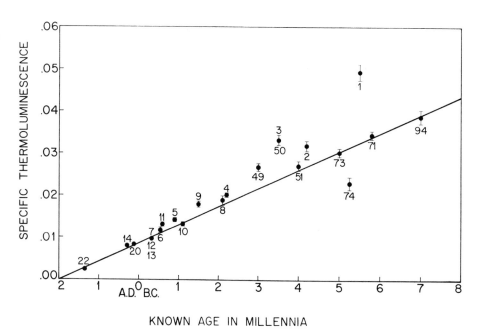

KNOWN AGE IN MILLENNIA

1,2,3,4,5,9,10 and 11 from Hasanlu, Iran
49,50 and 51 from Susa, Iran
8 from Baluchistan
6 and 7 from Plain of Sybaris, Italy (excavated
    from 4 meters below the water table)
12,13 and 14 from Torre Mordillo, above Plain
    of Sybaris, Italy
20 from Le Muraglie, above Plain of Sybaris,
    Italy
22 Pecos Pottery, from Southwest United
    States
71 and 73 from Çatal Hüyük, Turkey
74 from Haçilar, S.W. Turkey
94 from Suberde, Turkey

Finally, after the rate of α bombardment, the natural thermoluminescence, and the artificial thermoluminescence have been obtained, one may calculate the value of the specific thermoluminescence of the given potsherd as follows:

$$\text{Sp. TL} = \frac{R}{\alpha} \qquad (1)$$

where Sp. TL = specific thermoluminescence and R = the average ratio of (N-TL) to (A-TL). (The ratio of the peak heights of the glow curves.)

Results and Discussion

For age calibration there are two possible approaches. One is to determine the age directly from the ratio of natural thermoluminescence and natural irradiation multiplied by the inverse ratio of artificial thermoluminescence and irradiation dose as follows:

$$\text{Age} = \left(\frac{\text{N-TL}}{I_N}\right)\left(\frac{I_A}{\text{A-TL}}\right) \qquad (2)$$

where I_N and I_A = natural and artificial irradiations, respectively. This might be considered to be an absolute calibration, but, as already pointed out, there is a serious difficulty, namely, that it is not now possible to measure with precision the inherent radioactivity (plus possibly also the contribution from external surroundings).

Fortunately, there is another means of age calibration, namely, with samples of known age. This method may be considered an indirect approach, but all factors may be measured with greater precision. The specific thermoluminescence (Equation 1) is determined for each sample of known age, and this value is then plotted versus its known age as shown in Figure 18.5. The slope of the line drawn through the average values of these determinations provides a proportionality constant, and the ages of samples of unknown age may then be calculated by Equation 3:

$$\text{Age} = K\left[\frac{(\text{N-TL})}{\alpha(\text{A-TL})}\right] \qquad (3)$$

where K = proportionality constant and α = relative radioactive content determined by counting the rate of alpha disintegration.

In Figure 18.5 the calibration line is based upon samples from A.D. 1350 to 800 B.C. (Sample Nos. 6, 7, 12, 13, 14, 20, 22) which have been dated firmly by archaeological techniques. The earlier ones in this figure are plotted as samples of known age, but the ages of these are dependent upon C-14 dates of associated samples. In Figure 18.5, reasonably good agreement is noted between the specific thermoluminescence and known ages for samples later than 2500 B.C. Within this range the ages of most samples may now be determined with a precision of ±200 years. For samples earlier than 2500 B.C., we notice a scatter in the results which in some cases is much greater than the uncertainty of the measurements. Since the majority of the deviant values fall above the calibration line, it may be that this trend is a result in part of the discrepancy between C-14 dates and true ages in these earlier B.C. millennia. The largest discrepancies are most likely the result, however, of the inhomogeneity and coarser grain sizes of this earlier pottery. Unexpected situations may also affect thermoluminescence dates. For example, a series of 24 different sherds from the Agora excavations in Athens all showed abnormally low natural thermoluminescence. This was probably caused by subsequent ambient heating from later occupations at this site.

In regard to the dating of pottery of unknown age, which we are just beginning to do on a limited scale, most thermoluminescence dates have been in agreement with archaeologists' estimates or with comparative C-14 dates although there have been a few exceptions. We have received many requests to determine the authenticity of various objects, and in the course of making these tests, we have found that pottery made in the past several centuries can usually be dated with this method. A few specific examples are as follows:

1. Several supposedly Etruscan statuettes were found to be not earlier than A.D. 1850. These are reported in greater detail by E. L. Kohler (Reference 9.) These figures emitted natural glow curves which were readily measureable but, because of their high inherent radioactivities, were proved to be of very young age. One of these was an "Etruscan" figurine from the collections of our Museum, and another was one of the well-known big "Etruscan" warriors from the Metropolitan Museum in New York; both are about 100-years old.

2. A tile from Rome, purportedly of classical origin and found at a depth of 4.2 meters, was dated to approximately A.D. 1700, and therefore, is probably of the Renaissance period (unless it had accidently been reheated in A.D. 1700). This tile contained normal radioactivity, but as revealed in its artificial glow curve, was highly susceptible to radiation damage. It, therefore, was capable of accumulating a sufficient amount of metastable electrons within a relatively short time.

3. An Italic terracotta head was submitted to us to determine whether it was made in the fifth century B.C. or several hundred years later. Just to confuse matters, our thermoluminescence date is 900 B.C.

4. More satisfactory results were obtained with a cup from Haçilar, Turkey. The date obtained was 5100 B.C. which is in excellent agreement with the range of 5250 to 5000 B.C. anticipated from C-14 dates for

the Early Chalcolithic level, Period I, at this site. As a result of this test, the University Museum was happy about the purchase of the cup.

We feel that we have now demonstrated that thermoluminescence will provide a useful method for dating pottery. One of the next challenges is to find out what other materials exhibit natural thermoluminescence and how the technique may be applied for other purposes. In the first respect, measurements made with a piece of obsidian from El Chayal, Guatemala, produced natural glow curves which were 10 times greater in amplitude than normal pottery and with peaks at higher temperatures, about 400°C. This illustrates that it might be possible to use thermoluminescence to date comparatively recent volcanic eruptions which caused the formation of obsidian and would in turn provide another method to identify the sources from which obsidian artifacts were made, but its practical use would probably be limited to cases where there is ambiguity in the trace element analysis.

Another material, namely, glass, exhibits negligible thermoluminescence unless its inherent uranium content is sufficiently high. Experiments with samples from three different locations (submitted by Dr. Robert Brill, of The Corning Museum of Glass) which contain relatively high percentages of uranium show natural glow curves of good magnitude.

In regard to the application of thermoluminescence for other purposes, there are possibilities in fields related to dosimetry. One is the detection of radiation damage from C-14. We are now making a search for carbon compounds or mixtures containing carbon which are sufficiently sensitive to the weak betas emitted by C-14. It is hoped that it will be possible to detect natural C-14 by this method, but if not, there is a good chance that this principle will provide a new and completely different technique for the determination of the half-life of C-14.

Acknowledgment

We acknowledge with gratitude the financial support from the National Science Foundation (Current Grant GS-1568).

References

1.
Aitken, M. J.
"Thermoluminescence Dating of Pottery," *Proceedings of the 1967 International Conference at UCLA on the Applications of Science to Medieval Archaeology.* In press.

2.
Daniels, F., Boyd, C. A., and Saunders, D. F.
"Thermoluminescence as a Research Tool," *Science,* 117, 1953.

3.
Fleming, S. J.
"Study of Thermoluminescence of Crystalline Extracts from Pottery," *Archaeometry,* **9,** 1966.

4.
Fremlin, J. H.
"Effects of Non-uniformity of Material on the Thermoluminescent Method of Dating," *Thermoluminescence of Geological Materials,* edited by D. J. McDougall, Academic Press, New York, 1968.

5.
Han, M. C. and Ralph, E. K.
"Potential of Thermoluminescence in Supplementing Radiocarbon for Dating in the Middle Ages," *Proceedings of the 1967 International Conference at UCLA on the Applications of Science to Medieval Archaeology.* In press.

6.
Higashimura, T., Ichikawa, Y., and Sidei, T.
"Thermoluminescence Dating of Pottery Using Separated Mineral Fraction," *Thermoluminescence of Geological Materials,* D. J. McDougall, Ed., Academic Press, New York, 1968.

7.
Houtermans, F. G., Jäger, E., Schön, M., and Stauffer, H.
"Messungen der Thermolumineszenz als Mittel zur Untersuchung der thermischen und der Strahlungsgeschichte von naturlichen Mineralian und Gesteinen," *Ann. d. Physik,* **20,** 1957.

8.
Kennedy, G. and Knopff, L.
"Dating by Thermoluminescence," *Archaeology,* **13,** 1960.

9.
Kohler, E. L.
"Ultimatum to Terracotta-Forgers," *Expedition,* **9,** 1967.

10.
Mazess, R. B. and Zimmerman, D. W.
"Pottery Dating from Thermoluminescence," *Science,* 152, 1966.

Chapter 19

The Colonial Obsidian Industry of the Valley of Mexico

Joseph W. Michels
Pennsylvania State University

Introduction

In this paper I have attempted to illustrate an important use of obsidian hydration dating, namely, the identification of obsidian artifacts that belong to a cultural period for which we have few if any single component sites. The technique of obsidian hydration dating was developed less than ten years ago (Reference 3) and is already becoming a common laboratory capability among anthropology departments with a strong commitment to archaeology (Reference 8).

This paper is the first of a series of reports on the obsidian industry of the Valley of Mexico which I have been investigating since 1966 with the support of a National Science Foundation grant. Approximately 9000 obsidian specimens from thirty previously excavated sites are being used in this investigation. Over 3000 of these artifacts have been selected for obsidian dating. The ultimate objective of the project is to identify the role obsidian has played in the various subsystems of the Archaic, Formative, Classic, Postclassic and Colonial cultures known to have existed in the Valley of Mexico. This report deals exclusively with the obsidian industry of the Colonial period.

The Valley of Mexico (Figure 19.1) is situated in the central highlands at an elevation of 7000 feet above sea level. Technically it is not a valley but a basin, for it lacks a natural outlet. Volcanic eruptions beginning in the late Tertiary period gave it the form of an irregular elliptical depression extending 75 miles in a north-south direction and 40 miles from east to west surrounded by high mountains.

The archaeological record of the Valley of Mexico terminates abruptly with the fall of Aztec civilization at the hands of a Spanish army in 1519–1521. Most archaeologists have restricted their attention to the preconquest period and the Spanish did not record pertinent detailed information on rural Indian life during the three centuries of Colonial rule. Probably the most comprehensive summary of our present knowledge of the Colonial period is to be found in Gibson's very excellent history of the Indians of the Valley of Mexico from 1519 to 1810 (Reference 5). This volume excels primarily in its description of those aspects of Indian life that relate directly to Spanish Colonial society. The obsidian industry, so important in Pre-Hispanic times, is all but ignored.

At present, the archaeology of Colonial Indian culture in the Valley of Mexico is becoming better understood through an intensive study of ceramic and obsidian artifacts. Recent progress in the identification of the salient stylistic and technological aspects of Colonial ceramics has

encouraged investigators to reexamine existing archaeological collections in the expectation of finding previously overlooked data on Colonial occupation.[1] Similarly, with the aid of firm ceramic identification, new surface surveys in the Valley promise to produce numerous Colonial sites that merit archaeological excavation. Stone artifacts, on the other hand, are notoriously unreliable time markers when considered in terms of their stylistic and technological attributes. With the aid of the hydration dating technique, however, obsidian is one class of stone that can become an extremely sensitive indicator of time, often capable of revealing the presence of cultural episodes unrecognizable by conventional archeological techniques. It is from this standpoint that the present paper serves to illustrate the role of archaeological chemistry in present-day research. For those who have not had an opportunity to examine a hydration rim through the microscope, Figure 19.2 will show how clearly such a rim stands out in polished cross-section.

Physical scientists engaged in research on obsidian hydration dating have argued on theoretical grounds that the diffusion of water into obsidian should follow the diffusion law $M^2 = Kt$, where M is the depth of penetration of water in microns, K is the diffusion coefficient, and t is the time in years (Reference 4). Experimental research on obsidian hydration has focused on one or another of the multiple components of the diffusion coefficient. I. Friedman, R. L. Smith, and W. D. Long, for example, have conducted controlled experiments on the temperature dependence of diffusion (see Reference 4). They have made considerable progress but have not yet been able to formulate that dependence. W. Haller has argued that on the basis of his data it appears very likely that diffusion is exponentially concentration dependent (Reference 6). Finally, I. Friedman and the present author have established that diffusion is dependent upon composition, although the nature of this dependence remains to be formulated.[2]

Editor's note, added at the request of the author:

From what is known about the durability

Rate of Hydration of Obsidian

---

[1] Thomas H. Charlton, University of Iowa, is currently investigating Colonial ceramics using both original field data and existing archaeological collections, with the support of a National Science Foundation grant.

[2] I. Friedman established separate rates for rhyolitic and trachytic obsidians of Egypt (Reference 6); I have established separate rates for green and gray rhyolitic obsidians of the Valley of Mexico (see this report).

19.1
Map of the Valley of
Mexico in A.D. 1519.

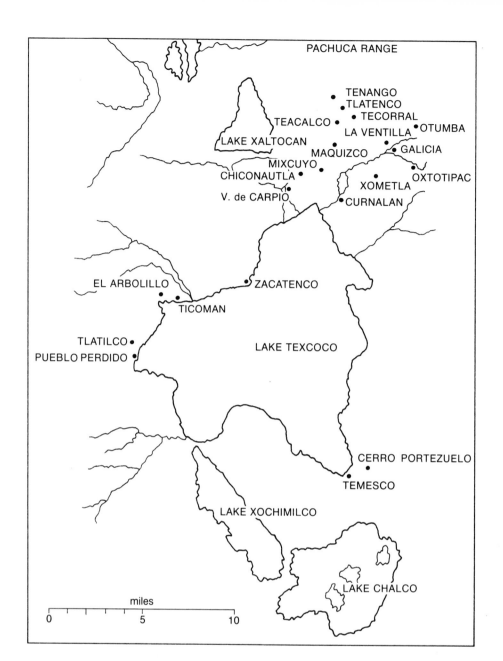

PACHUCA RANGE

TENANGO
TLATENCO
TEACALCO
TECORRAL
LA VENTILLA
OTUMBA
LAKE XALTOCAN
GALICIA
MAQUIZCO
MIXCUYO
CHICONAUTLA
OXTOTIPAC
XOMETLA
V. de CARPIO
CURNALAN

EL ARBOLILLO
ZACATENCO

TICOMAN

TLATILCO
LAKE TEXCOCO
PUEBLO PERDIDO

CERRO PORTEZUELO
TEMESCO

LAKE XOCHIMILCO

LAKE CHALCO

miles

0   5   10

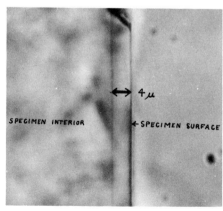

19.2
Hydration rim.

(or corrosion resistance) of man-made glasses, one expects that the rate of hydration of obsidians could depend rather sensitively upon the relative proportions of major ingredients, as well as upon those of certain minor ingredients. In general, it is the higher silica and alumina contents, coupled with lower alkali contents, which make natural glasses so much more durable than most of the ordinary man-made glasses. (For example, man-made glasses found in similar contexts may have weathering crusts some 500–2000 times as thick as the hydration rims on obsidian artifacts.) Thus, variations in the concentrations of the above elements in particular, as well as almost any others present at a level of a few percent, could well have a bearing on hydration rim dating. It should also be noted that all the elements affecting the diffusion constants are not necessarily the same as those which can be used for identifying geologic sources.[3]

The absence of precisely formulated relationships between these variables and the diffusion phenomenon of obsidian indicates the importance of further work in the physical chemistry of obsidian hydration. Several large-scale obsidian dating projects are currently in progress, (including the one being reported on in this paper) and we may shortly possess substantial field data upon which to prepare a thorough evaluation of obsidian chronometry and conventional archaeological dating. At present, the only recurring complaint among archaeologists is the unexpected antiquity of some of their artifacts. For the most part, obsidian dates are falling within time ranges archaeologists can accept without reservation.

Until the diffusion coefficient is more clearly understood, we will not know how great an error is associated with our present efforts at chronometric dating. As mentioned earlier, a casual evaluation of recent dating projects gives the hint that only an error factor within acceptable limits is likely to be discovered. In saying this I am, of course, presuming that the archaeologist has in all cases made a maximum effort to control for temperature and composition within the sample for which he is constructing a hydration rate. All of the obsidian dating for my Valley of Mexico project has been based on the application of hydration rates that rest upon the assumption discussed earlier, that the diffusion of water into obsidian follows the diffusion law $M^2 = Kt$.

[3] Recent interest in identifying the geologic source of an archaeological artifact of obsidian has led to the analysis of obsidian composition by means of neutron activation analysis and by X-ray fluorescence. See for example, the two chapters in this volume by A. A. Gordus, J. B. Griffin, and G. A. Wright, and also F. H. Stross and associates. (Chapters 15 and 16).

It appears that there are at least two rates for the Valley of Mexico, one for gray obsidian and one for green obsidian. As early as 1961, Donovan Clark cited evidence from the Yayahuala Site, Hidalgo, Mexico that led him to suggest that gray and green obsidian might have different hydration rates (Reference 1). Now, on the basis of over 2000 dates from the Valley of Mexico, we can confidently assert that they do differ significantly in rate.

A hydration rate for gray obsidian was tentatively established for the Valley of Mexico by Friedman and Smith in 1959 (Reference 3). The rate, $4.5\mu^2/1000$ yr, rests upon the assumptions stated earlier and, at this writing, continues to be archaeologically supportable. The rate for green obsidian has just been established by the present author. The rate is $11.45\mu^2/1000$ yr, and was derived from the diffusion formula ($M^2 = Kt$) using a known point on the curve (2.27μ, 450 BP). The known point was established for the Chiconautla Site by associating a tight, high-frequency cluster of obsidian measurements (47) with the primary occupational component (Aztec) and coordinating the approximate terminal date of that component (ca A.D. 1518) with the lowest hydration rim measurement value of the cluster (2.34μ), less 0.07μ for measurement error (2.27μ) (see Table 19.1). Thus, from the diffusion formula, we have

$$k = \frac{(2.27)^2}{450} = \frac{5.153}{450}\mu^2/yr$$

$$k = \frac{5.153}{450}\cdot 1000 = 11.45\mu^2/1000 \text{ yr}$$

Subsequent evaluation of the resulting congruency between obsidian dates and conventional dating for green obsidian from as many as 20 sites within the Valley of Mexico provides empirical support for the reliability of the new rate.

Table 19.2 illustrates the extent of correspondence for five archaeological sites, in addition to the Chiconautla site. Chiconautla is an Aztec site, and if we use the new rate on the green obsidian recovered from the site we have 71 percent of the obsidian falling within that period. Teacalco is the type site for the final or "Teacalco" Phase of the Aztec period. According to Tom Charlton,[4] the site also exhibits marked concentrations of early Colonial pottery. High correspondence is indicated, therefore, when we note that the combined Aztec and Colonial percentages constitute 78 percent of the dated green obsidian. Maquixco is an extensively excavated site known to have been occupied over a long period of time beginning in the late Formative and extending into the Aztec period. The Classic and the Aztec periods, however, stand out as being the principal occupational compo-

[4] Personal communication, 1968.

Table 19.1

Hydration Measurements of Green Obsidian Artifacts From the Chiconautla Site (G. C. Vaillant Excavation)* †

1.65μ	2.50
1.68	2.51
1.69	2.51
	2.51
2.00	2.51
2.06	2.51
2.07	2.51
2.07	
2.09	2.82
2.09	2.83
2.11	2.83
2.12	2.83
	2.83
If 2.34μ less 0.07μ = A.D. 1518	2.84
2.34	2.84
2.34	2.85
2.34	2.85
2.35	2.86
2.35	2.86
2.35	2.86
2.36	2.86
2.37	2.86
2.37	2.87
2.38	2.87
2.38	2.88
2.38	Then 2.89μ plus 0.07μ = A.D. 1202
2.42	by the formula $M^2 = Kt$
2.42	—
2.45	3.09
2.46	—
2.46	3.29
2.48	3.30
2.48	3.31
2.50	3.31
2.50	—
2.50	3.62
—	3.65
	—
	4.25

* The listing of measurements is interrupted at each point where two measurements are separated by 0.20μ or more.

† The Aztec period is believed to have begun about A.D. 1200 and to have terminated at the time of the Spanish Conquest, A.D. 1519.

Table 19.2

Percentage Distribution by Culture Period of Green Obsidian Hydration Dates for Selected Sites, Valley of Mexico*

Archaeological Sites	Archaic	Early Formative	Middle Formative	Late Formative	Classic	Early Post-classic	Aztec	Colonial	Number of Specimens†
Chiconautla	—	—	—	—	5%	7%	71%	16%	66
Teacalco	—	—	—	—	5%	16%	27%	51%	37
Maquixco	—	—	—	6%	30%	14%	32%	18%	195
Tenango	—	—	—	—	31%	20%	16%	29%	83
La Ventilla	—	—	—	10%	60%	26%	—	—	57
Venta de Carpio (green only)	—	—	—	13%	56%	22%	6%	—	46
Venta de Carpio (gray plus green)	5%	—	—	26%	45%	14%	5%	—	74

* All percentage values less than 5% are not shown.

† Number of specimens used is number of specimens dated less all gray specimens (with the exception of the final Venta de Carpio percentages) and less all green specimens that fall within exclusion intervals that separate the measurement boundaries of the culture periods used in the table.

nents of the site. The obsidian dates correspond very well with that characterization of the site, with 62 percent of the dated green obsidian falling within those two principal components. Tenango is a Classic period site, according to ceramic crossdating. The dating of green obsidian artifacts confirms the presence of a significant Classic occupation and, in addition, suggests the presence of important secondary occupations during the Postclassic. La Ventilla is also a Classic site, but in this case a full 60 percent of green obsidian artifacts date to the Classic period.

Venta de Carpio is believed to have had an important late Formative as well as Classic period occupation, on the basis of ceramic crossdating. By examining only the green obsidian dates, we fail to uncover a significant late Formative occupation, although we do observe a very large percentage of the specimens falling within the Classic period. This inability to detect a Formative component of any consequence is because of the fact that the Formative period is characterized by a heavy dependence upon gray obsidian. The Classic Period ushered in an era of progressively greater and greater popularity of green obsidian. We know this from studies of the numerous workshops and other high-density obsidian concentrations discovered within the City of Teotihuacan. An excellent discussion of this data and of this trend from gray to green obsidian can be found in a recent article by Michael Spence (Reference 10). Returning our attention to Venta de Carpio, if we add the obsidian dates of grey obsidian artifacts to those of green obsidian, and recalculate our percentages, we find that now 26 percent of the specimens fall within the late Formative period, and 45 percent fall within the Classic period.

The presence of a compositional variable for Valley of Mexico obsidian has been discovered and, we believe, controlled for by the calculation of two separate rates of hydration. No similar variable has been identified with respect to temperature. The Valley of Mexico appears to constitute a homogeneous climatic environment; permitting us to treat temperature as a constant for the total sample.

Identification of Colonial Artifact Sample

On the basis of the two hydration rates discussed earlier, it is possible to assign each artifact to its appropriate archaeological period. The dating of the periods is already well established in the literature (Reference 9). Table 19.3 gives the chronometric scale for Valley of Mexico hydration measurements in regard to the principal cultural periods of that culture area. A total of 2036 artifacts from 20 sites have been dated and analyzed as of this writing. Table 19.4 gives the distribution of dates by site for the Aztec and Colonial periods. One hundred and forty

artifacts were identified as belonging to the Colonial period (see Table 19.5), and these constitute our Colonial artifact sample. All subsequent discussions focus upon these artifacts and upon the contiguous Aztec period specimens. It will be noted that both the number of specimens dating to the Aztec and Colonial periods and the relative percentage of the total site sample they represent vary significantly among the 20 sites. This is believed to correlate with the nature of Aztec and Colonial utilization of the site locality, and to justify a certain range of behavioral interpretation. Column 2 of Table 19.6 reveals the primary occupational episodes of each site, based on ceramic typology and sherd densities. The greatest percentage of obsidian dates for each of the 20 sites falls within the primary occupational period (or periods) listed in Table 19.6 for each site.

It will be noted that there is a high correspondence between sites which have a ceramically defined Aztec occupation of considerable prominence and sites which have more than 9 percent of dated obsidian falling within the Aztec period. Nine of the 20 sites appear to have had significant Aztec occupation. Seven of these exhibit Aztec obsidian percentages in excess of 15 percent, and one (Chiconautla) almost 50 percent.

Our knowledge of Colonial ceramics is just developing, and very little solid information is yet available regarding the presence of Colonial ceramics at archaeological sites within the Valley of Mexico. We are therefore unable to inspect the extent of correspondence between Colonial obsidian artifact frequencies and Colonial sherd densities. However, by inference from the relationship shown between these two sets of data for the Aztec period, it appears reasonable to argue that Colonial artifact percentages which exceed 9 percent may very likely signify Colonial occupation. Percentages between 2 percent and 9 percent for either Aztec or Colonial samples seem to signify real traces of utilization, perhaps for some special activity and perhaps for only short, temporary durations which are of too low a magnitude to imply residential use.

It is important to point out that the sites represented by these artifact collections were selected for excavation on the basis of their primary occupational component, rather than for their potential contribution to the establishment of a general historical sequence for the area in which they are located. A period not represented in the Cuanalan site excavation, for example, may be heavily represented at a site locality only a few hundred meters away. This fact limits the range of behavioral interpretation permissible on such a sample. We will therefore concentrate our attention upon the functional and technological

Table 19.5
Colonial Period
Hydration Measure-
ments

Period	Subdivision	Date	Grey Obsidian ($4.5\mu^2/1000$ yr)	Green Obsidian ($11.45\mu^2/1000$ yr)
		A.D. 1821	0.88 micron	1.37 microns
	Late			
Colonial		A.D. 1669	1.08	1.77
	Early		1.23	1.92
		A.D. 1519	1.34	2.19
	Aztec		1.49	2.34
Post-classic		A.D. 1200	1.78	2.89
	Early		1.93	3.04
		A.D. 900	2.12	3.42
Classic			2.27	3.57
		A.D. 300	2.66	4.29
	Late		2.81	4.44
		600 B.C	3.32	5.35
	Middle		3.47	5.50
Formative		1500 B.C.	3.88	6.23
	Early		4.03	6.37
		2500 B.C.	4.41	7.08
			4.56	7.23
Archaic		7200 B.C.	6.35	10.17
			6.50	10.32
Paleo-indian				

* Chronometric scale for Valley of Mexico Cultural Periods is based on that of Sanders and Price (Reference 9). Period boundaries are identified by an 0.14μ exclusion interval to insure that assignment of artifacts involves no overlapping of periods as a result of measurement error (standard deviation $\pm0.07\mu$).

Archaeological Site	No. Artifacts Dated	No. Aztec	Percent	No. Colonial	Percent
1. Maquixco	397	83	20.9	37	9.32
2. Temesco	96	2	2.08	1	1.04
3. Cerro Portezuelo	43	6	13.95	1	2.32
4. Teacalco	65	10	15.38	19	29.23
5. Oxtotipa	119	35	29.41	23	19.33
6. Xometla	62	10	16.13	7	11.29
7. Cuanalan	131	5	3.81	3	2.29
8. Mixcuyo	76	4	5.26	3	3.95
9. Venta de Carpio	104	4	3.84	2	1.92
10. Galicia	37	0	0.0	0	0.0
11. Tenango	153	18	11.74	21	13.72
12. La Ventilla	100	3	3.0	1	1.0
13. El Arbolillo	105	0	0.0	2	1.9
14. Tecorral	43	2	4.65	2	4.65
15. Tlatilco	45	0	0.0	1	2.22
16. Pueblo Perdido	64	6	9.38	3	4.69
17. Tlatenco	64	12	18.75	2	3.13
18. Chiconautla	102	47	46.1	11	10.75
19. Zacatenco	111	2	1.8	0	0.0
20. Ticoman	119	2	1.68	1	0.84
Totals:	2036	251	12.32%	140	6.82%

Site	Laboratory Number	Hydration Measurement (microns)	Obsidian Color	Site	Laboratory Number	Hydration Measurement (microns)	Obsidian Color
1. Maquixco	3	1.64	green	4. Teacalco	230	1.67	green
	28	2.00	green		237	2.17	green
	29	1.98	green		238	1.76	green
	34	2.09	green		239	1.50	green
	37	2.07	green		243	1.88	green
	40	1.76	green		245	1.68	green
	58	2.02	green		246	1.70	green
	61	1.28	gray		247	1.86	green
	66	2.15	green		252	1.60	green
	67	1.91	green		255	1.65	green
	69	2.01	green		256	1.91	green
	74	2.12	green		259	1.78	green
	79	1.98	green		265	1.61	green
	98	1.71	green		266	1.76	green
	104	1.83	green		270	2.01	green
	113	1.97	green		280	1.86	green
	147	2.12	green		282	2.09	green
	149	1.60	green		284	1.96	green
	166	2.01	green		288	1.62	green
	174	1.68	green	5. Oxtotipac	290	1.30	gray
	178	2.01	green		292	1.21	gray
	179	2.04	green		294	1.30	gray
	183	1.98	green		299	1.33	gray
	185	2.15	green		311	1.61	green
	194	1.99	green		323	1.32	gray
	195	1.82	green		326	1.25	gray
	202	1.80	green		333	1.26	gray
	204	1.73	green		337	1.60	green
	207	2.01	green		338	1.39	green
	216	2.17	green		340	0.97	gray
	217	1.89	green		344	1.33	gray
	221	2.03	green		348	1.84	green
	222	1.99	green		351	0.97	gray
	224	1.88	green		362	1.18	gray
	226	2.05	green		368	1.67	green
	1020	1.24	gray		369	1.47	green
	1164	1.22	gray		370	1.00	gray
2. Temesco	666	1.18	gray		381	1.19	gray
3. Cerro Portezuelo	999	1.90	green		386	1.84	green
					392	1.30	gray
					394	0.89	gray
					400	1.05	gray
				6. Xometla	425	2.01	green
					430	1.20	gray
					436	1.34	gray
					437	1.24	gray
					453	1.16	gray
					463	1.59	green
					468	2.07	green
				7. Cuanalan	531	1.30	gray
					1912	2.04	green
					1949	2.07	green
				8. Mixcuyo	552	2.01	green
					575	0.95	gray
					580	1.88	green
				9. Venta de Carpio	712	2.02	green
					801	1.18	gray

Table 19.5
Colonial Period
Hydration Measure-
ments (Continued)

Site	Laboratory Number	Hydration Measurement (microns)	Obsidian Color
10. Galicia	—	—	—
11. Tenango	851	1.81	green
	856	1.54	green
	857	1.68	green
	860	2.05	green
	864	2.03	green
	866	2.03	green
	874	2.02	green
	887	2.14	green
	890	1.52	green
	892	1.09	gray
	907	2.14	green
	916	1.70	green
	921	1.97	green
	931	1.70	green
	937	1.69	green
	939	0.91	gray
	957	1.68	green
	958	2.08	green
	968	2.05	green
	972	1.69	green
	988	2.07	green
12. La Ventilla	1338	1.69	green
13. El Arbolillo	1422	1.22	gray
	1457	1.70	green
14. Tecorral	1524	0.93	gray
	1532	2.06	green
15. Tlatilco	1576	1.26	gray
16. Pueblo Perdido	1615	1.25	gray
	1633	2.10	green
	1646	1.87	green
17. Tlatenco	1693	2.19	green
	1703	2.07	green
18. Chiconautla	2025	2.11	green
	2029	2.00	green
	2030	1.68	green
	2035	1.65	green
	2042	2.07	green
	2049	1.69	green
	2052	2.09	green
	2077	2.06	green
	2084	2.12	green
	2102	2.07	green
	2103	2.09	green
19. Zacatenco	—	—	—
20. Ticoman	2512	1.17	gray

Table 19.6
Definition of Primary Occupational Episodes Based on Ceramic Typology

Archaeological Site	Primary Occupational Period(s)	Aztec Obsidian Above 9%	Aztec Obsidian 2% to 9%	Colonial Obsidian Above 9%	Colonial Obsidian 2% to 9%
1. Maquixco	Classic / Aztec	X		X	
2. Temesco	Formative		X		
3. Cerro Portezuelo	Late Classic / Early Postclassic	X			X
4. Teacalco	Aztec	X		X	
5. Oxtotipac	Early Postclassic	X		X	
6. Xometla	Late Classic / Early Postclassic	X		X	
7. Cuanalan	Formative		X		X
8. Mixcuyo	Classic		X		X
9. Venta de Carpio	Formative / Classic		X		
10. Galicia	Classic				
11. Tenango	Classic	X		X	
12. La Ventilla	Classic		X		
13. El Arbolillo	Formative				
14. Tecorral	Classic		X		X
15. Tlatilco	Formative				X
16. Pueblo Perdido	Early Postclassic / Aztec	X			X
17. Tlatenco	Classic-Aztec	X			X
18. Chiconautla	Aztec	X		X	
19. Zacatenco	Formative				
20. Ticoman	Formative				
Totals:		9 Aztec Site	6 Aztec Use	6 Colonial Site	7 Colonial Use

Table 19.7
Colonial Artifact Types

Type of Blank Used in Manufacturing of Tool	Numerical Designation of Type	Artifact Type Name
Prismatic Blade	1	Knife
	2	Scraper
	3	Serrated knife
	4	Knife / scraper
	5	End scraper
Flake	6	Knife
	7	Scraper
	8	Pointed knife
	9	Graver
	10	Rasp
Biface	11	Arrow point
	12	Dart point
	13	Perforator
Unmodified	14	Core residue
	15	Flake detritus

Summary Artifact Categories		Artifact Types Included
A.	Rasp	10
B.	Knife	1, 3, 6, 8
B./C.	Knife / scraper	4
C.	Scraper	2, 5, 7
D.	Graver	9
E.	Perforator	13
F.	Projectile point	11, 12
G.	Manufacturing debris	14, 15

259

attributes of the artifacts themselves, and on inferences that can be drawn from the total valley-wide Colonial artifact sample. We are proceeding on the assumption that the obsidian industry of the Colonial period, and the manner in which it articulates with the various cultural subsystems of that period, are intelligible in terms of this limited but valley-wide sample.

Colonial Artifact Types

Introduction

The manufacture of useful implements of obsidian involves a preliminary step that transforms the quarried nodule or river-worn cobble into units that can be conveniently modified for use in a specific task. This preliminary step is the production of artifact "blanks" or "preforms." There are three general preform classes represented in our Colonial artifact sample: (1) prismatic blades, (2) flakes, (3) bifaces. Table 19.7 lists the artifacts produced from each preform class.

Prismatic blades are long, delicately thin slivers of obsidian that have been removed by an arduous pressure-flaking technique from the body of a specially prepared polyhedral core (Reference 2). They have razor-sharp edges which are very fragile. Without any modification, they can be employed in cutting and scraping tasks of great variety.

Flakes vary considerably in form and size and serve as blanks for a wide range of implements, both heavy and light duty. They are irregularly shaped units that are removed from a core of obsidian by percussion flaking. Usually, the edges of a flake are naturally sharp, and the blank can be applied as a knife or scraper without prior modification. A large number of artifact types, however, do require some modification of the shape of the flake, or of the characteristics of the edge. Such modification is referred to as "retouch" and occurs much more often on flake preforms than on prismatic blade preforms. The most prevalent obsidian tool within our sample dating to the Colonial period is the rasp end scraper produced by retouch of large thick flakes.

Implements that are manufactured out of obsidian with an eye to aesthetic considerations as well as those of function are often produced on a biface preform. A biface preform is a flake that has undergone extensive retouch of all surfaces usually in order to render it symmetrical in all dimensions. Biface blanks are usually lenticular in cross-section and are often lanceolate or leaf-shaped in outline. Convenient modification of the size, form, and edge characteristics by means of retouch will transform a biface blank into any number of artifacts, including knife blades, spear and dart tips, arrowheads, perforators, and figurines. The ceremonially important sacrificial knives of the Aztecs were often made from obsidian biface blanks. Throughout the entire prehistory of

central Mexico, projectile points were commonly made from biface preforms.

There are no utilitarian implements made from stone that require biface preforms for functional reasons; flake or prismatic blade preforms will always suffice. This is evidenced by the fact that the archaeological record reveals flake and blade analogs for all bifacial implements. Hence, implements that are manufactured with biface preforms are very likely employed in prestige-connected tasks where embellishment of equipment can be expected. Another important factor in selecting an implement preform is whether or not the implement will be disposed of after completion of the task. The extra labor involved in producing biface blanks would tend to limit their use to the production of implements which have a high probability of being reusable or, in the case of projectiles, recoverable. The Colonial era appears to have lacked prestige occupations that required obsidian implements, for our artifact sample reveals few biface preforms, and these are very rudimentary.

The following paragraphs describe the individual artifact types represented in the Colonial artifact sample. Their functional and technological attributes are discussed in some detail, since these descriptions do constitute an important part of our functional analysis of the obsidian industry for this period. Refer to Table 19.8 for location of types by site. Figure 19.3 illustrates the way in which wear marks and surface examination can be used to identify the uses to which the tools were put.

Prismatic blade knives require no retouch of the preform or blank (Figure 19.4). The entire original length of the blade is often exploited, and when blades snap into smaller sections they continue to be used. Our Colonial sample includes five specimens that range in length from 54 to 70 mm. They were struck from both gray and green polyhedral cores. Both edges of each blade exhibit tiny, irregular bifacial spalls that we have experimentally established as signifying use on woody plant material, bone, or some other equally resistant material, in a sawing or shaving motion. These implements appear not to have been hafted to handles but simply held by the fingers in a precision grip (use of thumb, index, and middle fingers). Prismatic blade knives that have been used on nonwoody plant material or flesh do not exhibit any noticeable wear or spalling. The fact that our sample does not include any specimens lacking evidence of wear does not mean that none were used on such soft materials but only that the negative evidence for such use is concealed by the wear pattern described earlier.

Prismatic blade scrapers are hand-held (precision grip) side scrapers that were put

Prismatic Blade Knives

Prismatic Blade Scrapers

Table 19.8
Frequency Distribution of Colonial Artifacts

Archaeological Sites*	Artifact Types*															Totals
	1	2	3	4	5	6	7	8	9	10	11	12	13	14	15	
1						1	2			28		2		3	1	37
2	1															1
3						1										1
4		6	1	2	4		2			4						19
5						3	1	3		15		1				23
6										4	1		1	1		7
7						1	1				1					3
8	1									2						3
9		1										1				2
10																0
11	1	5		8			4		1			2				21
12						1										1
13							1		1							2
14									1						1	2
15	1															1
16			1							2						3
17	1						1									2
18		2		2	1					2	1	3				11
19																0
20											1					1
Totals	5	12	4	10	6	8	12	3	3	57	4	9	1	4	2	140

* Refer to other tables for archaeological site names and artifact type names.

19.3
Wear marks and surface examination are identifications for the original use of tools.

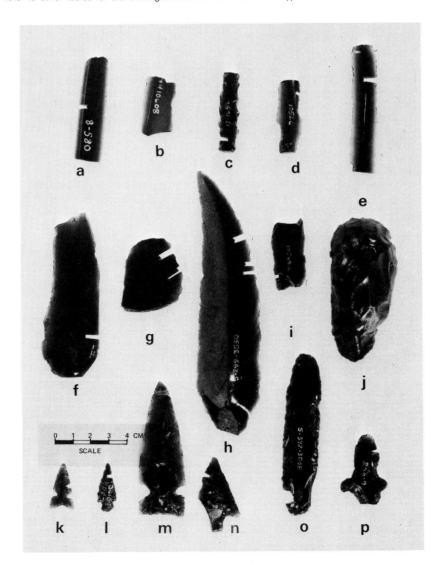

to use directly, without prior retouch. (See Figure 19.5.) A unidirectional scraping motion is signified by the production of tiny regular spalls along one face of the used edge. The edge is gradually eroded away by this unifacial spalling, and the general size and form of the material being scraped is often revealed as a result. Extensive scraping of cylindrical shafts will produce a concavity in the edge of the blade scraper. Similarly, extensive scraping of a straight surface will erode a portion of the edge proportional to the width of the object being scraped. In the case of objects of greater width than the length of the blade, the entire edge of the scraper will undergo erosion. A number of these scrapers exhibit alternating wear faces as a result of the artisan's habit of rotating the blade in his hand while continuing to scrape in the same direction. Such wear patterns demonstrate the absence of hafting. Most such scrapers exhibit two or three loci of use, each ranging between 10 and 20 mm in length. The blades themselves range in length between 25 and 58 mm. The length of the scraping bits suggest use on relatively narrow objects such as cylindrical shafts, tool handles, tree branches, or bone.

The characteristic wear pattern of these implements can best be reproduced experimentally by scraping fresh bone or woody plant materials. It is for such materials that the tool is most efficient. The resistance of the surface of the object produces unifacial spalling as the scraping blade is drawn across it. This spalling automatically resharpens the scraping edge, permitting the artisan to work without interruption and without having to change blades. A generous section of a two-by-four pine plank can be planed down a half inch or more in a matter of minutes using one of these delicate prismatic blade scrapers. Our Colonial sample includes twelve specimens, all but two of which were produced from green polyhedral cores.

Prismatic Blade Serrated Knives

Prismatic blade serrated knives are relatively thick (4 mm) prismatic blade blanks which were notched repeatedly along both edges, producing a double-edged serrated cutting tool. (See Figure 19.6.) The edges, however, exhibit little or no erosion caused by cutting or scraping. Such a lack of conspicuous wear on edges made so vulnerable through multiple notching suggests that these tools were used on nonwoody plant materials or flesh. Although the entire lengths of the two edges have been modified, there is a good possibility that these implements were hafted to some kind of handle. Hand-held in a precision grip, the sharp teeth of the edge would tend to bruise or cut the artisan's hand. The fact that both edges were prepared also suggests that the artisan may have wanted to exploit both edges simultaneously, in a manner similar

to our own fruit coring tool. In the literature, these implements are sometimes referred to as Chiconautla blades since they are found in considerable quantity at that site. During the Aztec period Chiconautla, located near Lake Texcoco, is reported to have been the residence of a large number of professional fisherman (Reference 5, page 340). It is possible that this tool is some sort of fish gutting implement used by these specialists. Our Colonial sample includes four of these artifacts, two of which come from the Chiconautla site. All are made of green obsidian.

Often a prismatic blade preform will exhibit both scraping and cutting wear at various loci around the edges. Such tools are referred to as composite tools in archaeological literature and testify to the necessity of both operations in the execution of many tasks. Ten of these specimens are included in the Colonial sample, and all but one are of green obsidian. These specimens range in length from 22 to 59 mm. The original length of the blades was in the 40 to 60 mm range; smaller ones appear to be a result of the blade snapping during use. The cutting bits and the scraping bits reveal patterns of wear that signify use on wood or bone or some equally resistant material. All ten specimens in the Colonial sample come from only two sites, both of which are located on the Cerro Gordo north slope at the northern end of the Teotihuacan Valley, close to mountain slopes that provided a plentiful wood supply. The fact that so many of this type of specimen are broken, that they show evidence of use on hard surfaces, and that they come from selected sites near timberland, suggest that they may belong to a special woodworking tool kit.

Prismatic Blade Knife/Scraper

The natural curvature of long prismatic blades struck from relatively fresh polyhedral cores was exploited in the production of this remarkably efficient tool (Figure 19.7). The blade tip opposite the end that formed part of the striking platform is used as a very sharp rasp without any prior retouch. Unidirectional scraping motion automatically resharpens the edge by producing tiny pressure spalls on one face of the edge. The long, slender blade body can be comfortably held in the hand in a firm precision grip, while the rasp bit engages the surface of the object to be worked at an efficient cutting angle. The use of hafted handles is not unknown for this tool type. Two of the Colonial specimens exhibit side edge blunting through retouch that usually signifies preparation for hafting to a handle. Experiments attempting to reproduce the wear pattern of this artifact type point unambiguously to use on wood or bone. These end scrapers turned out to be the most efficient woodworking tools of all tested. The angle of cutting is easier to control than is the case for most scrapers, and it cuts

Prismatic Blade End Scraper

19.4
Close-up of prismatic blade knife-edge. Note extensive edge-on erosion and blunting. Length of segment shown, 29mm.

19.5
Close-up of prismatic blade scraper-edge. Note presence of spalling is restricted to one face of the edge. Length of segment shown, 20mm.

19.6
Close-up of multiple notching on prismatic blade. Length, 44mm.

19.7
Close-up of prismatic blade end scraper-bit. Note that spalling is restricted to upper face of scraping edge. Width of end scraper-bit, 9mm.

19.8
Close-up of flake knife-edge. Note extensive edge-on erosion and blunting. Length of segment shown, 29mm.

19.9
Close-up of flake scraper edge. Note presence of spalling is restricted to one face of the edge.

19.10
Close-up of graver teat. Length, 41mm.

19.11
Close-up of flake end scraper rasp, depicting prepared scraping bit. Note the presence of retouch on upper face. Width of flake end scraper, 45mm.

19.12
Close-up of edge of biface perforator. Note absence of wear on edge (in focus, foreground). Length, of segment shown, 23mm.

deeper. Six prismatic blade end scrapers are included in our Colonial sample, and they are all made of green obsidian.

Flake Knife

Flake blanks employed as cutting implements vary considerably in size and shape (Figure 19.8). In our sample, they range in length from 40 to 110 mm and exhibit great variability in the size and shape of the cutting edges. All specimens in the Colonial sample, however, do possess a similar wear pattern which has been shown experimentally to signify use on wood, bone, or other similarly resistant surfaces. Very large flake knives can be held in the hand in a pressure grip (as you would hold a hunting knife) and can be used efficiently on large objects. With thicker blanks, flake knives may require edge retouch for sharpening purposes. Their ruggedness, as compared to the delicate character of prismatic blade knives, would suggest that they can be applied to heavier duty tasks. The Colonial sample includes eight specimens of this type, three of which also exhibit minor episodes of scraping activity at selected loci along the edge.

The flake knives in our Colonial sample all exhibit edge erosion resulting from use on hard materials. This does not mean that these knives were not used to cut soft materials (flesh, hides, nonwoody plant objects), for any such use would be concealed by the wear pattern of the harder materials. The ability of the knife edge to cut soft materials is not impaired by the kind of edge erosion that cutting harder surfaces produces. In fact, the bifacial spalling characteristic of knife edges after use on hard objects contributes a mild but noticeable serration to the edge that is very efficient in cutting such objects as uncooked flesh, hide, and fibrous plant material.

Flake Scraper

Flake blanks employed in scraping activities also vary considerably in size and shape (Figure 19.9). One of the more ubiquitous tools in our Colonial sample, and in archaeological assemblages generally, flake scrapers exhibit light to heavy scraping wear on one or more segments of their edges. Wear is conspicuous, taking the form of unifacial spalling at the cutting edge, and can be reproduced experimentally by scraping wood, bone, or other equally resistant surfaces. As in the case of prismatic blade scrapers, the flake scraper automatically resharpens itself during use. Examination of the scraping segments on flake blanks suggests that they are functionally equivalent to prismatic blade scrapers, for the length of the bit and the nature of the wear are identical. Like all of the artifact types discussed so far, flake scrapers can be classified as disposable tools. That is, since there has been no expenditure of effort in converting the blank to a tool, and since the production of the blank is itself a rapid, if arduous task, the artisan can afford to discard it upon completion of the job for which it was made. Our sample contains 12 specimens of this type, and all are of green obsidian.

Flake Pointed Knives

Flake pointed knives are the closest thing to our hunting knife or kitchen knife in the archeological record of the Colonial period. Large flakes with one end assymetrically tapering to a point were apparently hafted to handles (two of the three specimens show evidence of rubbing wear on the medial ridge of the outer face at the bulbar end). Their exposed blades range between 50 and 70 mm in length. A handle would be a positive aid if the pointed end of the knife was actually employed in a stabbing motion. The edges of this type of knife are not as sharp as edges on smaller flake or prismatic blade knives, but the additional pressure that can be applied with the superior grip of a hafted handle appears to have been satisfactory compensation. Edge wear on the Colonial specimens suggests application to variable materials—both soft and hard—and seems to suggest an all-purpose knife. Two of the three Colonial specimens are of gray obsidian, and one is of green obsidian.

Flake Gravers

Flake gravers are probably one of the most disposable and least detectable implement types within any archaeological assemblage (Figure 19.10). The artisan generally selected a discarded flake on which he would produce a graver teat by notching or with a burin blow. This teat would be used for incising or grooving of resistant surfaces. Since considerable downward pressure was employed in this process, the graver teat was usually stubby in form to avoid fracture, and hence quickly dulled. In some instances, a flake blank would undergo retouch that produced several separate graver teats. Three gravers are included in the Colonial sample. They all vary considerably in the form of the flake blank upon which they were fashioned. Although gravers can be used to work a large number of materials (stone, wood, bone, bottle gourd) for both ornamental and utilitarian purposes, they occur in low frequency during the Colonial period.

The Flake End Scraper Rasp

The flake end scraper rasp is one of the most ubiquitous tools in our Colonial sample (Figure 19.11). This implement is produced from flake blanks that are unusually thick (over 15 mm at some point and never under 10 mm in average thickness) and which exhibit the appropriate shape before retouch. The shape sought by the artisan is that of a tear drop with the maximum thickness located at the wide end and tapering gradually down to a narrow tail. The head, or working bit, of the rasp is blunt, somewhat convex, and has a cutting edge that is oriented 90 degrees from the axis of the scraper body. The width of the head varies between 20 and

50 mm. The implement appears to be designed to effect a very shallow cut during the scraping stroke and to pull at the surface of the object rather than to cut into it. The tail end of the flake functions as a hafting tang for deep insertion into a handle; leaving only 20 or 30 mm of head protruding. Evidence of hafting is in the form of rubbing abrasion marks that occur on the medial ridge of the upper face of many of the specimens. Such marks appear to be produced by contact between the stone and the wooden handle under the stresses of use. In addition, the tapering ends all show side edge blunting by percussion retouch which, as we mentioned earlier, is often a preparation for hafting. Retouch is also extended to the working head, where it is employed in achieving the proper cutting angle and the proper head curvature. There is thus an investment of labor in the production of this implement, and it cannot be regarded as a disposable tool. Its seemingly very specialized design, its evident reusability, and its ubiquity would strongly suggest a function of some economic importance for communities widely distributed throughout the Valley of Mexico.

Our experiments with this implement type have shown it to be admirably designed to effect the separation of pulp from the fiber of maguey cactus leaves. Maguey fibers were used extensively during the sixteenth century for the production of cloth used for dress by the Indians (Reference 5, p. 318). Such fibers were also employed in the production of cordage, netting, and other textiles. Maguey cactus also contributed to the Indian economy in a variety of other ways: the maguey leaves, when dry, were used as roofing material and as fuel; and the juices of the maguey plant were used to manufacture a highly nourishing as well as intoxicating drink called pulque (Reference 5, p. 318). The maguey plant thrives in all soils found within the Valley of Mexico and became the second most important cultivated plant (after maize) in this area. Although grown principally in the northern communities of the Valley of Mexico, the area devoted to maguey cultivation underwent considerable expansion during the Colonial period (Reference 5, p. 318). Fifty-seven specimens of this artifact type are included in the Colonial sample, and there are twice as many of green obsidian as of gray obsidian. The ratio only reflects the greater popularity of

green over gray obsidian during the Colonial period. At the Oxtotipac site, located very close to extensive deposits of gray obsidian in the Otumba region, the ratio is just the reverse.

Weight is the criterion used in this study to distinguish between points hafted to arrow shafts and points hafted to short spears (darts) propelled with the aid of atlatls. All points weighing two grams or less are classified as arrow points and all points weighing more than two grams are classified as dart points. Evidence supporting the validity of this criterion, or any other criteria for that matter, is difficult to collect. My choice of weight as the criterion is based on a study of projectile points of the western periphery of the United States great basin. The study, which uses obsidian-dated artifacts, demonstrated a gradual reduction in the weight of projectile point types from four grams to less than one gram during the late prehistoric period (Reference 7). It was during this period that the bow and arrow began to compete with the dart and atlatl as a hunting weapon. Prior to this time all point types consisted of specimens weighing more than two grams. I have therefore fixed the boundary between the two artifact categories at two grams for the purposes of the present study.

Five basic projectile point types are represented in the Colonial sample, and all but one have exhibited both arrow and dart variants during the Aztec-Colonial era (see Table 19.9). Projectile point types are distinguished on the basis of form, especially the form of that portion of the artifact that is secured to the projectile shaft by means of hafting, i.e., the "base." The first type is identified by its concave basal edge and by the side notching of an otherwise lanceolate or triangular bifacial blank. Type 2 has a symmetrically shouldered basal stem. The shoulder is either straight or sloping. Type 3 specimens are also side notched, and possess straight or convex basal edge form. Type 4 points are corner-notched, with well-defined barbs and stems. Type 5 consists of simple leaf-shaped points of variable size.

Thirteen points from the total dated sample have been assigned to the Colonial period. Six are of gray obsidian, and seven are of green obsidian. Workmanship on the Colonial specimens of what is often a

Biface Arrow and Dart Points

Table 19.9
Projectile Points: Type and Period Distribution

	Aztec Period		Colonial Period	
	Arrow Point	Dart Point	Arrow Point	Dart Point
Type 1	2	1	2	2
Type 2	0	2	1	0
Type 3	0	3	0	1
Type 4	1	6	0	5
Type 5	0	2	1	1

highly crafted artifact type is generally poor. One-half the time, very little facial retouch is in evidence, and the blanks often still retain their original warping or assymmetry. Little of the traditional aesthetic treatment seems, on the basis of our small sample, to have been applied to this class of artifacts during the Colonial period.

There are specific references in the historical record of the Colonial period to the use of the bow and arrow in hunting deer, and of the use of the dart and atlatl in hunting water fowl and fish (Reference 5, pp. 340–343). Wild game contributed to the diet of the Indian population, and in the markets of the Colonial period flesh of deer, rabbit, hare, gopher, and weasel could be obtained. Large flocks of ducks and geese wintered on the lakes of the Valley of Mexico; during the period extending from October to March, the shooting and snaring of these animals was an important economic occupation. Fish were also an important marketable commodity. It has been estimated that over one million fish were taken annually from the Valley lakes during the early Colonial period (Reference 5, p. 340). Fishermen in boats employed line rods, hand nets, and atlatl darts in their recovery. Hunting appears, therefore, to have been a diverse, widespread activity involving several recovery techniques, including the use of stone-tipped projectiles, that contributed significantly to the subsistence base of the Indian population.

Biface Perforator

Only one specimen of this type is included in the Colonial sample (Figure 19.12). It was produced on a green biface blank. The blank was extensively retouched in shaping, and the resulting form is similar to a Christian cross. The artisan would employ the tool by gripping the upper three extensions in a precision grip and force the penetration of the long pointed bit into the item being worked with downward pressure and a twisting motion. The present dimensions of the artifact are 10-mm thick, 27-mm wide (at horizontal grip extensions), and 38-mm long (incomplete because of fracture). This specimen shows no evidence of wear on the remaining segment of the bit, which suggests that it was used on materials with a low resistance to penetration.

Core Residue and Flake Detritus

The prismatic blade, flake, and biface preforms associated with the Colonial artifact types were derived from a variety of cores. Prismatic blades are struck from specially prepared polyhedral cores. Tabular cores contribute wide, parallel-sided flakes that are sometimes referred to as macroblades since they possess many of the functional characteristics of prismatic blades. Nodule cores, consisting of irregular polyhedral nuclei of variable size, produce our widest range of flake preform shapes. Very few cores were selected for dating during the early part of the research project, and therefore few appear in the Colonial sample. Of these, three specimens are nuclei of quarried green obsidian nodules, and one is a fractured segment of a river-worn cobble of gray obsidian.

In the preparation of a core, or in the preliminary fashioning of a flake preform, thick, irregularly-shaped flakes of varying size are produced, often in great quantities. If these are not subsequently utilized, they are classified as detritus and signify to the archaeologist a stone tool fabrication activity. Two detritus flakes, one gray and one green, have been dated to the Colonial period.

Economic Analysis

Raw Material

Obsidian outcroppings are concentrated in the northern perimeter of the Valley of Mexico. Natural veins and riverworn cobbles of gray obsidian are extensively distributed around the vicinity of Otumba, while extensive veins of green obsidian are to be found in the Pachuca range and on Cerro de las Navajas. Aboriginal mining and quarrying operations are documented for the veins of green obsidian,[5] suggesting that extraction of the raw material may have involved occupational specialists. Substantial quantities of the gray obsidian, however, were obtainable by means of mining and surface collection in areas far more accessible to the population centers of the Valley.

Processing and Distribution

Inspection of the Colonial artifact sample for each of the sites in our study suggests that communities outside of the Teotihuacan Valley were within a distribution network that encompassed both varieties of obsidian. Within the Teotihuacan Valley, sites located in the vicinity of Otumba show noticeably greater use of gray obsidian, while sites located on or near the piedmont of the Pachuca range show similarly disproportionate use of green obsidian.

Indian markets must have played an important role in the distribution of green obsidian, since the source was not conveniently accessible and the extraction techniques favor occupation specialization. Green obsidian was the primary material out of which cylinder cores were fashioned. From a single such core, hundreds of prismatic blades could be produced, each constituting a highly versatile blank or preform for the production of cutting and scraping implements. It seems reasonable to suppose that quarried nodules of green obsidian were brought to market and sold by the miners themselves. Other craftsman, skilled in the preparation of cylinder cores and in the pressure-flaking technique of blade production, would very

[5] For discussion of obsidian mines see Holmes, W. H., *Amer. Anthro.*, n.s., **2**, 1900, p. 405 and Spence, M. W., and Parsons, J., *Amer. Antiquity*, **32**, 1967, p. 542.

likely purchase a portion of these for further processing and resale. The balance of the nodules would then be sold to individual users who would fashion a limited variety of implements (e.g., maguey rasps) and retain the flake detritus as preform material for subsequent modification into selected flake tools. Gray obsidian, being more accessible and not necessarily requiring arduous extraction, may have achieved valley-wide distribution through the separate collecting efforts of many individuals aimed at satisfying their own needs. Distribution via the Indian market, however, cannot be ruled out.

Range of Products

The range of products for the Colonial period is given in Table 19.7. Basically, they consist of various types of cutting and scraping tools that can be used on a variety of hard and soft materials. Many of them functioned as manufacturing implements in various tool-producing industries. In carpentry, for example, they were used to fashion a wide variety of wooden implements: the digging stick, the bow and arrow, the atlatl and dart, stone tool handles, wooden parts for animal and fish traps, fishing rods, poles for house construction, net supports, boat paddles, and wooden components of the weaving loom. The remaining obsidian artifacts were most likely employed directly in various domestic activities unrelated to manufacture. Virtually no evidence has been found of obsidian products that functioned ornamentally, ceremonially, as money, or which are associated with prestige-connected occupations.

Product Manufacture and Distribution

It appears that, with the exception of the manufacture of certain types of preforms, all artifacts fashioned from obsidian were the work of individual users. As such, no distribution of finished artifacts can be said to have occurred during the Colonial period. The manufacturing process was at most perfunctory, requiring little more than lateral retouch at the locus of the bit or hafting tang. Often, preforms were applied to tasks without preliminary retouch.

Social and Economic Impact of Industry

During the Colonial period, the roles played by obsidian artifacts were not as varied as in previous periods. In Pre-Hispanic Mexico, obsidian was used ornamentally (lip and nose plugs, stylization of functional artifacts), ceremonially (figurines, eccentrics, mirrors, sacrificial knives), as a status symbol in high prestige occupations (hunting and warfare), and as a commodity in interregional barter transactions (Valley of Mexico green obsidian is found widely traded throughout southern Mexico). The social and economic impact of the obsidian industry during the Colonial period was confined to such industries as food production, food collection, housing, clothing, and household maintenance. None of the activities utilizing obsidian artifacts (hunting, maguey fiber extraction, woodworking, bone and gourd working,

fishing, food preparation) appear to have been notably prestigious during this period.

In summary, then, obsidian cannot be associated with prestige occupations, is marketable only as raw or preliminarily processed material, is processed by craft specialists only with regard to its recovery as a raw material, and articulates with most other industries only indirectly through the manufacture of industry-specific tools. As such, obsidian cannot be said to have had much of a social impact on Colonial Indian society.

Economically, however, obsidian appears to have made a very significant impact. A wide range of industries made use of stone and wooden implements. The efficiency of obsidian tools, their cheapness and their abundance, made them a vital asset to the manufacturing sector of the Indian economy which relied so heavily on wood as a raw material. However, since the products manufactured with obsidian tools were intended, in most cases, for personal use and only secondarily for sale in the Indian market, little commercial (i.e., market) value can be assigned to them. In consequence, the obsidian artifacts used in their manufacture also had little commercial value since they failed to play a significant role, either directly or indirectly, in market transactions.

Level of Product Consumption

The all-pervasive role of stone and wooden implements in Indian life, the exhaustibility and breakability of obsidian artifacts, the short distances between user and source of supply, and finally the cheapness of the implements, all conspired to make the level of obsidian artifact consumption very high. Obsidian artifacts are second only to pottery sherds in their abundance at archaeological sites in the Valley of Mexico.

Long-Term Trends

Table 19.10 gives the artifact frequency distribution for the Early and Late Colonial Periods. The sample is too small, however, to permit us to detect significant differences in composition between the artifact assemblages of the Early Colonial and Late Colonial Periods. What is noticeable, however, is a progressive reduction in number of artifacts as we move from early to late Colonial times.

Colonial Period Site Analysis

Up until now, we have been discussing the Colonial period artifact sample as a whole in an attempt to identify the structural and functional nature of the obsidian industry for the Valley of Mexico during that period. We have been limited largely to a qualitative analysis since our sample is so small (140 specimens). It seems desirable, however, to make some provisional interpretations regarding the nature of each of the 20 sites in our sample during the Colonial period. Table 19.6 gives the primary occupation period or periods

Table 19.10
Early/Late Colonial
Artifact Frequency
Distribution

Site	Early Colonial (artifact categories)								Total	Total Excluded	Late Colonial (artifact categories)								Total
	A	B	B/C	C	D	E	F	G			A	B	B/C	C	D	E	F	G	
1	19			2			1	2	24	7	4	1					1		6
2									0	1									0
3									0	1									0
4			3	1					4	5	3	1	1	5					10
5	4	1	2				1		8	5	7	2	1						10
6	3				1				4	2							1		1
7		1		1			1		3	0									0
8	1								1	1	1								1
9				1					1	1									0
10									0	0									0
11			4	4			2		10	2		1	4	3	1				9
12									0	0	1								1
13									0	1				1					1
14				1					1	0								1	1
15		1							1	0									0
16	2								2	1									0
17		1		1					2	0									0
18	2	2		2			2		8	0	1						2		3
19									0	0									0
20									0	1									0
	31	6	9	12	1	1	7	2	69	28	15	7	6	9	1	0	3	2	43

Table 19.11
Interpretive Key to
Colonial Period Site
Analysis

Artifact Category	Activity	Nature of Site
A. Rasp	1. Fiber and pulp extraction from maguey leaves	Residence/ Agricultural field
B. Knife	2. Light manufacturing and/or	Residence/ Agricultural field/
B./C. Knife/scraper		Food gathering theatre
C. Scraper	3. Household maintenance	
D. Graver		
E. Perforator		
F. Projectile Point	4. Food gathering (hunting, fishing, fowling)	Residence/ Food gathering theatre
G. Manufacturing Debris	5. Stone artifact manufacturing	Residence/ Agricultural field/ Food gathering theatre

Table 19.12
Colonial Period Site
Analysis

Site No.	Artifact Code	Inferred Activities	No. of Artifacts	Nature of Site Utilization
1	ABCFG	12345	37	Residence
2	B	2	1	Unspecified nonresidence
3	B	2	1	Unspecified nonresidence
4	ABB/CC	123	19	Residence
5	ABB/CCF	1234	23	Residence
6	AEFG	1245	7	Residence
7	BCF	24	3	Food gathering theatre
8	AB	12	3	Agricultural field
9	CF	24	2	Food gathering theatre
10	—	—	—	Not utilized
11	BB/CCDF	234	21	Residence
12	B	2	1	Unspecified nonresidence
13	CD	2	2	Unspecified nonresidence
14	DG	25	2	Unspecified nonresidence
15	B	2	1	Unspecified nonresidence
16	AB	12	3	Agricultural field
17	BC	2	2	Unspecified nonresidence
18	ABCF	1234	11	Residence
19	—	—	—	Not utilized
20	F	4	1	Food gathering theatre

of each of the sites based on established ceramic chronology. In addition, Table 19.6 lists the sites that appear to have witnessed occupation during the Colonial period on the basis of the Colonial percentage of the dated sample of each site (above 9 percent). If, however, we draw upon our preceding analyses of artifacts and of the obsidian industry as a whole, it appears possible to push our interpretation of the sites a little further.

Table 19.11 gives a key to the interpretation of sites based on the artifacts collected from them (refer to Table 19.8 for information on the artifact assemblages for each site). It seems possible, on a very gross level, to discriminate between three types of sites—residential, agricultural field, food-gathering theatre—when diagnostic artifact combinations are present. Examination of Table 19.11 will reveal that the key elements in the artifact combinations are projectile points and rasp end scrapers. Manufacturing tools (knives, scrapers, gravers, perforators) are treated as a single element that can infer either light manufacturing or household maintenance, or both. Artifact combinations denote activity configurations for each site, and these in turn suggest the nature of site utilization.

In order to analyze the twenty sites in our sample, we can use the key together with the following assumptions: First, cutting and scraping tools denote only light manufacture if rasps and projectile points are both absent. Second, the same implements denote both light manufacture and household maintenance if rasps and projectile points are both present. Third, if at least three of the five cutting and scraping artifact categories are represented, then they denote both light manufacturing and household maintenance, even if only rasps or only projectile points are present. Finally, if less than three of the mentioned artifact categories are present, then they denote only light manufacturing, providing that they are associated with only rasps or only projectile points but not both. By manipulating the cutting and scraping instruments in this fashion, the artifact combinations yield plausible activity configurations that discriminate between possible forms of site use, albeit in a very gross and tentative fashion. Table 19.12 gives the results of the application of the interpretative key of Table 19.11 to the sites included within our sample.

It is interesting to note, first of all, that those sites which were declared residential in Table 19.6 on the basis of percentage of sample dating to the Colonial period are also classified as residential on the basis of their artifact combinations. Table 19.12 indicates that our sample of twenty sites consists of six residential sites, three food gathering theatres, two agricultural fields, seven localities that did not witness residential utilization but which were exploited for some other unspecifiable purpose, and two localities that do not appear to have been used at all during the period in question. It will be interesting to re-examine these interpretations after we have obtained more adequate control of Colonial Aztec pottery. Pottery sherd densities are often excellent indicators of the nature of site utilization, and we would expect that such information would serve as a means of testing the validity of these very tentative interpretations.

Conclusion

By enabling us to assemble a large collection of archaeologically contemporaneous specimens out of previously excavated sites, obsidian dating makes it possible for us to conduct explicitly problem-oriented research. The reader will note that lengthy chronological considerations are virtually absent in this study which involves an assumption of contemporaneity among the artifacts of twenty sites, excavated by almost as many different archaeologists. The reader will also note that little attention has been directed to matters of artifact style—a necessary topic when questions of contemporaneity through cross-dating are raised. Instead, we have been able to concentrate on the behavioral aspects of the data almost exclusively.

The principal limitation of the data used in this study is, of course, the small size of the Colonial artifact sample. This can be overcome to some extent by additional large-scale dating programs that focus on late Aztec sites, which our evidence suggests offer the best opportunity for discovering Colonial occupations. The smallness of the sample severely restricted the application of quantitative techniques in our study of the structure and function of the Colonial obsidian industry and in some instances limited us to highly tentative interpretations. Future work connected with the completion of this research on the Valley of Mexico will continue to focus upon the behavioral topics raised in this paper.

Acknowledgments

I wish to acknowledge with thanks all of those individuals who generously made their artifact collections available for this study: William T. Sanders, Gordon F. Ekholm (G. C. Vaillant's collections), Jose Luise Lorenzo, Evelyn Rattray, Juan Vidarte, Pina Chan, Keith Dixon, and Henry B. Nicholson.

This study was supported by NSF grant GS 1256 to J. W. Michels.

References

1.
Clark, D. L.

"The Application of the Obsidian Dating Method to the Archaeology of Central California." Thesis, Stanford University, 1961.

2.
Crabtree, D. E.

Amer. Antiquity, **33,** 446, 1968.

3.
Friedman, I., and Smith, R. L.

Amer. Antiquity, **25,** 476, 1960.

4.
(a) Friedman, I., Smith, R. L., Long, W. D.;
(b) Katsui, Y., and Kondo, Y.;
(c) Haller, W.

(a) *Bull. Geol. Soc. Amer.,* **77,** 323, 1966; (b) *Jap. J. Geol. Geography,* **36,** 45, 1965; (c) *Physics and Chem. of Glasses,* **1,** 46, 1960.

5.
Gibson, C.

The Aztecs Under Spanish Rule, Stanford University Press, Stanford, California, 1964.

6.
Haller, W.

Physics and Chem. of Glasses, **4,** 217, 1963.

7.
Michels, J. W.

"Lithic Serial Chronology Through Obsidian Hydration Dating," Thesis, Univ. of California, Los Angeles, 1965.

8.
Michels, J. W.

Science, **158,** 211, 1967.

9.
Sanders, W. T., and Price, B. J.

Mesoamerica, The Evolution of a Civilization, Random House Inc., New York, 1968, p. 15.

10.
Spence, M. W.

Amer. Antiquity, **32,** 507, 1967.

Chapter 20

Gas Chromatography Methods for Bone Fluorine and Nitrogen Composition

Donald W. Groff
Western Connecticut State College

Introduction

History has shown us that chemistry often progresses by the development of new techniques and tests of their applicability in specific areas. Indeed this is in evidence at present in modern archaeological chemistry where many advances are being made through the application of new analytical instruments and methods in the field of archaeology. This is a report of findings to date on just such an application, that is, the use of gas chromatography for the analysis of fluorine and nitrogen in bones.

A discovery report by James and Martin (Reference 22) and many subsequent papers have described the use of gas-liquid partition chromatography. With simple modifications one may quickly and conveniently analyze for ammonia (hence, nitrogen) and silicon-tetrafluoride (hence, fluorine) values in a large number of samples.

Review of Chemical Bone Dating

Previously some of these analyses have been done employing a volumetric fluoride technique by Willard and Winter (Reference 37), a technique reviewed in detail by McKenna (Reference 26).

Fluorine is separated from interfering substances by distillation of the sample with perchloric acid in the presence of a silicate. The fluorine then escapes as hydrofluosilicic acid. Armstrong (Reference 3) showed that the liberated fluorine ion would react with thorium nitrate in aqueous solution to form a thorium fluoride precipitate. Excesses of the remaining nitrate give a pink color with sodium alizarin sulfonate, the titration indicator. Armstrong (Reference 4) showed that virtually the same method is suitable as a microchemical technique with error not exceeding 0.2 percent using a 5 mg sample. Hoskins and Freyd (Reference 21) further refined the technique by introducing an internal blank. Heizer and Cook (Reference 19), Oakley and Hoskins (Reference 28) in a celebrated Piltdown test, and others have used this basic method effectively to learn the fluorine content of fossil bone.

The Kjeldahl nitrogen analysis method is well known in analytical chemistry. Contributors to chemical archaeology have used it to test for nitrogen in bone and teeth. It is considered to be a test for amino acid (protein) and is so employed in the foods processing and agricultural chemistry fields today. Strictly speaking, the method does not determine amino acid amounts but merely its nitrogen content. Investigation has shown that in spite of the complex amino acid composition, 16 percent of it is nitrogen. Chemists have adopted this figure to convert from percent nitrogen to percent amino acid by multiplying the former by 6.25 to determine the latter.

In the Kjeldahl determination, bone material is digested with H_2SO_4 in the presence of a catalyst and the nitrogen goes to NH_4HSO_4. The NaOH added to the resulting solution liberates ammonia gas which passes into an absorbing agent and is titrated. Hamilton and Simpson (Reference 16) reported this technique, adding that the liberated ammonia may be caught in a boric acid solution and titrated directly with standard acid without bringing the amount of boric acid into the calculations. The most common catalysts for this test are mercuric oxide, metallic mercury, and copper sulfate.

Investigators have recently sought the identity and quantity of certain amino acids from the total organic protein content in the hope that these may give a better measure of fossil bone antiquity. Abelson (References 1, 2), Ho (Reference 20), and Ezra and Cook (Reference 15) cite the presence and abundance of amino acids in fossil shell and bone as determined by using standard thin layer chromatographic methods after hydrolysis in HCl.

Total organic content may be learned by weight loss through ignition. Although this technique is a test for labile organics, it is not a test for nitrogen alone. The results are a gravimetric summation of all organic constituents. Ordinarily nitrogen content alone in fresh bone approximates 5 percent by weight (Reference 25). Total organics (carbon, nitrogen, and organically bonded water) approach 19 percent in fresh bone. The relationship between total organics and nitrogen is not consistent as shown by Cook and Heizer (Reference 10) and Cook (Reference 9). The latter is an excellent review of the chemical analysis of bone and the problems of chemical interference by phosphates and calcite inherent in fossil bone materials.

Optical, radiochemical, and X-ray methods have been used to learn the antiquity of bone materials. Baud (Reference 6) reviews these and the efforts of other contributors. The optical index of refraction and birefringence of bone changes with compositional changes from collophane to apatite as suggested by Rogers (Reference 31). Bone opacity to X-rays decreases with loss of collagen and the degree of loss may be measured by comparison with standards. Increases in bone fluorine increase its opacity and may similarly be used as an index of age. X-Ray diffraction may be used to learn the unit cell dimensions of the primary mineral, apatite. As hydroxyapatite changes with time to fluorapatite, its cell dimensions show a marked decrease in the length of its ''c'' axis. In situ conversion to fluorapatite is an important time process underlying relative age dating by fluorine analysis. Unfortunately, other solid-state diffusion processes may prompt similar unit cell changes. See Joffe and Sherwood (Reference 23) and Davidson and Atkin (Reference 14).

Relative and absolute bone dating methods and results have been reviewed in Oakley (Reference 27), Cook (Reference 8), Ho (Reference 20) and in several other important papers. No one element or method is a recognized panacea to chemical bone dating, but fluorine, uranium, and nitrogen are often named as the elements sought in relative and absolute bone dating.

Bone dating methods depend upon postburial accumulation of substances uncommon in living bone and/or depletion of substances native to it. Ion exchange between buried bone and its matrix (soil) occurs bringing about these gains or losses, but the nature and kinetics of such are unknown and vary from soil to soil. McConnell (Reference 25) and Ezra and Cook (Reference 15) show nitrogen-bearing amino acids in fresh bone approaching 5 percent (by weight) but fluorine only in trace amounts. Bones of great antiquity show fluorine occurring at 4 percent (by weight) with nitrogen absent or in traces.

The status of modern chemical bone dating is reviewed by Cook and Heizer (Reference 10), Race et al. (Reference 30), Tax et al. (Reference 34), Heizer (Reference 18), Verzar (Reference 35), Cook (Reference 8), and others. Each relate the loss of bone collagen and the accumulated fluorine with time, but fail to cite *rates* of loss or gain of these materials. Cook and Heizer (Reference 10) show that fossilization is a logarithmic function with time that cannot be quantitatively generalized. Furthermore, they show that attempts to cross-apply results of one region with those of another are foredoomed to failure. Rate of fossilization depends upon burial conditions.

Cornwall (Reference 12) and Robinson and Edgington (Reference 29) have found that those conditions most favorable for fossilization are rapid burial, deep overburden, low temperatures, and alkaline conditions. Factors favoring rapid decay are acid ground conditions, exposure to oxygen, and periodic waterlogging. Cook and Cohn (Reference 9) and Cook (Reference 8) discuss bone complexity, chemical alternation, and chemical limits imposed by the burial environment on fossilization. Geochemical controls in the same region which operate longer on older bone should have altered it more

profoundly than younger bone with which its association is being sought. On this premise chemical relative age dating is built.

The rate of alteration after burial is determined by the rate of fluoride penetration and protein leaching. Calcite deposition, however, may seal bone and protect its interior from further destruction. A calcite seal may forever give bone the chemical illusion of recency or youth, a gift not available to the animal which produced the bone.

Baud (Reference 6) reviews the mechanisms of bone fossilization. Rogers (Reference 31) and McConnell (References 24, 25) review the crystallography of the minerals present in fresh and fossil bone. Studies by Ezra and Cook (Reference 15), Armstrong (Reference 5), Rogers (Reference 32), and Race (Reference 30) show it to be a complex of collagen (90 to 96 percent), fats, tissue, and bone with water attached in various ways. Initial bone decay is found to be rapid, but glycine, aspertic acid, ananine, and glutamic acid (all nitrogen bearers) are long retention proteins reported by these investigators. These undoubtedly yield the nitrogen found in tests of the fossil bone.

Discovery

In order to evaluate the usefulness of gas chromatography for bone analysis, the author has used it in the analysis of several mastodon bones. These came from a mastodon bone cache uncovered in the basement diggings for the dwelling of Mr. John Lindy in ancient Monongahela River gravels near Redstone Schoolhouse by Pennsylvania Route 711 not far from Fayette City, Pennsylvania.

After the original discovery of ''peculiar fossil horse hoofs'' (teeth) by Mr. Lindy, more precise identification and excavation of the site was begun by Pittsburgh's Carnegie Museum staff in April 1961 under the direction of Mr. Allen D. McCready. His associate, Mr. John Guilday, identified the bones and teeth as from *Mastodonus americanus*. From the degree of ossification he estimated the bones to be Sangamon or Illinoian in age and from dentation wear, or lack of it, it was judged to be a teen-aged monster at death. See Figure 20.1 for a dorsal ''molar'' which shows no wear and which probably never extruded through its gum encasement. The museum soon abandoned the excavating, and the author and several of his students, in cooperation with the Lindys, continued this effort for several years until the productive horizon was depleted. Upon recovery the bones were identified and mapped according to their excavation position, elevation, and orientation (a study to be reported on later). The Carmichaels, as the gravel formation from which the bones were taken is called, has never been dated. Spores which would allow

273

20.1
Dorsal ''molar'' of *Mastodon americanus*. The lack of crown wear prompts the suspician that the owner had been young at death.

20.2
Teeth, bone, and tusk cache. The teeth show different degrees of abrasion.

20.3
Restored mandible with teeth in place. Two smaller mandibular tusks appear at left. A large maxillary tusk is shown in the center.

20.4
The meter stick separates rib bones (below) from vertebrae units (above). Leg bones appear at left and knee-cap, toe, and a leg bone are shown above.

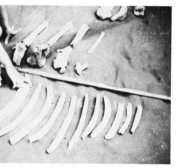

20.5
Carmichaels formation.

20.6
Chromatograph flow system.

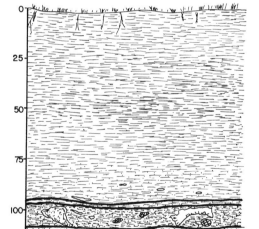

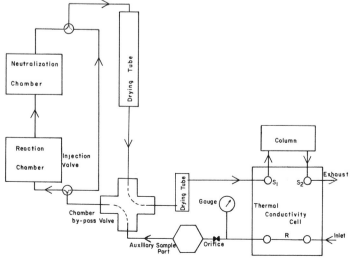

such dating were not found in these sediments.

Figure 20.2, taken shortly after recovery, shows bone, teeth, and tusk parts exactly as they were found. Figures 20.3 and 20.4 show bone, teeth, and tusk parts after restoration of many units which had been broken or badly abraded.

The Carmichaels formation has three general compositions in the bone-rich zone. All are silty or clayey. By examination and coring, the uppermost (Unit A) is found to be roughly 91 inches deep and is a fine-sandy clay. Unit B, immediately underlying Unit A, is a silt. Unit C, immediately beneath Unit B, is a silty clay. All three zones were found to contain mastodon bone materials. Units B and C produced the largest pieces. Unit B was measured and found to be from 0 to 3 inches thick and Unit C from 0 to 9 inches thick. A thick sand was found to underlie all of these units and a cobble layer occurs with Unit C and immediately above the sand (see Figure 20.5).

Gas Chromatographic Technique

To the organic chemist, the gas chromatograph has been a chemist's dream—a continuous magical tube into which a complex group of chemicals is placed and from which a completed analysis may emerge. The system used in this work is a Fisher gas partitioner (modified) with a stainless, teflonized pyrolizer (or reaction chamber) with neutralization chamber used in both the fluorine and nitrogen analyses. Columns were prepared to dry and separate the gases evolved in the analysis (see Figure 6).

The fluorine analysis is run isothermally at 80°C. A 20 foot by 0.25 inch column was prepared with 15 percent Kel-F, 40 oil over a T-6 (teflon) support of 80–100 mesh. Helium is used as the carrier gas. Silica sand is placed in the neutralizing chamber; 0.01 gram of crushed bone at 100 mesh size is placed in the reaction chamber and the chamber then closed. Approximately 2 cc of concentrated H_2SO_4 is syringed into the chamber. A sulfate salt is produced and HF released. The pyrolizer and its contents are purged with a helium stream moving at 25 ml/min, and HF is forced into the neutralizing chamber where SiF_4 is produced. At $T - 7.5$ minutes, the conductivity cell recognizes the SiF_4 and measures it.

Equilibrium favors a high SiF_4 solubility in water. In the reaction chamber (where HF is neutralized) the SiF_4 is purged from that solvent by the continuous flow of carrier gas at a great rate. Moisture from the system is removed in the drying tubes beyond this chamber, and the silicon tetrafluoride concentrated in the long column (Figure 20.6).

Hamlin (Reference 17) devised a gas-fluid chromatographic analytical method for inorganic fluorides and noted:

No material was found that was completely inert to all possible combinations of inorganic fluorides although nickel, Monel, . . . and teflon were reasonably resistant.

Not "all possible combinations" were sought in this gas chromatography application, and the author found no measurable HF loss nor fluoride contamination using teflon and a rapidly flowing carrier gas. Blanks were run to verify this. The HF transport occurred only into the next (neutralizing) chamber where relatively stable SiF_4 was generated eliminating the nuisance of HF handling beyond that point.

The inert helium carrier and the small sample tend to prevent formation of fluosulfonate. McKenna (Reference 26) recommends that a small amount of pure sulfur (mixed with the catalyst, a sulfate) may be prevented in the reaction:

$$2HSO_3F + S \longrightarrow 3SO_2 + 2HF$$

The nitrogen content is obtained by a modified Kjeldahl method for ammonia. A microsample (0.01 gm) of crushed bone of size -100 mesh is mixed with an approximately equal volume of $CuSO_4$ and placed into the reaction chamber. These are dissolved with strong H_2SO_4 producing NH_4HSO_4. The chamber is then closed and purged with the helium carrier gas. An excess of strong NaOH (at 70°C) is syringed into the chamber producing ammonia. The reaction and analysis are performed isothermally at 70°C with a helium feed at 20 ml/minute. A 9 foot by 0.25 inch separation column similar to that devised by Sze and others (Reference 33) was used with a 15 percent (by weight) THEED (tetrahydroxyethylenediamine) and 5 percent TEP (tetraethylenepentamine) liquid phase on a 60–80 mesh chromosorb-W solid phase.

The ordinary drying agents would absorb both the moisture and the ammonia gas. Whitfield (in an unpublished thesis, Reference 36) evaluated various anhydrous salts as drying agents blind to ammonia. His results are in part reproduced in Table 20.1.

From Table 20.1, it can be seen that ammonia losses were not detected through a CaO drying tube. Quick lime (CaO) used originally as a drying agent was soon replaced by CaC_2 which responds to moisture,

$$CaC_2 + H_2O \longrightarrow C_2H_2 + CaO,$$

without absorbing NH_3 giving an effective double drying agent. Carbide was used in the drying columns and neutralization chamber.

Table 20.1
Drying Agents Blind
to Ammonia

Anhydrous Compounds	Percent NH_3 Absorbed
$PbCl_2$	46.2
$PbSO_4$	51.9
K_2CO_3	31.9
NH_4Cl	20.7
KCl	9.0
CaO	0.0
Na_2SO_4	0.6
Cotton	14.7

The analysis for fluorine and nitrogen by this method is rapid, but the machinery for analysis must be kept "running." A positive pressure from the carrier gas, helium, purging the separation column for no less than a half hour after each test prevents ghosts of former analyses from appearing in later analyses. Moisture tends to dampen the responses of the separation column. Therefore, drying columns must be serviced or replaced frequently. In spite of these obvious disadvantages, gas chromatography methods in bone dating are quite rapid when compared with standard wet chemistry techniques and especially the modified fluorine technique of Willard and Winter (Reference 37).

Results and Interpretation

Analysis of bone from each stratigraphic unit in random sequence by this method showed the fluorine content to be somewhat higher than anticipated for bone material of Sangamon age interred in the clay matrix. From Oakley (Reference 27), unpublished work of Jack Allen, R. P. Bullen (personal communication), and the log-decline rate of Cook and Heizer (Reference 10), the author expected about 1.4 percent of fluorine in the suite of fossil bones if they are Illinoian in age.

Cook and Cohn (Reference 9) have stressed the importance of soil ions which contribute to the fossilization of bone material. They note that Ca^{2+}, Na^+, K^+, NH_4^+, CO_3^{2-}, F^-, and PO_4^{3-} are those which greatly affect fossilization. The alkalis named are abundant in montmorillonoid clays. Potash and fluorine occur with the flexible and brittle micas and are loosely held in their crystal sites. The remainder of those named have probably migrated from the bone, yielding the high carbonate, organic, and phosphatic soils observed by Cook and Treganza (Reference 11). Generally speaking, quartzose and kaolinitic soils contain fewer mobile ions than those with clay zeolites, feldspars, montmorillonites, and chlorites. The former are also more in equilibrium with lower pH conditions. Cornwall (Reference 12) reviews the role of pH and mineralogy in the physical environment of soils in a way that supports this notion.

A quantitative vertical mineral profile is needed through the productive horizons that contained mastodon bone to learn what measurable physical characteristics exist between the bone nitrogen and fluorine compositions and the soil. (See Table 20.2.) From the studies of Robinson and Edgington (Reference 29), it is learned that up to 7000 ppm fluorine occurs in soil. Minerallogically, fluorine is most apt to occur sequestered in the hydroxyl sites in the flexible micas, particularly in muscovite and lepidolite, and may be responsible for slightly higher than anticipated values for fluorine in the Carmichaels sediments of Unit C. Waterlogging from the porous lower sands may have provided the media for ion exchange causing the lower units to show less nitrogen (by leaching) and more fluorine than the upper units. The standard deviation σ of the fluorine and nitrogen compositions varies directly with the percentage concentration for unknown reasons.

Standard deviation σ values show that concentration variability increases systematically down-column. It may be that these trends are connected with difference in the mineralogical makeup of the surrounding clay-rich gravels. Clay types present suggest mixed-layering in montmorillonites and a mixed layering between illite and montmorillonite clays in Unit C. The texture and clay mineralogy of each clay unit (A to C) is shown as Table 20.3. The units correspond to those shown in Figure 5. The "stable" clay phases of Unit A predominate and are in minor concentration and are of presumably little consequence in Unit B. Unit C houses montmorillonoids and illite, possible ion exchangers. The entire Unit C is in contact

Table 20.2
Fluorine and Nitrogen Concentrations and Their Variation in Mastodon Bone Parts from Three Carmichael "Gravel" Zones

Carmichaels Formation	Percent Concentration Fluorine	Nitrogen
Unit A	(1) 1.35	0.221
	(2) 1.40	0.222
	(3) 1.51	0.222
	(4) 1.47	0.220
	(5) 1.49	0.219
	$\overline{X} = 1.44$	$\overline{X} = 0.2208$
	$\sigma = 0.059$	$\sigma = 1.1 \times 10^{-3}$
Unit B	(1) 1.48	0.180
	(2) 1.42	0.182
	(3) 1.46	0.190
	(4) 1.55	0.186
	(5) 1.58	0.179
	$\overline{X} = 1.498$	$\overline{X} = 0.183$
	$\sigma = 0.088$	$\sigma = 4.1 \times 10^{-3}$
Unit C	(1) 1.78	0.170
	(2) 1.76	0.188
	(3) 1.71	0.175
	(4) 1.77	0.174
	(5) 1.77	0.170
	$\overline{X} = 1.758$	$\overline{X} = 0.1754$
	$\sigma = 0.260$	$\sigma = 6.6 \times 10^{-3}$

Table 20.3
Analysis of Carmichaels Formation Samples

	Fraction	Weight Percent	Content
Unit A	Sand	36	Quartz. Minor feldspar.
	Silt	25	Quartz. Minor illite and montmorillonite.
	Clay	39	Illite and kaolinite montmorillonite (10–15%).
Unit B	Sand	15	Quartz.
	Silt	67	Quartz. Minor illite and kaolinite.
	Clay	19	Illite and kaolinite. Quartz (20–30%). Minor montmorillonite.
Unit C	Sand	12	Quartz. Minor illite.
	Silt	39	Quartz, kaolinite, and illite. Minor amounts of montmorillonite.
	Clay	49	Kaolinite and illite. Mixed layered illite and montmorillonite.

with a porous, semipermeable fine sand layer beneath it. During burial, it appears likely that bones from the same animal might gain fluorine and lose nitrogen (from protein matter) at a rate controlled by the matrix clays and gravels. The presence of a semipermeable, wet horizon below Unit C, and the increased presence of ion-exchangers in that horizon, leads to speculation that the bone composition gradients and variation from Units A through C is a result of local stratigraphic geochemical control. Furthermore, ground waters migrating upward from the underlying sands may be responsible for the systematic variation in nitrogen and fluorine data as well as the extreme deviations found within Unit C and the alteration of clays there. It will be noted that the trends in fluorine and nitrogen concentrations in this study vary in the directions indicated by this hypothesis. That is to say, the fluorine (taken up by the bones) is greater near the bottom, whereas the nitrogen (depleted due to the removal of protein) is in lesser abundance near the bottom. Further work is required on the natural apatite content of the lower sands, and a more quantitative study of percentage of each clay type of each unit.

These results emphasize the importance of local geochemical control over the ion interchange with fossilization and the contribution to that interchange by each stratigraphic unit involved. Before exploiting a bonebed, it may be advisable for archaeologists to take cores of the material (soil) in the region of the find for geochemical analysis should the find prove to be worthwhile. A hand coring device was used to take cores through the bone-rich units. Mineral analyses from samples selected as representative of Units A through C are shown in Table 20.3.

In these results we see encouragement that gas chromatography may prove very useful for bone analysis, and we are continuing research along these lines. The technique for fluorine may be improved with the use of 15 percent Kel-F, 10 oil on Chromosorb T 40–60 mesh materials and tested isothermally at 100°F. These substrate materials have been improved and Kel-F oil will easily withstand this temperature. Dibutylphthalate may also be used in the fluoride analysis as a liquid phase on the same chromosorb substrate. Silicone rubbers such as Plastisol or Dow Corning Silicone Silastic 588A may be used to some advantage in the reaction chamber. The chamber lining should be removed for cleaning after each test. A chamber coated with a silicone rubber lining may be not only effective (as is teflon) but removable as well.

With the same preparation both fluorine and nitrogen content may be obtained. Sulfuric acid treatment is common in each test, as is the bone pretreatment and amount of sample required. After the HF is purged from the reaction chamber, the micro-Kjeldahl technique could be employed. The gases liberated by that method may be directed into a separate neutralization, drying, and separation chamber system. This may greatly reduce the laboratory time but would require two recorders and a "double-barrelled" chromatograph.

Acknowledgments

The author is indebted to Mr. and Mrs. John Lindy for permitting the excavation of bone materials, the continued cooperation of the Lindys and scores of students in the digging and classifying, Dr. James Witt and Mr. James Whitefield for their work in chromatography, and the patient editor of this work without whose council it might never have been completed.

This paper is Contribution #3, Earth Sciences Department, Western Connecticut State College.

References

1. Abelson, P. H. ''Paleobiochemistry,'' *Carnegie Institute of Washington Yearbook*, **53**, 1953, pp. 97–101.

2. Abelson, P. H. ''Paleobiochemistry,'' *Carnegie Institute of Washington Yearbook*, **54**, 1954, pp. 107–109.

3. Armstrong, W. D. *J. Amer. Chem. Soc.*, **55**, 1933, pp. 1741–1742.

4. Armstrong, W. D. *Ind. Eng. Chem., Anal. Ed.*, **8**, 1936, pp. 384–387.

5. Armstrong, W. G., and Tarco, L. B. H. *Nature*, 1966, pp. 481–482.

6. Baud, C. A. *The Application of Quantitative Methods in Archaeology*, R. F. Heizer and S. F. Cook, Eds., Viking Fund Pub. in Anth., 28, 1960, pp. 246–264.

7. Bowen, R. N. C. *The Exploration of Time*, Newes, London, 1958.

8. Cook, S. F. *The Application of Quantitative Methods in Archaeology*, R. F. Heizer and S. F. Cook, Eds., Viking Fund Pub. in Anth., 28, 1960, pp. 223–245.

9. Cook, S. F., and Cohn, H. C. Ezra *Southwestern J. Anth.*, Univ. N. Mex., **15**, 1959, pp. 276–290.

10. Cook, S. F., and Heizer, R. F. *Southwestern J. Anth.*, **9**, 1953, pp. 231–238.

11. Cook, S. F., and Treganza, A. E. *Amer. Antiq.*, **13**, No. 2, 1948, pp. 135–141.

12. Cornwall, I. W. *The Application of Quantitative Methods in Archaeology*, R. F. Heizer and S. F. Cook, Eds., Viking Fund Pub. in Anth., 28, 1960, pp. 265–299.

13. Cornwall, I. W. *Bones for the Archaeologist*, Phoenix House, Ltd., London, pp. 204–205.

14. Davidson, C. F., and Atkin, D. *Proc. 19th Int. Geol. Conf., Algiers*, 11, 1953, pp. 13–31.

15. Ezra, H. C., and Cook, S. F. *Science*, **126**, p. 80, 1957.

16. Hamilton, L. F., and Simpson, S. G. *Quantitative Chemical Analysis*, 12th ed., Macmillan and Co., New York, 1964, pp. 501–502.

17. Hamlin, A. G., Iveson, G., and Phillips, T. R. *Anal. Chem.*, **35**, 13, 2037, 1963.

18. Heizer, R. F. *Anthropology Today*, Univ. of Chicago Press, Chicago, 1953, pp. 3–42.

19. Heizer, R. F., and Cook, S. F. *Amer. J. Phys. Anth.*, **10**, 1952, pp. 289–303.

20. Ho, Tong-Yun *Proc. N. A. S.*, **54**, 1965, pp. 26–31.

21. Hoskins, C. R., and Fryd, C. F. M. *J. Appl. Chem.*, **5**, 1955, pp. 85–87.

22. James, A. T., and Martin, A. J. P. *Biochem. J.*, **50**, 1952, p. 679.

23. Joffe, E. B., and Sherwood, A. M. *A. E. C. Tech. Info. Serv.*, TEM 149, Oak Ridge, Tenn., 1951.

24. McConnell, D. *Amer. Min.*, **23**, No. 1, 1938.

25. McConnell, D. *Science*, 136, 1962, pp. 241–244.

26. McKenna, F. E. *Nucleonics*, **9**, No. 1, 1951, pp. 40–49.

27. Oakley, K. P. *Framework for Dating Fossil Man*, Aldine Pub. Co., Chicago, 1964.

28. Oakley, K. P., and Hoskins, C. R. *Nature*, **165**, 1950, pp. 379–382.

29. Robinson, W. O., and Edgington, G. *Soil Science*, **61**, 1946, pp. 341–353.

30. Race, G. J., Fry, E. I., Matthews, J. L., Wagner, M. J., Martin, J. H., and Lind, J. A. *Amer. J. Phys. Anth.*, **28**, No. 2, 1968, pp. 157–162.

31. Rogers, A. F. *Bull. G. S. A.*, **35**, 1924, pp. 535–556.

32. Rogers, H. J., Weidmann, S. M., and Parkinson, A. *Biochem. J.*, **50**, 1952, pp. 537–542.

33. Sze, Y. L., Borke, M. L., and Ottenstein, D. M. *Anal. Chem.*, **35**, No. 2, 1963, 240.

34. Tax, S., Eiseley, Y. C., Rouse, I., and Voegelin, C. F. *An Appraisal of Anthropology Today*, Univ. of Chicago Press., Chicago, 14, 1953.

35. Verzar, F. *Scientific American*, **208**, No. 4, 1963, pp. 104–114.

36. Whitfield, J. R. ''Ammonia Losses by Adsorption and Absorption of High Alkaline Salts in Gas Chromatography,'' Unpublished M.S. Thesis, Indiana Univ. of Penna., Indiana, Pa., 1966.

37. Willard, H. H., and Winter, O. B. *Ind. Eng. Chem., Anal. Ed.*, **5**, 1933, pp. 7–10.

Chapter 21

Applications of Solid-State Nuclear Track Detectors to Archaeology[1]

R. Walker, M. Maurette
R. Fleischer, and P. Price
Washington University;
General Electric Research and Development Center

Introduction

Although photographic emulsions have been used for many years to record the tracks of individual nuclear particles, it has only been realized relatively recently that many common materials such as minerals, glasses, and plastics also have the ability to record nuclear tracks. In such materials, called Solid-State Track Detectors (S.S.T.D.), the individual tracks can be seen in an ordinary optical microscope following a chemical etching treatment of the substance.

The subject of S.S.T.D. has been reviewed elsewhere in detail. (References 5,6) The purpose of this paper is to call attention to their applications to archaeology for those who have not been previously introduced to them, and to highlight certain recent developments. Although S.S.T.D. have not yet had a major impact on archeology, the techniques have considerable potential and it is our hope that this note may also serve to stimulate further work in this area.

Absolute Age Dating Using Stored Nuclear Tracks

Fission Track Dating

Laboratory heating experiments show that the latent track images produced by the passage of nuclear particles are very stable. For example, in many substances the extrapolated fading times at room temperature exceed, by far, the age of the solar system! It might therefore be expected that natural radioactivities would produce tracks that would be stored up in a sample, the total density of tracks increasing with time.

This is, indeed, the basic idea of track dating. However, it turns out that most of the natural radiations that are found in an earth-bound sample do *not* produce tracks. For example, electrons, alpha particles, and most cosmic rays never produce enough atomic disruption to register tracks *directly*. In fact, Price and Walker (Reference 13) in their original paper on track age dating argued that the overwhelming majority of tracks found in terrestrial samples must be caused by fission fragments produced by the spontaneous fission of uranium impurity atoms. The age dating technique based on these tracks has consequently come to be called the "fossil fission track method." In Figure 21.1, we show an example of fission tracks in mica and in Figure 21.2, we show the considerably different appearance of etched tracks in glass.

Although subsequent work has shown that there are other important sources of fossil (stored) tracks (Reference 11), this has

not invalidated the fission track dating method. The other kinds of fossil tracks are extremely short and special techniques must be used even to see them; they cannot be confused with the much larger and easier to observe fission tracks.

The fission track dating method is extremely simple. The density of stored tracks is proportional to the product of the uranium concentration and the total storage time. The uranium concentration can be separately determined by irradiating the sample in a known flux of thermal neutrons. The age is thus determined by making track counts before and after a reactor irradiation. The method has been shown to give general agreement with other dating techniques for times as long as 1×10^9 years. (References 5, 6)

The basic difficulty in applying the fission track method to archaeological problems is its lack of sensitivity. In their original paper on the application of fission track dating to manmade glasses, Brill et al. (Reference 2) showed that it was possible to get the correct ages for artifacts that were ~20 to 100 years old. However, the samples that were studied all contained large amounts of uranium—a practice that did not become important in glass making until the end of the 1830s.

The typical concentration of uranium of ~1 ppm gives a track density of only $0.3/cm^2/1000$ yr. Since it is very difficult to work with samples containing as few as $10t/cm^2$, this effectively limits the fission-track dating to times $> 10^4$ to 10^5 years for "typical" specimens.

Future application of fission-track dating to archaeology can take either the direction of working with samples of high-uranium content or working with samples that are very old, as has already been done in several problems dealing with prehistoric man. (References 3, 7) Another application of the latter approach would be to identify the geographic locations of the obsidian used in artifacts by dating the obsidian flows from various sources. Such a technique should complement the existing techniques of trace element identification developed by Renfrew (Reference 14) and others.

It may also prove possible to develop techniques for working with very low track densities. Obviously, this would open up a much wider range of archeological interest.

Recently Huang and Walker (Reference 11) showed that fossil tracks are also

Alpha-Recoil Dating

[1]Work supported by N. S. F. Grant GA-1460 and McDonnell Contract Z80058T.

21.1
Fission tracks in mica.
The tracks are about
10μ long and have a
fairly uniform, diamond-
shaped cross section.
The revelation of tracks
is accomplished by etch-
ing in concentrated HF.

21.2
Fission tracks in glass.
In contrast to their ap-
pearance in crystalline
materials (see Figure
21.1) fission tracks in
glass appear as oval
shaped etch pits. These
corrosion figures are
very characteristic and
can be recognized even
in the presence of a
large background of
round bubbles. Etching
is done with concen-
trated HF.

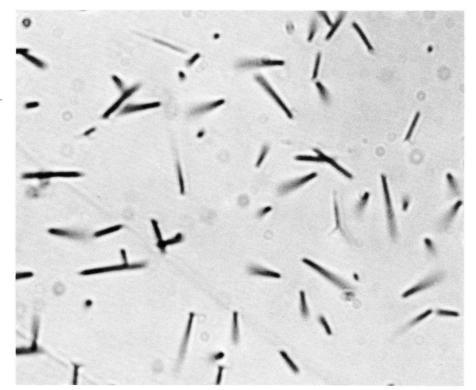

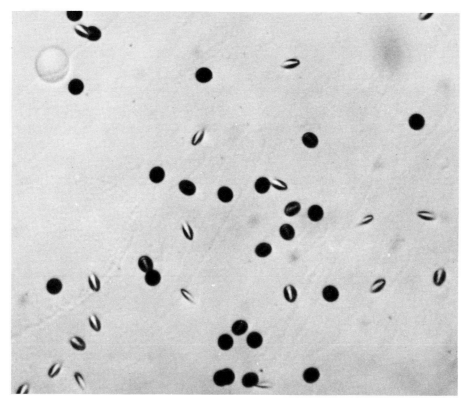

21.3
Uranium map of a terra-cotta sample. To obtain this photograph a mica detector was placed next to a sample of terra-cotta and the sandwich was irradiated with thermal neutrons. The mica was then unfolded from the terra-cotta and etched in HF acid. It can be seen that most of the coarse grains in the terra-cotta (bottom) show up as clear areas on the mica detector (top). In contrast, the fine-grained matrix material has given rise to many fission tracks, producing a consequent obscuration of the mica detector.

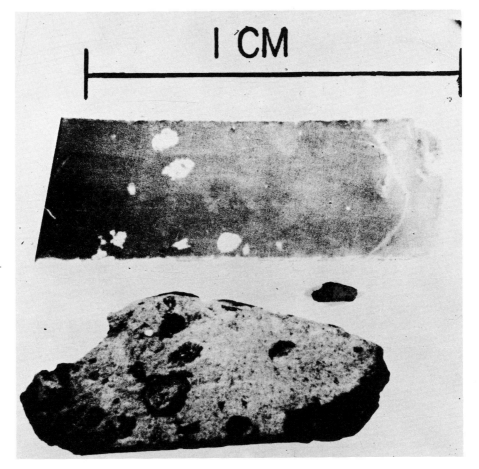

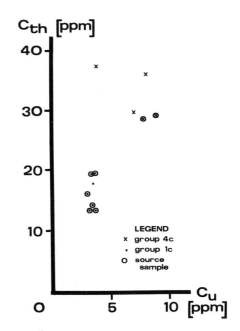

21.4
The U-Th correlation plot for obsidians from the Middle East. These obsidians had previously been divided into separate groups 1C and 4C by C. Renfrew et al (Reference 14) who based their groupings on detailed trace element analyses. The circled points show samples that were obtained from two different obsidian mines.

produced by the recoiling heavy nuclei that accompany the alpha particle decay of U and Th. However, the alpha-recoil tracks are very short ($\sim$100 Å) and can only be seen using special techniques such as electron-microscopy or phase contrast microscopy. Because the lifetime for alpha decay is very short compared to that for spontaneous fission, there are thousands of times as many alpha-recoil tracks as fission tracks. Therefore, in principle, these new tracks form a highly sensitive new tool for age dating that could be extremely interesting for archaeology. Their utility in practice has, however, not yet been demonstrated.

The basic method of alpha-recoil dating is more complicated than that of fission-track dating since it requires independent determination of both U and Th. Track techniques have now been developed for the microscopic measurement of Th concentrations (References 1, 8) and the α-recoil method should soon be tested.

Contrary to an abstract published in the bulletin of the A. G. U., (Reference 10) there now appears to be no evidence for the existence of α-recoil tracks in glass. It is possible to produce another kind of track in glass (and other materials as well) from recoiling Si nuclei that have been struck by incident α-particles. This third kind of fossil track, the α-interaction track, is produced in low density and has no obvious interest for dating purposes.

Determination of U and Th Using Track Techniques

Although we believe that the measurement of ages is by far the most important application of track studies to archeology, there is also a domain of applications based on the ability to measure distributions of U and Th using track techniques. (References 1, 8, 12)

The U concentration may be useful as a crude indicator of the origin of an artifact (Reference 4) or it may be needed as input information for another measurement, such as thermoluminescence. In Figure 21.3, taken from previously unpublished work by Hair et al. (Reference 9), we show one of the unique advantages of the track method of U determination, namely, the ability to make a detailed *map* of the U distribution. To obtain Figure 21.3, a piece of mica was laid next to a section of terra-cotta from a statue of disputed authenticity. The mica-sample sandwich was irradiated in a reactor and the mica was subsequently etched. It can be seen that the coarse-grained material in the terra-cotta gave out very few fission tracks and hence is relatively depleted in U. The U-rich matrix gave a large density of induced tracks. The inhomogeneous distribution of U shows that the fine-grained matrix and the coarse-grained structure should be treated separately in thermoluminescent age determinations.

The Th concentration of an unknown can be determined by two separate irradiations: one with fast nuclear particles, such as 30 MeV α-particles, the other with thermal neutrons. The fast particles fission both Th and U with about equal probability, while the thermal neutrons fission only U.

Apart from the interest for α-recoil dating, the Th and U concentrations can potentially be used to characterize the geographic origins of various materials. In Figure 21.4, for example, taken from unpublished work by Hair et al. (Reference 9), we show the U concentration plotted versus the Th concentration for various obsidian samples from the Middle East. It can be seen that the obsidians fall into two distinct Th-U groupings. These groupings correspond to chemical groupings that had previously been determined by Prof. C. Renfrew (Reference 14) of the University of Sheffield, from whom the samples were obtained.

Those interested in pursuing any of the methods described in this paper should be aware of the existence of a series of standard glasses containing calibrated, trace quantities of U and Th. Information about these glasses, which were developed by a collaboration between groups at Argonne National Laboratory, Corning Glass Works, and Washington University (Reference 15) are now available from Dr. Robert Brill of the Corning Museum of Glass.

Acknowledgments

We would like to thank our colleagues J. Kaufhold and M. Hair for permission to quote their unpublished results. Prof. Colin Renfrew of the University of Sheffield called our attention to the potential interest of dating Middle East obsidians and has kindly provided us with samples.

References

1.
Bimbot, R., Maurette,
M., and Pellas, P.
''Description d' une Nouvelle Méthode pour Mesurer le Rapport des Concentrations Atomiques du Thorium et de l'Uranium,'' *Geochim. et Cosmochim. ACTA*, **31,** 263, 1967.

2.
Brill, R., Fleischer,
R., Price, P. B.,
Walker, R.
''The Fission-Track Dating of Man-Made Glasses,'' *J. Glass Studies,* **VI,** 1964, pp. 151–155.

3.
Fleischer, R. L.,
Leakey, L. S. B.,
Price, P. B., and
Walker, R. M.
''Fission Track Dating of Bed I, Olduvai Gorge,'' *Science* **148,** 72, 1965.

4.
Fleischer, R., and
Price, P. B.
''Uranium Contents of Ancient Man-Made Glass,'' *Science* **144,** 841, 1964.

5.
Fleischer, R., Price,
P., and Walker, R.
''Tracks of Charged Particles in Solids,'' *Science* **149,** 383, 1965.

6.
Fleischer, R., Price,
P., and Walker, R.
''Solid State Track Detectors: Applications to Nuclear Science and Geophysics,'' *Ann. Rev. Nuc. Sci.,* **15,** 1, 1965.

7.
Fleischer, R. L., Price,
P. B., Walker, R. M.,
and Leakey, L. S. B.
''Fission Track Dating of a Mesolithic Knife,'' *Nature* **205,** 1138, 1965.

8.
Hair, M., Kaufhold,
J., Maurette, M.,
and Walker, R.,
''Precision Micromapping of Th using Cyclotron-Induced Fission Tracks,'' to be published.

9.
Hair, M., Kaufhold,
J., and Walker, R.
''Fission Track Studies in Archaeological Materials,'' to be published.

10.
Huang, W., Kaufhold,
J., Maurette, M., and
Walker, R.
''Alpha-Recoil Dating of Young and Old Glasses'', *Trans. A. Geophys. Union* **49,** P105, 1968.

11.
Huang, W., and
Walker, R.
''Fossil Alpha-Particle Recoil Tracks: A New Method of Age Determination,'' *Science,* **155,** 1103, 1967.

12.
Price, P. B., and
Walker, R. M.
''A Simple Method of Measuring Low Uranium Concentrations in Natural Crystals'', *Appl. Phys. Letters* **2,** 23, 1963.

13.
Price, P., and
Walker, R.
''Fossil Tracks of Charged Particles in Mica and the Age of Minerals,'' *J. Geophys. Res.,* **68,** 4847, 1963.

14.
See for example,
Renfrew, C., Dixon,
J. E., and Cann, J. R.
''Obsidian and Early Cultural Contact in the Near East'', *Proc. of the Prehistoric Society,* **2,** 30, 1966.

15.
Schreurs, J., Friedman, A., Hair, M.,
Kaufhold, J., and
Walker, R.
''Calibrated Glasses for Fission Track Experiments,'' to be published.

283

Index